Aggression and Crimes against Peace

In this volume, the third in his multi-volume project on the philosophical and legal aspects of international criminal law, Larry May locates a normative grounding for the crime of aggression – the only one of the three crimes charged at Nuremberg that is not currently being prosecuted – that is similar to that for crimes against humanity and war crimes. He considers cases from the Nuremberg trials, philosophical debates in the Just War tradition, and more recent debates about the International Criminal Court, as well as the hard cases of humanitarian intervention and terrorist aggression. May argues that crimes of aggression, sometimes called crimes against peace, deserve international prosecution when one State undermines the ability of another State to protect human rights. His thesis refutes the traditional understanding of aggression, which often has been interpreted as a crossing of borders by one sovereign state into another sovereign state. At Nuremberg, charges of crimes against humanity were pursued only if the defendant also engaged in the crime of aggression. May argues for a reversal of this position, contending that aggression charges should be pursued only if the defendant's acts involve serious human rights violations.

Larry May is professor of philosophy at Washington University in St. Louis and Research Professor of Social Justice, Centre for Applied Philosophy and Public Ethics, Charles Sturt and Australian National Universities. He is the author or editor of numerous books, including *The Morality of War; Crimes against Humanity*, which won an honorable mention from the American Society of International Law and a best book award from the North American Society for Social Philosophy; and *War Crimes and Just War*, which won the Frank Chapman Sharp Prize for the best book on the philosophy of war from the American Philosophical Association.

Aggression and Crimes against Peace

LARRY MAY

Washington University
and
Centre for Applied Philosophy and Public Ethics

CAMBRIDGE
UNIVERSITY PRESS

CAMBRIDGE UNIVERSITY PRESS
Cambridge, New York, Melbourne, Madrid, Cape Town, Singapore, São Paulo, Delhi

Cambridge University Press
32 Avenue of the Americas, New York, NY 10013-2473, USA

www.cambridge.org
Information on this title: www.cambridge.org/9780521719155

First published 2008

Printed in the United States of America

A catalog record for this publication is available from the British Library.

Library of Congress Cataloging in Publication Data
May, Larry.
Aggression and crimes against peace / Larry May.
p.   cm. – (Philosophical and legal aspects of war and conflict series)
Includes bibliographical references and index.
ISBN 978-0-521-89431-9 (hardback) – ISBN 978-0-521-71915-5 (pbk.)
1. Aggression (International law)   2. Crimes against humanity.   3. Criminal intent.
4. International criminal courts.   I. Title.
KZ6355.M39   2008
341.6′2–dc22   2007037935

ISBN   978-0-521-89431-9 hardback
ISBN   978-0-521-71915-5 paperback

Contents

v

Acknowledgments

With this volume, I bring to completion the third of a multi-volume project discussing critically the moral foundations of international criminal law. I began this project shortly before the Rome Conference that adopted the Statute of the International Criminal Court in the summer of 1998. The previous summer, I had been asked to address the topic of reconciliation at a conference in Calgary. There I met Richard Goldstone, the first prosecutor of the International Criminal Tribunals for the Former Yugoslavia and for Rwanda. It was during a lengthy after-lunch walk that I discussed some of my ideas with him and began to see the beginnings of a single-volume study of how collective liability becomes translated into individual criminal responsibility. Then right after the Rome Conference, I took an excellent course with Leila Sadat on the emerging field of International Criminal Law, and I was hooked.

What started out to be a one-volume study was transformed into a multi-volume work, the first three volumes of which tracked the crimes originally charged at the Nuremberg trials. The first volume, *Crimes against Humanity: A Normative Account* (2005), and the second volume, *War Crimes and Just Wars* (2007), have won awards in philosophy and in law. Both volumes were published by Cambridge University Press, whose editors, especially Beatrice Rehl, have been a pleasure to work with. Over the ten years I have been involved with these volumes, my work has gone from being about a fringe topic to the very center of public policy debates across the globe. I feel lucky to have stumbled on this topic just as it was about to catch fire – nearly every morning at the breakfast table there is a news story that inspires me to get down to the business of finishing this trilogy with the hope that I can contribute something positive to the search for international justice today. The fourth volume of this multi-volume work will concern genocide.

Various versions of these chapters have been read at colloquia or con-
ferences in Canberra, College Station, DeKalb, Greensboro, Helsinki,
Louisville, Oslo, New York, Portland, St. Andrews, St. Louis, St. Peters-
burg, and Washington, DC. I am very grateful for comments from the
following: Sharon Anderson-Gold, Michael Blake, Chris Brown, Allen
Buchanan, Deen Chatterjee, Michael Cholbi, David Copp, Cindy Holder,
Jan Klabbers, Martti Koskenniemi, Hugh LaFollette, Bruce Landesman,
David Lefkowitz, David Luban, Anthony Lang, Jeff McMahan, Steve
Ratner, Andrew Rehfeld, David Rodin, Leila Sadat, Don Scheid, David
Schweikard, Ken Shockley, Jim Swindler, John Tasioulas, and Kit Well-
man.

Earlier versions of these chapters appeared in *Midwest Studies in
Philosophy, 2006; Studies in the History of Ethics*, February 2006; *Journal
of Social Philosophy*, Winter 2007; and *The Journal of Political Philosophy*,
Summer 2007. I am grateful to be able to reprint some of this material in
my book. Indeed, the opportunity to publish what are effectively chapters
rather than completely free-standing papers has made it possible for me
to continue in a nearly uninterrupted fashion to complete the current
book.

My greatest debts are to my colleagues and friends, Marilyn Friedman
and Kit Wellman, who read the first draft of the book and did so quickly
enough that I could make changes before I embarrassed myself. As usual,
Marilyn was especially helpful at discussing the ideas behind these chapters over many a meal. I am also grateful to Martti Koskenniemi, who
took the time to debate my approach with me one summer afternoon in
2006 in Helsinki. The final chapter of this book is, in part, a response
to some of his criticisms of those of us who have attempted to provide
normative arguments supporting international criminal law. I am also
enormously grateful to Mark Drumbl and Steve Lee, who read a late draft
and provided excellent suggestions, especially concerning often very difficult legal and philosophical issues, respectively. My department chair,
Mark Rollins, and our department secretary, Mindy Danner, are also to be
thanked for providing financial and clerical support, respectively. Zach
Hoskins has provided an excellent index for which I am very grateful.

PART A

PACIFISM AND JUST WARS

1

Introduction

Between the Horrors and Necessity of War

This book is about the normative grounding of crimes of aggression, or what are sometimes called crimes against peace. The crime of aggression is the only one of the three crimes charged at Nuremberg (the other two being crimes against humanity and war crimes) that is not currently being prosecuted. The ensuing discussion of the crime of aggression is timely since the International Criminal Court (ICC) has jurisdiction to prosecute such crimes, as they were prosecuted at Nuremberg, but the ICC currently lacks, and is now seeking, a mechanism for international trials for the crime of aggression. I will examine the justifiability of initiating war, as well as who should be held liable for initiating or waging an unjustified war. I will focus on issues in international criminal law, that is, on when and whether individuals should be prosecuted for initiating and waging aggressive war, rather than on the more traditional question of when or whether States are to be criticized or sanctioned for waging aggressive war.

My view is that crimes of aggression are deserving of international prosecution when one State undermines the ability of another State to protect human rights. This thesis runs against the grain of how aggression has been traditionally understood in international law. Previously, it was common to say that aggression involved a State's first strike against another State, where often what that meant was simply that one sovereign State had crossed the borders of another sovereign State. In this book I argue that the mere crossing of borders is not a sufficient normative rationale for prosecuting State leaders for the international crime of aggression. At Nuremberg, charges of crimes against humanity were pursued only if the defendant also engaged in the crime of aggression. I now argue for a reversal of this position, contending that aggression charges should be pursued only if the defendant's acts involved serious human rights

3

violations. Indeed, I argue that aggression, as a crime, should be defined
as not merely a first strike against another State but a first wrong that
violates or undermines human rights.[1]

My strategy is to find a normative grounding for the crime of aggression that is similar to that for crimes against humanity and war crimes.
Today, crimes against humanity and war crimes are considered *jus cogens*
crimes, that is, crimes that are of such paramount wrongness that States
are universally bound not to commit them.[2] If there are to be prosecutions for crimes against peace (or the crime of aggression) that are similar
to prosecutions for crimes against humanity and war crimes, then there
must be a similarly very serious violation that aggression constitutes. Mere
assaulting of sovereignty does not have the same level of seriousness and
is not as universally condemned as are the other crimes. For this reason,
among others, I argue that aggression, as a crime, needs to be linked
to serious human rights violations, not merely to violations of territorial
integrity.

A decade ago, I first conceived the idea of writing a book on the normative and conceptual issues in international criminal law. That project
has grown into a series of volumes, of which this is the third. The first two
volumes were on crimes against humanity and war crimes, respectively.[3]
In the current volume, I focus on the normative principles and conceptual assumptions of prosecuting individuals for crimes against peace. The
concept of humanity plays an important role in each of these volumes.
In the first volume, a particular kind of crime is identified, crimes against
humanity, that harms humanity, as opposed to individual States or persons. In the second, a type of crime is identified, war crimes, that assaults
humaneness, as opposed to more traditional assaults on justice. And in
this third volume on the crime of aggression, I argue that aggressive
wars are best understood as wars that undermine the ability of States,
and hence of the human community, to protect human rights. In all
three books, as is increasingly seen in debates about international law,
the focus is on the "laws of humanity": a set of rules meant to govern the
international community, that is, the obligations and rights of humanity,
although in each type of crime humanity is harmed differently.

---

[1] In a different context, David Rodin has also argued for a similar view of aggression. See
his book, *War and Self-Defense*, Oxford: Oxford University Press, 2002.

[2] See Alexander Orakhelshvili, *Peremptory Norms in International Law*, Oxford: Oxford University Press, 2006.

[3] *Crimes against Humanity: A Normative Account*, New York: Cambridge University Press,
2005; and *War Crimes and Just War*, New York: Cambridge University Press, 2007.

Crimes against peace assault humanity by undermining human rights protections that States normally can provide, but crimes against peace do not harm humanity the way that crimes against humanity, such as ethnic cleansing campaigns, do. Crimes against peace also are not like war crimes in assaulting humaneness, since all wars, not merely aggressive wars, are inhumane, and aggressive wars are not necessarily more inhumane than defensive wars. For this reason, I will speak of the harm of crimes against peace as involving the abrogation of human rights, rather than as directly harming humanity or humaneness.[4] Of course, there are States that have been massive violators of human rights, and wars waged to stop such States are not generally aggressive in my view.

Most of the book uses examples from the International Military Tribunal sitting at Nuremberg and the subsequent proceedings by the American Military Tribunal also sitting in Nuremberg under the auspices of Control Council Law Number 10, since these are the most important international trials that have occurred for crimes against peace.[5] In the end I offer some strong cautions for contemporary lawyers about how the Nuremberg model is increasingly being used today. Nonetheless, I argue that prosecutions of State leaders for crimes against peace can be justified and should go forward today where the undiluted elements of State aggression as well as the subjective and objective elements of individual criminality are present.

In this first introductory chapter, I will set the stage for the later chapter-length discussions by trying to indicate the considerations that allowed both the Just War tradition and contemporary international law to come to similar understandings about which wars were clearly aggressive and which were not. I will also explain the methodology of the book: normatively minimalist and also defendant-oriented throughout. In general, I wish to indicate why there is a problem about war over the centuries, namely, that war is strongly condemned but also seen as allowed, or at least excusable, in some few cases. Indeed, in those few cases, such as when a State uses military force in self-defense or defense of others, these wars are not only justified but may even be required. This is because war is

---

4 See Lawrence Douglas, *The Memory of Judgment*, New Haven, CT: Yale University Press, 2001, pp. 45–46.

5 The other main trials for crimes against peace were those held in Tokyo, but the judgments reached there did not provide us with a very rich analysis of this international crime, as well as in Poland (the Greiser trial) and in China (Chinese War Crimes Military Tribunal). See Mark Drumbl's discussion of these latter trials in his paper presented to the 60th Anniversary Conference on Nuremberg held at Washington University in the fall of 2006.

often paradoxically something that is needed to restore human rights protection and peace in a region of the world. That some wars may be justified or at least excused will have a strong impact on when and whether individuals should be prosecuted for such wars.

I. Condemning War but Fighting for Peace

War is a horrible thing and only in the most extreme cases can it be justified. Given the likelihood that innocent people will be killed in war there remains a strong contingent presumption that all wars are unjustified. In his essay "The Grotian Tradition in International Law," Hersch Lauterpacht described the 17th-century philosopher and founder of international law, Hugo Grotius, as someone whose writings displayed "a disapproval, amounting to a hatred of war."[6] And yet, according to Lauterpacht, Grotius also "does not deny that war is a legal institution . . . war is not inconsistent with the law of nature and with many other kinds of law."[7] I will also explain that war is needed in certain cases since international solidarity seems to require that a State be willing to go to war in order to aid States that are protecting human rights, or to prevent harm to individuals in oppressive States. In this way we confront the problem that all wars seem to be condemnable but that some wars may be justified or at least excused.

One normative difficulty is that if what makes war immoral is the killing of people, then all wars are immoral and there is no relevant moral distinction between aggressive wars and defensive wars. If one wants to maintain a distinction of this sort and punish people for waging aggressive wars but not for waging defensive wars, focusing on killing alone will not work. One strategy is to see that some wars destabilize a sovereign State and other wars do not; indeed, purely defensive wars shore up rather than destabilize. But this turns on the ability to explain why sovereign States matter morally. The difficulty is that today not all sovereign States are worth preserving morally since some States are the worst human rights abusers. Yet in most cases the world is better off with stable rather than destabilized States, as the problem of failed States as a haven for terrorist groups so vividly indicates. My view is that aggression is morally wrong because it destabilizes States that generally protect human rights more than they

---

[6] Hersch Lauterpacht, "The Grotian Tradition in International Law," *British Year Book of International Law*, vol. 23, 1946, p. 47.

[7] Ibid., p. 46.

curtail them.[8] If a given State is not generally protecting human rights, it will be less clear that war waged against such a State is indeed best labeled aggressive and unjustified war. Indeed, if States systematically violate the basic human rights of their citizens, then those States have no right to insist that other States respect their sovereignty.[9]

State aggression is a resort to the means of war not justified by reference to self-defense or defense of others. Normally, State aggression is a form of war, that is, the violent use of force by one State (or State-like entity) against another. The most obvious way that State aggression causes harm concerns the loss of life, and risk to loss of much of what is valuable to many other lives, that is a consequence of any war. But this strategy, as I said above, will not allow us to distinguish aggressive from defensive wars. In all wars, many people are either killed or placed in serious jeopardy of being killed, and it does not matter whether the war is aggressive or defensive. Instead, one might try to show that humanity is harmed in aggressive but not in defensive wars. This would mean that it is not the violence per se that is the wrong-making characteristic of State aggression but the effect on humanity.

One clear way that humanity might be harmed by some, but not all, wars concerns the significant violation of human rights that sometimes occurs when one State destabilizes another State. Of course, not every destabilizing of a State does cause significant violation of human rights since some States are major abusers of human rights and destabilizing them would seemingly have a positive effect on the protection of human rights in the world. But in at least some of these cases, having a failed State may make for much broader human rights abuses than was true when there was, for instance, an authoritarian State that significantly abused human rights. In many cases, though, destabilizing a State not related to self-defense or defense of others seems to be a harm to humanity in that significant human rights are abused, or made much more likely to be abused.

Traditional Just War theory argues that some wars can be justified, even required, out of respect for the protection of innocent life. Self-defense and defense of others are the key bases for the justification of war. This position was historically articulated in opposition to strict pacifism, although it ended up calling only for a kind of limitation on certain

---

[8] See Allen Buchanan, *Justice, Legitimacy, and Self-Determination*, Oxford: Oxford University Press, 2004.

[9] See my discussion of this issue in chapter 1 of my book *Crimes against Humanity*, 2005.

versions of pacifism. If pacifism is itself grounded in respect for life, especially innocent life, then it appears that some wars may be justified, from
the standpoint of certain versions of pacifism, if those wars will prevent
massive loss of innocent life without risking a corresponding loss of life
that occurs as a result of waging the war itself. Indeed, the early Church
Fathers saw themselves as sympathetic to pacifism and yet also thought
that some wars could be justified on just the grounds we have been discussing, namely, concern or respect for the lives of fellow humans. Of
course, we may want to question whether the early Church Fathers really
were pacifists, but my point is only that war can sometimes be justified
on the same grounds on which certain forms of pacifism are themselves
grounded.

Strict pacifists will not support any war since war involves the intentional
taking of human life. But few would follow these strict pacifists in saying
that one should not use violent force to defend an innocent person's or
one's own life from mortal attack. As an analogy, think of the abortion
debates. Strict adherents to a pro-life position will argue that all abortions
are unjustified. But they do not gain many adherents to their position
when the focus is on those cases of abortion that are necessary to save
the life of the pregnant woman. And the reason regarding abortion is
similar to the case of war. It seems odd to think that abortion or war
should be condemned in all cases on grounds of protecting life and yet
not recognize the conflicting intuitions that many people have about the
cases in which abortion or war is necessary to protect innocent life as well.
Except in the most extreme view of it, the principle of respect for life does
not seem clearly to require that all wars or all abortions be prohibited.

As we will see in later chapters, another strategy in these debates is
to maintain a strong condemnation of all wars, and yet allow that some
individuals who initiated war can be excused if the reason that war was
initiated had to do with the protection of innocent life. Once again, strong
pro-life adherents in the abortion debates sometimes take the view that
abortion is morally impermissible even to save the life of the pregnant
woman. Yet some allow that the woman or her doctor may be excusable
for what they have done. This recognizes the distinction, which is very
important in legal theory, between a justification and an excuse.[10]

To say that war is justified is to say that the moral or legal reasons in
support of waging war in a given context outweigh the moral or legal
reasons against waging war in that context. To say that waging war might

---

[10] See Thomas Franck, *Recourse to Force*, Cambridge: Cambridge University Press, 2002,
   ch. 10.

be excused is to say that even though the balance of reasons weigh against waging war, special considerations might warrant that waging war in this case not be blamed or punished. Think of the example of murder. One can say that a person is guilty of murder even though he or she had some reason to engage in this act. But one can also say that a person is guilty of murder and yet his act can be justified or excused, such as in the case of killing in self-defense. One can be guilty of murder and yet excused from punishment.

One strong strain of the Just War tradition has taken off from the above position, namely, that some wars can be allowed or at least excused even if one is generally sympathetic to pacifism. This is the position of Augustine and of Thomas More, as well as some of the followers of Thomas Aquinas, who specifically discuss abortion as well as war in just these terms – that some wars may be justified out of respect for life. The extreme pacifist early Church Fathers began to lose adherents throughout the Roman era, and it seems likely that the Just War doctrine came into being as a way to save much of the sentiment behind the pacifist position, especially the strong support for life, by admitting that some, but only very few, wars could be justified or excused. Contrary to what is often thought today, I read the Just War tradition as continuing a tradition of generally condemning war. And in this respect, Just War theory and contemporary international legal theory are quite similar to each other. Indeed, there are very similar debates today in legal circles about how to regard recourse to force, and whether and when war can be justified or at least excused if it seems necessary to use even lethal force to restore or maintain the peace.[11]

II. War and Contemporary International Law

International law and the Just War tradition share many things in common, and perhaps the most important is the general condemnation of war and yet the recognition that war may be justified or excused in certain cases. One way to think about wars that might be justified is to think of the use of violence by individuals instead of by the State. Self-defense and defense of others seem to be grounds for the use of violence by individuals; and when violence is used for other reasons it seems prima facie unjustified in the sense that it is aggression. Self-defense has been recognized in domestic laws for hundreds, if not thousands, of years and is now also recognized in international law. The United Nations Charter,

[11] See Franck, *Recourse to Force*, 2002, ch. 2.

as we will see in this section, seems to recognize a self-defense basis for justified resort to war even as it purports to outlaw the use of force by one State against another State.

After the Second World War, there was an attempt to instill the idea that waging war is against international law. Article 2(4) of the United Nations Charter reads as follows:

> All members shall refrain in their international relations from the threat or use of force against the territorial integrity or political independence of any State, or in any manner inconsistent with the purposes of the United Nations.

The Charter is, at the very least, a multilateral treaty that is binding on all of the States that ratified it, which includes all but a handful of the States in the world at present. Depending on one's view of customary international law, it may be that the Charter is now also customary law and binding on all States, not merely those that ratified it. The prohibition on the use of force, though, is not absolute here, since the Charter only prohibits the use of force against "the territorial integrity" or "political independence" of another State. And while this covers an enormous amount of ground, it certainly falls short of the complete prohibition on war that many hoped for when the United Nations was formed.

Indeed, self-defensive wars and wars fought in defense of others appear not to be subject to the prohibitions of Article 2(4) since arguably they are not *aimed* against the territorial integrity or political independence of another State. Unless all crossing of borders, for whatever reason, is such a violation, there appears to be a kind of loophole in Article 2(4). If force is used to stop aggression, it is not itself aimed against the territorial integrity or political independence of a State. And while the only way to stop aggression may be to violate the political independence of a State, this need not be the primary aim and indeed may not be the aim at all if lesser measures of force may do the trick. In any event, Article 2(4) has not achieved what many hoped, namely, the unambiguous and unqualified outlawing of all wars.

The opening for some legally justifiable or excusable wars is seen most clearly in another part of the United Nations Charter, Article 51, which reads as follows:

> Nothing in the present Charter shall impair the inherent right of individual or collective self-defense if an armed attack occurs against a Member of the United Nations, until the Security Council has taken measures necessary to maintain international peace and security.

This article appears to allow for self-defensive wars, or at least to indicate that nothing else in the Charter (especially Article 2(4)) will rule them out. The interpretation of this Article, especially in light of Article 2(4), as actually allowing certain wars is controversial to say the least. But it certainly seems that wars waged in self-defense, if the United Nations does not quickly act, are not clearly unjustified or inexcusable in international law, as was also true for the Just War tradition.

The United Nations Charter has been interpreted by customary international law over the last sixty years. But the core consideration regarding war is that the use of force is generally disallowed unless the State using force has itself been attacked and needs to use force to defend itself or to defend one of its allies. In later chapters we will have occasion to wonder about the use of customary international law in international criminal proceedings. Suffice it here to note that, at least outside of the context of international *criminal* law, there has been wide consensus in thinking that a State could go to the defense of another State, especially if these States were in some kind of collective security organization, such as NATO. So defense of self and perhaps defense of others has been the basis for legally waging war, and all other, or nearly all other, recourse to war is considered aggression.

Aggression has thus been mainly defined negatively. It is the use of force by one State against another State neither in self-defense nor defense of others (within a collective security arrangement). But there has not been a formal recognition of this standard. At the moment, the International Criminal Court lists the crime of aggression as one of the four crimes falling under its jurisdiction. Yet, until the elements of this crime can be agreed to, no prosecutions for this crime can be engaged in by the Prosecutor's Office of the ICC. In my view, there is considerable agreement about how to understand the crime of aggression, or at least the State aggression element of this crime. As we will see, though, there is considerable controversy in international law today about how to understand the place of the State aggression element in the crime of aggression, that is, in the crime for which individuals, as opposed to States, may be punished for having waged aggressive war. Indeed, unlike other international crimes, if there will eventually be prosecutions for the crime of aggression, there will only be major State leaders in the dock.

In very recent years an International Criminal Court has evolved that will allow for the prosecution of individuals for international crimes. We can learn quite a bit about the status of aggression in international law today from this source. The debates about the crime of aggression during

the Rome drafting convention of the ICC Charter and subsequently have
called attention to some of the problems in providing a legal definition of State aggression and in delineating the elements of the crime of
aggression. Article 5 of the Rome Statute and the Final Act of the Rome
Conference called for a Preparatory Commission to convene in the last
years of the twentieth century and the beginning years of the 21st century.
The task of what came to be called the PrepCom was

> To define the crime of aggression and to set out the conditions under which
> the Court shall exercise jurisdiction with respect to this crime.[12]

Within the PrepCom, there was consensus on many things, including that
the crime of aggression is a crime that should primarily be prosecuted
against State leaders. There was also agreement about the most obvious
cases of aggression. I hope that what follows will contribute to the ongoing
debate about how to define aggression and how to delineate the elements
of the crime that must be proved to convict State leaders for waging
aggressive war.

The members of the PrepCom took as their point of departure the 1974
UN General Assembly Resolution 3314, as well as the 1986 International
Court of Justice ruling in the Nicaragua case, the case that held the United
States to have acted aggressively in the mining of Nicaragua's harbors.[13]
The General Assembly Resolution, as we will see, used the idea of "first
strike" as the core idea in delineating aggression. One of the main things
that the members of the PrepCom, and others in the international law
community, seem to agree on is that aggression should be defined, if it is to
be defined at all, by reference to the principle of priority, namely, "that the
aggressor in an international conflict shall be considered that State which
is the first to take certain actions."[14] There is also an emerging consensus
about examples of aggression. But there is still controversy about how to
think about hard cases such as humanitarian wars and terrorist wars. I
devote two of the last chapters of this book to these especially hard cases.

---

[12] Mauro Politi, "The Debate within the Preparatory Commission for the International
Criminal Court," in *The International Criminal Court and the Crime of Aggression*, edited by
Mauro Politi and Giuseppe Nesi, Burlington, VT: Ashgate, 2004, p. 46.

[13] See ibid., pp. 47–48 for a good, brief discussion of these sources on aggression. This will
be taken up in much greater detail in later chapters.

[14] Mohammed M. Gomaa, "The Definition of the Crime of Aggression and the ICC Jurisdiction of that Crime," in *The International Criminal Court and the Crime of Aggression*, edited
by Mauro Politi and Giuseppe Nesi, p. 68. It should be noted that PrepCom did not in
the end reach consensus about how to define aggression.

In 2009, seven years after the Rome Statute entered into force, the International Criminal Court will consider amendments to the Charter and will be open specifically to amendments about substantive crimes such as the crime of aggression.[15] My hope is that this book will contribute to the review process and will help establish jurisdiction to prosecute the crime of aggression. But I also suspect that there will be a continuing debate on this very controversial crime that is likely to last for centuries, just as debate about the *jus ad bellum* component of the Just War tradition has already lasted for several centuries, arguably for millennia. As we will see in subsequent chapters, especially Chapter 10, one of the main problems is that any attempt to label the actions of one State as aggressive will be inevitably tied up in political considerations that courts have been notoriously bad at adjudicating. It is for this reason that many have proposed that the determination of whether a State has indeed engaged in aggression, as the first element in establishing the prima facie case of an individual committing the crime of aggression, should not be decided by a court but instead by a political body such as the Security Council of the United Nations. While this will politicize the trials, perhaps those trials will be less politicized than if the International Criminal Court itself is the entity that engages in what will inevitably be a political decision about whether a State has engaged in an aggressive as opposed to a defensive war against another State.

III. Many Unjustified Wars but Few Criminal Leaders

While recognizing some wars as legitimate, both the Just War tradition and contemporary international law have seemed to agree that very few such wars are indeed justified. Part of the explanation for this agreement is that there has been a consensus that war is horrible and that wars should be considered justified only if there is an impending crisis that needs to be confronted and is so grave that those also grave consequences of waging war might be justified to accomplish this objective. Wars waged for territorial gain or for converting the heathens have been condemned in the Just War tradition for at least five centuries. And in contemporary international law, there is not currently agreement that humanitarian wars are justified, even in the case of waging war to stop genocide.

---

[15] See Article 121 of the Rome Statute. Article 123 also says that seven years after entering into force there will be a review of the Statute to consider amendments.

In both Just War theory and contemporary international law, only a limited number of wars are prima facie justified. In the Just War tradition, a fairly strict standard of just cause was employed, greatly limiting which wars were considered legitimate. "Cause" refers to the reasons that a State has to wage war against another State, and "just cause" refers to the legitimate reasons that would warrant going to war and for that waging of war not to constitute "aggression." In contemporary international law, there are also requirements that are difficult to meet. Most important is that a State generally should not be the first to strike, that is, the first to use unjustified force against another State. In most cases, the use of force can be justified only if another State has already employed force against a State and that State is merely using force as a reaction, and typically only as a means of self-defense.

One of the main reasons that so few wars are justified is that there are normally reasonable alternatives to a State's use of violent force in thwarting threats from other States. Consider the controversy over the centuries about how strong a threat has to be before violent force can be resorted to. If this is not specified with some precision, many, if not most, wars would seem to be justified. We need to be able to distinguish, for instance, between an imminent threat and a distant threat. And we also need to distinguish between mere fear and justified fear of attack. Here we will want to know whether enemy troops are massing on the border or merely that an enemy's military expenditures are increasing. We should not require that a State wait passively until troops are marching on its capital; but neither should we allow a State to march against the enemy State's capital just on the basis of vague fears. I will say much more about these issues in Part B of this book.

There has been much more controversy about who should be held liable when States engage in aggression than about when and whether a State has committed aggression. While many if not most States that wage war are condemnable, few individuals will be held criminally liable for waging unjustified or aggressive war. This is because of the difficulty of linking the acts of the individual to the State aggression. But even more than this, there is considerable difficulty in establishing the *mens rea* requirement for criminal liability when we are discussing members of a State who are often not aiming to harm other States. So, if anyone is held criminally liable it should be the aggressive State's leaders, whose *mens rea* often most closely parallels the guilt of the aggressive State. But as we will see, many leaders are often also merely aiming to advance what they regard as the legitimate interests of their

State rather than to do anything harmful to other States and their members.

In international criminal law, as in any other type of criminal law, the defendants are punishable only if it can be proved that they have both a guilty act and a guilty state of mind. It is not justifiable to subject individuals to punishment if they have merely done what they thought was right or that they were acting from noble reasons. Mere guilt by association is not sufficient. No matter how notorious the defendant, it is always possible that the defendant did not do what he or she is accused of doing. And in any event, principles of due process require that every person is entitled to a fair trial as a matter of respect for that person, if not out of respect for humanity. This is especially true when the crime that the defendant is accused of is the waging of aggressive war. I will say much more about these issues in Part D of this book.

War is waged by a series of acts, many of which are not themselves otherwise criminal. In crimes against humanity or war crimes, the individual acts are normally themselves criminal, such as murder, torture, and rape. Crimes against humanity and war crimes are largely the aggregated acts of individuals that are seen as somewhat different from normal when in the international context, but that could have been the subject of domestic criminal prosecutions even outside of the context of armed conflict. In crimes against humanity, the context is an assault on a population; in war crimes the context is acts that were part of an armed military action. In the crime of aggression, the context is that of State aggression, which is not simply the aggregated acts of individuals. Of course, killing is a wrong that could be prosecuted; yet the international crime is not just killing, but killing that is part of State aggression as opposed to defensive killing.

The waging of war starts with the issuing of an order, not in itself already a criminal act. What the orders require people to do might be criminal in other contexts, but indeed even this is not always true. Many of the other acts in waging war are also not themselves criminal outside of the context of war, such as marching, the maintenance of weapons, and even the crossing of borders. Of course, war normally involves killing. But in an important sense, it is the State that wages war, not individuals, and there is a sense in which the acts of individuals that make up war are conceptually and normatively distinct from the State aggression. And it is significant that not all wars are illegal, so even when the acts of soldiers are clearly aimed at waging war, these acts are not always illegal or criminal either. Indeed, since some wars are legally or

morally required, such as certain self-defensive wars, the acts of participating in war could be morally required rather than acts that should be
prosecuted.

The collective element of crimes of aggression, namely, that the acts
in question constitute aggressive war, transforms the acts of individuals,
such as massing at borders and aiming weapons, from acts that are often
not criminal to acts that are. In other international crimes, the collective
elements, such as assaults on a population or assaults against protected
categories of people such as POWs, enhance the harmfulness of the acts of
individuals, such as murder, rape, and enslavement, which are themselves
normally already criminal. What many soldiers do in wars of aggression
is often not different from what other soldiers do in legal, that is, non-
aggressive, wars. On the other hand, short of killing, it is not true that
those individuals who commit war crimes are acting in the same way as
soldiers who do not commit crimes. And this is also true of those who
perpetrate crimes against humanity, since it is wrong to rape and torture
whatever the circumstance. On the other hand, individuals whose acts
could be said to be part of the crime of aggression will often not know
that they are indeed committing that crime, or any crime.

It is for this reason that the individuals in the dock charged with crimes
of aggression will not often look like the "moral monsters" of war crimes
and crimes against humanity, except for the rare Hitlers who are at the top
of the State's leadership hierarchy. Only the leaders typically understand
that the acts they are doing are clearly illegal, with nearly everyone else
thinking that the war they participate in is defensive or at least not clearly
aggressive. The highest-ranking State leaders should be the main, if not
the only, people prosecuted for the crime of aggression, if anyone is. War
is not something that soldiers or even lower-ranking officers commit. And
for this reason, to be explained in Chapter 11, there should be very few
individuals prosecuted for the crime of waging aggressive war as opposed
to other international crimes.

Thus, for this and the other reasons mentioned above, it will turn out
that we have a very puzzling situation: few wars will be waged justifiably,
and many wars will be aggressive wars; but very few individuals should
be prosecuted for the crime of waging aggressive war. In this sphere of
international criminal law, there will be a lot of impunity in the sense that
many individuals who participate in this crime should not be prosecuted,
even though State aggression will be quite common. Of course, it is still
true that States, as opposed to individuals, can be held liable for waging
aggressive wars and monetarily penalized in various ways. It is just that

States cannot be put in the dock, and in addition, it is not clear what sort of monetary penalty would be adequate, especially since the members of the State who are least well-off and also least responsible for State aggression are the ones most hurt by monetary penalties directed at States.

IV. Minimalism, Consensus, and Solidarity

In this work, as in my other books on international criminal law, I will take a moral minimalist approach. I will proceed from a position that seeks the least controversial assumptions – that is, assumptions that might achieve international consensus. Consensus is not unanimity, and this is especially true in the international arena. But there are reasons to think that consensus, at least minimalist consensus, may be possible there. One reason has to do with globalization. As structures and institutions develop that cross borders and encompass an increasingly large swath of the globe, there are opportunities for individuals to meet and cooperate with each other – surely one of the first signs that a limited consensus could emerge. A second reason is that in the international arena, what we all have in common is our humanity. And our humanity can be a source of solidarity, as, for example, when we have deep feelings of empathy that could lead to fellow feelings of the sort that might support duties among members of that international community, as we'll see in Chapter 3.

Those who think that people's interests are mostly in conflict have a lot of explaining to do. Hobbes may have been right to say that if people travel into foreign lands they keep their chests locked and their hands on their swords. This is normally true, if it is, when people have no sense of connection with each other – that is, if they feel they cannot predict whether people in foreign lands will attack them.[16] In addition, even if goods are scarce and people are in competition for them, as Jack Knight has argued, institutions can provide answers to the question of whom we can rely on in situations of uncertainty.[17] And both international law and Just War theory can be cited, at least in their large areas of convergence, as a basis upon which people's ideas about what constitutes State aggression, of the sort that could give rise to prosecutions of individual leaders for the crime of aggression, might achieve a rudimentary consensus within an international community.

[16] Thomas Hobbes, *Leviathan*, 1651, ch. 13.
[17] Jack Knight, *Institutions and Social Conflict*, New York: Cambridge University Press, 1992, ch. 1.

One place where there has not been much agreement concerns the use of force in insurgency or terrorist actions, which have increasingly been the source of wars in the world today.[18] As we will see, there is concern among lawyers and philosophers that the international community display solidarity toward those States that are victimized by other States. There is an emerging view that such solidarity should extend to those peoples that are victimized by their governments or by majority groups within their States. Indeed, while there has been hot debate about such an issue, many States nevertheless agreed that NATO's bombing of Serbia for having led an ethnic cleansing campaign in Kosovo was the epitome of international solidarity, especially in its manifestation of the duty to go to the aid of those who could not defend themselves and faced extermination. In Part E, we will examine so-called humanitarian wars as well as wars against terrorism. But it should be noted that such wars are controversial today in international law, and in some philosophical circles.[19]

Despite the lack of agreement about whether States are justified in intervening in the affairs of other States where there is civil strife, there has been an emerging consensus about other sorts of wars or armed conflicts. Indeed, even the United States seems to admit that it needs some kind of Security Council authorization before it invades another State that has not struck first against it, as it did before invading Iraq in its vaunted war on terrorism. Such attempts at global recognition are a good indication of a possibly emerging global solidarity of the sort envisioned when the United Nations Charter was first proposed in San Francisco in 1945. The United States has played an important role in the legal limitation of war, both in San Francisco and later in Rome at the drafting of the ICC Charter, and it is indeed odd that it is the United States, at least in the decade starting in 2000, that has been the greatest obstacle to the International Criminal Court (the ICC), which will surely play a very large role in subsequent generations in limiting war. For like the Nuremberg Tribunal, the ICC might be able in the future to hold individuals liable for the waging of aggressive war, probably making it less likely that wars will indeed be waged.

---

[18] See Christine Gray, *International Law and the Use of Force*, 2nd ed., Oxford: Oxford University Press, 2004, ch. 1.

[19] See *Humanitarian Intervention: Moral and Philosophical Issues*, edited by Aleksandar Jokic, Orchard Park, New York: Broadview Press, 2003; *Ethics and Foreign Intervention*, edited by Deen K. Chatterjee and Don E. Scheid, New York: Cambridge University Press, 2003; and *Humanitarian Intervention: Ethical, Legal, and Political Dilemmas*, edited by J. L. Holzgrefe and Robert Keohane, New York: Cambridge University Press, 2003. Also see *Terrorism and International Justice*, edited by James P. Sterba, New York: Oxford University Press, 2003.

I agree with the critics of international criminal law that it is hard to show that the sparse number of international trials conducted to date has deterred many State leaders from waging aggressive war. And I agree that there are problems with retribution and reconciliation in international criminal law as well. My view is that it is not possible to provide a justification of international criminal law based on only one of these traditional justifications for criminal trials. But, as I argue in Chapter 15, a hybrid justification is possible. Concerning deterrence in particular, there is reason to think that State leaders can be deterred in some cases since they are rational beings like everyone else.

In this book, I take a defendant-oriented approach to the questions of which individuals should be prosecuted, and by what criteria, for the waging of aggressive war. The vast majority of literature on international criminal law is victim-oriented. To a certain extent this makes sense. The perpetrators of aggressive wars are some of the worst of offenders. One need only list people like Adolph Hitler, Joseph Stalin, Slobodon Milosevic, and Saddam Hussein to elicit an immediate condemnation. Those people waged aggressive war, often ruthlessly against all of their neighbors. For this reason, it is easy to see why so many international legal theorists and political philosophers are victim-oriented. Indeed, it is unlikely that trials will proceed against leaders who did not also commit other heinous crimes. But for this same reason we should proceed with caution and respect for the rights of these leaders, since extreme reactions often generate abuse or at least neglect the possibility of innocence on the part of those who are strongly vilified.

Even among non-governmental groups, such as Amnesty International and Human Rights Watch, which are famously sensitive to the plight of domestic defendants, when we move to the international arena these groups are more victim- than defendant-oriented. In order to correct this apparent imbalance, I will not take a victim-oriented approach here, although I do not mean to show any disrespect for the victims, and the families of victims, of aggressive wars. Aggressive wars should be condemned in the strongest terms, and in some circumstances I think that State leaders should be prosecuted and punished for initiating or waging aggressive war. My defendant-oriented approach does not deny that the crime of aggression should be vigorously prosecuted. Rather, I wish merely to correct an imbalance and pave the way for greater safeguards against the abuse of defendants' rights in international prosecutions.

I will defend the idea that some State leaders, both military and civilian, can and should be prosecuted for crimes of aggression and crimes against peace. In this sense my position is in between those who, on the one hand, argue that the crime of aggression is the worst of all crimes and that many individuals should have to stand trial for it, and those who, on the other hand, argue that it is States rather than individuals that should be sanctioned for waging war. As with all good middle-ground positions I will have to defend myself from both flanks, probably never fully satisfying any of my critics from either camp. Middle positions are not exciting, but they are often where the truth lies.

While not taking a victim-oriented approach, I certainly recognize that the horror of aggressive war is that many innocent civilians will be the victims of those wars. If and when deterrence works in international criminal law, the harms to victims must be at the forefront of our concerns. But in many cases, especially in prosecutions for the crime of aggression, it will not be clear whether deterrence is likely. And then, it seems to me, a focus on the defendants makes as much sense as a focus on the victims. And our guide should be concern for the rule of law. Of course, the rule of law also protects victims and can even be consistent with prosecution of victimless crimes in some restricted cases. But the goals advanced by such prosecutions make the most sense to pursue when there is a strongly regulatory governmental structure – which is surely not the case at the international level.

The guiding idea of the book is that prosecutions for the international crime of aggression can be very important, but part of this importance is that the international community should treat even those who seem to be the greatest enemies of international peace according to the rule of law. And this is true even though threats to the peace of the international community are indeed very significant. Prosecutions of State leaders, or lower ranking individuals for that matter, not only act as a possible deterrence; they also speak to the way the international community regards its members in general. When individuals, no matter who they are and no matter what they are accused of, are not treated according to the rule of law, with all of its attendant due process constraints on arrest, incarceration, prosecution, and punishment, a message is sent that is as damaging as if the defendants were given outright impunity for what they are accused of having done. We will all be the losers when the rule of law is weakened, especially at the international level. My book is, if nothing else, a cautionary note for the time when we move forward, as we should, to prosecute State leaders for the horrific crime of waging aggressive war.

V. Summary of the Arguments of the Book

In this final section I will provide a summary of the main arguments advanced in the rest of the book. In general, I argue that some, although quite few, prosecutions against State leaders for waging aggressive war can be justified. As I have indicated, I take a somewhat unusual position on these controversies: an explicitly minimalist and defendant-oriented approach to this topic. In the first part of the book I discuss in some detail the Just War tradition's condemnation of wars, and also the strong sense in this tradition that international solidarity calls for military intervention by some States against other States in limited cases. I also indicate that this view is the predominant one today in international law as well. We thus begin with a normative problem to be solved: how war can be condemned but also allowable, or at least excusable, in certain cases.

In the second part of the book, I examine three of the normative principles thought to be crucial for *jus ad bellum* considerations in justifying war. First, I look at the principle of priority or first strike and argue that this principle is really only one of several tests for just cause. I then reexamine the idea of what constitutes a just cause for waging war. This idea is crucial to determining which wars are aggressive and which are defensive. I argue that just cause is limited by a rudimentary consideration of proportionality. Finally, I try to reframe the idea of proportionality, a normative principle crucial for both *jus ad bellum* and *jus in bello* branches of the Just War tradition and for the establishment of a legitimate basis for contemporary international criminal trials. I argue that proportionality is far more important than is normally thought.

In the third part of the book, I discuss some of the case law from Nuremberg and begin to focus on the specific charges of aggression in these trials. I directly address the main conceptual puzzle I find in this area of law: how do we prosecute individuals for a crime that is committed by States, or at least State-like entities? And how do we link the State plan to the criminal intent of the defendants? I delve into some metaphysical issues to try to frame the debate, namely, the issue of how to conceive of the relationship between the State and its members, especially its leaders. Regardless of whether we are methodological individualists or collectivists, discrete, isolated individuals do not seem to be responsible for waging war, aggressive or not. I spend time on each of three different kinds of defendants prosecuted at Nuremberg: two military leaders (Admirals Doenitz and Raeder), a group of middle-level political leaders (the Ministries case), and wealthy civilians whose businesses strongly supported the war effort (the Krupp and I. G. Farben cases). At Nuremberg, the top political and military leaders, as well as middle-level political leaders, were often convicted, but the business leaders were often acquitted largely because a sufficient link was not established between the State aggression and the acts of the individual in the dock. I argue that the Nuremberg precedent is not sufficient as a grounding for trials of State leaders for the crime of aggression today. I then ask what is the precedent value of the Nuremberg judgments and examine what customary rules were created by that precedent.

In the fourth part of the book, I try to say something about how to define State aggression and the elements of the crime of aggression. The idea is to follow Thomas More's lead and think of aggressive war as any war not waged for self-defense, defense of another State, or to prevent oppression or other humanitarian crises. I refer to this in a shorthand way as wars waged in self-defense or defense of others. I want to make a simple point about how some trials might be able to proceed even if the international community couldn't agree about all possible cases. I also defend a set of subjective and objective elements that would be necessary for the successful prosecution in the International Criminal Court or other bodies that might prosecute the crime of waging war that is not in self-defense or defense of others. And I look at several important defenses that could be used by State leaders accused of the crime of aggression.

In the fifth part of the book I examine the two most difficult cases: humanitarian wars and terrorist wars. Humanitarian intervention is especially problematic because the justification or excuse of waging war is the protection of innocent life and yet wars also threaten the loss of innocent life. Humanitarian wars are, on one hand, the easiest to understand since they are aimed at stopping human rights atrocities. On the other hand they are the hardest to understand since they do not involve a response to State aggression, at least understood militarily, and they risk doing even more harm than they seek to prevent. I also discuss whether terrorist leaders and other non-State leaders should be prosecuted for the crime of aggression. I am not opposed to prosecuting the Slobodan Milosevics or Saddam Husseins of the world, but if we also prosecute leaders not at the very top we should prosecute them for what they did and intended, and not for what others did or intended. In general I provide a defense of certain limited international trials for the crime of aggression and crimes against peace. And such a defense is not limited to State leaders, although the prosecutions against non-State leaders should, in my view, be even rarer than against State leaders. Finally, I mount a normative defense of some international trials for aggression in light of some of the most astute challenges that have been brought in the last few years.

In Section I of this current chapter, I quoted Hersch Lauterpacht on the dilemma posed by Grotius, namely, that war is both hated and also seen as legal in some cases. As we have seen, the legality of war is due to its necessity in preventing certain kinds of tragedies from occurring. As I have previously argued, military necessity is a very slippery concept.[20] The idea that certain tactics, such as torture, could be necessary for achieving a certain military objective is fraught with problems. Very few tactics are militarily necessary, since there are often other tactics that could be employed instead with no significant loss in effectiveness. The idea that certain wars could be necessary for achieving a certain objective, such as preventing genocide, is fraught with the same problem as that concerning the necessity of tactics. Very few wars are necessary for achieving certain objectives, since there are often other strategies, especially diplomatic ones, that could be employed instead without significant loss in effectiveness.

As the United Nations gains strength, it might gain the ability to threaten a State on the brink of a genocidal campaign or of invading its neighbor, in a way that makes the recourse to war on the part of the defending State less likely to be grounded in necessity. This gives new meaning to the provision in Article 51 of the United Nations Charter, according to which even self-defensive wars are justified only until the United Nations takes action. A strong UN would be able to take quick and effective action, thereby blocking the loophole created in Article 51 to the more general prohibition on war that is contained in Article 2(4). And while we are still some years away from seeing this effective strength in the UN, we can contemplate how this change will affect the status of war as grounded in necessity. Perhaps there will be a time in the not-too-distant future when we can, on Grotian grounds, decry war as being always unjustified.

In this book, I will discuss the idea of waging aggressive war as well as the more recent idea that individuals can be prosecuted for such wars by international tribunals. In the next two chapters I will explain the two main competing factors in the moral and legal analysis of war. First, I will explain that war is a horrible thing and that only in the most extreme cases can it be justified, and given the likelihood that innocent people will

---

[20] Larry May, *War Crimes and Just War*, New York: Cambridge University Press, 2007, ch. 9.

be killed in war there remains a strong contingent presumption that all wars are unjustified. Second, I will explain that war is nonetheless needed in certain cases to prevent the destruction of a State or of a significant portion of its people, and that international solidarity seems to require that a State be willing to go to war to aid other States or their people from harm and hence to preserve peace and human rights. In this way we confront again the problem that wars are condemnable but that some wars may be justified or at least excused. In any event, when wars are clearly aggressive, some State leaders may be prosecuted for initiating or waging such wars. But there are significant conceptual and normative hurdles in doing so.

2

Grotius and Contingent Pacifism

In general, there breathes from the pages of *De Jure Belli ac Pacis*, a disapproval amounting to hatred, of war.

Hersch Lauterpacht[1]

De Jure Belli ac Pacis reminded his audience that he was still an enthusiast for war around the globe.

Richard Tuck[2]

Grotius's great work, *De Jure Belli ac Pacis*, an 864-page work published in 1625, is still considered to be the single most important work in international legal theory.[3] Grotius is the great modern defender of the Just War tradition, but he is also a kind of pacifist. This is an uneasy alliance within the same thinker. But such is the history of the Just War tradition, whose adherents maintained the same dual ideas: that war was evil, but that it could be, indeed must be, justifiable in certain cases. In this chapter I will attempt to explain how Grotius reconciled the various elements of his political and moral philosophy. And then, by building on Grotius's ideas I hope to provide the beginning of an account of a doctrine I will call "contingent pacifism."[4] Contingent pacifism is opposed to war not on absolute grounds but on contingent grounds, namely, that war as we have known it has not been, and seemingly cannot be, waged in a way that

---

[1] Hersch Lauterpacht, "The Grotian Tradition in International Law," *British Year Book of International Law*, vol. 23, 1946, p. 47.

[2] Richard Tuck, *The Rights of War and Peace: Political Thought and the International Order from Grotius to Kant*, Oxford: Oxford University Press, 1999, p. 95.

[3] Hugo Grotius, *De Jure Belli ac Pacis* (On the Law of War and Peace) (1625), translated by Francis W. Kelsey, Oxford: Clarendon Press, 1925.

[4] As far as I am aware, Jeff McMahan first coined this term but employed it in another context. See Jeff McMahan and Robert McKim, "The Just War and the Gulf War," *Canadian Journal of Philosophy*, vol. 23, 1993, pp. 501–541.

is morally acceptable. As we will see, *jus ad bellum*, the morality of initiating war, is thus dependent on *jus in bello*, the morality of waging war.

The early Church Fathers, especially Tertullian,[5] were pacifists, taking quite literally the pronouncements of Jesus that even if you have been directly attacked, you must turn the other cheek rather than fight back. This is the Western origin of the prohibition against engaging in war. The early Just War theorists already framed their ideas in serious debate with such pacifist ideas. Augustine argued strongly against such pacifist religious views,[6] as did the seminal proponents of modern international law. Indeed, Grotius devoted thirty-four pages to showing that some wars could theoretically be justified despite the difficulty of reconciling war with what Jesus and the early Church Fathers had said.[7] Contemporary Just War theorists seem to have lost sight of the fact that Just War theory was initially devised as a response to, though not a complete rejection of, pacifism. It is interesting to speculate on why contemporary Just War theorists do not see their views as being as close to pacifism as did the early Just War theorists. One possible explanation is that contemporary Just War theorists largely define themselves in opposition to realists who deny that morality has any connection to war, not in opposition to pacifists who are few in number in the modern era. When Just War theory is understood as it was in its early years, contingent pacifism could be merely a variation of this doctrine, as we will see.

In this chapter I will discuss the limits of the Just War doctrine, as well as Grotius's contribution to a somewhat different, although related, doctrine that I am calling contingent pacifism. The chapter is paired with the next chapter in setting out the conflicting ideas in Just War theory as well as contemporary international law on the legality of war. In the current chapter I set out the strong prohibition on war; and in the next chapter I explain why some wars nonetheless may be justified or at least excused. The first section of the current chapter explicates Grotius's general view of what makes a war just. In the second section, I set out Grotius's reasons for supporting contingent pacifism, namely, the view that, in most if not all wars, out of a concern for the innocent, it will not be justified to risk the killing of noncombatants or even most soldiers. In the third section, I step back from Grotius and try to develop a coherent modern position

---

[5] Tertullian, "The Soldier's Chaplet" (c. 210), chs. 11 and 12, in *Disciplinary, Moral and Ascetical Works*, translated by Rudolph Arbersmann, Sister Emily Joseph Daly, and Edwin Quain, New York: Fathers of the Church, 1959, pp. 255–260.

[6] Augustine, *The City of God* (c. 420), translated by Henry Bettenson, New York: Penguin Books, 1984, Book XIX, chs. 1, 7, and 12, pp. 843, 861–862, and 866–867.

[7] Grotius, *De Jure Belli ac Pacis*, Book I, ch. 2.

on contingent pacifism that is in keeping with Grotius's views. In the fourth section, I discuss an objection to contingent pacifism. In the final section I give reasons to think that international law is also committed to a form of contingent pacifism, explaining what is worth preserving and admiring about the doctrine. Throughout I examine a doctrine that has largely been neglected in the literature about the morality of war.

I. Grotius on Just Wars

In Chapter 2 of Book I, Grotius stakes out a rather common Just War position. He says:

> In the first principles of nature there is nothing which is opposed to war; rather, all points are in its favor. The end and aim of war being the preservation of life and limb, and the keeping or acquiring of things useful to life, war is in perfect accord with those first principles of nature. If in order to achieve these ends it is necessary to use force, no inconsistency with the first principles of nature is involved, since nature has given to each animal strength sufficient for self-defense and self-assistance.[8]

From the beginning of the Just War tradition, self-defense or defense of the rights of others was seen as an obvious basis for justifying some wars. Early Just War theorists thought that defense of others was the most important of these claims, because it was more selfless, but by the beginning of the modern era, self-defense was seen to be the most obvious rationale for some wars, and Grotius seems to follow in this vein.

But there is a second consideration that also supports war, yet causes significant worries down the road for Grotius. On the very next page he says:

> Right reason, moreover, and the nature of society, which must be studied in the second place and are of even greater importance, do not prohibit all use of force, but only that use of force which is in conflict with society, that is which attempts to take away the rights of others.[9]

This looks like a simple restriction on which wars can be justified in self-defense, but, much later in Grotius's book, it turns out to be of major importance. Indeed, I will argue that it is the consideration of the rights of others, along with humanitarian considerations developed by Grotius, that transform his otherwise conventional Just War views into a position that is quite close to pacifism, if not itself a nontraditional form of pacifism.

[8] Grotius, *De Jure Belli Ac Pacis*, p. 52.
[9] Ibid., p. 53.

Grotius provides three claims that are meant to summarize his over-all position in early passages from his book. First, he cites, approvingly, Galen's natural law comment that "man is an animal born for peace and war."[10] Second, Grotius also provides a rational grounding for the use of force when he says:

> It is not, then, contrary to the nature of society to look out for oneself and advance one's own interests, provided the rights of others are not infringed; and consequently the use of force which does not violate the rights of others is not unjust.[11]

And third, Grotius claims that his "thesis is also proved by the general agreement of all nations, and especially among the wise."[12] Here the laws of nations join forces with the laws of nature and the precepts of right reason to confirm that some wars can be justified.

The structure of the early parts of Grotius's book is to develop each of these lines of argument by reference to the chief sources of justice: natural law, right reason, and international custom. It is in this way that Grotius seems to establish the justifiability of war on firmer grounds than previous theorists who drew on only one or another of these sources. Grotius even seems to engage in overkill when he argues, at very great length, that the Gospels are also not inconsistent with the idea of war.[13] He then summarizes this argument by saying: "Now it is in the love of innocent men that both capital punishment and just wars have their origin."[14] However we should note that Grotius here turns from self-defense to defense of others as the best "just cause" for war.

So far, Grotius espouses a line quite consistent with standard Just War theory. But we should pause to note that just a few years earlier, the great Scholastic philosopher Francisco Suarez had added to the Thomistic ver-sion of Just War theory a new element. Aquinas had listed the elements in a just war to be

1. the authority of the sovereign
2. a just cause
3. a rightful intention.[15]

---

[10] Ibid.
[11] Ibid., p. 54.
[12] Ibid., p. 55.
[13] Ibid., pp. 57–85.
[14] Ibid., p. 75.
[15] Thomas Aquinas, *Summa Theologica*, Pt. II-II, Qu. 40, Art. 1, trans. by Fathers of the English Dominican Province, London: Burns, Oates and Washburn, 1936.

Suarez adds to this

4. a proper method[16]

Yet, this addition, as we will see, changes everything. There is good reason to think that Grotius followed Suarez in this respect.

The first major indication that Grotius is worried about how tactical concerns can undercut support for initiating war comes when Grotius is already deeply immersed in *jus in bello* concerns. In Chapter 10 of Book III of *De Jure Belli ac Pacis*, Grotius surprises his readers by saying: "I must retrace my steps, and must deprive those who wage war of nearly all the privileges which I seemed to grant but did not grant them." This all falls under the label of "With what meaning a sense of honor may be said to forbid what the law permits."[17] And while most of what Grotius takes back has to do with privileges concerning the tactics of those who wage war, it also appears that he wants to take back some of what he said about the justifiability of initiating or waging war at all.

This comes out most clearly when Grotius talks, as he does in the next chapter, Chapter 11 of Book III, about the right of killing.[18] As it turns out, most forms of killing violate the rights of others. Combining this point with the previously noted one – namely, that war cannot be justly waged if it violates the rights of others – gets us a draconian requirement that most wars will be hard-pressed to meet. For if there are violations of rights in many, if not most, cases of war, then the situations where war might be justified shrink, perhaps to the vanishing point.

The point here is that Grotius denies that otherwise prohibited tactics are justifiable merely because one fights with a just cause. One might have thought that Grotius would not maintain this position, since he clearly acknowledged that wars can be just. If a war can be just in that one side fights for a just cause and the other side fights unjustly, then it would seem to follow that any tactic that advances the side fighting for a just cause would itself be justifiable. To stop an unjust invasion, it seems odd to say that I cannot use tactics that seem to be the most efficacious. Yet Grotius's discussion of this point, which I will explicate later, comes under the label of what type of killing might be unjust even in a just war.

---

[16] Francisco Suarez, "On War," in *Selections from Three Works* (Disputation XIII, *De Triplici Virtute Theologica: Charitate*), (c. 1610), translated by Gwladys L. Williams, Ammi Brown, and John Waldron, Oxford: Clarendon Press, 1944, p. 805.

[17] Grotius, *De Jure Belli ac Pacis*, p. 716.

[18] Ibid., p. 722.

Grotius's discussion of unjustifiable killing in war could be only a very straightforward discussion of what types of killing cannot be justified by those who fight without just cause – that is, of the *jus in bello* restrictions that are in place even after *jus ad bellum* concerns have seemingly been addressed. But since he places many restrictions on killing even in a just war, so that use of certain tactics can turn a just war into an unjust war, *jus in bello* considerations appear to place restrictions, at least at the limit, on what counts as a just war. And in this sense, Grotius may be following Suarez in thinking that if one is unable to wage a war with justified methods or tactics then one is unjustified in initiating the war at all.

II. Grotius on Justifiable Killing in War

In the first step down the road to what I will call contingent pacifism, Grotius says that "it is necessary that he who is killed shall himself have done wrong."[19] Grotius also says that killing can be justified if there is no other way to save one's own life or property, but he later argues that wars rarely have this character. The category of killing, as punishment for wrong done, seems to be the most important. And yet, according to Grotius, few soldiers have done anything personally wrong, even on the battlefield. Soldiers typically just follow orders, often out of a patriotic feeling. And even leaders act in ways they think will advance the interests of their States, thereby keeping to their primary obligations as rulers. So, for Grotius, it is hard to see why these soldiers, or leaders, would be thought to have done wrong even during war.

In this discussion, Grotius refers his readers to his earlier discussion of punishment. There he had said that punishment can be justified only if the one punished displays "a base or malicious nature."[20] This require-ment will make it very hard for many wars to be justified as forms of punishment; while every war will have at most one side that is in the right and one side that is in the wrong, those who fight on the wrong side do not necessarily fight with base or malicious motives. Indeed, it will often be very hard for soldiers to figure out whether their side is in the right or in the wrong, since most soldiers are not privy to their leaders' reason-ing. For punishment to be justified, the one punished must deserve to be punished, and no one deserves to be punished who is without malice or guilt.

[19] Ibid., p. 723.
[20] Ibid., p. 488.

Grotius makes it explicit that he will follow this line of reasoning when he says, "No man may rightly be killed because of his ill fortune, for example those who take sides under compulsion."[21] And in a very important passage, Grotius then also distinguishes between wrongs and faults. One cannot be rightly killed, in war or in capital punishment, for misfortune or for fault, but only for having done wrong. Grotius defines fault and wrong by quoting Aristotle as follows:

> Now misfortunes are things which could not have been foreseen, and are not committed with evil intent; faults things which could have been foreseen, yet are not done with evil intent; wrongs things done purposely and with evil intent.[22]

This leads Grotius to draw a firm line between those "who are responsible for a war . . . [and] those who follow them."[23]

For Grotius, it is unjustifiable to kill a soldier who is merely following orders, especially if that soldier is fighting out of a "sense of duty and righteous zeal." These soldiers are not cruel or inhuman and do not deserve to be killed. According to his earlier doctrine, Grotius could say that it would be a violation of their rights for people who are merely following orders to be killed, even in a just war. Indeed, the killing of these people in violation of their rights would seemingly make the war itself unjust. Remember that Grotius had declared that "the use of force which does not violate the rights of others is not unjust."[24] So, it appears that the key is to figure out whether soldiers violate the rights of others in determining whether their actions are just.

The cornerstone of Grotius's doctrine calls for the prevention of the death of the innocent during war, as he says "no action should be attempted whereby innocent persons may be threatened with destruction."[25] Here the innocent are merely those who during war have not done wrong. But Grotius goes even further than this restatement of the principle of discrimination or distinction. He says that it is our duty "to spare those who are guilty for the sake of the innocent."[26] This means that the prohibition on not killing the innocent extends so far as not to kill even the guilty if doing so might jeopardize the innocent.

[21] Ibid., p. 723.
[22] Ibid., p. 727, quoting Aristotle's *Rhetoric*, I, xiii.
[23] Ibid., p. 729.
[24] Ibid., p. 54.
[25] Ibid., p. 734.
[26] Ibid.

Grotius clearly indicates what he means by the innocent whose lives should not be taken even in a just war. "Children are always to be spared," as are old men. Women are to be spared "unless they have been guilty of an extremely serious offense."[27] Grotius also follows other theorists in arguing that members of religious groups, those who are in arts or letters, farmers, merchants, and prisoners of war all should not be killed.[28] These individuals have not done wrong, at least in regard to the war, and cannot justifiably be killed. Such restrictions place quite severe limits on the waging of war. According to Grotius's criterion, it is likely that most wars violate the rights of individuals, and hence likely that most wars are unjust to begin with.

But the crucial piece of the puzzle, that moves Grotius toward a form of pacifism, comes when he says that it is not legitimate to argue "that by a sort of fiction the enemy may be conceived as forming a single body."[29] Instead, we must consider whether any given soldier has "done wrong" as an individual before he or she may be justifiably killed. If the requirement is that each person killed must have done wrong, then virtually no war could be regarded as justified, since it would be almost impossible to determine whether all those soldiers – on the battlefield, for instance – have done wrong and hence could be justifiably killed.

At this stage of Grotius's argument, it appears to me and to some other commentators, such as Hersch Lauterpacht quoted at the beginning of this chapter, that Grotius moves very close to a form of pacifism. This is not an absolute principled pacifism, where he is opposed to all violence. But it is a "contingent pacifism" according to which killing the innocent is nearly always wrong. In this view, justified war is nearly impossible because nearly all war involves killing those who are innocent, that is, those who have not personally done wrong in war.

Grotius sometimes seems to modify his claims in ways that run contrary to my interpretation of him as a contingent pacifist. But he also returns to his main theme, often in the same paragraph, as when he says:

> Against these precepts of justice and the law of nature frequently exceptions are offered, which are by no means just; as for example, if retaliation is required, if there is need of inspiring terror, if too determined a resistance has been offered. Yet he who recalls what has previously been said for putting to death will easily perceive that such exceptions do not afford just grounds for an execution.[30]

[27] Ibid.
[28] Ibid., pp. 736–737.
[29] Ibid., p. 741.
[30] Ibid., p. 740.

Retaliation, he tells us here, can only be justified "against those who have done wrong."[31] In non-retaliatory cases, we similarly can only justifiably kill those who have done wrong. Yet any military unit will have a mixture of those who are innocent and those who are not.

But as the other quotation at the beginning of this essay, from Richard Tuck, indicates, some scholars have seen Grotius as only too ready to justify a whole assortment of wars. So, we must consider the possibility that Grotius did not fully understand the implications of the extended discussion we have just seen in Book III, Chapter 11, from *De Jure Belli ac Pacis*. My view is that Grotius was at best a "contingent pacifist" of the sort who does not fully realize that his views have committed him to the condemnation of virtually all wars, even as he is otherwise disposed to think that they could be justified. Indeed, even as they recognize that such wars are not currently justifiable, contingent pacifists must keep open the possibility that wars in the future could be waged in such a way that they could be justified, in case weapons become so precise that they can be targeted exactly and intelligence becomes so good that we can pick out and kill only the guilty and not the innocent soldiers.

III. The Idea of Contingent Pacifism

The view that I call contingent pacifism, which I derive from Grotius's remarks, can be initially summarized as follows:

> Rarely, if ever, is it morally permissible to kill the innocent.
> All wars involve killing, or the risk of killing, the innocent.
> Rarely, if ever, are wars morally justified.

This simple argument admits that it may be possible for some wars to be morally justified in principle. Since there have been few if any wars in the past that were justified, and since there is no conclusive reason to think that the future will not resemble the past, this view nonetheless comes very close to being, if it isn't already, a nonstandard form of pacifism.

One could argue that contingent pacifism calls only for looking at wars on a case-by-case basis to see whether there is unjustified killing of the innocent, and that this is consistent with what Just War theorists have often argued over the centuries. In response I would have to agree – contingent pacifism is consistent with some forms of Just War theory. This is why Grotius could be both a Just War theorist and yet also a supporter of contingent pacifism. The two quotations at the beginning of the chapter,

---

[31] Ibid., p. 741.

one pointing out that Grotius disapproved of and even hated war and the other that Grotius was an enthusiast for war, could be reasonable interpretations of Grotius's texts. Grotius is a defender of war in theory; yet he finds wars in practice to be subject to strong disapproval. However the view I call contingent pacifism is different from other views that allow for the possibility of justifying some wars.

To get an initial idea of what is involved in contingent pacifism, consider a parallel idea concerning the justifiability of capital punishment. Today many theorists and politicians are not opposed to all cases of capital punishment; indeed, the hypothetical case of the child molester who also kills his victims is often mentioned as a case in which capital punishment is regarded as justified even by those who have serious principled reservations about capital punishment. But when it comes to actual cases, the problem is that trial procedures do not guarantee accurate verdicts even in capital trials. Indeed, the chances that an innocent person, or at least the wrong person, will be convicted or that the jury will fail to see significant mitigating factors, or overstress aggravating factors, are so great as to undermine any warrant for thinking that capital punishment will be used only for guilty persons. Even though one might recognize the moral justifiability of capital punishment for some types of case in theory, one can become a contingent opponent of capital punishment, or as it might be called, a contingent abolitionist. According to this view, capital punishment should not be employed if it looks as though defendants will be executed when they do not deserve to be. A similar position could be taken on the justifiability of war, resulting in what I have been calling "contingent pacifism."

Contingent pacifists, by analogy, do not have absolute principled objections to war; indeed, they forthrightly acknowledge that in theory wars can be justifiably waged, especially in cases of self-defense and defense of others. But contingent pacifists follow Francisco Suarez in thinking that wars can only be justifiably initiated and waged if it is clearly foreseeable that justifiable tactics can be employed. And contingent pacifists follow Grotius in understanding that justifiable tactics are those that do not violate the rights of the innocent. Wars cannot justifiably be initiated or waged if it is likely that doing so will result in serious violations of the rights of the innocent. Thus the objection to war is contingent rather than absolute; but the contingencies may occur so often that one would become a de facto pacifist by maintaining this objection.

Contingent pacifists blur the border of *jus ad bellum* and *jus in bello*, but they do it in a way that is different from the currently popular view that also blurs the distinction. Several leading theorists have argued, only somewhat plausibly, that contrary to several thousand years of theorizing within the Just War tradition, the morality of tactics should be determined by whether war is just. Different rules concerning the morality of tactics should be in place for the side that wages a just war as opposed to the side that wages an unjust war.[32] Indeed, some have argued that there should be few if any restrictions on those who fight on the side that wages a just war, and that very strict restraints should apply to those who fight on the side that wages an unjust war. I will not here go into the merits of this new doctrine, except to say that I disagree strongly with its conclusion and have argued against it elsewhere.[33] My point in bringing it up, however, is to observe that contingent pacifists will offer another kind of argument for revisiting the separateness of *jus ad bellum* and *jus in bello*, and hence will also mainly be swimming against several thousand years of Just War theorizing.

Instead of basing *jus in bello* on *jus ad bellum*, contingent pacifism does the reverse. Contingent pacifism does not call for, indeed does not countenance, the weakening of *jus in bello* rules of war for those who fight in a just war. But contingent pacifism does call for determining whether a war is just in light of *jus in bello* considerations regarding how the war is conducted. Specifically, contingent pacifism adds a significant condition to the requirements for the initiating and waging of a Just War, based on Suarez's requirement that "the method of its conduct must be proper."[34] The problem with this requirement is that we cannot determine whether it has been met in advance of fighting the war, since our ability of prediction is always fallible. The requirement must be reformulated, as I have suggested, to be something like "it must be likely that the conduct of the war will be proper." But once formulated in this way, the new requirement folds *jus in bello* considerations into the requirements for *jus ad bellum* and disrupts the separateness of these branches of the Just War doctrine.

It is possible to reach the same conclusion I have been defending while maintaining the separation of *jus ad bellum* and *jus in bello*. Suppose one holds that the justness of initiating or waging war (*jus ad bellum*) is

[32] See Jeff McMahan, "The Ethics of Killing in War," *Ethics*, vol. 114, Summer 2004, pp. 693–733; and Lionel McPherson, "Innocence and Responsibility in War," *Canadian Journal of Philosophy*, 2005, pp. 485–506.

[33] See my book *War Crimes and Just Wars*, New York: Cambridge University Press, 2007, ch. 2.

[34] Suarez, "On War," p. 805.

independent of the tactics or means used in conducting the war (*jus in bello*). One could still agree that any military tactic that was quite likely to kill innocent people is unjustified. However, war itself is not thereby rendered unjustified. But if it turns out that because of the restrictions on tactics there are no justified tactics left, then war would be rendered so restricted tactically as not to be one that can be morally fought. By this I mean that if people who want to fight a just war cannot find any morally permissible tactics, then there really isn't any morally justifiable war that they are morally permitted to fight. To say that the war is just but there are no morally permissible tactics to use in that war is equivalent to saying that the war cannot be permissibly fought. This form of contingent pacifism would hold that while war can be morally justified in theory, the fighting of war is not and is unlikely to be morally justified, and hence that most if not all wars are morally impermissible.

Some contemporary authors have seemed to see the Grotian point that I have been developing. Jenny Teichman, for instance, says the following:

> If all the soldiers on the morally right side are thereby innocent, then to kill them is murder and on a par with killing children (say). Those on the morally wrong side who cannot know that their rulers are engaged in an unjust war are also innocent, and to kill *them* is murder and on a par with killing helpless old peasants, or priests, or nuns. Rulers, who after due consultation and after taking counsel from wise men come to believe sincerely, albeit wrongly, that their cause for war is a just cause, are also innocent; to kill them, if one could get hold of them, would be murder. But who then *may* be killed in a just war justly fought? Only those few rulers who have either failed to take proper consultation (negligence) or know themselves that their cause is not just (guilty mind). But a war with so few protagonists is not a war at all.[35]

Here we can see a version of contingent pacifism. War is not immoral, for it could be based on self-defense or defense of others. But so few people can be justifiably killed in such a war that war is nonetheless all but extinguished from the moral universe, or at least war, in the forms that we have known and are foreseeable in the future, is rendered immoral.

Other theorists in recent times have held views that are similar to contingent pacifism. Robert Holmes argues in a similar vein when he says:

> If the means necessary to waging war cannot be justified, then war cannot be justified and no war can be just. Not only must there be moral constraints upon the conduct of war even if the war is in all other particulars justified; the possibility must be recognized that there are moral restraints upon the

[35] Jenny Teichman, *Pacifism and the Just War*, Oxford: Basil Blackwell, 1986, p. 64.

treatment of persons that prohibit the waging of war in the first place, that is, even engaging in the limited killing and destruction that otherwise just wars entail.[36]

And James Sterba argues that anti-war pacifism can be rendered consistent with certain strains of Just War theory.[37]

Writing before the beginning of the Just War tradition, Seneca said that it is odd that "actions forbidden of private citizens are committed in the name of the state." Governments try hard "to restrain murders and the killing of individuals" and yet "wars and the crime of slaughtering nations [are] full of glory."[38] But more than reiterating the abhorrence with war, contingent pacifists argue that war may turn out not to be justifiable even in those cases that seem to be paradigmatic ones where we might think it to be justified despite its abhorrence, namely, in cases of self-defense or defense of others. Such a view gives rise to a major objection against contingent pacifists that I will next consider.

IV. An Objection to Contingent Pacifism

One of the chief objections to contingent pacifism can be explained by reference to a non-war example. Imagine that someone points a gun at you. As far as you can tell, your life will be extinguished in the next few minutes unless you shoot and kill this person. Yet, as far as you can tell, your attacker may be innocent and not responsible for his actions. If the attacker is innocent, it seems unjustified to kill him. But if you do not kill him, you in effect sacrifice your life, which is also an innocent life and importantly your own life. If similar results are reached about States, then contingent pacifism seems to entail that a State is blocked from trying to defend itself from attack and to save the lives of its members. If it makes sense to say that we can kill someone who might be innocent in the personal case, why does it not make sense in the case of war? And if killing the innocent in war can indeed be justified, then contingent pacifism is undermined.

---

[36] Robert L. Holmes, *On War and Morality*, Princeton: Princeton University Press, 1989, p. 183.

[37] See James Sterba, "Terrorism and International Justice," *Terrorism and International Justice*, edited by James P. Sterba, New York: Oxford University Press, 2003, pp. 206–228, for a good summary of his view; and James P. Sterba, *Justice for Here and Now*, Cambridge: Cambridge University Press, 1998, ch. 7.

[38] Seneca, *Letters*, xcvi [xcv 30], quoted in Grotius, *De Jure Belli ac Pacis*, p. 170.

There are several things to say about this objection. First, while it is true that Just War theory has often relied on just such an example to get its foot in the door against pacifism, it is not at all clear that the personal case is sufficiently analogous to war to be helpful. Notice that in the example the possibly innocent attacker is poised to attack and hence is clearly jeopardizing your life. There are circumstances in which enemy armies are also poised to attack and are thereby jeopardizing lives or even the "life" of the State.

However, things are normally much more complicated in the multi-person case than in the personal case. For one thing, the "killing" of a State may result in no one's loss of life, since one State is merely replaced by another. The main complication is that the individual soldier is not normally in the position of being attacked outside the context of war. Some soldiers volunteer to be put in harm's way or choose to act in ways that have that risk as one clear option. If the soldier had not placed himself on the battlefield, or its equivalent, the soldier would not now be in need of defending himself against an enemy soldier. In a sense, some soldiers are complicit in their current predicament in ways that are rarely true in the personal case. A similar situation often holds for a State that is threatened by another State. A State that is likely to be "killed" if self-defensive violence is not directed at members of an attacking army is usually not completely innocent. For these reasons the personal case and the war case are not parallel. And even in situations where it seems that utilitarian considerations would weigh heavily in favor of self-defensive violence, the individual soldier is often better off not engaging in such violence.[39]

The objection urges us to treat a State as if it were a single entity that, like a human person, can be harmed or killed. I follow Grotius, who cautions against taking a collectivist position on such issues. Here is the key quotation from Grotius again: "It is not sufficient that by a sort of fiction the enemy may be conceived as forming a single body."[40] If we are launched into the discussion of who can justifiably be killed, we must look at the wrongness of the actions or the innocence of the persons, one by one. To do otherwise is to engage in a pernicious form of guilt by association, that is, to hold one person guilty for what the other members of the group are doing. For such a view fails to take into consideration

---

[39] See my essay "Collective Responsibility, Honor, and War Crimes," *Journal of Social Philosophy*, Fall 2005, pp. 289–304.
[40] Grotius, *De Jure Belli ac Pacis*, p. 741.

the key ingredient in guilt and responsibility, namely, whether individual persons have a guilty state of mind that warrants loss of immunity that could then warrant wartime violence.

The analogy also fails because the innocent soldiers who are likely to be killed during war are not the ones who are threatening the lives of those most likely to kill them. The soldiers who do not fire a shot and may have no desire to do so are not innocent threats, at least not in any direct sense, against the lives of the soldiers who fight for a just cause and who would take their lives, or risk doing so, if war is allowed. And those who do threaten the lives of others are often very hard to separate from those who do not. We should not hold people responsible for what others are doing unless there is very good reason to think that all are involved in a task that cannot have its parts separated from one another.

Even if the above argument does not convince, there is another perhaps more plausible response. Contingent pacifists do not necessarily dispute the justifiability of war on grounds of self-defense or, even better, on grounds of defense of others. Indeed, contingent pacifists have no absolute principled way to rule out such wars and are critical of normal pacifism for ruling out such wars as unjustifiable in all cases. Contingent pacifists are not pacifists in the normal sense in that they do not rule out the justifiability of every type of war. Instead, contingent pacifists consult the context in each case to see if there are justifiable ways to wage the war in question. They become a kind of pacifist since people cannot know in advance whether a proposed war can be conducted rightly. In war where there is so much violence, the benefit of the doubt must always go to restraint. As Grotius said: "war is of the utmost importance, seeing that in consequence of war a great many sufferings usually fall upon even innocent persons. Therefore in the midst of divergent opinions we must lean toward peace."[41] Whether it is because of lack of knowledge, or divergent opinions, contingent pacifists rarely if ever think a proposed war is prima facie justified.

Again, consider the case of capital punishment. The contingent abolitionist about capital punishment does not say that all cases of capital punishment are morally unjustified. Indeed, there may be cases, at least in theory, in which the evidence is nearly unassailable that a defendant, who is about to be executed, is the one who committed an especially egregious murder. What drives the contingent abolitionist to a position similar to the opinion of those who on absolute principled grounds oppose

[41] Ibid., p. 560.

all capital punishment is a belief that in most if not all cases there is a significant risk that an innocent defendant will be falsely convicted and then executed. The contingent abolitionist, however, remains open to the possibility that some cases of capital punishment are justified. The contingent abolitionist allows that capital punishment can be legitimate and worries only that innocent persons might mistakenly be convicted of capital crimes.

In a similar vein, the contingent pacifist, like the traditional Just War theorist, believes that some wars are, at least in theory, morally justified, especially wars waged for self-defense or defense of others. The contingent pacifist might not oppose such wars as those waged against Nazi Germany's aggression, at least initially thinking that such wars are surely justified, if any wars are. Indeed, the contingent pacifist believes that the world would be a better place if such wars were fought, assuming that tactics could be devised that did not risk the killing of the innocent. Yet the contingent pacifist recognizes that even the war fought against Nazi aggression was conducted with incomplete information and did result in the killing of many innocent people. But such wars could do considerable good if only the risks of killing the innocent were not so high.

The justification for war based on a need for defense of others or self-defense, first mounted by those like Augustine against the early Church Fathers who were pacifists, is something that contingent pacifists take very seriously. But the concern for not killing the innocent is the overriding concern and one that is very hard, but not impossible, to overcome. Reasonable contingent pacifism requires only that it is not foreseeable that the tactics chosen will put innocent lives at risk; it does not require certainty that no innocent people will be killed. When innocent lives are on both sides of the balance sheet, as we will see in subsequent chapters, a door is open for justifiable war, but there will probably be few such cases.

V. Contingent Pacifism and International Law

Since the establishment of the United Nations Charter in 1945, there has been a strong prohibition on the use of force by States. Many international lawyers think that the strong prohibition on the use of force should remain in place in international law, despite the problem of humanitarian intervention. I began this chapter by quoting remarks from Hersch Lauterpacht about Grotius. Those same comments could be used to summarize Lauterpacht's own views on the international law of armed force. In his classic work, Lauterpacht argued that the "fundamental precept" of international law is "there shall be no violence."[42] Lauterpacht's remarks were addressed to the League of Nations, but we can find many, indeed most, international lawyers who would say the same thing about the United Nations concerning whether there is a prohibition on the use of force by States.

There is then a strong sense that international law has a pacifist flavor to it. But since some exceptions are allowed, such as for self-defense when authorized by the United Nations, international law can hardly be said to be pacifist in the traditional sense. In this section, I will give some reasons for thinking that contingent pacifism best captures the current position in international law as well as the position of many legal scholars since at least Lauterpacht's influential articulation of the "no violence" principle of international law. Indeed, it might turn out that the contingent pacifism of contemporary international law is even stronger than the Grotian form of contingent pacifism I defended above, which was based on a concern that during wars the innocent are placed at risk.

The international law version of contingent pacifism is based on a concept of collective security that replaces the older idea of States being left largely alone to look out for their own security. The older international order was based on the idea that States were sovereign and should not ever invade one another's territories. There is a bit of the old order in the newer UN idea of collective security, for the idea is that States should not attack each other, and that if they do the response should come under international auspices. The newer international order calls for a kind of contingent pacifism that has to do with the need for maintaining international peace, which on first sight might appear to be a stronger basis for a kind of contingent pacifism than that grounded in concern for the possible death of innocent persons.

The Preamble to the Charter of the United Nations sets out quite clearly a type of pacifist agenda for the nations of the world:

> We the People of the United Nations determined to save succeeding generations from the scourge of war, which twice in our lifetime has brought untold sorrow to mankind . . . and for these ends to live together in peace with one another . . . and to ensure by the acceptance of principles and the institution of methods, that armed force shall not be used, save in the common interest. . . . [43]

---

[42] Hersch Lauterpacht, *The Function of Law in the International Community*, Oxford: Clarendon Press, 1933, p. 64.

[43] Charter of the United Nations, T.S. 993, 59 Stat. 1031, 1976 Y.B.U.N. 1043 (June 26, 1945).

Article 1(1) calls for the "suppression of acts of aggression" and calls for the "settlement of international disputes or situations that might lead to a breach of the peace" by "peaceful means." And then, in Article 2(4) of the United Nations Charter, it is declared:

> All members shall refrain in their international relations from the threat or use of force against the territorial integrity or political independence of any state, or in any other manner inconsistent with the purposes of the United Nations.

Of course some exceptions are allowed, as I indicated in Chapter 1, chiefly through the reference in Article 51 to individual and collective self-defense. But even this exception is controversial since it seems to call for a State to wait to see whether the United Nations will take action before the aggrieved State or its allies can use military force.

Even in the Preamble to the Charter, it is recognized that force could be used for the common good. Yet, since it is unclear whether this is a recognition of the justifiability of war or whether mere "police action" at the international level is contemplated, the UN Charter can be read as a document that endorses a type of contingent pacifism. And since the Charter is considered about as solid a source of international law as one can get, it is fair to say that a form of contingent pacifism is at least contemplated if not institutionalized in contemporary international law. It is possible to design weapons that will diminish the risk of innocent loss of life, perhaps even to diminish it to the vanishing point, and hence allow for some wars to be fought that do not violate the prohibition on the loss of innocent life that was the chief concern of Grotian contingent pacifism. But if our concern is with maintaining peace in the international arena, as is the chief concern of international law's version of contingent pacifism, it appears that it will be harder to envision a time when wars might be justified. In the next chapter, I will sketch an argument to the contrary, indicating how the maintenance of international peace might indeed call for certain wars to be waged.

Thomas Franck has argued that the drafters of the United Nations Charter failed to make allowance for the dramatic rise in public support for human rights and for public outcry in favor of humanitarian wars to defend human rights.[44] The Charter's Preamble says that it "reaffirms faith in fundamental human rights, in the dignity and worth of the human person, [and] in the equal rights of men and women." It is of course also

---

[44] Thomas Franck, *Recourse to Force*, Cambridge: Cambridge University Press, 2002.

true that another important United Nations document, the Universal Declaration of Human Rights, itself drafted just three years after the UN Charter, has greatly fueled the public support for human rights. In the next chapter, I will explore the reasons for thinking that some use of force by States might be allowed, perhaps even required, despite my support for some version of contingent pacifism. I here wish to indicate that I share Thomas Franck's concerns and do not disagree that one plausible position is to continue to maintain the strong prohibition on the use of force and yet to acknowledge certain excusing conditions, although not justifying conditions. I agree with Franck that the United Nations Charter seems to contemplate a prohibition on the use of force by States but also seems to allow that defending human rights could be an excuse to the charge of aggression.

Before leaving this topic I wish to mention a prudential form of contingent pacifism that even those international law scholars and State leaders who are realists might embrace, having to do with the high costs of waging any war. This is not a new idea by any means. Indeed, there is some reason to think that Erasmus had a similar view.[45] The idea is that wars are hugely costly in terms of human as well as material resources lost. To initiate war is almost always, indeed perhaps always, a bad risk. There are almost always, and perhaps always, diplomatic alternatives, especially once there is in place a body like the United Nations that can be employed both for intense diplomatic pressure and for spreading the cost of an armed response across other States under the collective security umbrella.

Realist concerns about the cost of war were surely also at the forefront of the considerations that led to the formation of the United Nations. In the aftermath of World War II, two things were obvious to most State leaders. The human cost of war in the technological age was enormous; and the economic cost was in many ways just as great. Europe was devastated by that war, especially by the aggressiveness of the way it was waged by Nazi Germany. A certain kind of prudential contingent pacifism was in the air, and it manifested itself in the call for an international order that would prevent mass wars in the future. But it soon became clear that there was a problem as well – for not all State leaders saw that waging war was too horrible to contemplate, even after the reality of World War II. And the

---

[45] See Sissela Bok's essay, "Early Advocates of Lasting World Peace: Utopians or Realists?" in *Ethics and International Affairs: A Reader*, 2nd ed., edited by Joel H. Rosenthal, Washington, DC: Georgetown University Press, 1999, pp. 124–147. Bok writes, "Even on the strictest strategic grounds of national self-interest, Erasmus insists, a truly realistic look at the costs of war should dissuade a prince from just about all recourse to arms," p. 130.

question then had to be raised again about whether war in defense of peace was ruled out by the same United Nations documents that meant to preserve peace.

If we focus on the prohibition on the killing of the innocent as the main normative principle for assessing the legality and morality of war, then all wars are morally suspect and virtually to the same degree, as our discussion in this chapter has shown. So, if we are to save the moral and legal distinction between aggressive, and unjustified, versus defensive, and justified, wars, some other normative basis must be found than a concern for the killing of the innocent. In the next chapter we will engage in such an effort by identifying a different concern for individuals, namely, the violation of their basic human rights that is made more likely when previously stable governments that protected those rights are destabilized. Indeed, as we saw, Grotius often describes his own position in rights terms rather than protecting the innocent terms. I will address this issue in terms of the normative principle of solidarity between people. The distinction between aggressive and defensive war is a normative marker to stand for the difference between those wars that attack, versus those that support, States that protect the human rights of their people.

If the idea of aggression is linked with jeopardizing human rights, then there is a sense in which the idea that aggression alone, understood as merely crossing borders in an unprovoked way, is not ultimately to be seen as the most serious of international crimes, as was alleged in the Nuremberg trials. Instead, it is the linking of war with human rights violations that is the normative harm done by aggression. And this allows us to see why it is that the Nuremberg "precedent" is so often misunderstood today. The genocide that was epitomized by the Holocaust is thought to be the supreme crime that triggered the trials at Nuremberg, when in fact it was Nazi aggression. Today it is hard to see how aggression could have been thought to be more important than genocide. And indeed, it is my contention that unless putative aggression is linked with serious human rights deprivation, such as occurs in genocide, it is hard to explain why aggression should be strongly condemned normatively.

The key consideration is that stable States that respect and protect the basic human rights of their people should not be destabilized, and that the international community, such as it is, can come to the aid of States against their attackers. Rawls argued that some that were not democratic liberal States deserved to have their sovereignty respected. He called such States minimally decent. One can certainly wonder whether democracy is crucial for the long-term protection of basic human rights.[46] But I think it is uncontroversial that at least in the short term some non-democratic States can, and do, protect the basic rights of their people. War waged against such States, as well as war waged against those States that are both democratic and protectors of the basic human rights of their people, could count as the kind of aggressive wars that should be condemned. Indeed, one of the lessons learned by thinking about wars of humanitarian intervention is that otherwise aggressive wars are not necessarily normatively problematic if the aim of such wars is to protect a people from assault by its own government. To be sure, there are other problems with wars of humanitarian intervention that will be explored in Part E of this book, such as that they risk the lives of more civilians than they potentially save. But one of these problems is not that they are unjustifiably aggressive. In what follows in the next chapter, the full-scale argument for such a conclusion will be spelled out.

Like Grotius, I am of two minds about the morality of war, wanting to support certain wars, at least in theory, but also disapproving of wars, at least the way they are typically waged. Contingent pacifism does not rule out the moral justifiability of any war in advance, that is, in advance of examining the specific context and circumstances of a given war. Hence, the view I have defended here appears to be not really a form of "pacifism" at all, at least as that term has been traditionally understood. But insofar as contingent pacifism might indeed lead to no wars being justified, it might still be called a form of pacifism, although nontraditional. The contingent pacifist is a nonstandard kind of pacifist, just as the contingent abolitionist is a nonstandard kind of opponent of capital punishment. That a view is nonstandard is, of course, not a mark against it. In the next chapter, I will explore the arguments in favor of some wars on grounds of the duty to go to the aid of those who are fellow members of the international community. That chapter will complete the first part of this book on the origins of the idea of aggressive war and its prohibition in philosophy and international law.

---

[46] John Rawls, *The Law of Peoples*, Cambridge, MA: Harvard University Press, 1999.

3

International Solidarity and the Duty to Aid

> There exists a solidarity among men as human beings that makes each co-responsible for every wrong and every injustice in the world, especially for crimes committed in his presence or with his knowledge.
>
> Karl Jaspers[1]

In the 17th century Grotius argued that States exist in a loose community, but there may be enough of an international community to generate duties of mutual aid. In the 18th century Vattel argued that States clearly owe each other assistance because they are all part of a larger community of States. Today, we also speak of an international community, as when it is said that crimes against peace or crimes against humanity harm the international community. In those historical and contemporary cases, theorists have sometimes tried to defend such claims by reference to the idea of solidarity among States. I will argue that solidarity is importantly associated with minimal duties of mutual aid within that community. But solidarity has too many conceptual and normative problems to be a strong grounding for such duties.[2] Nonetheless I employ the idea of solidarity to defend a minimal duty of mutual aid of States that is able to justify some wars, although not as robust a duty as many human rights theorists seem to want today.

The duty of mutual aid of States is the counterpoint to the general prohibition on war that pacifists and even Just War theorists have defended over the centuries. In Just War theory the general prohibition on war was a contingent prohibition, and such prohibitions can sometimes be

---

[1] Karl Jaspers, *The Question of German Guilt*, New York: Capricorn Books, 1947, p. 36.
[2] On the status of the contemporary debate about associational duties, see Christopher Heath Wellman, "Relational Facts in Liberal Political Theory: Is There Magic in the Pronoun 'My'?" *Ethics*, vol. 110, no. 3, April 2000, pp. 537–562.

outweighed by other considerations. We here confront a problem that has plagued theorists since at least the time of Augustine: war is both so horrible that it should generally be prohibited on moral grounds, but also sometimes necessary for us to meet our moral obligations of mutual aid. According to this construal, if war is to be justified it will be on grounds of defense of innocent others.

I will focus on the crime of aggression, and on whether some acts of initiating war without provocation could be seen as non-aggressive or at least justified on grounds of defense of others. So-called humanitarian war is the classic case of a war that seems to be aggressive but which many people see as nonetheless justified, if not sometimes required of States. In the previous chapter, I defended contingent pacifism according to which any waging of war that kills innocent people is unjustified.[3] But in international criminal law, at least since the time of the Nuremberg trials, only waging aggressive war is seen as clearly unjustified waging of war. What makes a war aggressive is an unprovoked attack by one State against another. I will investigate the difficult question of what the foundation is of a State's duty to aid another State, and why it may be justified for that State to engage in an unprovoked attack on a State that is itself attacking another State, or some of its own people.

The chapter proceeds as follows. I begin with a discussion of Augustine and Vattel, surely the two most significant thinkers in the historical Just War tradition to have addressed our topic. In the second section, I examine the very idea of there being an international community in which there are legal duties. In the third section, I spend considerable time trying to explain what solidarity is and why it might be the key to understanding the duties of aid of the members of the international community. In the fourth section, I tackle some of the main objections to the idea of international solidarity. Finally, I discuss the idea that there are natural duties of justice that call for States to go to the aid of one another, especially when there are serious human rights abuses. Throughout, I discuss how the solidarity among people and among States might support peace and yet call for certain wars to be waged to sustain that peace.

I. A Historical Note

The Just War tradition is normally traced back to Augustine, although there are surely similar ideas expressed already in Cicero and even Plato.

---

[3] Also see my paper, "Grotius and Contingent Pacifism," *Studies in the History of Ethics* (an online journal), February 2006, pp. 1–24.

In Augustine's writings we find explicit discussion of "laws of war": rules concerning the initiation of war as well as rules that prevent the commission of wrongs during war.[4] Augustine stipulates that "concern for the interests of others" not "lust or domination" must be the grounding of just wars.[5] The justification of wars grounded in concern for the interests of others follows from the two main principles of morality that Augustine articulates: "First, to do no harm to anyone; and secondly, to help everyone wherever possible."[6] Typically, killing someone does them harm and must be prohibited. But in rare cases in order to help others and prevent graver injustice, it may be necessary to kill during war. It is for this reason that it is possible for some wars to be "just wars."[7]

Because of his discussion of "just wars" Augustine is considered the founder of Just War theory, the theory that some wars can be morally justified to prevent consequences that are themselves worse than the violence of war itself. Augustine develops his doctrine in reaction to the early Church Fathers, who were largely pacifists. Thinkers like Tertullian had argued that all wars were immoral, at least for those who are Christian.[8] It is not implausible to think of war as always unjustified, given the horrors of war. Even for Augustine, there will be few wars that meet his standards of justification. Most wars have been fought for territorial expansion, and these wars would generally not be justified on Just War theory. But when wars are fought for attaining peace, or for preventing peace from deteriorating, they might be justified. And Augustine initiates a long historical line of theorizing by claiming that the best justification is framed in terms of the interests of others, rather than even the intuitively plausible self-defensive wars.

Hugo Grotius, writing in 1625, adds a layer of support to Augustine's idea by proposing that there is an "association which binds together the human race, or binds many nations together" and that such an association "has need of law."[9] Grotius then famously defends the idea "that there is

---

[4] Augustine, *The City of God*, selections reprinted in *The Morality of War*, edited by Larry May, Eric Rovie, and Steve Viner, Upper Saddle River, NJ: Prentice Hall, 2006, p. 19.

[5] Ibid.

[6] Ibid., p. 18.

[7] Ibid., p. 16.

[8] Tertulllian, "The Soldier's Chaplet," (c. 210), chs. 11 and 12 in *Disciplinary, Moral, and Aesthetic Works*, translated by Rudolph Arbermann, Sister Emily Joseph Daly, and Edwin Quain, New York: Fathers of the Church, 1959, pp. 255–260; reprinted in *The Morality of War*, pp. 12–14.

[9] Hugo Grotius, *De Jure Belli Ac Pacis* (On the Law of War and Peace) (1625), translated by Francis W. Kelsey, Oxford: Clarendon Press, 1925. 17.

a common law among nations, which is valid alike for war and in war."[10]
As one commentator has recently noted:

> Grotius, too, is of course fully aware of the importance of independent
> nations. . . . However his ultimate frame of reference remains the Ciceronian
> *humani generis societas* inherited from Stoicism, a society of mankind rather
> than States.[11]

And another commentator has claimed that there is a "solidarism of
Grotian doctrine."[12] This view is based on seeing in Grotius a support for a
"conception of international relations which regards them as taking place
within a real society where rules and institutions confine the behavior of
individuals and States alike."[13]

Thirteen centuries after Augustine, Emer De Vattel expands on the
Just War ideas, as follows:

> Since Nations are bound by the Law of Nature mutually to promote the
> society of the human race, they owe one another all the duties which the
> safety and welfare of that society require. The *offices of humanity* consist in
> the fulfillment of the duty of mutual assistance which men owe to one
> another because they are men.[14]

These duties of humanity are matters of charity for Vattel, and hence not
as strongly binding, as are duties of justice, but the duties of humanity
are duties nonetheless. So Vattel argues that it may be our duty to go to
war to prevent others from being harmed even though "to neglect or to
refuse to further the advancement of a Nation does not constitute an act
of aggression."[15]

Contrary to many others who have written on these topics at his time
or before, Vattel argues that the duties of humanity are binding and may
even override a State's sovereignty.

---

[10] Ibid., p. 20.

[11] Peter Haggenmacher, "Grotius and Gentili," in *Hugo Grotius and International Relations*,
edited by Hedley Bull, Benedict Kingsbury, and Adam Roberts, Oxford: Oxford University
Press, 1990, p. 172.

[12] R. J. Vincent, "Grotius, Human Rights, and Intervention," in *Hugo Grotius and International
Relations*, p. 252.

[13] Ibid., p. 241.

[14] Emer de Vattel, *Le Droit des Gens, ou Principes de la Loi Naturelle* (The Law of Nations or
the Principles of Natural Law) (1758), translated by Charles G. Fenwick, Washington:
Carnegie Institution, 1916, p. 113; reprinted in *The Morality of War*, edited by May, Rovie,
and Viner, p. 100.

[15] Ibid., p. 119; and reprinted in *The Morality of War*, p. 106.

> To give help to a brave people who are defending their liberties against an
> oppressor by force of arms is only the part of justice and generosity. Hence
> whenever such dissention reaches the state of civil war, foreign Nations may
> assist that one of the two parties which seems to have justice on its side.[16]

The key is to make sure that one is assisting the side of a conflict that
has itself been the victim rather than the perpetrator of rights violations.
Sometimes both sides are perpetrators, or even victims. And many times
it will be difficult to determine which State is which. But in clear-cut cases
States are bound to intervene on the side of the victims.

Vattel cautions though that the exercise of one's duty to aid normally
requires military intervention into a sovereign State only when a full-scale
civil war has broken out and two sides may equally claim the mantle of
sovereignty. As was common at his time, Vattel argues that sovereignty
has many advantages in the world such that we should be reluctant to
intervene except where sovereignty is unclear, as in a full-scale civil war.
Yet, he also allows that in certain extreme cases, full-scale civil war is not
a required condition of humanitarian intervention:

> if a Nation, by its accepted principles and uniform policy, shows clearly that
> it is in that malicious state of mind in which no right is sacred to it, the safety
> of the human race requires that it be put down.[17]

Notice, though, that this is only in the case where the safety of the human
race depends on military action, not merely where there is oppression of
a segment of a State's population by the rest of the State's population.
For otherwise the State would still have the right of self-defense against
the intervening States that supposedly were attacking for humanitarian
reasons.[18]

Vattel seems to be overly concerned about the rights of sovereign States,
at least by today's standards. But some recent theorists have attempted
to revive concern for the rights of States by arguing, in a similar vein to
that of Vattel, that some individuals can have their rights violated when
the sovereign government they have put in place is overthrown by outside forces, despite the fact that their State is oppressing other people
and war would stop the oppression.[19] The majority of people in a State
have a kind of collective right of self-determination against those, from

[16] Ibid., p. 131; and reprinted in *The Morality of War*, p.108.
[17] Ibid., p. 135; and reprinted in *The Morality of War*, p. 110.
[18] Ibid.; and reprinted in *The Morality of War*, p. 109.
[19] On this point see Allen Buchanan, *Justice, Legitimacy, and Self-Determination*, New York: Oxford University Press, 2004.

within or without, who try to dispossess them of the government they have chosen for themselves. This is one way to think of Vattel's worries about intervention into a State that is not in full-scale civil war.

The main idea that Vattel gives us is that humanitarian considerations, especially defending the liberty of peoples, can sometimes provide a justification, indeed even a duty, to go to war. One of the chief reasons to support such a view has to do with the solidarity that is owed to people in other States simply by virtue of their being fellow humans. So, even as Vattel worries about State sovereignty, he also supports a rudimentary cosmopolitan ideal of each person being obligated to go to the aid of those who are being victimized, regardless of where they happen to reside. Vattel also supports a duty of States. His position has much plausibility if one thinks that there is anything to the idea that there is such a thing as humanity or the international community. Wherever humans suffer there is a sense that other humans, as well as States, who can go to their aid should do so. Of course, there are many limitations on this principle of mutual aid, as we will explore below.

The defenders of humanitarian intervention today are often also cosmopolitan in thinking that it is justifiable to cross State borders to protect the innocent from harm. There is a growing recognition of an international harm principle that calls for all States to be ready to go to the aid of people who are subjected to genocide or torture. The major conventions on genocide and torture call on all ratifying parties to be ready to enforce the terms of the convention regardless of where the breach occurs. The general idea here is called universal jurisdiction.[20] Unfortunately, humanitarian war also often threatens the lives of the innocent as well, as is true of all wars. Once again we face a seeming dilemma where to protect the innocent, innocent lives need to be threatened.

II. The Idea of an International Community

These days, talk of a global community, especially globalization, is omnipresent. But while such talk seems to be everywhere, there is little discussion of what exactly it means for there to be an international legal community. A good place to start is with Hersch Lauterpacht, who says: "The first function of the legal organization of the community is the preservation of peace. Its fundamental precept is, 'there shall be no violence.' But this primordial duty of the law is abandoned and the reign

[20] See Luc Reydams, *Universal Jurisdiction*, New York: Oxford University Press, 2003.

of force is sanctioned as soon as it is admitted that the law may" require violence for the purpose of enforcing the law's proscriptions.[21] Peace is the goal of law, but violence must sometimes be used to maintain the peace.

For there to be an international legal community, according to Lauterpacht, there must be two conditions met: first, there must be rules that prohibit the use of violence; and second, the enforcement of the "no violence" principle should not have gaps, that is, there should be no sections of the community that fail to recognize the principle or where the principle is not enforced. This second condition sets the stage for a variation on the dilemma that traditional Just War theory had discussed, namely, that violent force must sometimes be used to enforce rules of peace. The international community sometimes requires violence to enforce its laws, even though its laws have as their main aim the curtailment of the realm of force, just as is often true in the domestic sphere as well. Just as the police must sometimes use violent force to maintain the domestic peace, so sometimes armies must use violent force to maintain the international peace.

International law is premised on the idea that all political communities have a strong interest in peace and in the protection of basic human rights, and that the interests of the members are greater than what divides them. These are the guiding ideas behind the founding of the United Nations (in the late 1940s) and fifty years later the International Criminal Court (in the late 1990s). Crimes against humanity jeopardize that peace and undermine basic human rights. In this sense, crimes against humanity adversely affect the common interests of the political communities of the world.[22] One way to think of harms to humanity is as harms to these common interests, and to the solidarity of the international community. Similar things could be said about aggression and crimes against peace.

Because of the shared interests in peace and basic human rights protection, of all humans in all political communities, we can speak non-metaphorically about the human or international community. Individuals could come to see that the interests of others overlap sufficiently with their own interests to create common interests.[23] And something similar might be said about the interests of States of the world, although it will

---

[21] Hersch Lauterpacht, *The Function of Law in the International Community*, Oxford: Clarendon Press, 1933, p. 64.

[22] See my essay, "Humanity, International Crime, and the Rights of Defendants: Reply to the Critics," *Ethics & International Affairs*, vol. 20, no. 3, 2006, pp. 373–382.

[23] See the discussion of solidarity in my book, *The Socially Responsive Self*, Chicago: University of Chicago Press, 1996.

be harder to talk of common interests of States than of individuals. It seems to me that the solidarity many people feel with fellow humans is based on common vulnerability to violence and harm; and the shared interests are based on just these characteristic features of being human as well. In this sense there is an international community of humans, a humanity in which individual humans identify. But since not all humans so identify, the idea of an international community is still normatively weak and problematical.

Even though the international community – that is, humanity – is not a political community, it is a community that can be harmed.[24] Humanity is not a fiction if we mean by it a non-political community composed of all humans who share interests of peace and protection of human rights that arise from the shared vulnerabilities that all humans experience. Humanity can be harmed when some of its members are harmed in certain ways that prey on the common vulnerabilities of all humans. In addition, there is a non-political community of States insofar as States, like individuals, have some common interests. Indeed, the rise of international organizations may have facilitated a kind of global civil society that makes it possible for common interests to be identified.

Common interests are not merely aggregated interests of individual human persons. Security can only be attained collectively, and it is very hard to maintain security in an isolated part of the world where the areas around you experience insecurity. This is due, at least in part, to the increasing globalization that all parts of the world are experiencing. Regional stability is necessary for long-term security of a particular State in the region; and international stability is necessary for lasting security in nearly every corner of the world.

Akira Iriye has argued that if we look initially not at how governments behave but at the non-governmental organizations of the world we can already see a global community emerging.[25] There is a sense, he says, that international society "has always existed," in the sense that States have cooperated with each other in forming alliances and making treaties about a large range of matters.[26]

> Through treaties and agreements, the nations of the world periodically sought to establish an international system, however fragile and temporary it might prove, but much more would be involved if they were to organize a global community, what Hedley Bull terms an "international society." Such a community would arise only if nations and their people recognized that

---

[24] See my book, *Crimes against Humanity: A Normative Account*, ch. 5.
[25] Akira Iriye, *Global Community*, Berkeley: University of California Press, 2004. ch. 6.
[26] Ibid., p. 10.

some issues affected them equally... [such as] to standardize weights and measures, to adopt uniform postal and telegraphic rates, and to cope with communicable diseases.[27]

These are obviously very modest and tentative connections, but they do turn on a common interest among all States.

What makes a more stable basis for international community, says Iriye, comes from non-governmental organizations.

It was against the background of these developments that international non-governmental organizations began to be created in the second half of the nineteenth century.[28]

Indeed, by 1910, 90 percent of international organizations were non-governmental and that figure has continued to grow throughout the past century.[29]

Iriye ends his study by citing a statement supporting the idea that globalization may lead to a world community that is far more than a transitory collection of common interests. Iriye writes:

A realization may emerge that all organizations – the state, business enterprises, international organizations, and nongovernmental associations – will form what Kofi Annan, secretary general of the United Nations, has called a strategic partnership in the service of all people as the world becomes more globalized.... If these separate communities were to come closer together, then there would truly emerge a human community that would consist of various complementing organizations sharing the same concerns and seeking to solve them through cooperative endeavors.[30]

Iriye says that we are not there yet and would hence agree with me that there is not yet a political world community, but that we are perhaps closer than many imagine.

International law, especially international criminal law, can be seen as the law of the international community, or of humanity. Violations of international criminal law can be seen as violations of the rules or laws of humanity, one possible translation of *jus gentium*. International crimes concern atrocities that are so serious that the international community, and even the peaceful existence of humanity, is jeopardized. The common interests that bind together the peoples of the world, and their States as well, concern the desire and need for peaceful relations, where

[27] Ibid.
[28] Ibid., p. 11.
[29] Ibid., p. 28.
[30] Ibid., p. 209.

subgroups of humans are not attacked because of their ethnic, racial, religious, or national characteristics. International crimes assault the common vulnerabilities of humans. Thus, international crimes are, in some sense, violations of the human condition.[31]

Let me close this section by briefly restating how the three primary international crimes are connected to the idea of humanity. Crimes against humanity harm humanity by treating a subset of humanity as if they were not humans, as not deserving of the protection humans should have as unique individuals.[32] War crimes are crimes against humaneness, against what is often called the principle of humanity – that is, crimes that fail to treat humans with mercy and compassion as are deserved by all humans.[33] Crimes against peace are crimes of aggression where one State or State-like entity attempts to destroy another State or State-like entity, thereby undermining one of the chief human institutions that promotes peace and protects human rights. All forms of international crime can be assimilated to this model and understood as some kind of harm to humanity, although each category of international crime harms humanity differently.

III. Solidarity of the International Community

Grotius and Vattel, as we saw, talked of an international community bound together by solidarity. Yet, there is a conceptual puzzle about whether attitudinal and behavioral states like solidarity can be ascribed to collectivities like the international community. One possible solution to this puzzle is to claim that collective solidarity is merely shared solidarity, that is, the ascription of solidarity to a collectivity is merely the shorthand way to talk about what each member of the collectivity displays, with the added condition that the attitudes and behavior be expressed toward the group or at least toward each member of the group. This of course stops short of ascribing attitudes and behavior to the collectivity itself, although it depends on what we think of the metaphysical status of collectivities, a subject that I have explored elsewhere.[34] I will take up some of these

[31] Hannah Arendt makes a similar argument in her book *Eichmann in Jerusalem*, New York: Viking, 1963.

[32] See my book, *Crimes against Humanity: A Normative Account*, New York: Cambridge University Press, 2005.

[33] See my book, *War Crimes and Just War*, New York: Cambridge University Press, 2007.

[34] See my book, *The Morality of Groups*, Notre Dame, IN: University of Notre Dame Press, 1987.

metaphysical issues aimed at understanding the forms of solidarity that could apply to the international community, and perhaps ground duties of mutual aid among States.

Emile Durkheim has done the most to make the idea of solidarity theoretically respectable and to explain how solidarity grounds institutions, such as when "law reproduces the principal forms of social solidarity."[35] Social solidarity is an attitudinal and behavioral state that Durkheim ascribes to a group. There are two sorts of solidarity: mechanical and organic. Mechanical solidarity depends on a cohesiveness that is "the result of resemblances" whereas organic solidarity results from a "division of labor," where different organs of the community have a different role to play.[36] Mechanical solidarity seems to be what an international community at the moment might be based in, although Durkheim thinks that in mechanical solidarity the resemblances and common interests are so strong that they override individuality, making the collective an entity that exists independently of its members.

I do not share Durkheim's view that social groups have independent existence, but I do agree that social groups cannot be reduced merely to the features of the members. For social groups are, on my account, individuals in relationships, and the relationships are not reducible to the features of the individuals, but they also do not constitute independently existing things. So, in my view, the best way to understand social groups is as entities that emerge from the conjunction of individuals and relationships.[37] The solidarity of the international community does not eliminate individuality, but nonetheless there may be relationships created when the members recognize that they have common interests, even in the minimal way that Iriye indicated, such as concerning the need to prevent communicable diseases or, I would add, also the need to prevent atrocities.

One might object that the spread of communicable disease is not sufficiently analogous to the spread of atrocities across borders. Yet, NATO felt that it needed to mount an armed intervention into Kosovo in the early part of the 21st century because of significant fears that atrocities

[35] Emile Durkheim, *Division of Labor in Society*, New York: Free Press, 1964, p. 68.
[36] Emile Durkheim, *Emile Durkheim on Morality and Society*, edited by Robert Bellah, Chicago: University of Chicago Press, 1973, pp. 63 and 69. Also see my discussion of Durkheim's view of solidarity in my book, *The Socially Responsive Self*, Chicago: University of Chicago Press, 1997, ch. 2.
[37] See my books *The Morality of Groups*, Notre Dame, IN: University of Notre Dame Press, 1987; *Sharing Responsibility*, Chicago: University of Chicago Press, 1992.

committed by Serbs against Kosovar Albanians would spread to other European States. And the United States has consistently given a similar rationale for invading countries in its part of the world, such as Cuba and Nicaragua, to prevent the spread of social chaos to the rest of the hemisphere and ultimately across the United States' borders. Perhaps some of the politicians' speeches made about this issue involve hyperbole. But the analogy between the spread of communicable diseases and the spread of violence and social chaos across borders is not so easy to dismiss as it might first appear.

In my view, to say that a group or collectivity has solidarity need not be to say that there is an independently existing thing that has the feature of solidarity. It may be merely to say that there are individuals related in various ways, and that one of the ways they are related is in solidarity with each other. Solidarity is a potentially interesting relation to constitute a social group since it is both a behavioral and attitudinal state and a way individuals are related in groups. But solidarity, on my account, is not itself a behavioral or attitudinal state of the group but rather a way that the members of the group are related. Solidarity arises from a shared sense of common interest and is expressed or felt by individuals who see their fates linked.

This poses a puzzle for how to think about solidarity in the international community. It is common to think, as Vattel did, that the members of that community – namely, States – can have, or display, solidarity with one another. But that would then mean that the members, that are also social groups, would have the attitudinal and behavioral state of solidarity. And yet, this would deny the methodological individualism that I and many other theorists subscribe to. Another way to conceive of the international community is that members of the social groups called States could have a second-order attitudinal and behavioral state. Not only do they have attitudes that when shared in sufficient numbers constitute a social group, such as the State, but they also can have or display attitudinal or behavioral states about how their social groups should interrelate to other social groups within a larger social group, such as the international community.

It seems to me that the international community can have solidarity mainly in this extended sense. That community, which is itself composed of social groups, has solidarity mainly insofar as the members of the social groups that form the international community have attitudinal and behavioral states of solidarity primarily toward their own social groups, their States, and then secondarily toward the larger social

group that encompasses these primary social groups, that is, toward the
international community. These are best thought of as second-order attitudes since they are attitudes about what "attitude" their social groups
should display toward larger social groups such as international communities. Think of the common interest in the prevention of atrocities.
Since most atrocities are committed by States and can be prevented only
by other States, the common interest is an interest in having States act
in certain ways, and secondarily in having the community of States put
pressure on these States to act in these various ways. Of course, it may
be that not all members display such attitudinal and behavioral states,
and we would then have to assess how many members were sufficient to
constitute a kind of consensus of solidarity representing the international
community.

Returning to Durkheim's remark, we can say that law may follow the
solidarity of societies and communities in that there will be recognized
duties that are associated with being a member of a social group, primarily
in States and secondarily in the international community, that is bound
together by solidarity. As Hart once observed, there is a minimal moral
basis for law in that all law contains duties restricting the free use of violence, for instance.[38] Some law reflects the need for social harmony that
motivates people to constitute social groups. And some law is a reflection
of the principal forms of social solidarity. At the international level, the
same will hold true. So, there will be various rules and laws that reflect
the solidarity, if any, that is felt or manifested by the members of States
toward the international community. International law will reflect the
social solidarity of the various groups that make up that international
community.

Groups are constituted by individuals in relationships. And solidarity
is one kind of relationship. Solidarity is the kind of relationship that is
deeply dependent on the mental and behavioral states of the members
of the group. In this sense, solidarity is both an attitude of fellow feeling
and a kind of glue that holds the group together, for instance, by making
it more likely that members will come to each other's aid. Unlike other
relationships, such as a hierarchical organization, solidarity not only is a
form of relationship but is also associated with a motivation to form and
stay formed in that relationship. This is because solidarity associates with
duties that motivate individuals to do things that initiate or perpetuate
group formation, as we will see in greater detail later.

[38] H. L. A. Hart, *The Concept of Law*, Oxford: Oxford University Press, 1961, 1994, p. 172.

In a previous work, I argued that the kind of solidarity that connects to moral motivation normally involves five overlapping factors:

1. conscious group identification
2. bonds of sentiment
3. interest in the group's well-being
4. shared values and beliefs
5. readiness to show moral support[39]

I also argued that humanity doesn't involve this kind of solidarity, although there may be weaker bonds of solidarity that occur in the human community. But our deep sense of moral commitment will not arise unless these factors are present.

Even if all humans identify with each other as humans and display empathy toward each other, this will not normally be enough to ground strong duties of mutual aid in the human or international community. This is because our deepest moral commitments come from our sense of self, and solidarity provides grounding for similar deep moral commitments only when it makes an individual feel that his or her group affiliation is as important as his or her sense of self. There can be a kind of extended self, mediated through social groups, that motivates individuals, but the more extended things get, the weaker are the commitments that one feels. If, as I argued, an individual human's commitment to the international community is mainly second order, then the ensuing sense of obligation will be weak. There are duties of mutual aid that are associated with solidarity in a human community, but the solidarity is not enough to ground strong obligations or duties.

The major problem with the idea of the international or human community is that the group in question is so amorphous. It is unclear what the features are of this community that would be important to its well-being. Normally, for a group to have interests the group must have features that could be harmed. And while I think that humanity or the international community can indeed be harmed, it is really only when people are denied equal treatment as members of this community that this chiefly occurs, rather than in virtue of an injury to the group per se. The harm to the international community can be group-based harm, but not full-blown harm per se. Consider the contrast between a family and the international community. The family may have assets, a reputation, and a distinct identity that could be adversely affected; in that way,

[39] Larry May, *The Socially Responsive Self,* Chicago: University of Chicago Press, 1996, p. 44.

the interests of the family as a whole could be harmed. It is very unclear whether there is anything comparable to these features in the human or international community.

Despite the problems in identifying the features in virtue of which the international or human community can be harmed, there is enough group identification and bonds of empathy among many of the individuals who ultimately constitute this group to think that there may be weak duties associated with membership in this group, and that the solidarity of the group plays a role in the formation of those duties, although commonality of interest is surely even more important. A kind of solidarity exists at the international level, but many individuals do not feel the tug of that solidarity to be very strong at all. There are various problems, both ontological and normative, that make it very hard to ground strong moral duties in the solidarity of the international community. I will attempt to address some of these objections in the next section. And then, at the end, I will explain the basis in solidarity of minimal duties of mutual aid nonetheless.

IV. Objections

The first objection to what I have set out in the previous section is that I have not recognized the true reality of social groups, such as the international or human community. According to this objection, the ontology of social groups is to be understood according to a "Hegelian" approach. Of course, even Hegel did not embrace a full-blooded collectivism, and the new followers of Hegel are more careful yet to try to carve out a kind of middle ground between individualism and collectivism. Indeed, I would contend that the new movement is really very much like the 1950s position that embraced emergent properties.[40] I have no trouble thinking that there are emergent properties, and I think of relationships as just this kind of thing.[41]

In any event, few would argue today that social groups have a reality independent of the individuals who make up those groups. Of course,

---

[40] I'm thinking of May Brodbeck's work in this respect.

[41] I have said that relationships like solidarity can constitute social groups, and now I am opening up the possibility that relationships like solidarity also might be emergent out of groups. This seems puzzling. I don't think it should be, though. Some relationships are constituted by solidarity relationships, but solidarity could itself emerge out of our social relationships. I am grateful to David Schweikard and Ken Shockley for help in sorting out this problem.

one of the things in question is whether individuals are the firm foundation of the social world. And I would join in this questioning. For it may be that individuals are themselves just nodes or intersections of group characteristics. In this sense, individuals have no unique characteristics that are not shared with some others; but rather what makes individuals unique is the particular combination of otherwise shared characteristics. But talk of group characteristics does not mean that they must be ontologically firm. Indeed, my view is that we may find that there are no firm ontological foundations in the social world, but perhaps an ontological boot-strapping, where group characteristics only manifest themselves when they are shared by two or more individuals.[42]

The second objection is that I have recognized too much reality of social groups. A strict methodological individualist will say that relationships are merely properties of individuals, and hence they cannot constitute anything else. And in answer to the question of how a relationship can be merely a property of one individual, a minor retrenchment might be made only to admit that relationships could be properties that two or more individuals have in common. However, there is nothing ontologically significant about this since many properties such as being bald are held by many people at once without us thinking that baldness must be seen as a mysterious property that cannot be reduced to properties of individuals. On this account, solidarity cannot constitute groups, let alone duties to groups, since solidarity is merely a feature of how one and another person feel and behave.

My response here is to admit that solidarity, in a sense, might be reduced to the attitudes and behaviors that several individuals have in common. But "in common" cannot be reduced to properties that individuals have. If I am in solidarity with you, both you and I feel and display certain things toward each other. We are also, because of this, in a relationship to each other and so solidarity goes beyond merely the individual attitudes and behaviors that each of us has. The relationship we are in, the solidarity relationship, is not completely reducible to the properties that I have, or that you have.[43] Yes, it is true that the relationship can be nearly reduced to the attitudes and behaviors that I have *and* the attitudes and behaviors that you have. But once again, the "and" here is quite important and cannot easily be reduced to properties of me or properties of you. And

---

[42] See my discussion of this issue in my book, *The Morality of Groups*, 1987.
[43] Indeed, while solidarity is primarily a relationship between or among individual people, it can be sometimes also be a relationship between or among social groups.

for this reason I remain resistant to the suggestion that I should embrace a full-blooded individualism.

The third objection is that I have not seriously considered the possibility, actively pursued by cosmopolitans, that the international community is directly constituted by the attitudes and behaviors of solidarity of individuals rather than of States and other social groups. I do not have strong objections to seeing the international community as a social group that has as its members individuals rather than States, but as I said this is only true secondarily. And in any event, we then need to figure out how States fit into this picture. For my larger project, on the crime of aggression, we need to understand how States are to relate to each other in the international sphere. It may be that individuals have duties directly as members of the international community, but in understanding war, which is primarily a matter of the interrelations of States and non-State actors, it is essential to understand how these social groups relate to the larger international community. The crucial question is how States can have duties to one another.

Of course, it could be argued that individuals have duties directly to the international community and that one of these duties is to influence their States to act in ways that are supportive of international peace. This way of understanding things would make individuals and their relationships the constituent members of both States and the international community. There would not be a relationship between States and the international community except in that extended sense in which they are both mediated by individuals. Of course, as a methodological individualist, I must recognize the sense to this idea, for I really can't say that any social group is anything other than individuals and the relationships of individuals. So the international community must ultimately be a function of individuals in relationships, even if they are secondary or iterated ones.

A fourth objection could be registered at this stage. If the international community is not an entity that exists apart from its members, and if the members are primarily States and State-like entities, then ultimately the international community is twice removed from but not ontologically independent of individuals. Why think that the individuals in question must be human persons? Why can't States be individuals, or at least be so thought of, when we are discussing legal and not moral matters? It is well known that the law has recognized various types of individual, including corporations and churches, as individuals, at least as legally fictitious individuals. Why should we not follow this lead, especially with an entity like the State that so many people readily recognize? And why not take this analysis a step further and allow that the international community could be a fictitious legal individual as well?

I also have no strong objection to this line of approach. Of course, where I might disagree is in the analysis of what it means for something to be a legal fiction. I have suggested, from the very beginning of this chapter, that there certainly is sense to be made of the idea of an international community. I have said that it is not a full-blown political community, but we can talk of "it" as instantiating normative principles such as that peace should be pursued and atrocity prevented. But for me the crucial thing is what we can say normatively of those who constitute the international community. Do they, the States or human individuals, have duties by virtue of being members, or parts, of the international community? In the next section I take up this question, readily recognizing that the international community itself might be thought to have obligations or duties as well, but perhaps only if we treat that community as a legal fiction.[44]

A fifth and final objection is that I have not properly understood how strong solidarity is among individual members of the human or international community and hence how strong the duties associated with human solidarity might be. As we will see below, I do recognize that there are duties associated with solidarity in the human or international community, but that these are relatively weak. The objection is that some of these obligations can be quite strong. Indeed, in my book *Crimes against Humanity*, I recognized just this point when I said that there is enough of a social group at the international or human level to think that the group can be significantly harmed. If a group can be harmed then it seems that it can also have stronger associational duties than I have here allowed. And even if the group cannot have duties, perhaps individuals can have duties to it, especially the duty not to harm it.

This objection sets the stage nicely for our final section on the status and extent of the duties that are associated with solidarity in a human or international community. Let me only note at this stage that one can think that a group can be harmed without thinking that the group has, or can be the object of, duties or obligations. In this respect, consider animals or very young children. In both cases we can say that they have sufficient capacities to be harmed and yet lack other capacities that would be necessary for them to have duties or obligations. Similarly, some groups

---

[44] For more on this topic see Lon Fuller, *Legal Fictions*, Stanford, CA: Stanford University Press, 1967.

can be harmed, perhaps because they achieve enough identity through the way that others come to think of these members, but that the members do not have sufficient group consciousness so that the group could have duties or obligations. I explore these issues in more detail, and also discuss the type and strength of duties that might be associated with solidarity of the human or international community, in the final section of this chapter.

V. The Duties of Solidarity

In this final section, I wish to explore the moral duties that are associated with solidarity in the international community. The question is whether solidarity can ground a strong or merely a weak duty to aid other States against violent force perpetrated against them that they cannot resist. And another question is whether solidarity helps ground a duty on States to go to war to prevent authoritarian States from repressing their own people. To overcome the prima facie duty not to engage in violent force that all States have, perhaps only a weak duty to aid will be sufficient in some cases. But even if humanitarian wars of various sorts may be justified on broad grounds of solidarity, as we will see at the end, solidarity poses a hurdle to such humanitarian wars as well.

I have been treating humanity as a distinct group that potentially has moral duties and rights of its members. Many people will undoubtedly wonder why I do not proceed in a more straightforward, universalistic manner rather than trying to create particularistic duties and rights from membership in humanity. Why not merely say that every person has duties and rights to every human as a matter of objective morality? I have not proceeded in this way because I regard such claims to be contentious and not in keeping with the moral minimalism to which I subscribe. If individuals see that they share enough in common to have solidarity with the rest of humanity, it may be easier to get them to see that they have duties as well as rights vis-à-vis these others than if such duties and rights are merely postulated universally. In any event, both universalistic and particularistic moral considerations can be appealed to in order to argue for restraints on what individuals would do in their own pure self-interest.[45] Even if one disagrees with my preferred particularistic strategy

[45] See David Miller, *On Nationality*, Oxford: Clarendon Press, 1995, pp. 54–55. Also see Nicholas D. Kristof's op-ed essay, "Save the Darfur Puppy," in the *New York Times*, Thursday, May 10, 2007, on how hard it is to motivate people to give to those suffering in Darfur if that appeal is universalistic as opposed to particularistic.

for arguing for this thesis, one should see that a universalistic strategy could be mounted to support the same result.

The appeal to human solidarity, as well as to the related moral idea of common interests of humanity, is meant to bridge the gap between universal and particular moral appeals. Solidarity involves the linking of individuals by a common bond of fellow feeling and reciprocity of attitude. If one feels connected to another through common interests, then one also will tend to support the other similarly to how one would want oneself supported. In particular, there will be a close association between self-defense and defense of the other with whom one is bound in solidarity. So, while there are not the strong relations between solidarity and the duty to aid others that Vattel envisioned, the association between solidarity and the duty to aid others does seem to exist nonetheless. But the normative grounding of such an association is not obvious.

If there is an international community that is at least partially constituted by attitudes of solidarity, then there might be duties associated with being a member of that community. And the duty to aid fellow members of the international community seems like a good candidate for such a duty. Indeed, many philosophers have signed on to the idea that we have associational duties merely by virtue of our memberships in various groups. Again, think of the analogy to the family, perhaps the paradigmatic community for which the members have strong duties to one another. Children have duties to their parents, and parents have duties to their children; siblings have duties to each other, as do spouses. Like members of the family, members of a State have duties to one another, as do members of a corporation or an army. All of these associational duties are grounded in mere membership. If there is such a thing as an international community, then membership in that community might also be associated with, or generate, duties to aid fellow members who are in distress.

The common interests of humanity are well illustrated in the three main types of crime that were charged at Nuremberg. All three crimes (crimes against humanity including genocide, violations of the rules and customs of war, and the crime of waging aggressive war) speak to the human interest that atrocities not occur. These crimes seem to speak to a universal principle – that individuals should not harm each other – and indeed this is true. But it is also true that these crimes speak to a common interest that all members of humanity have and that is infringed when an atrocity occurs in any part of the world. When ethnically or racially motivated atrocities occur, the members' individuality is being denied and there is a high likelihood that other humans could experience this denial and harm.

There is a sense in which harming any member of humanity, as a member, harms humanity. By this I mean that harming some human by failing to take seriously what makes that person human harms humanity. Harming one human being by failing to take account of that person's uniqueness is what is key to harming humanity, because of the likelihood that others might be mistreated as well. This is perhaps an odd claim. I am trying to get beyond merely the aggregate claim that when humans are harmed *en masse* humanity is harmed. Indeed, I'm not sure how this could work even in the case of the bombing of Hiroshima. Rather, it seems to me that harming individuals harms humanity when these individuals are treated in ways that deny them their individuality, which is itself one of the hallmarks of being human. I suppose I am making a claim similar to that made by Martin Luther King, Jr., that certain harms to individual humans also harm all other humans because they are put at risk of similar harm as well.[46]

Solidarity is a mechanism by which individual interests are transformed into common interests through an expanding of a person's sense of self. When the person recognizes herself as a member of a family, this pulls her into the affairs of fellow family members and makes their interests, at least to a certain extent, her own interests. In the international domain, as I have admitted, the bonds of solidarity are much weaker than in most families. Indeed, many members of humanity do not feel solidarity with other humans at all; and those that do feel this solidarity experience it as considerably weaker than that experienced as family members. But some people can and do feel solidarity with fellow humans. And it is not inconceivable that this solidarity would motivate or be associated with, or ground, some relatively weak duties. It is also not inconceivable that human solidarity could be strengthened especially as the advantages of belonging to an international community become clearer over time.

There is a good question, however, about who the members of a putative international community are, as I have already indicated. It may be that the members are States. In his book, *Justice, Legitimacy, and Self-Determination*, Allen Buchanan argues that there is an international community and that there are duties that all States have toward that community, chiefly in terms of the creation of global institutions that protect

[46] Martin Luther King, Jr., "Letter from the Birmingham City Jail" (1963), reprinted in *Applied Ethics: A Multicultural Approach*, edited by Larry May, Shari Collins-Chobanian, and Kai Wong, 4th ed., Upper Saddle River, NJ: Pearson Prentice-Hall, 2006, pp. 353–363.

human rights. In general, Buchanan argues "that for the most part the same basic criteria of legitimacy that are appropriate for individual states are also appropriate for the international legal system, even though the latter is far from being a global state."[47]

It may also be that the members of the international community are States but that States are merely placeholders for collections of individuals. In that sense, we could say that, at least derivatively, the members of the international community are individual human persons. The international community might be just a shorthand expression for humanity, that is, the community of all humans. We could then say that humans have duties to all fellow humans, where perhaps these duties have correlative rights that we could call human rights. Both human rights and duties would be based on membership in the human community. Of course this doesn't yet tell us how extensive those duties, and rights, would be.

We could begin with a quite modest duty that calls on fellow humans to go to the aid of those who are facing mass atrocity or wars of annihilation. It is hard to imagine being in solidarity with others and yet not feeling that one should act to prevent mass atrocity or annihilation of those with whom we have common interests. While the global goal of the international community is peace, the duty to aid means that there will be some wars, namely, those that are necessary for maintaining the peace, that will be justified by reference to shared interests and especially the desire for peace. The duty to go to war to support those who are in need of help is associated with global solidarity, but there is also a problem in that the States that one needs to attack are also part of the international community and hence may themselves be owed restraint on the part of a fellow State that might be tempted to attack on grounds of solidarity. This has been one of the strongest strands in the Just War tradition and also in contemporary international law, namely, that States owe it to their fellow States not to attack them unless they are about to be attacked themselves.

So there is a potential conflict between, on the one hand, the duty that the members of the international community have to go to the aid of fellow States that are being attacked, even if this means going to war to protect them, and, on the other hand, the duty the members of an international community have not to attack each other. Of course, these

---

[47] Allen Buchanan, *Justice, Legitimacy, and Self-Determination*, p. 291. And in a series of more recent essays, Buchanan has argued that forcible democratization and other humanitarian wars can be justified by broadly liberal and cosmopolitan principles relating to the legitimate use of force to advance important human rights. See especially Allen Buchanan, "Institutionalizing the Just War," *Philosophy & Public Affairs*, vol. 34, no. 1, Winter 2006, pp. 2–38.

are almost surely prima facie duties, and we might make some headway on this issue if the list of reasons to go to another's aid is a short list and only when things on that list occur can the duty not to attack other members be overridden. The result is once again that States have a weak duty to aid other States, but that this duty may be sufficient to overcome the prima facie duty not to employ violence against others and hence give a grounding for the idea that some, seemingly aggressive, wars are just wars.

Mark Osiel has written extensively about a related issue that connects solidarity and international criminal law.[48] Osiel is mainly concerned with the way that trials in general may advance social solidarity within a society rather than within the world. But there is no reason not to contemplate the idea that there might be an extension of the arguments he considers to the world society. Rather than defend criminal trials as grounded in substantive shared interests, or consensus, of a community, Osiel is highly suspicious of the idea that there is such a substantive consensus in any particular pluralistic society, and we can add that this would be even more the case in the world community. Instead, Osiel grounds the normative support for criminal trials in the kind of consensus that comes from dissensus, that is from the way that people come to accept shared procedural values – as a way to resolve at least temporarily their substantive differences so that the society can go on.

> Prosecuting wrongdoers also evokes – more important to Durkheimians – an awareness of *sharing* these sentiments with others, that is, of belonging to a community whose members are united by this very convergence and periodic reinvigoration of moral sentiment. In criminal trials, prosecutors – as spokesmen for "the people" – tell the stories through which such sentiments are elicited and such membership consolidated. In affirming criminal convictions, appellate courts draw upon "the ritual attitude of sacred respect" for themselves and for the moral traditions they invoke.[49]

Ultimately, Osiel finds even this much substantive consensus too much to expect in deeply divided societies, settling instead for the kind of minimal respect that comes from accepting the same procedures, with a heavy dose of procedural civility, that allow for temporary settlement of deep differences. International criminal trials might aid in the effort to instill a deeper sense of solidarity in the international community and perhaps a greater respect for the international rule of law.

[48] Mark Osiel, *Mass Atrocity, Collective Memory, and the Law*, New Brunswick, NJ: Transaction, 1997.
[49] Ibid., p. 29.

As I indicated at the beginning of this chapter, there is a tension in both traditional Just War theory and also in contemporary international law about whether non–self-defensive wars can be justified. I follow in a long line of theorists, including Augustine, Grotius, and Vattel, in thinking that wars can be justified, on grounds of preventing harm to others, even when a State is not attacked or in imminent threat of such an attack. But this position is not antithetical to the Just War tradition. While there are very strong reasons against all wars, there are also sometimes sufficient reasons to go to war in order to prevent mass atrocity or to protect people from other serious harms, including those harms that occur when a state is mounting a campaign of aggressive war.

I have tried to indicate that while there is tension among these normative principles some wars may be justified as a response to aggression, and international criminal proceedings can also be justified to prosecute those who wage aggressive rather than defensive wars. Solidarity can help us see the plausibility of both these claims. In the next part of the book I will examine the normative principles held in law and philosophy to be important *jus ad bellum* principles that determine which wars are justified, or defensive, and which wars are unjustified, or aggressive.

PART B

RETHINKING THE NORMATIVE
AD BELLUM PRINCIPLES

4

The Principle of Priority or First Strike

In the next three chapters, I will reconceptualize several of the traditional *jus ad bellum* principles for use in international criminal law.[1] In this respect, I will return to the discussions in the first chapters about how to justify war morally and legally. The guiding idea will be that for purposes of criminal trials of individuals for the crime of aggression, a somewhat different standard of what counts as defensive and what counts as aggressive war may be advisable. We may want a more expansive idea of aggressive war if what we are interested in is merely condemning States for their behavior. But when we come to the question of what standard to use in criminal trials there may be good reasons to focus only on the most egregious cases of aggression. In this respect, then, it also would make sense to reconceptualize the traditional principles of *jus ad bellum* that mark the divide between aggressive and defensive war.

I will begin with a normative principle that is not normally listed as a *jus ad bellum* principle, the principle of priority or first strike. This principle is often cited as one of the main normative principles in international legal discussions, but as we will see properly it is really a preliminary way of understanding the just cause principle, the subject of the next chapter. In the legal and moral debates about the justifiability of initiating war, two powerful ideas are dominant: the State that strikes first is normally thought to initiate an aggressive war, and the State that goes to war as a last resort to stop the assault is normally thought to initiate a defensive war. These temporal signs are only prima facie indicators of justifiability

---

[1] Bruce Landesman claims that Just War theory is really an amalgam of views that have changed over time. Hence, in his view it is somewhat misleading to say that I am reconceptualizing *jus ad bellum* principles. Perhaps, in his view, I should say that I am providing a new conceptualization here.

of initiating war, but they are omnipresent in the literature of at least the last 500 years.

The intuition behind the priority principle is based on the analogy between war and the two-person altercation. To decide in a preliminary way who is the aggressor in a barroom brawl, we typically ask, "who threw the first punch?" Similarly, when investigations are launched into police shootings, we also ask, "did the police shoot first or were they first shot at?" And if the barroom brawler or the police officer did eventually strike, we would next ask: "was there any other reasonable alternative to stop the assault?" If there was a reasonable alternative, then the shootings were not a last resort, and hence not defensive.

One of the most difficult questions posed by these simple intuitive approaches to the justifiability of initiating war concerns the State that strikes first but also had no reasonable alternatives to prevent an assault. This case is often labeled "anticipatory self-defense" or "preemptive strike." Ian Brownlie says that there is opposition by some

> to the principle of the first attacker, the "priority principle," in definitions of aggression. To describe any act is to determine when it was committed and to enumerate its characteristics, and it would seem that the "priority principle" is inherent in all definitions. The question is of course closely related to that of anticipatory self-defense.... When the justification of self-defense is raised, the question becomes one of fact, viz., was the response proportionate to the apparent threat.... The whole problem is rendered incredibly delicate by the existence of long-range missiles ready for use: the difference between attack and imminent attack may now be negligible.[2]

Brownlie here seems to think that considerations of first strike are now nearly obsolete. I will offer a partial response in this chapter. I will also explain why the idea of last resort may not do the work that it was once thought to do, at least in the case of anticipatory self-defense.

In this chapter I wish to reassess the doctrine of anticipatory self-defense and the larger question of the justifiability of preemptive and preventive war. In the first and second sections, I will rehearse an important debate between Alberico Gentili and Hugo Grotius from 400 years ago on our topics. Then I will spend sections three and four looking first at "first strikes" and then at "last resorts" to see what, if anything, is to be said for these as markers of aggressive or defensive war. In those sections, I will address directly the justifiability of preemptive war. In the fifth section,

[2] Ian Brownlie, *International Law and the Use of Force by States*, Oxford: Clarendon Press, 1963, pp. 366 and 368.

I will briefly explain why most theorists, myself included, condemn the idea that preventive war is nonaggressive, although the line between pre-emptive and preventive war is indeed hard to draw, especially, as Brownlie notes, since the advent of "long-range missiles ready for use." I will argue that the claim of anticipatory self-defense makes the most sense when we are talking of the crime of aggression but does not make nearly as much sense when we are merely talking of whether a State's aggressive use of force should be condemned. Throughout, it will turn out that these topics are harder to resolve than most people today seem to think, especially when we are thinking about the crime of aggression, and even harder yet than those writing in the 16th and 17th centuries thought.

I. Gentili and the Justification of Offensive War

Two of the leading figures at the end of the 16th and beginning of the 17th centuries in effect debated the issues I will address in this chapter.[3] Their views are often clearer and more cogent than those presented today, although often not presented with as much subtlety. Gentili and Grotius disagree about most things, beginning with whether it matters that one is engaging in a defensive or offensive war. Both agree that defensive wars can, and should, be seen as justified wars. But they clash over the justifiability of offensive wars, and their disagreement is insightful for debates today about how best to understand first strikes and last resorts as well as anticipatory self-defense and preventive war generally. In this first section I will deal with Gentili's arguments and in the next section take up the arguments of Grotius.

Alberico Gentili wrote at the end of the 16th century. He was a trained lawyer who became one of the most prominent members of the faculty at Oxford University in his time. Gentili's views, as we will see, are quite nonstandard, even as they seem to arise out of engagement with the Just War tradition. His views can best be seen, I believe, as embodying a kind of commonsense approach that clearly resonated with his students and readers. He was not the theoretician or historian that Grotius was, but his views have held up surprisingly well over the centuries and to my ear have a distinctly contemporary ring. Indeed, Gentili could have been one of the advisors in U.S. President George W. Bush's cabinet when the

---

[3] For a good historical discussion of the views of those who came before and those who came after Gentili and Grotius, see Gregory M. Reichberg, "Preventive War in Classical Just War Theory," *Journal of the History of International Law*, vol. 9, 2007, pp. 5–34.

decision was made to attack Iraq because of a fear that it had weapons of mass destruction that could be used against the United States.

Gentili said that wars can be divided into offensive and defensive ones. Defensive wars are waged for either self-defense or defense of others. And the best argument in support of defensive wars is derived from necessity, that is, "when one is driven to arms as a last resort."[4] But it also turns out, in Gentili's view, that even "an offensive war may be waged justly . . . there is always a defensive aspect, if they are just."[5] Gentili supports this claim by the following argument:

> we have discoursed at length of the law pertaining to every kind of defense. . . . As a matter of fact, offensive warfare has the same motives, arising from necessity, expediency, or honor. Necessity, however, we understand in the sense that we cannot maintain our existence without making war. . . . A second variety of this necessary warfare will be found in the case of those who, because they have been driven from their own country or are compelled to leave it through some emergency and to seek another home, from necessity make war upon others. . . . the destruction of their cities has driven them into the lands of others.[6]

As we will see, Gentili goes on to argue that many forms of offensive war, not just that waged by exiles trying to support their own livelihood, can be justified. If offensive wars can be waged for necessity, then there is a sense in which offensive wars can be waged as a last resort and can be justified. This curious position requires explanation.

Concerning the case of exiles who must fight a war to preserve themselves from destruction, Gentili says:

> Or do we think it right for men to have no pity for their kind, and allow nothing but death for these exiles, who have been driven from their fatherland? Yet care must be taken lest those wanderers grow discontented with the humble means which of course they can acquire for themselves without war.[7]

Underlying Gentili's general position here is the idea that people should not be forced to do what is opposed to their sense of honor and dignity. In a very curious passage, Gentili says:

---

[4] Alberico Gentili, *De Jure Belli* (On the Law of War) (1598), translated by John C. Rolfe, Oxford: Clarendon Press, 1933, p. 15.

[5] Ibid., p. 30.

[6] Ibid., p. 79.

[7] Ibid., p. 80.

> Suppose that some one desires to issue a scurrilous book against you, and that there are no available magistrates to whom you may appeal. I maintain that it is your right to protect yourself from insult by force of arms.[8]

Apparently, Gentili thinks that generally one should not have to flee rather than use violent force to defend what is valuable to you.

By taking the position that he does, Gentili disputes the age-old idea that those who strike first are prima facie in the wrong, even as he supports the idea that last resort is of key, although not of completely overriding, importance for determining when offensive war might be justified. Gentili maintains that "to kill in self-defense is just, even though the one who kills may flee without danger to himself"[9] for "every method of securing safety is honorable"[10] and that it is almost always dishonorable to be forced to flee rather than to stay and defend one's rights.[11] Indeed, Gentili defends the idea that wars can be fought in anticipation of "dangers already meditated and prepared" but not yet launched.[12]

Concerning this latter doctrine, Gentili is justly famous for providing two key analogies to explain why first strike as anticipatory defense is justifiable. First, he argues that

> we ought not to wait for violence to be offered us, if it is safer to meet it half way... one may at once strike at the root of the growing plant and check the attempts of the adversary who is meditating evil.[13]

And employing another metaphor he says:

> That is an excellent saying of Philo's, that we kill a snake as soon as we see one, even though it has not injured us and will perhaps not harm us. For thus we protect ourselves before it attacks us.[14]

These two powerful images, of stopping the growing plant before it is a major problem for us to weed out, and killing a snake that has not yet shown any signs of harming us but might eventually do so, play into deep-seated intuitions of many people. Indeed, Gentili drives this point home when he says: "No one ought to expose himself to danger. No one ought to wait to be struck unless he is a fool."[15] It is only reasonable that

[8] Ibid., p. 84.
[9] Ibid., pp. 58–59.
[10] Ibid., p. 59.
[11] Ibid., p. 83.
[12] Ibid., p. 66.
[13] Ibid., p. 61.
[14] Ibid.
[15] Ibid., p. 62.

precautions of various types be taken, "even though there is no great and clear cause for fear, and even if there really is no danger, but only a legitimate cause for fear."[16] Gentili adds further support by saying that it is also reasonable that "while your enemy is weak, slay him."[17] And he then concludes this discussion by saying that "a defense is just which anticipates dangers that are already meditated and prepared, and also those which are not meditated, but are probable and possible."

Gentili does his best to blur the line between regular self-defense and anticipatory self-defense by urging us to think about long-term issues, not merely the short-term. He also tries to undermine the distinction between dangers that are impending and those that are probable or even only possible. In some ways, Gentili then sets the stage for the Bush Doctrine of seeing war as a legitimate means of self-defense even if there is little or no evidence that a danger is impending. Gentili accomplishes these tasks by relying on evocative and intuitively plausible examples. He thus makes significant inroads into the traditional doctrine of seeing first strike and last resort as the key factors to consider in determining whether war was justifiably initiated.

II. Grotius on Fear of Attack

Hugo Grotius wrote at the very beginning of the 17th century and is today considered to be the founder of international law. While not a trained lawyer, Grotius lectured extensively in law and religion, and held an important professorship at Leiden in the Netherlands. Like Gentili, Grotius also represented various States in international disputes, most famously defending the Dutch for seizing pirate ships that contained vast fortunes that had been stolen from other European countries and not returning the stolen goods to those countries. His book, *De Jure Belli ac Pacis* is still one of the most often cited texts in all of international law, both in legal scholarship and court opinions.

With Gentili's arguments clearly in mind, Grotius argues that it is very difficult to justify offensive wars, even in anticipation, or fear, of attack. Grotius maintains that "those who accept fear of any sort as justifying anticipatory slaying are themselves greatly deceived."[18] For, as he says, "there are certain causes which present a false appearance of justice" and

---

[16] Ibid., pp. 62–63.
[17] Ibid., p. 65.
[18] Hugo Grotius, *De Jure Belli ac Pacis* (On the Law of War and Peace) (1625), translated by Francis W. Kelsey, Oxford: Clarendon Press, 1925, p. 173.

that "such a cause is the fear of something uncertain." Grotius develops an example here that is also quite telling:

> Wherefore we can in no wise approve the view of those who declare that it is a just cause of war when a neighbor who is restrained by no agreement builds a fortress on his own soil, or some other fortification which may some day cause us harm. Against the fears which arise from such actions we must resort to counter fortifications on our own land and other similar remedies, but not to force of arms.[19]

This example, perhaps not as powerful as those of Gentili, clearly seeks to counter the intuitive support that Gentili's own examples had received. Fear may justly motivate to do something but not necessarily justly motivate to go to war when less lethal means are available.

Another example that is directed specifically at first strikes Grotius takes from Gellius, a 2nd-century Roman author.

> When a gladiator is equipped for fighting, the alternatives offered by combat are these, either to kill, if he shall have made the first decisive stroke, or to fall, if he shall have failed. But the life of men generally is not hedged about by a necessity so unfair and so relentless that you are obliged to strike the first blow, and may suffer if you shall have failed to be first to strike.[20]

Grotius then adds this gloss on our theme: "while it is permissible to kill him who is making ready to kill, yet the man is more worthy of praise who prefers to be killed rather than to kill."[21]

When Grotius talks of those who are most worthy of praise, he often engages in this discussion in terms of honor and virtue rather than in terms of the dictates of justice. Honor is a key component in war for Grotius because when soldiers do not act from honor they are nothing but simple killers. Acting in a severely restrained way, even as one does kill, makes one more than a simple killer who strikes for greed or hatred. Killing only in certain situations when one is required to do so raises the act of the soldier onto a higher plane for Grotius. Gentili also speaks of honor but is primarily concerned with not shaming oneself by allowing oneself to be pushed into a corner. Grotius employs a broader notion of honor that is connected to the restraints of mercy that display one's true virtue.

[19] Ibid., p. 549.
[20] Ibid., p. 174.
[21] Ibid., p. 176. This passage should remind us that, as I argued in chapter 2, Grotius seems to adopt a nonstandard form of pacifism that I called contingent pacifism.

At another point in his seminal work on the laws of war and peace, Grotius argues

> that the possibility of being attacked confers the right to attack is abhorrent to every principle of equity. Human life exists under such conditions that complete security is never guaranteed to us. For protection against uncertain fears we must rely on Divine Providence, and on a wariness free from reproach, not on force.[22]

Equity here is that gap-filler that gives us a fair and reasonable way to act when there do not seem to be rules that prevent violent conduct. Grotius then puts his position in stark contrast to that of Gentili when he says: "I maintain that he cannot lawfully be killed either if the danger can in any other way be avoided, or if it is not altogether certain that the danger cannot be otherwise avoided."[23] And Grotius provides us with the simple formula that is still the doctrine in international law today: "The danger, again, must be immediate and imminent in point of time."[24] To establish this condition, evidence of planning that is virtually completed needs to be shown.

One of the main reasons that Grotius argues against the position Gentili had defended is that Grotius believes it is too easy to speak of fear as a mere "pretext" for clearly unacceptable grounds for going to war.[25] Pretexts are the publicly declared reasons for going to war, but behind them lurk other reasons that are hidden and would be considered unjustifiable grounds for going to war if exposed to the public light of reason. Grotius argues that it is important not to confuse "the terms 'cause' and 'pretext,'" for example, "the 'pretext' of the Second Punic War was the dispute over Saguntum, but the cause was the anger of the Carthaginians at the agreements that the Romans had extorted from them in times of adversity."[26] The difficulty of distinguishing "pretext" from "cause" makes Grotius much more cautious than Gentili, especially in respect to anticipatory attacks.

For example, some have said that the Iraq War of 2003 was started on a pretext, namely the fear of attack by Saddam Hussein's use of weapons of mass destruction (WMDs), but that the hidden cause was merely the desire of the United States to gain control over Iraq's extensive oil reserves.[27]

---

[22] Ibid., p. 184.
[23] Ibid., p. 175.
[24] Ibid., p. 173.
[25] Ibid., p. 169.
[26] Ibid., p. 546.
[27] Seymour Hersch, among many others, has defended this view. See his series of articles in *The New Yorker*, as well as his book, *Chain of Command*, New York: HarperCollins, 2004.

We should here recall what was earlier cited by Ian Brownlie, namely, that the having, or apparently having, of long-range missiles allows almost any State to say that another State presents a threat to it, thereby undercutting any restraint on what would count as a just cause for anticipatory attack. WMDs ratchet up Brownlie's concern about long-range missiles, since WMDs are, as the name implies, meant to be even scarier than regular weapons launched from one State into another unsuspecting State.

One possible way to bring Gentili and Grotius together, explored in much more detail at the end of this chapter, would be to have two different standards for the principle of priority. We could follow Grotius when we are asking when a State should be condemned and sanctioned for acts of aggression, and follow Gentili when we are asking when the State aggression element of the crime of aggression is satisfied and individuals can be prosecuted and punished. The reason for such a bifurcation is that there are two quite different reasons to appeal to the priority principle, one having to do with States and another having to do with individuals. I would argue that we should be more cautious in the case of individuals than in the case of States, as we will see in the final section of this chapter. Before taking up that topic, I return to Brownlie in the next section and to the last resort principle, which qualifies the first strike principle, in the fourth section.

III. First Strikes: The Priority Principle

In contemporary politics and international law there is a debate about the very same issues that vexed Gentili and Grotius. In this section I wish to give the flavor of that debate before I return to the conceptual issues and attempt a moderate resolution of the debate. Let us begin this section by returning to Ian Brownlie, one of the most respected theorists of international law. He says:

> In all probability the question which should be posed is not when is antici-
> patory action justified but, when has an attack occurred? This is a question
> which is not solved by reference to the "priority principle."... Thus if an
> unexplained force of warships or aircraft approached a state via the high
> seas and the superjacent airspace, this will constitute a threat to the peace
> but, it is submitted, does not itself justify forcible measures of self-defense
> since there is no resort to force by the putative aggressor and there is no
> unequivocal intention to attack.[28]

[28] Brownlie, *International Law and the Use of Force by States*, p. 367.

This is the standard "Grotian" approach taken by contemporary international law scholars, at least until quite recently.

The Grotian approach was to recognize that there is a right of self-defense for States but to see such a right as severely limited by certain temporal and spatial considerations, that is, following Grotius's injunction that "the danger, again, must be immediate and imminent in point of time."[29] Yoram Dinstein talks of the "immediacy condition," which he finds articulated most recently in the International Court of Justice's Nicaragua case.

> Immediacy signifies that there must not be an undue time-lag between the armed attack and the exercise of self-defense. However this condition is construed "broadly." Lapse of time is almost unavoidable when – in a desire to fulfill letter and spirit the condition of necessity – a tedious process of diplomatic negotiations evolves, with a view to resolving the matter amicably.[30]

Immediacy has to do with how close in time an attack *has occurred* for the State attacked to claim that it can engage in a reprisal war as a means of self-defense.

Imminence concerns responding to an attack that is seemingly *about to occur*. There is a lively debate in international legal circles about whether the doctrine of imminence countenances anticipatory self-defensive acts. Dinstein, like Brownlie, argues that threats of attack, even if imminent, only allow counter-threats, not anticipatory attacks. But he does allow for a category he calls interceptive self-defense.

> Interceptive, unlike anticipatory, self-defense takes place after the other side has committed itself to an armed attack in an ostensibly irrevocable way. Whereas a preventive strike anticipates an armed attack that is merely "foreseeable" (or even just "conceivable"), an interceptive strike counters an armed attack which is "imminent" and practically "unavoidable." It is the opinion of the present writer that interceptive, as distinct from anticipatory, self-defense is legitimate even under Article 51 of the Charter [of the United Nations].[31]

Dinstein joins the majority of contemporary international law scholars in thinking that imminence must be read very narrowly. The example that

---

[29] Hugo Grotius, *De Jure Belli ac Pacis*, p. 173.

[30] Yoram Dinstein, *War, Aggression, and Self-Defense*, 3rd ed., Cambridge: Cambridge University Press, 2001, p. 184.

[31] Ibid., p. 172. The first part of Article 51 of the United Nations Charter says: "Nothing in the present Charter shall impair the inherent right of individual or collective self-defense if an armed attack occurs against a Member of the United Nations until the Security Council has taken measures necessary to maintain international peace and security."

he gives is telling: if the United States had miraculously figured out that the Japanese carrier striking force was on its way to Pearl Harbor and the U.S. Navy had destroyed it while still on route, this would be justified as a form of interceptive rather than anticipatory self-defense. Notice that the United States would have to know that the Japanese had irrevocably begun their attack.

Another excellent example, written about by both Dinstein and Michael Walzer, is Israel's Six Days War in 1967. Dinstein agrees that the first strike by Israel was justified as interception of Egypt's forces massing on the border, even as Dinstein recognizes that this case is somewhat different from the Pearl Harbor case.

> True, no single Egyptian step, evaluated alone, may have qualified as an armed attack. But when all of the measures taken by Egypt (especially the peremptory ejection of the United Nations Emergency Force from the Gaza Strip and the Sinai Peninsula; the closure of the Straits of Tiran; the unprecedented build-up of Egyptian forces along Israel's borders; and constant saber-rattling statements about the impending fighting) were assessed in the aggregate it seemed to be crystal clear that Egypt was bent on an armed attack, and the sole question was not whether war would materialize but when.[32]

By contrast, in the hypothetical Pearl Harbor case, there was no question of when the attack would occur. Similarly, Walzer uses Israel's Six Days War to illustrate what he calls "just fear" because the massing of Egypt's forces at Israel's border "served no other more limited goal."[33]

Walzer differs from Dinstein, though, in recognizing that his conclusion about the justifiability of Israel's Six Days War requires a "major revision" of the Just War doctrine, as it is understood today.

> For it means that aggression can be made out not only in the absence of a military attack but in the (probable) absence of immediate intention to launch such an attack or invasion. The general formula must be something like this: states may use military force in the face of threats of war, whenever the failure to do so would seriously risk their territorial integrity or political independence.[34]

Walzer is thus not clearly still working within the Grotian tradition, perhaps moving closer to Gentili but nonetheless still keeping to the spirit of Grotius's concerns about limiting self-defense.

---

[32] Ibid., p. 173.
[33] Michael Walzer, *Just and Unjust Wars*, Boston: Basic Books, 1977, 2000, p. 84.
[34] Ibid., p. 85.

Recently, a clearer shift away from the Grotian tradition occurred when the United States declared a new doctrine, largely in response to the September 11, 2001, terrorist attacks on its shores. Here is the key provision of the so-called Bush Doctrine:

> Nations need not suffer an attack before they can lawfully take action to defend themselves against forces that present an imminent danger of attack.[35]

This statement might not have been all that different from Grotius's own view, especially given the reference to "imminence." But the Bush Doctrine also includes a claim that "uncertainty and lack of evidence should not preclude preemptive action where a serious threat to America's security is deemed to exist."[36] With the addition of this dimension, the Bush Doctrine looks much more like something that Gentili could have penned, allowing for preventive attacks, not merely those that were interceptive or even anticipatory.

The Bush Doctrine is also clearly different from the Grotian tradition in that it calls for war to be used as an instrument of United States foreign policy. The Grotian tradition sees war as a last resort, not as a part of normal policy. War can only be justified, in the Grotian view, when diplomatic efforts have been extensively tried and come up wanting. So, regardless of how we understand the priority principle, the use of this principle will be at odds with the Bush Doctrine and any other attempt to expand the domain of self-defense to include anticipatory or preventive attack. We next turn to the idea of last resort, perhaps the least well-discussed condition of the Just War tradition.

IV. Last Resort as the Ultimate Restraint

Let us begin with one attempt to define the principle of last resort. Douglas Lackey says that it involves this consideration: "If the just cause might be achieved by other means that have not been attempted, then war for that just cause is not just war."[37] Yet this is highly problematical. For in some sense "there are always other means, more or less dangerous,

---

[35] National Security Council, The National Security of the United States (2002).

[36] Amy E. Eckert and Manooher Mofidi, "Doctrine or Doctrinaire – The First Strike Doctrine and Preemptive Self-Defense under International Law," *Tulane Journal of International and Comparative Law*, vol. 12, Spring 2004, p. 122.

[37] Douglas P. Lackey, *The Ethics of War and Peace*, Upper Saddle River, NJ: Prentice Hall, Inc. 1989, p. 40.

more or less effective."[38] The idea of last resort is initially quite baffling. If the doctrine says that there must be no other means of defending oneself before one can be justified in using armed attacks to secure your State, then the principle appears to set an unlimited restraint since there are always other means available. But the principle is not utterly without limits, for as Paul Christopher has argued,

> The "last resort" condition is meant to restrain nations that are considering initiating hostilities – it is not relevant to nations that have already been attacked! . . . The condition of last resort was met [in the first Iraq War] as soon as Iraqi soldiers invaded Kuwait.[39]

Even when so limited, the principle of last resort, on almost every interpretation, seems to place very severe limitations on self-defense. And in any event we might wonder why minor attacks by one State against another shouldn't also have to pass the test of diplomatic alternatives. In this section I will explore whether the principle of last resort is plausible, and then in the next section I will examine whether this principle does indeed place severe restraints on the initiating of war.

On one level, last resort seems quite intuitively plausible. If I am in a barroom brawl and wonder whether I can throw the first punch, it is not enough to think that doing so will attain security for me. In addition, there must be no other reasonable steps I can take that would attain my security. In this sense, last resort is quite similar to necessity, for one way to show that striking first was a last resort is to show that it was necessary for one's self-defense. For if it is necessary to throw the first punch for self-defense, then there are no other alternatives that could have achieved this result. If there is an alternative that truly could attain the same result of self-defense, then the alternative that involves the least suffering and typically the least violence is the one that should be chosen on a doctrine of last resort.

The latter part of the doctrine, that one should choose the least violent means that can achieve a given permissible end, needs some additional support – for Gentili's comments make one wonder about seeing a snake, perhaps near the open front door of one's house. Even if one could avoid the snake's bite by leaving the room by the back door rather than confronting and killing the snake, doesn't it make more sense to take the more violent action and kill the snake thereby eliminating any future

---

[38] Walzer, *Just and Unjust Wars*, p. 213.
[39] Paul Christopher, *The Ethics of War and Peace: An Introduction to Legal and Moral Issues*, 3rd ed., Upper Saddle River, NJ: Prentice Hall, Inc. 2004, p. 88.

threat? One could ask in general whether retreating should always be attempted first before confronting a hostile threat. If one sees a very large menacing person at one's front door and one can leave by the back door without risking injury to self or the menacing person, must one take that option rather than confront the menacing person? Again doesn't it make sense to try to eliminate any future threat, especially since it is one's own home?

One way to respond to these questions is to insist that the alternatives that should be pursued as a last resort really are likely to accomplish the same self-defensive goals. Going out the back door or generally retreating often does not gain one self-defense except in the very short term. Self-defense often requires long-term planning. Think of the Six Days War between Israel and Egypt. It certainly was possible for Israel to mass its own troops at the border where Egypt was massing its troops, or to build up armaments at the point where these troops were massing. But such a strategy is only likely to have rendered Israel temporarily secure. Since Israel's forces were much smaller than Egypt's, attacking first with the element of surprise seemed best for Israel's long-term security. If last resort cannot accommodate such thinking, then perhaps it is shortsighted.

Last resort is only opposed to acting on long-term security interests if there are options, either short or long term, that have not been seriously contemplated, and that involve less violent means. So considerations of last resort are not going to block nearly as many actions as one might at first suppose. One of the chief things that last resort forces a State to contemplate is diplomacy, something that it is sometimes hard to contemplate in the midst of bellicose talk on both sides. But that is just the point. In the barroom brawl example, it is indeed difficult to take a breath and try to reason with the person who is acting in a menacing manner. But it is indeed a very good thing to take a breath, to stop and think, before acting violently in most situations. Of course, the problem is that in some other situations stopping to think may not be reasonable since, as in the Israeli case, the moment of surprise may be fleeting. So part of the calculation has to be not only whether there are less violent alternatives that might achieve the same short-term goal, but also there must be long-term calculations as well as calculations about whether the element of surprise is so crucial that even such calculating might be too dangerous.

Last resort is mainly a restraint on calculations about self-defense and defense of others. Initially it merely says that in most cases alternatives that are less violent need to be seriously considered. If it is a true emergency, then last resort calculation is probably off the table. But in all other cases, last resort calls for serious consideration of less violent alternatives that might be able to accomplish the same objectives as the violent means. In part what this means is that one is caused to stop and think, where thinking more often results in coming up with alternatives to what first appears to be the only reasonable strategy. For self-defense and defense of others, it is not sufficient to show that a given strategy will indeed secure one's defense. And it is this part of the doctrine of last resort that has brought the most criticism.

As we saw, Gentili makes the obvious point that if it is in our self-defense then we should be permitted to do whatever will secure it. But even in the case of the snake, there is a lingering doubt that we should be permitted to kill merely for our own peace of mind if there are other less violent options easily at hand. For the snake, like our opponent in the barroom brawl, has rights or interests just as we do. Last resort begins to make sense by urging that whenever violent means are contemplated, because of the effects of such means, we need to make sure that there isn't some way of resolving the problem by nonviolent or less violent means. But as with the case of the snake at the door, we need not risk long-term security in order to protect our potential attacker. What last resort calls for is a serious consideration of alternatives. Last resort does not dictate that we must always choose the least violent means, but only the least violent and equally efficacious means, time permitting. In this sense, last resort is like first strike, a kind of rule of thumb that guides us initially in thinking about what is a just cause to initiate or wage war. But as we will see in later chapters, the various proportionality principles will further restrict the last resort principle.

V. Contemporary Warfare and the Priority Principle

Ian Brownlie provides us with a very good example to consider that brings together the various considerations of the chapter and also points out the difficulties in applying the principles of first strike and last resort today. In previous times, States had to bring their armed forces to the border of a State that they wished to attack, and to do so took time allowing the target State to build up its own forces in anticipation of the attack, perhaps similarly moving its troops to the border as well. If the State that wished to attack was not adjacent to the target State, then other problems were posed, namely, having to move one's forces across a neutral State's borders, which was itself an act of war against the neutral State. And even if the States were adjacent, it might be too costly for States to keep their forces on active alert at the geographical fringes of its domain.

With the fairly recent development of long-range missiles, things have changed dramatically. States no longer have to mass forces at the border of target States, or to cross the border of a neutral State to threaten target States. States that are contemplating attacking target States need only point their long-range missiles at the target State, giving them a trajectory high enough not to violate the airspace of the neutral State that the missiles will pass over. And most important, missiles launched from far away have the element of surprise, giving the target State perhaps only minutes to try to marshal forces to stave off the attack. In addition, long-range missiles could be pointed at the target State for a very long time at little cost to the State wishing to threaten attack. And the target State will not know whether or when an attack is likely to occur.

One way to guard against such an attack is for the target State to mount its own missiles, either long-range missiles pointed back at the putative attacker, or intercepting missiles ready to strike invading long-range missiles. As it turns out, missile defense is much more costly than long-range attack missiles. One of the reasons for this also points to one of the other major problems of long-range missiles, namely, that long-range missiles can often be easily hidden from sight – for instance, in silos – making it very hard for target States to know how much defensive missile force is needed for retaliatory strike threats, or to intercept enemy missiles. Unlike the massing of troops on a target State's border, long-range missiles can be ready to strike and yet hidden from view.

In a sense, long-range missiles are a bit like the development of blitzkrieg strategies by Nazi Germany. The Nazis realized that they could move their troops very quickly in relatively lightweight armored vehicles and thereby gain the advantage of surprise as they attacked target States. And after a few such successful attacks, the blitzkrieg forces became like the long-range missiles, seemingly always aimed at potential target States. Germany did not have to mass forces at the target State's borders nor did it have to worry about neutral States since its forces would be in and out of the neutral States before anyone knew much about it. Thus, the Nazi use of blitzkrieg strategies was somewhat like the use of long-range missiles.

Long-range missiles, as well as blitzkrieg forces, pose special problems for the principle of first strike as well as for last resort. If a State knows that an enemy State has long-range missiles and believes that these weapons are aimed at it, then this could make first strikes justifiable to preempt the use of those missiles, even though they have not yet been launched, and perhaps even if there is no indication that they will be launched in the near future. And concerning last resorts, it appears that when long-range missiles enter the picture, nearly every scenario resembles an emergency situation since it is impossible to judge how much time, if any, a State has to prepare for the attack. Indeed, when long-range missiles are present, attacks are imminent; it is as if the troops have been marshaled at the borders and may already have been given the attack order from the commanders.

Long-range missiles are probably here to stay, as a result, we need to rethink the ideas of first strike and last resort. Long-range missiles could call for a strategy much like that outlined by Gentili, namely, to uproot the weed at the beginning before it grows and becomes very hard to remove. While I would not follow Gentili here, in some cases his position becomes more plausible. Strategic first strikes aimed at destroying missile-producing factories are in this sense much easier to justify than other types of first strike. And in such cases, last resort considerations, as Gentili also argued, are seemingly less important. Once the long-range missiles are operational, the threat is imminent, as far as anyone can tell. And then even Grotius would recognize that first strikes on the missile sites do not necessarily mean that one is the aggressor.

The main thing to learn from the example of long-range missiles concerns when last resort is meaningful and when it is of limited meaningfulness. Is putting up a missile shield like having to leave your own house to prevent being bitten by a snake at the door, or is it more like building your own castle to protect yourself? I would follow Grotius rather than Gentili in thinking that a State often has nonviolent options for staving off aggression that are not repugnant. And in those cases, the principle of last resort certainly seems to be relevant in that these options need to be seriously considered and good reasons advanced if one nonetheless decides to take a violent tack and engage in anticipatory first strike.

Throughout this chapter I have tried to indicate that considerations of last resort normally place a strong constraint on States that are contemplating anticipatory first strikes. I agreed with Dinstein that the case of interceptive first strike is much easier to justify than normal anticipatory first strike. And I also agreed with Brownlie that first strikes to counter long-range missiles are easier to justify than the normal cases as well. But with these two cases, and ones like them such as blitzkrieg strategies, to one side, States need to take much more seriously than many presently do their obligations carefully to consider nonviolent alternatives to first strike armed force.

Another case to put on the table is that of weapons of mass destruction. Chemical agents can spread through the air or water, often undetected until they begin to have a deadly effect on a population.[40] Here it looks like we would need to think of imminence in a very different way than we have so far. A State that begins to stockpile chemical, biological, or nuclear weapons seems to be like a State that develops a long-range missile system, except that it is even harder to detect when or where an attack might come. Yet, unlike missile systems, chemical, biological, and nuclear agents can be used for non-military purposes. This is especially problematical in the case of nuclear development, since electricity plants can be the aim of nuclear development rather than weapons production. The priority principle will be strained by such examples of contemporary warfare, but as we will next see, the principle can be refashioned so as still to have contemporary relevance. But that relevance will require changes in the principle that recognize more than has been recognized in the past, namely, that the principle can be put to multiple uses and should be tailored to those differences.

VI. International Criminal Law and the Priority Principle

Now let us return to the issue of how we should regard the priority principle in international criminal law today. We might begin by proposing that the priority principle be reconceptualized as follows:

> The priority principle involves the first use of armed force by one State, or State-like entity, against another State, or State-like entity, that is not provoked by an imminent threat.

The idea of imminence will be the key component of the first strike principle that has to undergo change in light of the development of contemporary weaponry. Imminence should be understood to mean that all of the factors are in place for a first strike and there is some evidence that the State has the intention to engage in such a strike. It is not required, though, as it was in previous ages, that troops be literally marshaled at a neighbor's borders. In this respect, anticipatory self-defense will generally have to have a wider scope than in previous eras.

As will be discussed in a later chapter, both the priority principle and the just cause principle will factor into a definition of State aggression in the crime of aggression, or as it is sometimes called, the crime against peace.

---

[40] For a lengthy discussion of chemical weapons in *jus in bello* terms see my book, *War Crimes and Just War*, New York: Cambridge University Press, 2007, ch. 6.

In some legal characterizations, as we will see in Chapter 10, the aggressor is often simply identified with the State that strikes first. But this is not a satisfactory way to proceed. For it often turns out that provocation has occurred, and the provoker is better identified as the aggressor than the person, or State, that actually struck first. In a reconceptualized priority principle, as well as a reconceptualized understanding of aggression, how we deal with provocation will also be a key factor. Most difficult of all will be the question, addressed in a chapter-length treatment in the final section of the book, about how to understand humanitarian intervention wars. Is it provocation for one State to abuse its own population so that when another State intervenes, such intervention is not seen to violate the priority principle? I delay an answer to this vexing question until later.

I would also propose that close-call cases should not be regarded as sufficient to count as satisfying the State aggression element of the crime of aggression. Anticipatory self-defense, or invasions of unoccupied territory, might be condemnable but might then not satisfy the State aggression element of the crime of aggression because they are so often not clear-cut. In the anticipatory self-defense case, especially concerning long-range missiles or nuclear weapons production, we might not call these clear enough cases of putative aggression to warrant international prosecutions of State leaders since the leaders could so easily have mistakenly thought that their States were justified in defending themselves. In the case of invasion of unoccupied territory, since there was a clear trespass into the territory of another State, things are clearer than in anticipatory self-defense cases. But we might think that it is not a serious enough violation to trigger the very serious consequences that often follow from prosecutions. In the rest of this section, and in the next chapter, I will defend these proposals.

A critic of the above proposal could say that in the case of anticipatory self-defensive action, and even more in the case of invasion of unoccupied territory, the issue is not who is harmed but rather what are the risks of triggering all-out war with all of its attendant horrors that we discussed in Chapter 2. I agree that the most significant thing that is risked when States either engage in anticipatory self-defense or invasion of unoccupied territory is that such actions will trigger all-out war. As a contingent pacifist, I take this consequence extremely seriously. But the question is whether the marking of the seriousness of this action requires more than condemnation of the State. Should we also prosecute the leaders of the State that engages in these actions?

If the major reason to prosecute, and punish, individual leaders of a State is to deter future leaders, then it is unclear to me that prosecuting in close-call cases can be justified, despite the worries about triggering all-out war. If leaders mistakenly believe that their actions are advancing the legitimate goals of their States at the time that they act, they are unlikely to be deterred by the threat of prosecution. And leaders are much more likely to hold these mistaken beliefs when we are discussing close-call cases. Of course, if the penalties are very high indeed, then State leaders may be deterred from even thinking of initiating war. But we must balance the deterrence interest against the loss of liberty interest.

If the reason to prosecute, and punish, individual leaders of States is for retribution rather than deterrence, it is even less clear that prosecution in close-call cases can be justified. The wrong-making character of the actions of these leaders is so much less clear in close-call cases, at least to me; and again we need to weigh the retributive benefits against the very serious loss of liberty that is risked when trials occur. Think of the case of invasion of unoccupied territory. If there are no serious human rights abuses in such State action, why think that we should nonetheless punish the State leaders responsible for such "minor" transgressions? It can't be because of the human rights worries.

Of course, one may return to the issue of the risk of all-out war that an even minor act of State aggression risks to justify the retributive punishment of prosecutions. But here we have a mismatch. The retribution is sought not for harm actually done but for harm risked, whereas the punishment sought is in my view quite serious. I suppose one could tinker with the punishment schemes, adjusting them quite low for such "crimes." But as long as loss of liberty, the paradigmatic punishment in criminal law, is still on the table, I think there is a normative problem nonetheless. There is a mismatch in terms of proportionality between the punishment and the crime. I'll say more about this general issue in the final chapter of this section, Chapter 6.

One could argue that there is no need to adjust the priority principle as long as there are other factors that go into an assessment of just cause. I do not have a major disagreement with this objection. Indeed, I think that we should generally diminish in importance the priority principle and elevate the other components of just cause so that we do not end up prosecuting defendants for relatively minor transgressions of State sovereignty. If it seems better to leave the priority principle as it has been understood and yet diminish its importance even more than I have proposed, rather than to qualify the priority principle and leave it as a fairly important factor in just cause determinations, I will not object. In the end, I think these two ways of viewing things amount to roughly the same point practically in any event.

Finally, let me summarize the ways in which I think the *jus ad bellum* normative principle of priority or first strike should be reconceptualized for prosecutions concerning the crime of aggression. The idea has been that a State that strikes first, especially if not provoked by threat of imminent attack, is normally engaged in aggressive and hence unjustified war. The proposal of this chapter is that only clear-cut cases of first strike be thought of as satisfying the State aggression element of the crime of aggression. We can still condemn other cases of putative aggression, perhaps with sanctions levied against States, but the prosecution of individuals for the crime of aggression should require a higher bar to be crossed, that is, it must be proved that a State engaged in a serious violation of the priority principle. The priority principle is really only one of several preliminary tests in discerning whether a war is fought for a just cause. In that sense, the priority principle should not itself be regarded as an independent principle of *jus ad bellum,* despite the way that lawyers sometimes regard it. I will continue to investigate this issue in the next chapter where a more explicit link is made between the priority principle and the just cause principle for crimes against peace prosecutions.

5

The Principle of Just Cause

In the Just War tradition, a distinction is drawn between the justification of initiating and waging war, *jus ad bellum*, and the justification of tactics during war, *jus in bello*. The main *jus ad bellum* normative principle is called "just cause." Traditionally, just cause referred to a wrong that a State had committed, which initially legitimated war as a response.[1] The two main just causes were unprovoked attacks on either one's own State or another State. In the past, just causes could involve either the prevention of those attacks or the punishment of them. Today, punishment is a highly contentious just cause, whereas prevention of attack on one's own or another State is still considered to be the most important of the just causes to go to war. Just cause only addresses a prima facie case to go to war, where there are other conditions that also need to be satisfied, principally proportionality, in order for the war to be just.

The principle of just cause is also at the core of what constitutes an aggressive war in contemporary international law. Traditionally, *jus ad bellum* principles were employed to determine whether a State was justified in its use of force. In the trials at Nuremberg, *jus ad bellum* principles were employed to determine whether individuals should be prosecuted for initiating aggressive war, and more recently, the International Criminal Court is considering the prosecution of aggression as well.[2] In this chapter, I will argue that the principle of just cause needs to be

[1] See Stephen C. Neff, *War and the Law of Nations: A General History*, Cambridge: Cambridge University Press, 2005.
[2] Today there are no prosecutions of individuals for the crime of aggression, even though the International Criminal Court has jurisdiction to do so, because of a failure of the international community to agree about what constitutes State aggression, one of the elements in the crime of aggression.

reconceptualized especially when we are discussing responsibility of individual defendants rather than States.

In the Just War tradition, extending back at least to the time of Augustine, if not including Cicero and even Plato as well, war is thought to be justified in only a small number of cases, especially for self-defense or defense of others. In that tradition, the best-known theorist is Hugo Grotius, who wrote in the early 17th century, although there are many other important Just War theorists as well. I will sketch some of their views, contrasting them with pacifist views. The aim of the chapter is to reconceptualize what many in law and ethics think to be the main *jus ad bellum* normative principle, the principle of just cause. In this and the next chapter, I argue that while the principle of just cause is very important the principle of proportionality is at least as important.

Jus ad bellum principles originate in the Just War tradition, and State aggression is largely a subject of international law. There is quite a bit of overlap of categories between the Just War moral tradition and international law so that both traditions for instance talk about *jus ad bellum* principles, and both normally talk about just cause and proportionality, the subjects of our next two chapters, as the key principles in this set. I will argue that the principle of just cause should be seen as a bifurcated principle, with a different standard employed for States than for individuals.

There are three elements normally thought to constitute the individual crime of waging aggressive war: State aggression, individual *actus reus*, and individual *mens rea*. Just cause and proportionality, as well as the priority principle, all bear significantly on what counts as the State aggression element. In subsequent chapters I will also extensively discuss *actus reus* and *mens rea* in crimes of aggression, or what are sometimes called crimes against peace. I will say something at the end of this chapter about whether the problems I uncovered with the traditional understanding of just cause can be alleviated by simply changing how we view the other two elements rather than by changing the State aggression element of the crime of aggression. Suffice it here to say that State aggression is only one element of the crime of aggression, but it is the element most closely related to traditional *jus ad bellum* principles such as just cause and proportionality.

The structure of the chapter is as follows. In the first section I will discuss two examples of unjust war: conversion of the heathens and promoting democracy. Then I will begin to explain what is a just cause to wage war. In the second section, I will discuss two seemingly paradigmatic examples of just war, wars waged for collective and individual self-defense. In the third section, I will reconceptualize the principle of just cause. I argue that just cause is best seen as a wrong committed by a State that threatens the lives or human rights of a sufficiently large number of people to offset the threat to lives and human rights that waging war poses. In the fourth section I will discuss how we should understand just cause in criminal trials for waging aggressive war. In the fifth section of the chapter I defend the view that we should have a bifurcated understanding of just cause and of other principles of *jus ad bellum*. In the sixth section I will draw out some implications of my view for the relationship between *jus ad bellum* and *jus in bello*.

I. Conversion of Heathens and Promotion of Democracy

There are cases when intervention for seemingly good reasons should be condemned as not satisfying the just cause principle for waging war and that hence could count as aggression. In this section I will look at two such cases: the 16th-century case of wars fought by the Spaniards to convert the heathen Indians in South America, and wars fought by contemporary Western democratic States to promote democracy in non-Western States. I draw parallels between these two cases and then give a preliminary sense of what the principle of just cause should mean in determining when a State can justifiably resort to war and when its acts of war will not be considered aggression.

Let us begin with the 16th-century philosopher Franciso Vitoria's treatment of the Conquistadors' claim that they had a just cause to wage war against the Indians as a means to stop them from practicing the wrong religion and to convert them from heathenism to Christianity. Following the Just War tradition, especially that version espoused by Thomas Aquinas, Vitoria draws the following conclusion:

> if the faith be presented to the Indians in the way named only and they do not receive it, the Spaniards can not make this a reason for waging war on them or for proceeding against them under the law of war.[3]

The main reason that Vitoria gives in support of his claim is that the Indians "are innocent in this respect and have done no wrong to the Spaniards."

[3] Francisco Vitoria, *De Indis et De Ivre Belli Reflectiones* (On the Indians and Reflections on War) (1536), edited by Ernest Nys, Washington, DC: Carnegie Institution, 1917, p. 143.

Vitoria then gives a concise statement of the Medieval doctrine of just cause: "they who are attacked for some fault must deserve the attack."[4] Since the Indians are without fault in the sense that they have done no wrong to the Spaniards and their heathen practices are similarly non-faulty, their heathenism cannot be the ground for a just war against them. The latter claim is based on Vitoria's argument that the heathens do not have to convert because they "are not bound, directly [as] the Christian faith is announced to them, to believe it."[5] The heathens were not deserving of attack before they heard the word of Christianity, says Vitoria, and it is surely no different now that they have heard it. They have committed no wrong of the sort that warrants an attack because of their not believing what the Christian Conquistadors have told them to believe.

The first question to examine is whether it is defensible to think of "just cause" in terms of whether those attacked deserve to be attacked. In the next section I will discuss self-defense cases, but here I wish to note that there may be innocent threats that raise self-defense concerns, that is, a person who is a threat may not be aware that she poses this threat. Such a person may not intend to be a threat and hence may be innocent and not deserving of being attacked, and yet the person threatened may have a just cause to employ violent means to defend himself. Insofar as innocent threats are imminent and serious threats, self-defense concerns might be sufficient for a just cause to engage in war even though those attacked have not done anything wrong that would make them deserve to be attacked. Such considerations should make us reluctant to follow Vitoria in thinking that just cause must be linked to deservingness to be attacked. But in the case at hand, this will not be as important as it will turn out to be later since the Indians were certainly not a threat to the Spanish Conquistadors any more than they had done wrong to the Conquistadors by their continued adherence to a set of heathen religious beliefs. Of course, if the heathen religious beliefs were being evangelized the way that the Conquistadors evangelized Christianity, it might be a threat to Christian culture, but that was surely not the case in the middle of the 16th century in South America.

The second question to ask is what sort of wrongs or threats must the attacked State have engaged in that might justify the attacking State's waging of war. Could it ever be a wrong done to one State for another State to believe or practice the "wrong" religion? Let us imagine that

---

[4] Ibid.
[5] Ibid., p. 142.

the religion in question involved human sacrifice, as the Conquistadors claimed to be true of certain South American religions. Of course it would matter whether the human sacrifice was itself a wrong, not merely done out of the wrong beliefs. But if there was mass slaughter of innocents by the leaders of this religion, this could be counted as a wrong. Such a wrong would not necessarily be based on the "wrong" religious beliefs instead of the obviously wrong murderous practices.

The question is really whether the tenets of the religion themselves could constitute a kind of wrong that could be a just cause for war to be waged to force the Indians to change their religion. Let us assume, for the sake of argument, that the heathen religion is the "wrong" religion in the sense that it does not contain true beliefs about human nature and the normative relationship between God and humans. Is this the kind of wrong that could be a just cause for war? I agree with Vitoria that it could not be seen as a wrong done to the Spaniards, even though it might be a wrong in other respects. The Spaniards could still practice their own religion even living next to the heathens, unless the heathens did become evangelists like the Christians, but apparently there was no evidence of that either.

What of the wrong done to the Indians themselves by the perpetuation of a society-wide religion that was "wrong?" Is the wrong done to the Indians themselves grounds for the Conquistadors to wage war to change that religion? Vitoria says no, arguing that the wrong must be done to the Conquistadors for them to have grounds to wage war against the heathens. Is this a defensible view? Couldn't this be a case of "defense of others" as grounds for waging non-aggressive war? Is subscribing to the "wrong" religion a wrong or harm to the people who so subscribe, especially if they are forced to subscribe? It may be, but if the people themselves do not object to this imposition it certainly seems unjustifiably intrusive for the Conquistadors to force the Indians to stop practicing the religion they want to practice or at least do not object to.

We might also think about a more contemporary case, the waging of war to promote democracy. The administration of U.S. President George W. Bush stands in a long line of recent State governments that have openly suggested that promoting democracy can be a just cause to wage war. It seems to me that an interesting way to approach these claims is by comparison with the claims in the 16th century that converting the heathens could be a just cause to wage war. Let us ask the question concerning two different cases, those people who seemingly acquiesce in a non-democratic government and those people who rebel against the non-democratic government but seem to need help to achieve democracy. The first case seems closer to the converting the heathens case, whereas the second raises a separate set of problems.

Like holding the wrong religious beliefs, it might be said that a State that is non-democratic practices the wrong form of government. The people may be wronged or harmed by this, but it is surely not necessarily a wrong or harm to the State that wishes to wage war to change this form of government. And for this reason, and since the people in question do not complain, it would seem to be unjustifiably intrusive for one State to force the non-democratic State to change its form of government. It may truly be in the best interests of the people to have their government forcibly changed, but it seems non-democratic to do so unless the people themselves request such a change. And given that the issue is the promotion of democracy, it seems odd indeed to seek to justify war that non-democratically forces people to change their practices in the name of democracy itself. If there were some other human right at stake, such as in cases of genocide, there might not be much importance placed on whether the people want intervention to stop the abuse as is true if we are talking about lack of democracy.

Things are quite different if the people in question, say a sizable subsection of the population of a State, ask for help in overthrowing a non-democratic government and replacing it with a democratic government. Here you have the combination of a kind of wrong being done by a State, in that it represses a portion of its population and forces them not to live under a democracy, in combination with the fact that that population group complains and rebels against this policy. It no longer is clearly intrusive for another State to intervene to help them. This goes a long way to establishing that the intervention might be justified. But does it provide a just cause for war, given the enormous harm caused by war? I will delay giving a full answer to this question until the chapter in which we consider the principle of proportionality that forces us to ask these comparative harm questions. Suffice it here to say that this case will be easier to fit under the category of just cause than the case discussed in the previous paragraphs.

But the problem remains that the State being attacked has not done a wrong to the State doing the attacking – indeed, the attacking State looks like it is the first striker. Here is where the priority principle intersects with the just cause principle, as we saw in the previous chapter. While there may be a prima facie plausibility to say that the attacking State is justified because its cause of promoting democracy to those who ask for it is just, there is also a prima facie implausibility of such an attack since the attacking State has not itself been attacked first. We will need to figure out how to weigh such considerations in subsequent chapters. But my tentative conclusion is that it is not obvious that promoting democracy will always outweigh other considerations, and hence not obvious that promoting democracy is a clear-cut just cause to wage what would otherwise be unjustified aggressive war.

II. Paradigmatic Just Causes: Individual and Collective Self-Defense

In this section, I discuss seemingly paradigmatic cases of a war fought for a just cause, and hence wars that are generally believed not to be aggressive. I also will provide a preliminary conceptualization of what a just cause is in international criminal law and how this construal differs from a broader conception of just cause than one can find in the traditional normative principles of *jus ad bellum*. In the first chapter, I pointed to Article 51 of the United Nations Charter as providing a paradigmatic exception to the general prohibition on State use of force. That article says

> Nothing in the present Charter shall impair the inherent right of individual or collective self-defense if an armed attack occurs against a Member of the United Nations, until the Security Council has taken measures necessary to maintain international peace and security.[6]

This canonical statement seemingly sets up two situations that are clear-cut cases of waging war for a just cause in *jus ad bellum* normative principles of contemporary international law: individual and collective self-defense. In this section I will examine these two cases as aids to thinking about how we might want to reconceptualize the principle of just cause today.

Let us start with the seemingly simple case of self-defensive wars. Consider the problem of wars that are provoked. It sometimes appears that there is a conflict between the claim that a State acted in self-defense and the claim that that State was also the first to strike the other State. We could reflect again on the cases of anticipatory self-defense discussed in the previous chapter. We might want to say that States that engage in self-defensive wars that also are first strikes are still to be criticized, and perhaps sanctioned, but not that individuals who participate in such wars are to be prosecuted. In the next section I will argue that in general we should

---

[6] Charter of the United Nations, T. S. 993, 59 Stat. 1031, 1976 Y.B.U.N. 1043 (June 26, 1945), Art. 51.

set a lower just cause standard when we are discussing the elements of individual liability than if we are discussing State sanctions. In this respect, I agree with Jeff McMahan, who has recently written that just causes are multiple and serve multiple purposes.[7]

Let us examine what it is about self-defense, collective or individual, that has seemed to so many to be paradigmatic of a just cause for war, and then try to understand why even this may be problematic in certain cases. The seemingly simplest case is when a single State has been attacked and launches a war to defend itself against that attacking State. The attacked State seemingly has a paradigmatic just cause to wage war to stop the attacking State, namely, self-defense. But what if the initial attack is not followed by an invasion or even by any indication that there will be further attacks? If the border is crossed and no one is hurt, and the offending State quickly returns to its own territory, it is unclear why this attack would count as a just cause for waging war, given that war involves such horrible risks. I would say that we might not even want to call this single attack a just cause for war.

A more standard case of individual, as opposed to collective, State self-defense is the case of a State that is being attacked and needs to engage in war to repel the attack and prevent itself from being overrun by the attacking State. Here we clearly have a just cause for initiating war, but again, for how long? Once the attacking State has been stopped and pushed back across the common border, does the attacked State have a just cause to continue the war, now marching into the attacking State's territory until it has subjugated the attacking State? The intuitive answer to this question is not at all clear. In some contexts we might want to give an affirmative answer, and in other contexts a negative answer. The answer is not clear-cut because the first strike is not necessarily of such magnitude as to warrant using continuing rather than very temporary self-defensive measures, and yet we were supposedly considering a paradigmatic case of just cause to wage war.

Now think about a case of collective self-defense. Let us say that a State is in a collective security organization with other States, on the model of NATO, for instance. Its neighbor who is not in the organization attacks one of the States in this organization, and the attacked State requests help from the organization. Is this a just cause for a non-attacked State to initiate war against the attacking State? In part the answer will depend on

[7] Jeff McMahan, "Just Cause for War," *Ethics & International Affairs*, vol. 19, no. 3, 2005, pp. 1–21.

what other alternatives have been tried so far. Collective security organizations often have tremendous diplomatic clout, so diplomacy would have to be pursued first, if time allows, before a State could legitimately launch a war to defend its comrade State. In addition, we will need to know if the attacked State is trustworthy in reporting whether and to what extent it needs help to defend itself. Collective self-defense, despite being listed in the UN Charter, is nonetheless problematical since the testimony of attacked States is not always reliable, certainly not nearly as reliable as a State's own sense of the way it is being attacked and whether this requires it to launch a war to defend itself rather than to ratchet up diplomatic efforts and veiled threats.

Perhaps the clearest paradigmatic case would be when a collective organization is itself under attack and needs to defend itself from another organization or powerful State that is attacking it. And yet, there have been very, very few such historical cases and hence it is not at all clear what we can learn by examining such anomalous cases. Another possibility would be when the collective organization is threatened because of what is happening to one of its member States. But again we can ask for criteria for determining threats and run into significant controversy in deciding how to answer this question. And it is also true that defending against a threat may not give a just cause that has much lasting power, since the threat may be eliminated after just one show of force on the part of the collective organization.

Today, in international law the supremely clearest case of self-defensive war is one that has been authorized by the Security Council of the United Nations. Article 39 states:

> The Security Council shall determine the existence of any threat to the peace, breach of the peace, or act of aggression, and shall make recommendations, or decide what measures shall be taken in accordance with Articles 41 and 42, to maintain or restore international peace and security.

Article 42 says that the Security Council "may take such action by air, sea, or land forces as may be necessary to maintain or restore international peace and security." So the individual or collective self-defensive wars, discussed in Article 51, have their clearest expression when the Security Council has authorized them.

Why does Security Council authorization make the use of force, by a single State or a group of States, acting in individual or collective self-defense, not, or less of, an act of aggression than without such authorization? One possibility is the legalistic answer that without such authorization, a State will more clearly run afoul of Article 2(4)'s general prohibition on the use of force, unless not inconsistent with the purposes of the UN. But even from a strictly legal perspective, why think that the UN and only the UN has the power to determine what are the purposes of the UN? And from a moral perspective, why think that the UN, a clearly political body, can determine what is aggressive and what is not? If the UN authorizes use of force, is the waging of war clearly not aggressive, or is it aggressive yet nonetheless justified? These questions have no easy answers. Perhaps we can say that when the use of force has received UN authorization, then whatever the purpose of such a war it is a just cause. But this stipulative way of proceeding looks merely ad hoc and doesn't advance our understanding of just cause. In this section, our brief examination has revealed the conclusion that there are few paradigmatic cases of just causes to initiate a sustained war by one State against another, even on grounds of self-defense. I next turn to a reassessment of the idea of just cause in light of the examples discussed above.

III. Reconceptualizing the Principle of Just Cause

Traditionally, it was thought that invasion, or threatened invasion, gave the invaded State a just cause for waging war. I reject this way of understanding the principle of just cause. In my view, States are not justified in going to war against other States merely to protect territory or property, unless that territory was occupied. The reason for this is that war involves the killing of many people and it is not at all clear why it would be a just cause to wage a war that involved such killings merely to preserve territory. Indeed, if the State in question was not protecting the rights of its members, it is also unclear why a State would be justified in going to war to preserve its sovereignty. My proposal about reconceptualizing the principle of just cause is that we figure out a way to connect just cause better with what the principle is ultimately to justify, namely, the killing of many people in war.

Any plausible reconceptualizing of the principle of just cause must limit just cause to those circumstances where going to war will provide overriding reasons to counter the presumption that war is nearly always wrong because of the risk of killing the innocent. If we are going to go to war and risk killing many people, some of whom will surely be innocent, there must be something at stake that is at least as important as what is risked. Lots of killing is always risked when a State resorts to war, and this must be balanced against what is to be gained from the war. Here the most important consideration is that recourse to war not be even prima facie permitted unless what war aims at is truly significant, and on the order of preventing the killing of lots of people. We should restrict what counts as just cause to connect to the minimization of the destruction of human life or at least to the promotion of human rights.

Some, seemingly such as Vitoria, have argued that just cause should be seen as a kind of threshold consideration – whenever a wrong has been done then, prima facie, war can be initiated to stop or avenge that wrong. What I am suggesting is that this traditional way to understand the principle of just cause is too broad since the number of wrongs a State can commit is too large to warrant war even in a prima facie way allowed by the principle of just cause, given all of war's attendant horrors. Some wrongs are not sufficiently grave to count as just causes that warrant war as a response. A State, or person, may make itself liable to be blamed or even to be punished for a wrong committed, and yet such liability does not extend to being attacked as would occur during war. One can here think of the analogy to capital punishment – not all wrongs render one liable to be executed for what one has done; indeed, only the most serious of offenses, if any, will warrant the death penalty, and surely not such offenses as would occur in the mere destruction of property or the trespass on another's land. War, like capital punishment, involves the killing of people and needs justification that is as strong as what is being justified as a response.

My proposal is that just cause be reconceptualized to be preventing or stopping a wrong committed by a State, or State-like entity, against another State, or subsection of a State, which is sufficiently morally serious to be analogous to the risk of large loss of life that war involves. On my proposal, just causes for war concern preventing or stopping wrongs from occurring, not retaliating against States for committing wrong. Just causes for war are not merely violations of territorial integrity, but only ones that involve threats to the lives, or basic human rights, of the members of a State. Just causes for war are not merely violations of a State's sovereignty by another State, unless the State whose sovereignty is violated is protecting the human rights of its members and can no longer do so, or when the sovereignty violation jeopardizes human rights in some other significant way. Just causes for war thus involve only certain wrongs committed by the State that is to be attacked, namely, wrongs that threaten the lives or human rights of a sufficiently large number of people to offset the threat to lives and human rights that is involved in the waging of the war in question. This way of understanding the principle of just cause makes it intimately connected to the *jus ad bellum* principle of proportionality.

Just causes must be significant, and significance in my view involves a threshold proportionality consideration. Just causes must be significant in that they meet a minimum threshold of good that could outweigh the likely bad that war will bring. This is not completely to mix just cause and proportionality principles, since the proportionality component of just cause is only a prima facie, not an all things considered principle. Proportionality only enters into just war considerations initially in a determination of whether the causes in question are sufficiently significant to offset the initial presumption against war that holds true in all situations. In my view, mere violations of territorial integrity are not just causes because of a failure to meet this proportionality threshold of just causes. This is a radical break with many just war theorists since just cause is often conceptualized as completely separate from proportionality. I will argue in detail in the next chapter that proportionality plays two roles in *jus ad bellum* principles: a threshold consideration in the principle of just cause and a more robust role in the principle of proportionality itself.

One objection to my proposal, often made over the centuries, is that to allow one State ever to violate the territorial integrity or sovereignty of another State is indeed to risk major loss of life or violation of human rights, since any incursion by one State into another State's affairs has proven to be often a prelude to full-scale attack. And if one has to wait for the full-scale attack, it is almost always too late to prevent the attack. This is why traditional Just War theory and contemporary international law, as manifested in the UN Charter cited earlier, look only to whether territorial integrity or State sovereignty has been breached, not to the further question of whether there is significant harm to individuals that is risked by such an action. Indeed, it is very hard to predict what else will happen once the firm bulwark against rights abuse normally secured by State sovereignty has been breached.

If the right to self-determination is a human right, it may turn out that most invasions that threaten a people's right to determine how it governs itself could violate my reconceptualized just cause principle – although it should be noted that merely depriving a people of the right to have lots of unoccupied and unused land would not necessarily constitute a violation of the right to self-determination as a human right. In my view, normally the key consideration is whether the assault on a population is imminent. If there is no such imminent threat to a population, then normally there is not a sufficient threat to warrant a State's claim to have just cause to go to war merely because borders have been crossed or sovereignty breached.

A second objection is that I have not taken seriously non-consequentialist wrongs that would justify recourse to war. Violations of State sovereignty are wrongs in at least two senses: they risk harm to members of States, but they also are violations of a moral principle that undergirds sovereignty. The problem, that I have explored elsewhere, is to explain precisely what that moral principle is. I have argued that the best way to think about the moral principle of sovereignty is in terms of protection of security of the individual members of a State.[8] Of course, this is also ultimately a consequentialist idea as well. It is not at all clear to me what would be a purely deontological consideration in this domain. I suppose one could claim that States simply have duties not to invade other States, but surely the obvious question would be why they have such duties.[9]

A third objection arises when we think of punishment as a just cause for war.[10] If a State has indeed committed a wrong, there is a sense in which the State deserves to experience retaliatory punishment. War can be justified as a means of punishment since just cause focuses on wrongs, and punishment is just about the proper response to wrongs committed, whether by individuals or by States. Indeed, if there is no likelihood that a State that commits a wrong will get the punishment it deserves by any other means, war has seemed to be justified as a way to achieve such just deserts, just as is true today in arguments in favor of capital punishment for those who otherwise are likely to escape other forms of punishment.

But in the Just War tradition, punishment was normally discussed in terms of deterrence, at least long-run deterrence, rather than pure retribution. And in my view the reason is clear enough. Since Grotius, retributive punishment is seen as not the proper basis for waging war as opposed to conducting a trial.[11] War is not a good instrument to use to engage in retributive punishment because it is too broad a brush. It is too likely

---

[8] See my book, *Crimes against Humanity: A Normative Account*, New York: Cambridge University Press, 2005, ch. 1.

[9] In a later chapter, I will explore the idea that in some very limited contexts wars of humanitarian intervention can be seen as just wars, even though they involve the violation of sovereignty or territorial integrity of States. Indeed, many people today believe that it is not only justified but even required that States invade other States to prevent or stop genocides. But most lawyers continue to have trouble with such cases, and I will follow them in raising significant worries about humanitarian intervention. See the extensive discussion of this issue in chapter 13.

[10] See Kenneth W. Kemp, "Punishment as Just Cause for War," *Public Affairs Quarterly*, vol. 10, no. 4, October 1996, pp. 335–353.

[11] Hugo Grotius, *De Jure Belli ac Pacis*, pp. 502–503, and elsewhere.

that those who deserve to be punished will not be, and those who do not deserve to be punished will be. Those who are thought to be deserving of punishment are often so thought because of characteristics of the individual, namely, whether the person acted in a malicious way or from racial animosity. So, while just causes concern wrongs done, wars are not legitimately waged unless the point of the war is to prevent or stop the wrong from being committed, now or in the future, rather than merely as an act of retribution. In the next section I will say more about how just causes should be understood in contemporary international law.

IV. Just Cause and the Element of State Aggression

Despite my argument that we should not recognize as many just causes as were traditionally recognized in Just War theory, when we consider prosecutions of individuals for initiating unjust or aggressive war things get more complicated. When the principle of just cause is used to determine whether individuals should be prosecuted for State aggression, we should be more lenient than if we are considering whether the State itself should be subject to sanctions. The reason for this is well stated in the Ministries Case at Nuremberg.

> Obviously, no man may be condemned for fighting in what he believes is the defense of his native land, even though his belief be mistaken. Nor can he be expected to undertake an independent investigation to determine whether or not the cause for which he fights is the result of an aggressive act of his own government. One can be guilty only where knowledge of aggression in fact exists, and it is not sufficient that he have suspicions that the war is aggressive.[12]

The American Military Tribunal sitting at Nuremberg held that we should not expect individual defendants to do a full-scale investigation to determine whether their States are engaging in aggressive or defensive war. I would follow this sage advice and change the way we think of just cause as a basis for determining whether to prosecute individuals for waging aggressive war.

Let me respond to a possible objection to the strategy proposed above. One could argue that we should leave the just cause criterion alone and simply tinker with the idea of State aggression, or with the *actus reus* and *mens rea* elements. For instance, we could say that State aggression, as an element in the crime of aggression, is not as closely based on just cause as

---

[12] "The Ministries Case Judgment," *Trials of War Criminals before Nuremberg Military Tribunals under Control Council Law No. 10*, vol. 14, p. 337.

it was traditionally thought in that the State aggression element requires more than merely establishing lack of just cause. I am not opposed to this strategy, since it has the same effect as that which I advocate, namely, making the element of State aggression in prosecutions in the domain of international criminal law harder to prove than State aggression in the mere regulation of States in the domain of international relations. I think there are some practical reasons to prefer my original strategy but I have no in principle reasons to offer against this other proposal.

We also could merely insist that just cause remain the same for individuals and States but that we tinker with the other two elements in the individual crime of aggression: the *actus reus* or *mens rea* elements. We could say, for instance, that mere knowledge of State aggression is not enough, and there must be an intent to advance that State aggression, as indeed I will suggest in later chapters. But the question is this: why think that such a move reduces the charge of unfairness to the defendants when the trial is already under way for an act of State aggression that was such a close call that the defendant was thoroughly unsure that he or she was indeed participating in an unjust war?

When there are close calls, and when the defendant's personal liberty, not merely sanctions against the State, is on the line, then I believe we should give the defendant the benefit of the doubt. Since the State aggression element is the first hurdle that must be crossed by prosecutors, I would argue that it is important that this hurdle not be set so low that defendants are put in jeopardy for anything but very firmly established causes, namely, those that are clearly unjust. Merely adjusting the *mens rea* or *actus reus* elements, which would presumably be established later in an international criminal trial, would not be fully fair.

The reason for this, drawn in terms of the rights of defendants, is also a kind of proportionality consideration. When the rights of individual defendants, especially important rights to liberty, are at stake, rather than merely the less important considerations of possible sanctions against a State, then we need to adjust our understanding of just cause and State aggression accordingly. It is not common to spill much ink on the rights of defendants in international criminal law given the enormity of the harms, almost always correctly called atrocities, that are committed in these cases.[13] Yet it is my view that the rights of defendants are themselves

---

[13] Exceptions to this rule include Salvatore Zappala, *Human Rights in International Criminal Proceedings*, New York: Oxford University Press, 2003; and Michael Bohlander, Roman Boed, and Richard J. Wilson, *Defense in International Criminal Proceedings: Cases, Materials, and Commentary*, Ardsley, NY: Transnational Publishers, 2006.

human rights issues that must be taken into account if international criminal law's legitimacy is to be successfully defended. If we fail to take the rights of defendants seriously we will undermine the very fragile idea of the international rule of law and we might undermine the very legitimacy of international law itself.

In a later chapter, Chapter 10, I will develop the ideas discussed so far into a proposal about how in general to define State aggression. I will defend the idea that a State is engaged in illegal aggression when that State has been the first to use violent force in a confrontation against another State, not provoked, and not in self-defense or defense of other States, or subgroups of a State, and has not been authorized by the UN to use violent force against another State. This definition of State aggression is what needs to be established in the prima facie case for the first element of the crime of aggression. I now merely wish to thwart a possible misimpression of my proposal about the connection between just cause and the crime of aggression.

There may be a just cause to engage in some wars that turn out to be aggressive on my account. This is because of how first strike and provocation are understood. This is relatively clear, as we saw in the previous chapter, when we considered difficult cases of contemporary warfare such as the use of long-range missiles. States trying to defend against the possible use of long-range missiles may not be able to wait for an imminent threat and hence may act aggressively but may nonetheless act on a just cause for war in a broadened construal of just cause. We might even wonder whether there is a tight connection between what counts as aggressive war and what counts as just cause for initiating war.

Humanitarian wars fall into the class of those wars that in some cases could be aggressive on my account, but for which in some other cases it might be appropriate to say that there is a just cause sufficient for not allowing prosecutions to go forward. At least in part this could be because of the ambiguity or unclarity in the idea of defense of others. Defense of others could include not merely States that have been invaded, but subgroups within a State that are being persecuted. And there is evidence that the United Nations has sometimes discussed things in just this way. Indeed, the UN's at least tacit acceptance of NATO's war waged against Serbia to stop it from persecuting its Kosovar Albanian minority population is a case in point. My view is that we should not expect even most military and political leaders to be able to determine such close calls and that instead we should raise the bar of what counts as just cause sufficient to block the claim that the State aggression element of the crime of aggression has been met. I recognize that this must be done cautiously.

My proposal is that "just cause" be easier to prove, and aggression be correspondingly harder to prove, in international criminal proceedings than in discussion of possible sanctions against States for illegal use of force. In particular, in criminal proceedings I would widen the understanding of just cause to include any basis for going to war covered by most instances of defense of self or others, whereas I would restrict the idea in its use outside of international criminal law only to individual or collective self-defense, not to consideration of defense of others.

As I explained earlier, there are very serious problems of knowledge concerning whether it is true that a State is in need of military help when the State in question is not one's own, but a State in another part of the world. By widening the idea of just cause for prosecutions and narrowing it for State sanctions, we can better deal with the hard cases where provocation occurs or where the confrontation of terrorist groups or other groups causing a humanitarian crisis calls for intervention in the form of war. The cases we dealt with above can be handled in different ways given the context of the investigation. In the next section I will provide additional reasons in support of such a bifurcated understanding of the "just cause" element in the normative principles of *jus ad bellum*.

V. The Bifurcated Normative Principles of *Jus ad Bellum*

In this section I wish to defend the view that just cause and other *jus ad bellum* normative principles should have a different status depending on whether they are being used to determine if a State should be criticized, and sanctioned, for aggressive war, or whether these principles are used to determine if an individual should be prosecuted, and punished, for participating in aggressive war. The main reason for a bifurcated just cause test is that today the just cause test can be used for such different goals.

Throughout most of modern history, just cause has only been used to determine whether a State has engaged in immoral or illegal use of force in armed conflicts. When international law was solely focused on States, the principle of just cause was a major factor in aiding States to determine whether they should or should not use force against other States. One could say that the just cause principle was the main element in the regulation of State conduct, making sure that States by and large did not transgress against one another's sovereignty. Just cause played a role in a regulatory regime that aimed at minimizing interferences with a State's sovereign prerogatives. The main idea was to minimize wars and all of their attendant horrors.

In the latter half of the 20th century, the focus shifts to individual criminal liability for aggressive war, and the just cause principle comes to play a different role than it had traditionally played. Here the main focus is not on the regulation of States but on the assignment of individual responsibility. Part of this shift is unrelated to the regulation of States insofar as responsibility and punishment are understood retributively. Part of the shift is still related to State regulation, insofar as deterrence is also a goal of responsibility and punishment. But now the deterrence is at least once removed from state regulation, since it has to do with the regulation of individuals who are leaders of States rather than the regulation of States themselves.

A critic of my view could argue that the deterrence objective of criminal trials is still quite close to the earlier objective of State regulation, since both are premised on the avoidance in most cases of the horrors of war. To a certain extent I would agree with this point. Criminal trials at the international level are indeed primarily aimed at getting those who control States to change their behavior and to try harder to avoid war. But the consequence of such trials is that individuals are put in prison, not merely that States are encouraged to act more peacefully. And this added consequence of international criminal trials puts an added burden on the just cause principle in my view. To be fair to the person in the dock, we should make it easier to prove that one had a just cause for war in determining whether these individual State leaders committed the crime of aggression.

My view is that when the just cause principle is asked to do different jobs it is not inappropriate to have somewhat different threshold levels for when the principle reveals aggressive behavior. I worry, as do my critics, that some loss of clarity will result from such a bifurcation. The main response to such worries is simply to present the two tests in as clear a manner as possible and indicate also very clearly when one test is to be used and when the other is to be used. And at least this latter task should be relatively easy since we can simply stipulate that the one test is a test for criminal trials and the other test is to be used in all other settings. We would hence give a specialized, or technical, meaning to aggression and just cause in the criminal trial setting and a different meaning for the political discussions about the regulation of State behavior in international relations.

A bifurcated understanding of "just cause" seems consistent with the idea, not really anticipated in earlier times, that *jus ad bellum* considerations could be used as a basis for bringing individuals to trial and subjected to significant loss of liberty. In international criminal law very different considerations are on the table than in those of international relations. Think of an analogy. Many people today strongly support sanctions brought against corporations that break the law, but many people have strong reservations about throwing CEOs in jail for such corporate offenses. And here we do not even have the fog of war considerations.

What we do have is collective decision making and collective action rather than the normal criminal case in which a single individual has chosen to break the law. Leaders can accomplish much more than mere followers, but they also have different responsibilities and motivations for their actions. The case of CEOs is almost always even more complicated since if nothing else the CEO is morally required to act on behalf of the shareholders rather than on behalf of himself or herself. Such considerations are often quite similar to what we find with military or political leaders who think of themselves as primarily acting for the interests of the society or community that the State represents.

Even as we might partially reject this analogy because we think that war is much more important than mere corporate wrongdoing, there is a sense in which we might still want to have somewhat different standards when it is criminal liability rather than State sanctions that are on the table. So, my proposal in this section is that just cause to go to war not be treated as a univocal standard. Perhaps for clarity's sake we might want to come up eventually with different names for the two standards. But at the moment it seems to me that there isn't much confusion risked. Not only is just cause not a univocal standard, but as we will see in the next section, it is not the only important standard either in determining whether war is justified or whether war is aggressive. Indeed, it seems to me that proportionality will play as large a role in *jus ad bellum* judgments as will just cause in any event, as we will discuss in Chapter 6.

If we follow this proposal we can provide a partial answer to those who worry that it is unfair to hold individuals, even those in top leadership positions, responsible for starting wars. In narrowing the range of possible trials, we do not hold political and military leaders responsible for all aggressive wars and hence we do not have the counter-intuitive result that the Nuremberg Courts worried about, namely, holding individuals responsible for what they would have trouble figuring out. To hold these leaders liable we insist that the acts of State aggression be relatively uncontroversial. Yet we leave open the possibility of sanctioning States for a broader range of cases on grounds of both retribution and deterrence. In addition, we are able to deal more effectively with the worries that many people have about the fog of war that almost always is attendant on the conduct of war. We want to do all we can to urge States not to resort to war, but we also want to be as fair as we can to individual leaders of States who find themselves asked to account for the practices of their States, even as we also want to deter these leaders as well.

VI. Rethinking the Separation of *Jus ad Bellum* and *Jus in Bello*

Finally, I wish to discuss one of the implications of the view I have outlined above. I hold that the separation between *jus ad bellum* and *jus in bello* should be bridged in that one of the *jus ad bellum* conditions is that it must be likely that war will be fought with just means in order to be justifiable. Today, it is far more likely that theorists will argue that *jus in bello* restraints will depend on whether *jus ad bellum* conditions have been met, so that if the war is initiated as a just war, there will be fewer tactical restraints on how the war should be fought than if the war is unjust. I have argued strongly against such a position.[14] Instead, following Suarez, I wish to support a view, also defended more recently by William V. O'Brien, that "just conduct in war is a *jus ad bellum* requirement."[15]

Why should we think that a war that cannot or is unlikely to be waged with just tactics should ever be considered a just war from the outset? If it turned out that no wars could be waged with just tactics, because for instance tactics could not guarantee that innocent civilians would not be targeted to be killed in war, it hardly makes sense to say that some of these wars were nonetheless justified at the outset and others were not. What is supposed to turn on this determination about how to regard wars at the outset needs to be couched in such a way so that it would not be misleading to States and their leaders as they tried to determine whether it is justifiable to start a war. We must be careful not to make it seem that it is appropriate to plan to go to war merely on the basis of what other States are planning.

My proposal is that we focus as much on the likely consequences of war as on the impetus for war in thinking about just cause. To some

---

[14] Larry May, *War Crimes and Just War*, New York: Cambridge University Press, 2007.

[15] William V. O'Brien, *The Conduct of Just and Limited War*, New York: Praeger, 1981, p. 35, quoted in Paul Christopher, *The Ethics of War and Peace*, 3rd ed., Upper Saddle River, NJ: Prentice-Hall, 2004, p. 101.

people, this proposal no doubt sounds counter-intuitive. After all, the very term, "just *cause*," implies that we are looking only at the reasons that *caused* war not what *is caused* by that war. But of course there is a second term in this pair, namely, "*just* cause." It is true that normally the justice considerations are all applied to the reasons to go to war, but as I have indicated, some, including Suarez and O'Brien, have seen "just" as implying that we need to think about the kind of war to be waged and ask whether it is indeed likely to be waged as a just war. Terminology aside, I do not think it is counter-intuitive to bring some considerations of how the war is likely to be waged into the discussion of whether the war is justified in being waged at all. Think of a war that could be successfully waged only by annihilating the enemy State's cities, perhaps by the use of nuclear weapons. It is questionable that such a war is just given the horrific consequences of waging that war.

One of the sources of controversy actually concerns other traditional elements in the Just War theory. In Medieval Just War theory, two important considerations were that for a war to be justified there had to be some reasonable likelihood that its objectives could indeed be met, and that its objectives were sufficiently weighty to offset the likely costs of war. These elements proved to be controversial, at least in part because they looked like simple pragmatic as opposed to moral considerations.[16] In the next chapter, I will take up the issue of proportionality in much greater detail. Here I am merely indicating that the question of whether just cause concerns forward-looking considerations could be addressed by merely switching to a consideration of one of the other elements in the Just War theory. But then we will be thrown back on our current topic when the question becomes what is the relationship between the "just cause" element and these other elements in that Just War theory?

We should ask whether "just cause" itself needs to be reconceptualized so as to take into account, or to be linked with, at least some forward-looking considerations, and hence that a reconceptualized "just cause" could open the door for breaking the barrier between *jus ad bellum* and *jus in bello*. One of the main reasons for this is that some have argued that once a war can be justified by "just cause" considerations, then it matters less what moral considerations there might otherwise be concerning tactics and how the war is waged. Indeed, some politicians have recently suggested that if there is just cause to go to war – say, because an enemy

---

[16] See Douglas Lackey's interesting discussion of this issue in his book, *The Ethics of War and Peace*, Upper Saddle River, NJ: Prentice-Hall, 1989, pp. 39–43.

is unjustly attacking – it would be odd indeed to restrict the tactics that could be employed in self-defense.

Yet when the only tactics that will be successful in self-defense cause the annihilation of many combatants and noncombatants alike, it seems to me that likelihood of success and the moral weightiness of success are indeed important. Let's say that an unoccupied section of one's State, perhaps a very small island, has been invaded. To stop and reverse the invading troops, given their vastly superior traditional armed forces, nuclear weapons will have to be used. Surely it makes sense to wonder whether a nuclear war initiated to retain a small, unoccupied island within one's territory is worth the war. And raising this question is indeed, in my view, to raise the question of whether some forward-looking considerations should be written into the just cause principle in *jus ad bellum* considerations.

So, my proposal is to follow Suarez in making the likelihood of waging war justly one of the *jus ad bellum* conditions. What does such a proposal do to the status of "just cause" in the overall scheme of *jus ad bellum* normative principles? One thing that happens is that "just cause" then comes to have a less central role in *jus ad bellum* than it is often thought to have. Indeed, it might make sense to think of the "*in bello*" principle of the likelihood of waging war justly as nearly as important as the just cause principle. We might also think of the "*in bello*" principle of likelihood of waging war justly also to be a principle that identifies which preliminary strategies of war are acceptable in a just war. Just cause has even a less central role than before because many acceptable aims of war can be overridden by concerns about whether the war can be conducted justly.

Like proportionality, as we will next see, the "*in bello*" principle I advocate as an *ad bellum* principle will put severe restraints on just war since it will restrain traditional just cause considerations in many cases. Proportionality, like the concern about whether unacceptable tactics are likely to be used, places restraints on just cause considerations by asking whether the acceptable aims of the war are indeed weighty enough to make the war just overall, and here consideration of human rights protection enters back into our analysis. Contrary to the Just War tradition, then, just cause is important but not the cornerstone of the *jus ad bellum* normative principles. Indeed, it isn't clear to me that there is such a cornerstone principle rather than a collection of principles all operating at about the same level that together form a coherent set of principles for determining when a State's recourse to war is justified.

In this section, I have tried to indicate why it might make sense to knock down the barrier that has been constructed between *jus ad bellum* and *jus in bello*. I want just to note though that I only favor this as going in one direction. I favor making *jus ad bellum* assessments about when it is justifiable to initiate war depend at least on certain *jus in bello* assessments, such as whether that war is likely to be waged by justifiable tactics. But I do not favor the current movement to make *jus in bello* assessments of whether it is justifiable to use certain tactics depend on *jus ad bellum* assessments such as whether it was initially justified to initiate the war. In my view, that latter barrier should remain in place, as it has for several thousand years.

In this chapter I have tried to indicate just how problematic just cause can be and why there may be good reasons to restrict what counts as just cause for determining when to criticize or sanction a State for acts of aggression. But I have also given reasons for why we might want to have a broader sense of what counts as just cause in determining whether the State aggression element of the crime of aggression has been satisfied. When the sanctions are punishments of individual persons, I have argued that the restricted construal of just cause is not appropriate. In any event, we should see just cause as seriously limited by proportionality considerations, and we should break down part of the barrier that has traditionally separated *jus ad bellum* from *jus in bello*. I will next examine the principle of proportionality, the closest we have, in my view, to a cornerstone of *jus ad bellum* considerations applied to international criminal law.

6

The Principle of Proportionality

In this chapter I will reassess the *ad bellum* principle of proportionality, especially in light of the reconceptualized Just War theory I have defended in previous chapters, as well as by reference to contemporary international law. After setting out the *ad bellum* principle of proportionality, I will return to the question of whether the doctrine of self-defense can be used to justify a preventive or preemptive war. Within the Just War tradition, there are actually two principles of proportionality that are not necessarily related to each other. There is both a *jus ad bellum* and a *jus in bello* principle of proportionality. The *jus ad bellum* principle of proportionality, the focus of this chapter, primarily concerns limitations on when initiating or waging wars might be unjustified because the gains aimed at in the war do not outweigh the likely losses in that war. The *jus in bello* principle of proportionality, the subject of other writings of mine,[1] concerns tactical considerations during war, primarily whether a given tactic otherwise thought to be justified is rendered unjustified because it causes unnecessary or superfluous suffering. Both proportionality principles concern weighing, and both principles can render otherwise justified acts unjustified during wartime. But they are thought to be strictly unrelated to each other in that, at least according to traditional Just War theory as well as contemporary international law, no matter how disproportionate the tactics, the proportionality of initiating or waging war is not affected. At the end of this chapter I explain why I find this result unacceptable and once again suggest that *jus ad bellum* principles should be affected by some *jus in bello* considerations.

[1] See chapter 10 of my book, *War Crimes and Just War*, New York: Cambridge University Press, 2007.

The *jus ad bellum* proportionality condition takes on an added and perhaps central role in the idea of aggression. *Jus ad bellum* proportionality is the condition that one could appeal to in order to explain why waging war to regain uninhabited islands is not a just cause for war since the civilian lives risked by the war are not offset by the regaining of the islands to a State's territory. As I began to explain in the previous chapter, just cause is thus not something we can fully understand without considering proportionality. The killing that inevitably follows from the initiating of war must be offset by the greater prevention of killing. And this point roughly maps onto the distinction between aggressive and defensive war, or at least what is worth preserving in that distinction. As I will argue in more detail in later chapters, defensive war is waged to prevent loss of rights of members of a State, whereas aggressive war undermines the State's ability to protect those members' rights.

Proportionality in *jus ad bellum* plays a similar role to that played by proportionality in *jus in bello* considerations. Proportionality is not itself the key normative consideration but it is very closely allied with that key consideration – namely, humaneness in the case of *jus in bello* and human rights protection in the case of *jus ad bellum*. Proportionality, at least concerning how to treat civilian lives, is deeply rooted in a concern for the protection of basic human rights. It is sometimes thought that necessity can justify a State in using nearly any means it can to save the lives of even a few of its soldiers. Proportionality is a severe limitation on this understanding of necessity and for this reason forces us to think about the value of the lives that are lost in wars. There is a sense in which a strict concern for proportionality would rule out most wars, but there would still be some just wars, namely, those fought to save a greater number of lives than those that were risked by engaging in war.

In *jus in bello* normative principles, the principle of discrimination is indeed the chief principle that concerns the lives of civilians. In another work, *War Crimes and Just War*, I set out a revised understanding of the principle of discrimination, indicating how it is related to the principle of proportionality.[2] Both of these principles are ultimately grounded in what I called the principle of humane treatment. Humane treatment goes beyond just a concern for human rights. Both *in bello* and *ad bellum* proportionality considerations are firmly grounded in considerations of human rights, even though they are not deontological considerations. As will become clear later, I argue that *in bello* considerations, primarily

---

[2] Larry May, *War Crimes and Just War*, New York; Cambridge University Press, 2007, ch. 8.

proportionality but also the principle of discrimination, are important in *ad bellum* determinations.

Proportionality is a largely consequentialist concern added into largely non-consequentialist *jus ad bellum* principles, such as the principle of just cause or the priority principle. In traditional Just War theory, even if there seems to be a just cause to go to war, say, for reasons of self-defense, a State cannot seek to annihilate another State in defending itself when that defense could be effectuated with significantly less loss of life. In this sense the *ad bellum* principle of proportionality puts limits, which can be quite significant, on the other *ad bellum* principles. In this chapter I will explore the normative justification for having such a principle and also the consequences for certain controversial issues concerning aggressive war that result from the acceptance of such a principle today.

In the first section of this chapter, I will set out some of the main ideas about the *jus ad bellum* proportionality principle from the Just War tradition. In the second section, I will juxtapose the Just War tradition's understanding of proportionality with that in contemporary international law. In the third section, I will use the example of a self-defensive war to illustrate the differences and similarities between the traditional moral and legal approaches to proportionality, and I will explain why in the end I find neither to be fully satisfactory. In the fourth section, I contrast the *jus ad bellum* and *jus in bello* principles of proportionality and argue that they should not be kept completely separate from one another. And in the final section, I attempt to connect the three *ad bellum* normative principles I have discussed: priority, just cause, and proportionality in a way that makes for a coherent set. Throughout this chapter, I will endeavor to set out a justifiable principle of proportionality that is applicable to modern wars.

I. Proportionality in Traditional Just War Theory

Hugo Grotius, writing in 1625, has probably the most developed account of proportionality in the Just War tradition. I begin with an examination of Grotius's view as expressed in Book II, Chapter XXIV of *De Jure Belli ac Pacis*. The chapter's title already conveys the sentiment behind the principle of proportionality: "Warnings not to Undertake War Rashly, Even for Just Causes."[3] Grotius argues in this chapter that "war is not to

---

[3] Hugo Grotius, *De Jure Belli ac Pacis* (On the Law of War and Peace) (1625), translated by Francis W. Kelsey, Oxford: Clarendon Press, 1925, p. 567.

be undertaken for every just cause," for "it frequently happens that it is more upright and just to abandon one's right" in light of "other virtues." We need to ascertain not only "whether an injury has been done" as a just cause for war, but also "how great is the estimate of the damage done."[4]

Grotius regards the deliberative process of deciding whether to wage war as a process inevitably involving a weighing and comparing of ends. Grotius then proposes three rules for deciding whether one should wage war in light of what we now call proportionality.

1. If "the matter under consideration seems to have an equal effectiveness for good and for evil, it is to be chosen only if the good has somewhat more of good than the evil has of evil."
2. "If the good and evil . . . seem to be equal, it is only to be chosen if its effectiveness for good be greater than for evil."
3. "If the good and evil seem to be unequal . . . then the thing is to be chosen only if its effectiveness for good is greater when compared with its effectiveness for evil than the evil itself compared with the good."

This comparison and weighing is understood to require us to think about the context of the war and ask whether the risks involved in war will be outweighed by the goals.[5]

Grotius discusses several cases of "needless destruction" of human life as is found when a war leads to the "slaughter of a people."[6] And he also talks of war undertaken for "trivial reasons, or to exact unnecessary penalties," arguing that when war is undertaken for these reasons it is "a crime if not against the foe, yet against his own people by involving them in so serious an evil on such grounds." War undertaken for a good, which is outweighed by the known horrors of war is for Grotius a crime, indeed, the kind of crime we have been examining in this book. And Grotius makes the point quite clear when he employs yet another sectional title: "Again war is not to be undertaken save for a most weighty cause at a most opportune time."[7]

Grotius links proportionality with necessity in this chapter, quoting Maximus: "War seems not to be undertaken by the just except of necessity." The "slaughter of people and the wasting of cities" can only be

---

4 Ibid.
5 Ibid., p. 572.
6 Ibid., p. 574.
7 Ibid., p. 575.

justified if it is necessary to achieve an overwhelming good.[8] For Grotius, even if the war is not strictly speaking unjust, because there is a just cause underlying it, the war should not be engaged in if it is not done for an overriding good and there is no other way to achieve that good. This is the central idea of the Just War tradition concerning proportionality. Indeed, Grotius rightly traces this idea back to Cicero and Augustine, the main intellectual forefathers of the Just War tradition. And Augustine is one of the first to link the restraint of proportionality to the general "feeling for humanity"[9] that is also crucial to the Just War tradition's attempt to restrain war even when war seems to be just.

Elsewhere I have argued that *jus in bello* proportionality can be seen as closely allied with a concern for humanity, requiring that we not act inhumanely.[10] Similar considerations are also true of *jus ad bellum* proportionality. If a self-defensive war goes beyond what is proportionate and not only are the invading soldiers repelled but they are tortured and slaughtered, something inhumane has occurred insofar as these enemy soldiers are not treated as fellow humans but instead treated as if their suffering didn't matter. Grotius quotes Seneca to this effect: "it is not for a man to put his fellow man to a wasteful use."[11] For Grotius, humanity requires that wars generally be avoided, and if the wars cannot be avoided then human suffering during war must be minimized. Out of such a concern arose the idea of proportionality, that is, that no more suffering should be produced during war than that which is necessary to alleviate greater suffering.

Douglas Lackey, a contemporary exponent of Just War theory, clearly articulates the *ad bellum* proportionality principle and also states its chief conceptual problem:

> The rule of proportionality states that a war cannot be just unless the evil that can reasonably be expected to ensue from the war is less than the evil that can reasonably be expected to ensue if the war is not fought. The rule of proportionality is easy to state but hard to interpret, since there are no guidelines as to what counts as an "evil" when the rule is applied. Suppose we interpret an "evil" as a loss of value, that is, as a death, injury, physical and psychological suffering, misery, and so forth. On this view of evil the rule of proportionality implies that a war is just only if there will be more

---

[8] Ibid., p. 577.

[9] Ibid., p. 576, quoting Augustine from Book XIX, ch. vii, of *The City of God*.

[10] See May, *War Crimes and Just War*, chs. 4 and 10.

[11] Grotius, *De Jure Belli ac Pacis*, p. 577.

death, suffering, and so forth if the war is not fought than if the war is fought. Given the destructiveness of war, the rule of proportionality, on this interpretation, would declare that almost all wars, even wars with just causes, have been unjust wars.[12]

Lackey urges that the principle of proportionality be amended for this reason, but before considering his argument I wish to note that the above exposition of Grotius, in combination with the discussion in Chapter 2, makes it clear that Grotius would not be unhappy with the result that Lackey laments. Indeed, this construal of the principle of proportionality merely provides one more route to the contingent pacifism I discussed earlier.

We should also note that on Lackey's account, the *ad bellum* and *in bello* principles of proportionality in a sense merge. In assessing "the evil that might reasonably be expected to ensue from war" it will be very hard to make this calculation without considering what are the likely tactics that will be used during that war. Traditionally, the evils at stake in the *ad bellum* principle of proportionality are those of the ends to be achieved by the war. But ends do not come in isolation from certain tactical considerations, since some ends may not be likely at all unless certain tactics are used during the war. In this sense, even in traditional Just War theory, the *ad bellum* and *in bello* principles of proportionality are not utterly isolated from each other.

Lackey points out that if "evil" is defined in terms of loss of rights, then proportionality tells us nothing beyond that the war has a just cause since just cause is also defined in terms of the offsetting of violation of rights. So, Lackey argues, we should think of "evil" as having to do with destruction of value, but to make sure that we do not end up with what he calls "antiwar pacifism" he proposes that the *ad bellum* proportionality principle be amended to say that a war that has a just cause passes the proportionality test "unless it produces a *great deal* more harm than good."[13] Even with this amendment, Lackey admits that the proportionality principle "will declare that many wars fought for just causes have been unjust wars since many wars for just causes have in fact produced a great deal more harm than good." But some wars will meet the test on this "liberalized rule of proportionality."[14]

[12] Douglas P. Lackey, *The Ethics of War and Peace*, Upper Saddle River, NJ: Prentice Hall, 1989, p. 40.
[13] Ibid., pp. 40–41, italics in original.
[14] Ibid., p. 41.

I wish to suggest that the liberalized view of the proportionality principle not be accepted. One of the main problems with Lackey's proposal is that it makes the proportionality principle even more difficult to apply than it was under the traditional interpretation. Lackey admits as much when he says:

> No formula can be generated for weighing the justice of the cause against the harm that might be done in pursuing it; the question can be resolved only on a case-by-case basis, by persons with a grasp of the relevant facts and a sufficient strength of character to view the problem from an impersonal rather than a patriotic point of view.[15]

Lackey then runs through a number of cases where he provides a short description of highly complex historical cases and then gives us a judgment of whether the proportionality principle was satisfied. And while I generally appreciate analyses that are case sensitive, Lackey illustrates how difficult his liberalized principle of proportionality is to apply by making it seem as if the main consideration is merely an intuitive one, namely, whether the particular war seems unjustified.

Unless we can come up with an understanding of "a great deal more" that is still able to be quantified, Lackey's proposed amendment to the traditional Just War theory's construal of proportionality seems hopeless. The one part of Lackey's analysis that seems right to me flies in the face of some other contemporary views, such as that of Thomas Hurka to be explored later in this chapter. In discussing extreme emergency cases, when an innocent State cannot save itself without causing the loss of innocent lives, Lackey affirms that there are restraints on what can be justly done even in cases of self-defense.

> How many innocent people am I entitled to kill if their deaths are necessary for my own survival? Even for non-pacifists, the answer is "not many." It follows at the level of nations, that the right of a state to cause destruction in order to assure its own survival is not unlimited.[16]

This part of Lackey's view seems to me to be correct, but it is also more consistent with the traditional than with the liberalized view of the proportionality principle. The idea that the harm to be done by waging aggressive war must be a "great deal" more than the good to be done seems to have reduced to "not much more," which is quite close to "not more than" the good to be done, the position I advocated earlier. I will

---

[15] Ibid.
[16] Ibid., p. 43.

return to this issue in later sections of this chapter. Before engaging in that analysis, I want first to discuss the status of the a*d bellum* principle of proportionality in contemporary international law.

II. Necessity and Proportionality in International Law

Many of the same considerations that were in play in traditional Just War thinking about proportionality exist also in contemporary international legal thinking. Here is a recent attempt to articulate the consensus in international law about proportionality.

> The rationale behind proportionality in *jus ad bellum* . . . relate[s] to the minimization of the disruption of international peace and security. Proportionality in self-defense, for example, is designed to ensure that States are allowed the minimum that is required to defend themselves against an aggressor. To go any further and allow excessive destruction of another State is seen as destabilizing a system that is founded on the peaceful settlement of disputes and a collective security system. Thus, the conduct of self-defense in a disproportionate manner is likely to embitter relations between adversaries and other respective protagonists, with the inevitable consequences for the harmony of the international community.[17]

As it is normally explained, one of the main differences between Just War theory and international law is that the former is largely grounded in moral considerations whereas the latter is largely grounded in prudential considerations. Yet it seems to me that this supposed difference between the two ways to think about the *jus ad bellum* proportionality principle can be highly misleading as this quotation from Judith Gardam makes clear.

International law is grounded in considerations of peace and security, but it is a mistake to think of those considerations as merely prudential. One indication of the moral underpinnings of international law can be found in the debate about whether *ad bellum* proportionality is itself grounded in humanitarian and human rights considerations. As one might expect, advocates of a humane war such as the International Committee of the Red Cross (ICRC) take the view that there is a solid moral foundation to international law, whereas realists strive to deny this. Gardam, an Australian expert in international law, claims that there is "growing recognition of the potential of proportionality in *jus ad bellum* to incorporate overtly humanitarian considerations."[18] And while she

---

[17] Judith Gardam, *Necessity, Proportionality and the Use of Force by States*, New York: Cambridge University Press, 2004, p. 16.
[18] Ibid., p. 17.

admits that the majority of scholars remain in a kind of realist camp, she says that the humanitarian view "is gaining ground."[19] At least in part this is because human rights considerations are invading nearly all aspects of *jus ad bellum* principles. I have explored this view in a previous work and also raised some concerns about the intermingling of human rights theory and considerations of the rules of war.[20]

Both *jus ad bellum* and *jus in bello* proportionality principles, in contemporary international law and Just War theory, have as one of their main aims "to minimize the torment caused by war – to ensure that the suffering and loss of life of both combatant and civilian is not disproportionate to the legitimate ends."[21] This long-standing concern is surely both moral and prudential. It is moral in that minimizing suffering should be a goal of all humans, and it is prudential in that the world is generally a safer place when this idea is given pride of place. Indeed, the idea that wars can be fought and yet respect for human rights can be maintained is one of the main ideas in almost any proposal concerning justifiability of war, as we saw in the first chapter.

The difference between *jus ad bellum* and *jus in bello* proportionality principles in international law is that the latter is focused on individuals, especially civilians, whereas the former is focused on "the civilian population as a whole, the level of destruction of the enemy forces and damage to enemy territory, infrastructure and the environment generally."[22] This again tracks the Just War theory where collective destruction is the key to *jus ad bellum* and individual suffering the key to *jus in bello* proportionality. Indeed, there is so much overlap between Just War theory and contemporary international law that the very terms used, as we have seen, are virtually the same. And while *jus ad bellum* principles of international law are relatively recent, the debates mirror the much earlier debates, those that have been ongoing for several thousand years, about both *jus ad bellum* and *jus in bello* principles in the Just War tradition.[23] At least in part this is because of the importance of custom and long-standing practice to contemporary international law.[24]

---

[19] Ibid., p. 18.

[20] See Larry May, *War Crimes and Just War*, New York: Cambridge University Press, 2007, ch. 4.

[21] Gardam, *Necessity, Proportionality and the Use of Force by States*, p. 15.

[22] Ibid., p. 19.

[23] See Stephen C. Neff, *War and the Law of Nations*, New York: Cambridge University Press, 2005.

[24] See *The Handbook of Humanitarian Law in Armed Conflict*, edited by Dieter Fleck, Oxford: Oxford University Press, 1995, ch. 1.

As in Just War theory, in international law the principle of proportionality is intertwined with the principle of necessity. Some, such as Judith
Gardam, say that "what is now known as necessity in the modern law of
self-defense" is that the war must be "a last resort after all peaceful means
have failed."[25] As we saw in Chapter 4, last resort is not quite the same factor as necessity in traditional Just War theory. But clearly they are related,
especially in cases of self-defense. If a State cannot prevent itself from
being invaded except by waging war, such wars are seen as necessary and
at least part of the reason is that in this case war is a last resort.

Self-defensive wars are treated differently from other types of war in
international law in that proportionality is not supposed to play a major
role. If it is indeed necessary for a State to engage in war to prevent an
imminent attack, there is little sense that that State must also do a proportionality assessment.[26] Article 51 of the UN Charter, and the jurisprudence that has grown up around it, gives to both individual State self-
defense and collective self-defense a different status from other grounds
for war. The consensus is that States would still have to wait to see whether
the Security Council is going to act first, even in these cases of self-defense.
But at least initially a State can act in self-defense as long as the necessity
condition is met, even if there is a question of whether proportionality is
met. Of course, after the initial invasion has been stymied, proportionality considerations are again on the table. But this disconnection between
necessity and proportionality in international law does not really have a
parallel in traditional Just War theory.

In very recent times, several States have tried to extend the idea of the
exclusivity of necessity into areas other than purely self-defensive wars, or
at least to widen considerably the idea of a self-defensive war. And there
has been a parallel movement among contemporary Just War theorists
and other moral philosophers to expand the idea that some wars do not
need proportionality considerations, or that proportionality considerations are only weakly constraining in *jus ad bellum* determinations. In the
next section I will examine both of these recent movements, fueled by a
reassessment of the importance of self-defense.

III. Self-Defense and Proportionate Response

If this book were about *jus ad bellum* principles concerning State responsibility for waging aggressive wars, self-defense would play a very large, if not
the largest, role. But when we are considering individual criminal liability

[25] Gardam, p. 5.
[26] Ibid., p. 9.

for State aggression, self-defense is only one of many important issues. I will spend this section and the next taking up issues of self-defense in the context of a full understanding of the role of proportionality. I will ask whether the type of war planned, and even whether the planning of a war, should matter in the context of the self-defense claims of the State that the defendant belonged to. This question is especially significant in light of our earlier discussion of how State aggression should be viewed differently in punishing an individual as opposed to sanctioning a State for waging aggressive war.

As I suggested earlier, we will want to give more latitude to the possible defenses for waging aggressive war if we are in fact dealing with individual criminal trials since the individuals being tried often find it very difficult to tell whether their States are justified in engaging in war as a form of retaliation or defense. Nonetheless, we will have to discuss in some detail how to regard self-defense of States, and even more regarding collective self-defense claims. In this context we can also revisit the discussion in Chapter 4 of how to regard what counts as a first strike and also last resort.

The hard cases of self-defense, especially those concerning preemptive and preventive war, are made somewhat easier when we are considering responsibility of individuals rather than States. This is because we may wish to draw a line in the sand concerning States, only recognizing limited application of self-defense as justification for waging war, and yet be reluctant to do so when it is individual liberty that is being jeopardized in a criminal trial. Individual State leaders who participate in the planning of a preemptive or preventive war, because of concerns of State self-defense, should normally not be prosecuted since these are often close call cases where it will matter a lot what the individual leader knew or could reasonably have come to know about the true basis of the alleged self-defense claims made on behalf of the State.

Proportionate response generally has not played a large role when self-defense is the issue, and I think this should extend to the hard cases as well, with an exception for preventive war that is based on distant future considerations. Consider a war that is launched because a neighbor State increases its military budget or begins to build a facility that several years later could produce nuclear weapons. One can certainly see that such a war could be characterized as a self-defensive war. But whether that war is indeed justified, and not aggressive, will depend on whether the war had a reasonably limited objective or was disproportionate to the threat and its cause.

I do not think that we should be quite as lenient toward defendants when the war they participated in is a war of collective self-defense rather than one of individual State self-defense. Wars waged for collective self-defense are recognized in Article 51 of the United Nations Charter. But as Yoram Dinstein and others have pointed out, the meaning of collective self-defense is not entirely clear. Dinstein identifies four possible meanings of the term self-defense:

1. individual self-defense individually exercised
2. individual self-defense collectively exercised
3. collective self-defense individually exercised
4. collective self-defense collectively exercised[27]

In the second case, there appears to be something collective going on, but it is really only an aggregation of individual acts of self-defense. Surprisingly, Dinstein says that that was largely what happened in World War II. In his third category, one State that has not been attacked goes to the aid of another State that has been attacked; and in the fourth category, "two or more States ... act together in supporting the victim country."[28] Viewed in this way, collective self-defense is a close cousin to humanitarian intervention, the subject of a later chapter.

Individual self-defense can come in at least two varieties, as Dinstein says, and proportionality has a role to play, although a relatively limited role in each case. The reason is that self-defense already carries with it the idea of a kind of necessity when little time and few options are available to the State that is forced to defend itself. Of course, there will be controversial cases, but in true cases of self-defense where there is a necessity to act quickly, proportionality will have a limited, normally minor role. Collective self-defense is harder, because the State acting in self-defense is more distant from the actual causes of the need for self-defense and will hence be more governed by proportionality than in true cases of individual State self-defense. Since the first two categories are not really collective self-defense, I will focus on the third and fourth of Dinstein's categories.

It seems to me that Dinstein is wrong to think that just any State that goes to the aid of another State has engaged in collective self-defense, as in his category three above. If the States in question have no formal connection with each other, this looks exactly like simple humanitarian action on the part of the non-attacked State, not collective self-defense. For there to be true collective self-defense, the collectivity or one of its

---

[27] Yoram Dinstein, *War, Aggression, and Self-Defense*, 3rd ed., Cambridge: Cambridge University Press, 2001, p. 222.
[28] Ibid., p. 224.

members must be attacked. Over the years many treaties were designed to make certain States feel they had an obligation to aid other States that were attacked because those States were part of a collective security organization. NATO is perhaps the best example of this kind of collective security organization. But questions arise about whether NATO can use any means at its disposal to thwart enemy attacks on it as a collectivity or on one of its members.

Proportionality is a key normative restraint on collective self-defensive wars, just as it is on individual State self-defensive wars.[29] This is the holding of the Nicaragua case, and many international law scholars agree that this is the right disposition. Unfortunately, there is not such wide-scale agreement about the individual case as about the collective case, as we have seen throughout this chapter. Dinstein says that proportionality is a very flexible standard that simply calls for "reasonableness in the response to force by counter-force."[30] He implies that proportionality is intrinsically related to the very idea of self-defense. By this he means, I think, that for an act of war to be called an act of self-defense, the war must indeed be necessary for the State to defend itself. And this is merely to say that a war justified in terms of self-defense must be a war that somehow matches the force, which is a threat, by a counter-force, which involves the minimal suffering needed to thwart the threatening force.

In this section we have seen that proportionality still plays a role even in cases of self-defense, and especially in cases of so-called collective self-defense. As we will see, proportionality may not be the supreme *jus ad bellum* principle but it often is the most important one, restraining war often even more than the principle of just cause. Proportionality may sometimes be hard to assess, as is true of all future-oriented consider-ations, but a good enough sense of it can normally be obtained that proportionality will weigh heavily in the determination of whether a war is just. Before rehearsing that argument, I wish to discuss some of the *ad bellum* principles that we have omitted from our discussion so far and indicate how if at all these "minor" principles relate to proportio-nality.

IV. Proportionality and Minor *Jus ad Bellum* Principles

The three normative *jus ad bellum* principles we have discussed in this chapter are not the only principles that have been proposed over the

---

[29] Dinstein, p. 239.
[30] Ibid., p. 184.

centuries, but they are the ones that have had the most influence on contemporary international law, especially international criminal law. In this section I will say a bit about some of the other principles often mentioned and then in the final section I will provide an overarching framework for understanding the connections among the three principles we have focused on as well as some of the others. In providing this framework, I am focusing on prosecutions of individuals for the crime of aggression rather than on the criticism or sanctioning of States for aggression.

As we will see in a later chapter, one of the first *jus ad bellum* principles in the Just War tradition was that of legitimate authority. In most cases of prosecutions for the crime of aggression, the issue of legitimate authority will not arise. In the penultimate chapter, Chapter 14, I will discuss the special case of terrorist aggression. Some think that terrorist aggression is never justified because it does not meet the legitimate authority principle, namely, that the war is initiated by an entity that has the authority to wage war. I do not accept this argument, because it may be that some non-State actors have as much legitimacy as State actors to wage war to protect their populations. When we are considering individuals who may find it very difficult to ascertain whether the possible excusing conditions do in fact obtain, we should refrain from prosecutions altogether. In any event, legitimate authority does not really have application today since the very idea of legitimate authority has been rendered nearly moot by the international requirement that in most cases a war must be authorized by the United Nations Security Council for it to be justifiably waged.

Another traditional *jus ad bellum* normative principle that has some, although limited, applicability to criminal prosecutions for the crime of aggression is the principle of right intention.[31] As sometimes said, it is not enough that wars be waged that have a just cause but the reason to go to war also has to be rightful. Some have seen that this requirement is not itself a separate category of *jus ad bellum* but either merely a refinement of the just cause principle or something that is unnecessary. It is thought to be a mere refinement in that one could say, as I did in the chapter on just cause, that the war must be initiated "for" or "because of" a just cause. Critics of this strategy say that they mean to rule out mixed

[31] This really is best understood as right motive rather than right intention, since it involves reasons rather than aims. See the discussion of this general issue in my paper "Individual Motive, the Crime of Genocide, and the Destruction of a Group 'As Such'" in my draft book manuscript, "Genocide, Social Groups, and Criminal Trials."

motives. But mixed motives in going to war are probably inevitable, as they are in the rest of life. The idea that this principle is not required at all is propounded by those who think that motives and intentions don't matter in justification. But this idea will then resurface when we get to the element of *mens rea* and will there prove hard to ignore.

In prosecutions for the crime of aggression, mental elements will play a large role as we will see throughout the rest of this book. The question, though, is whether the State aggression element should also have a mental element as an integral part of its requirements. It was once thought that the State must have bad intentions for aggression to be established. International law has not followed this medieval model, nor has contemporary Just War theory. And even those who think there should be some kind of mental element at the level of the State argue that just cause can supply it. This is not to deny that just causes could be pursued for mixed motives and that a full consideration of justification of war would require some inquiry into whether a just cause was indeed the main motivation for a particular war being initiated.

Yet another *jus ad bellum* principle is likelihood of success. As with right intention, this principle has pretty much dropped out of the contemporary Just War theory. In international law, the last resort and necessity principles have captured much of what was most important in this principle and together seem to tighten up the requirement. It is not merely that success can be had by waging war, but that waging war is the only way to achieve that aim. It is of course also extremely difficult to assess whether a war can succeed, and it is a bit odd to say that wars, especially self-defensive wars, should not be initiated because a State cannot predict that the war will indeed succeed. Even if a war had a low likelihood of success, if it was needed for self-defense there do not seem to be strong normative grounds for abandoning it.

Proportionality does not play much of a role in relation to these minor *jus ad bellum* principles, although since these principles do not themselves today play much of a role in *jus ad bellum* determinations I suppose this is not a significant result. Proportionality does not play much of a role in relation to the legitimate authority principle, except that it continues to set limits on what even a legitimate State can do to another State. Proportionality is clearly more important than these other principles, especially since the right intention can be subsumed under just cause, and likelihood of success can be subsumed under last resort or under necessity. Yet if one wants to think in a highly systematic way about all factors that influence the justifiability of war, one will want to take into account even these minor principles, all the while recognizing that some are more important than others.

Before attempting to place the three *jus ad bellum* principles I have focused attention on into some kind of order, I wish to consider whether proportionality is itself a *jus ad bellum* consideration or merely a factor in just cause considerations. I wish to suggest again that proportionality plays two roles in *jus ad bellum* considerations. Not all seemingly just causes are significant enough to justify war, even in a prima facie way. Significance is a kind of proportionality consideration, but it operates as a restriction on the normal threshold considerations. There is also an all things considered way that proportionality in itself factors into the justification of war.

A war might meet a threshold determination of significance in that the goals of the war were indeed ones that *could* bring about more rather than less suffering in the world, and yet it might be that all things considered the war should not take place because the type of tactics needed to win such a war *would* likely produce suffering that is disproportionate to the aims of the war. In this way, proportionality considerations play two different, although related, roles in the moral assessment of the initiation or waging of war. I make a radical break with the Just War tradition in arguing, as I did in the previous chapter, that there is a rudimentary proportionality consideration even when assessing just causes. In the current chapter, I have suggested that proportionality by itself can also play a robust role in determining whether wars are justified as well.

Proportionality, as an all things considered *jus ad bellum* principle, will be closely linked to proportionality considered as a *jus in bello* principle. As I will next explain, wars are not justified unless the likely tactics to be used are themselves justified. And the justification of the tactics will have to be drawn in terms of whether those tactics are indeed proportionate to the particular aims of the tactics used in the war. This is also a departure from Just War theory, especially as that doctrine is understood today, although not as at least some of its adherents, such as Francisco Suarez, historically have regarded it.[32] I next take up the question of how to weigh the major *jus ad bellum* normative principles, and how *jus ad bellum* considerations relate to *jus in bello* ones in the all things considered justification of war.

---

[32] See Francisco Suarez, "On War," in *Selections from Three Works* (Disputation XIII, *De Triplici Virtute Theologica: Charitate*) (c. 1610), translated by Gwladys L. Williams, Ammi Brown, and John Waldron, Oxford: Clarendon Press, 1944, p. 800.

V. Connecting Proportionality, Priority, and Just Cause

The three *jus ad bellum* principles considered in detail so far are proportionality, just cause, and priority. I have spent the better part of a chapter on each of these principles. It is now time to try to indicate how the principles are related to each other and whether they form a coherent set of *jus ad bellum* principles. One way to think about the principles is that the priority principle provides one test for just cause and proportionality is a major restriction on just cause. By this I mean that wars are generally to be regarded as aggressive if they violate the priority principle. If a State meets the test of the priority principle, then all other things being equal, the State has a just cause to wage war. Even though there might be a kind of first strike or first wrong, there will be cases when the justness of the cause overrides and makes this kind of violation of the priority principle not an instance of aggressive war. In addition, the proportionality principle is then a restriction on just cause in that even if the cause is just the war may still be aggressive if the type of war waged is not proportionate to the cause.

If we were to accept the above characterization of the relations among these three normative *jus ad bellum* principles, it would appear that there is no priority among them. We could start with any one of the principles and then be drawn into a consideration of the others. Normally people take them in the order that I describe them – priority, just cause, and proportionality. But we could also take proportionality as our first consideration. After we assess the proportionality, we will not have finished since we will then need to know whether the proportionate response was one that was made for a legitimate goal, a just cause. And then we will need to ask who started the war to ascertain whether the other State involved was the aggressor – for it may turn out that a State has just cause, but that the other State was not the aggressor either.

In medieval and early modern theorizing, a hot topic of debate was whether both States waging war could be in the right, or whether neither of the States could be labeled the aggressor. Think of a State that attacks another State and hence seemingly violates the priority principle, making it the aggressor. If that State had a just cause to attack, it would not be the aggressor. And if the State attacked did not do anything to provoke the attack, it may not be the aggressor either. Perhaps it acted in ways that it judged, wrongly, were in its self-interest. Or perhaps it judged that the attacking State was waging war disproportionately, although again this assessment was wrong; that State might, due to its culpable ignorance, also not be an aggressing State. This particular example was discussed by Alberico Gentili at the very end of the 16th century.[33] Whether or not one accepts Gentili's reasoning, this kind of case illustrates how intertwined are the normative principles we have discussed in this section of the book.

The main idea I wish to argue for is that just cause is not the primary normative *jus ad bellum* principle in contemporary international law or in traditional Just War theory. As Jeff McMahan has said, it is only contemporary Just War theorists who have tried to elevate just cause into a position of pride of place, although McMahan thinks that just cause does have priority over proportionality in a certain sense, namely, in that the other conditions "cannot be satisfied even in principle, unless just cause is satisfied."[34] But he recognizes, as I have also been arguing, that there is another sense in which proportionality may have a kind of priority over the just cause principle:

> Because just cause is only a restriction on the type of aim that can justify war, the proportionality requirement may have a larger role than many people suspect. Suppose, for example, that the defense of a State's territorial integrity against even partial annexation by another State is a just cause for war, as many people believe. If just cause is not a matter of scale, then there would be a just cause for war if a neighboring country were about to capture an acre of our territory on its border – an acre that it regards as a holy site, but that we are using only as a garbage dump. In this case, the reason why it would be wrong for us to go to war to retain our possession of that acre is not that our aim would be too trivial to constitute a just cause; it is, rather, that our just cause would be too trivial for war to be proportionate.[35]

McMahan thus supports the view I have been advocating in this section, namely, that there is no overarching principle that has priority over other principles in *jus ad bellum* – although I have argued in the previous chapter that this kind of case may not meet the just cause principle because of lack of significance of the cause, which is itself a matter of a rudimentary proportionality assessment.

McMahan and I agree on something else, although there are many other things for which this cannot be said.[36] McMahan holds that just

[33] Alberico Gentili, *De Jure Belli* (On the Law of War) (1598), translated by John C. Rolfe, Oxford: Clarendon Press, 1933, Book I, ch. 6.

[34] Jeff McMahan, "Just Cause for War," *Ethics & International Affairs*, vol. 19, no. 3, 2005, p. 5.

[35] Ibid, p. 4.

[36] See the discussion of some of this debate in my book *War Crimes and Just War*, especially chapter 2.

causes must provide a justification for killing and maiming, for that is what war involves or risks. In this respect we return to the discussion begun at the beginning of the book, where I suggested that war was horrible and that it was not clear that the people who were typically killed or maimed in war could be justifiably treated in this way. McMahan says that individuals can make themselves liable to be killed or maimed in various ways, such as if they engage in wrongs of various sorts. He and I might part company on what precisely these wrongs are, but we agree that they must be significant or serious enough, in terms of rudimentary proportionality considerations, that is, "sufficiently serious and significant to justify killing" them.[37]

In the previous chapter I began to take McMahan's point further than he is apparently willing to go. I believe that his argument is consistent with the position of contingent pacifism[38] that I set out in Chapter 2. Proportionality considerations are very important and can sometimes place very severe limitations on just cause considerations. And for me anyway this means that the cause must not only be above some minimal threshold of justice, but that it must be above a much higher threshold, namely, that it is sufficient to make wide sections of a population liable to be killed or maimed. And yet hardly ever, if ever, is a cause sufficient to do this. Practically, though, when we are talking about prosecutions for the crime of aggression, even when it turns out that most wars are unjustifiable, we should still give individuals, although not necessarily States, the benefit of the doubt.

Proportionality is a major moral restraint on the justifiability of most wars. I do not wish to claim that proportionality is generally a much greater restraint than is just cause. But I do want to emphasize how important proportionality is and to reemphasize that this is at least in part because for wars to be justified the nearly inevitable killing that occurs in war must be offset by something at least as serious. The discussion earlier on the legitimate concerns about killing the innocent cannot be taken lightly, and proportionality forces us to take those innocent lives quite seriously indeed. In addition, proportionality considerations bridge the divide between *jus ad bellum* and *jus in bello*. And while there are two somewhat distinct proportionality considerations here, they have in common

---

[37] McMahan, "Just Cause for War," p. 11.
[38] And I remind the reader that that was a term I also borrowed from McMahan but with a somewhat different meaning than he was willing to give it.

the idea that even when the cause appears to be just there are severe restrictions on what a State can do to another State. One State cannot seek to annihilate another State, even for major wrongs done, and one State cannot use weapons that cause extreme suffering either. If it is likely that wars will be waged in this way, in my view, such wars cannot justifiably be initiated.

Most important, States normally cannot conduct wars that aim at or have as their intended effects large-scale loss of civilian life. I would go further yet and argue that if it is likely that a war cannot be waged successfully without significant civilian suffering, the war should not be initiated. The *in bello* principles of proportionality and discrimination, as they enter into *ad bellum* determinations, will rule this out. Many wars will simply not meet this requirement, even some wars of self-defense. In this way, proportionality is a major restraint on the use of self-defense as a justification for war as well.[39]

Because of proportionality considerations that span the divide between *jus ad bellum* and *jus in bello,* slightly more weight should often be given to the proportionality than to the just cause principle, and since the priority principle is just one of many tests for just cause, priority is less important than just cause. I realize that this is based on a relatively nonstandard view of things that I hold. As I indicated above, the mixing of *jus ad bellum* and *jus in bello* principles, in the way I have been defending them, is not completely anomalous. Indeed, I would say that any view that was also advocated by Suarez cannot be easily dismissed in any event.

All three *jus ad bellum* principles I have considered in this section form a set of concerns that taken together work to promote human rights. I will return to this topic often in the rest of the book. Here I just want to say that the normative principles we have discussed in this section are aimed at determining when States, which generally speaking are protectors of human rights, have engaged in practices that so threaten human rights that other States might be justified in invading those States. In the next section of the book, I will turn more explicitly to the idea of aggressive wars in international criminal law. And I will spend considerable time discussing several cases from the trials at Nuremberg at the end of the

---

[39] By this I do not mean to suggest that a State is held hostage to what its opponent State chooses to do in terms of tactics. The proportionality and discrimination considerations that are relevant to *ad bellum* assessments concern what harm to civilians is likely to be done by the State that is deciding whether to initiate war. I am grateful to an anonymous referee for raising this potential objection.

Second World War, although I will worry about whether the folk history of these trials has indeed conveyed the right message. Nonetheless, the trials at Nuremberg are the only major trials for the crime of aggression and serve as a kind of "precedent" for contemporary attempts to revive trials for crimes against peace and the crime of aggression.

PART C

THE PRECEDENT OF NUREMBERG

7

Custom and the Nuremberg "Precedent"

> International law is not statutory. It is in part defined by and described in treaties and covenants among the powers of the world. Nevertheless, much of it consists in practices, principles, and standards which have become developed over the years and have found general acceptance among the civilized powers of the world. It has grown and expanded as the concepts of international right and wrong have grown. It has never been suggested that it has been codified, or that its boundaries have been specifically defined, or that specific sanctions have been prescribed for violations of it.
>
> "The Ministries Case Judgment"[1]

There are currently no prosecutions of individuals for having committed the crime of aggression or what is sometimes called the crime against peace. One fairly good reason for this fact is that there is no treaty or international statute that defines this international crime and sets out the elements that a prosecutor would have to prove to convict someone of violating it. There were prosecutions by the International Military Tribunal at Nuremberg, and the subsequent trials at Nuremberg just after World War II, but for various reasons that I will rehearse in this chapter, the Nuremberg prosecutions for crimes against peace have not been seen as establishing a "precedent."[2] I will examine what the basis of such trials

---

[1] *Trials of War Criminals before Nuremberg Military Tribunals under Control Council Law No. 10*, vol. 14, pp. 317–318.

[2] I will place the term Nuremberg "precedent" in scare quotes. This is done for several reasons. First, in contemporary international law the idea that there are precedents is highly contested. Second, technically, the Nuremberg court was a military tribunal operating under the jurisdiction of the Allied Command's control over its occupied lands, not an international tribunal like the ICC. Third, there is a counter-custom that potentially upsets whatever precedent value Nuremberg could have created, as we will see.

was said to be and why there has been such reluctance to use similar rationales today. I will also ask whether it makes sense to hold individuals responsible for aggressive war even if there was a consensus about the normative basis for such trials. Given that aggression is a crime committed by a State, what is the rationale for holding individuals responsible for this crime?

For several thousand years, waging aggressive war against one's neighbors has been thought to be one of the worst of crimes a State can commit. States that engaged in aggression were often punished, chiefly by military or economic means, such as military subjugation or economic boycott. Only in the last century have individuals been prosecuted and punished for having led a State into aggressive war. At the Nuremberg trial, the crime against peace was said to be "the supreme international crime," deserving the most severe punishment for those individuals who perpetrated it. In any attempt to understand how the International Criminal Court might start prosecutions for such crimes, we will need to learn from the example of Nuremberg, but also from several earlier attempts in the Just War tradition to set out norms for holding individuals responsible for State aggression.

The structure of the chapter is relatively straightforward. First, I will look at several ideas from the Just War tradition on whether and why individuals should be held responsible for State aggression. Second, I will look at the Nuremberg "precedent" to see what went right in that trial and why it has not been followed. Third, I will move to the abstract level and ask about what sorts of rules one can expect at the international level that could ground international trials for the crime of aggression. Fourth, I will address the question of what sources could be drawn on, other than an explicit treaty, to authorize such trials. Fifth, I will address a very recent attempt to save customary rules of international criminal law by the distinguished jurist Theodor Meron. Throughout I will be interested in the interplay of international customary norms and explicit rules concerning the crime of aggression, about which I will draw some conclusions in the final section.

I. Just War Theory and Aggression

Grotius, writing in 1625, is one of the first in the modern age to speak of the responsibility of individuals for State aggression. In *De Jure Belli ac Pacis*, Grotius says:

those who order a wicked act, or who grant to it the necessary consent, or who aid it, or who furnish asylum, or those who in any way share in the crime itself . . . all these may be punished, if there is in them evil intent sufficient to deserve punishment.[3]

But like many in the Just War tradition, Grotius believes in State sovereignty and is especially leery of States that "cross their borders with an armed force for the purpose of exacting punishment." Indeed, Grotius urges that "the crimes of individuals, in so far as they properly concern the community to which they belong, should be left to the States themselves and their ruler, to be punished or condoned with discretion."[4] And even when it is the ruler who has done wrong, Grotius equivocates saying only that a people may not "suffer for the crimes of its king or its ruler."

Grotius does not commit himself to punishing subjects for what the rulers have done despite the fact that "the most grievous punishment of kings who have sinned is the punishment inflicted on their people."[5] And Grotius never expressly addresses whether there are other punishments that could legitimately be meted out against rulers for their acts of initiating aggressive war. So, we are left wondering whether Grotius believes that kings and other rulers should be punished for their wrongs even as he admits that they are in some sense responsible and punishable for them.

Grotius also provides a reason why he is not sure that kings and other rulers should be punished for their crimes by other States, or in some other manner, outside of the borders of their own State. He writes that it is unclear exactly when custom becomes law.[6] So, while it may be that there is a long-standing custom that rulers are to be held responsible for such acts as initiating aggressive war, punishment follows from the violation of a specific law. The problem in Grotius's time was that there were no treaties or other specific laws rendering State aggression illegal and criminalizing the acts of those individuals who initiated or perpetrated the war.

It is also true today that the "black letter" international law is inconclusive on this topic, even as there is by now a very long-standing custom against State acts of aggression and against those rulers who lead their States into aggressive war. Indeed, the relationship between custom

---

[3] Hugo Grotius, *De Jure Belli Ac Pacis* (On the Law of War and Peace) (1625), translated by Francis W. Kelsey, Oxford: Clarendon Press, 1925, pp. 522–523.

[4] Ibid., p. 527.

[5] Ibid., p. 544.

[6] Ibid., p. 223.

and international law remains quite controversial. Custom will often be enough if we are talking of moral responsibility, but criminal liability requires some violation of a law, among other things. And while customs often become the basis of law, the transition between custom and law is as difficult to ascertain as is the transition from a primitive legal system to a developed one. I will explore the contemporary debate on this topic in more detail in subsequent sections of this chapter.

Later writers in the Just War tradition also struggled with the issue that I am concerned with here. Pufendorf, echoing sentiments he shared with Hobbes, argues that princes cannot be punished. To be subject to punishment, says Pufendorf, there must be "a court and judge that can render and execute a judgment." Yet the courts that exist within sovereign States "concern only subjects," not rulers. And if any court outside a State should issue punishments of a prince, the prince would cease to be sovereign altogether. Judges must inflict punishment "as a superior," says Pufendorf.[7] Like Grotius, Pufendorf says that the various customs that speak of the responsibility of kings and princes address only the obligations that involve moral punishment or the punishment of God, not that recognized by courts. The difficulty is that only courts can properly administer punishment and there are no international courts.

Vattel, writing in the 18th century, marks a watershed in our historical narrative, for Vattel is forthright in saying that the sovereign "is answerable for all the evils and all the disasters of war."[8] Indeed, Vattel says that the sovereign who wages an unjust war "is guilty towards all mankind, whose peace he disturbs and to whom he sets so pernicious an example." The ruler is bound to repair the damage that has been done. Vattel says:

> the sovereign alone is guilty, and he alone is under an obligation to repair the wrong done. The subjects, and especially the military, are innocent; they have done no more than obey, as was their duty; and they are only called upon to give up what they have taken in such a war, since they hold it without lawful title. That, I believe, is the almost unanimous opinion of honest men and of officers of the highest honor and integrity.[9]

[7] Samuel Pufendorf, *De Jure Naturae et Gentium* (On the Law of Nature and Nations) (1688), translated by C. H. Oldfather and W. A. Oldfather, Oxford: Clarendon Press, 1934, p. 1056.

[8] Emir de Vattel, *Le Droit des Gens, ou Principes de la Loi Naturelle* (The Law of Nations or the Principles of Natural Law) (1758), translated by Charles G. Fenwick, Washington: Carnegie Institution, 1916, p. 302.

[9] Ibid., p. 303.

In this way, Vattel sets the stage for holding the sovereign legally liable for waging aggressive war, but he can do no more than call for the sovereign to choose to pay reparations since there is no court to which the sovereign must answer. And Vattel does not address what is today the crucial question, namely, whether a ruler can be held criminally liable for waging aggressive war if there is an international criminal court.

By the 19th century, Wheaton could claim that there was such a thing as "international responsibility" that in some limited cases could give grounding for international tribunals.[10] Wheaton was thinking of "boards of arbitration and courts of prizes," established by the joint consent of the States who sought a resolution of a conflict. But the idea that, on any ground at all, there could be international tribunals was relatively new to the 19th century. The problem was that such an international tribunal, like the contemporary International Court of Justice, relied for its legitimacy on the consent of the parties before it and hence was not a good basis for criminal prosecution, which must be non-consensual. Indeed, the very idea that criminal punishment could only be meted out if the defendant agreed to it goes against the very idea of criminality and perpetuates impunity.

The best-known contemporary Just War theorist, Michael Walzer, coined the phrase "the war convention" to stand for "the set of articulated norms, customs, professional codes, legal precepts, religious and philosophical principles, and reciprocal arrangements that shape our judgments of military conduct."[11] Walzer, though, recognizes that the war convention is mainly social and moral, even though his own method is to look to the law first to try to ascertain the contours of the war convention. And because the war convention is social and moral, it is unclear in what sense the convention is binding in a way that would be the basis for criminal trials for those who violate the convention.

The Just War theorists from Grotius to Wheaton and then to Walzer came to the understanding that rulers could be held responsible for waging aggressive war, but they did not have a clear sense of what, if anything, followed from this legally. Legal rules were emerging out of the customary norms over the centuries, but corresponding legal institutions did not come on the scene until the middle of the 20th century, and then only fleetingly until emerging perhaps permanently at the century's end. Yet the question remained as to what value these emerging legal rules had

---

[10] Henry Wheaton, *Elements of International Law*, Boston: Little Brown, 1836, p. 22.
[11] Michael Walzer, *Just and Unjust Wars*, New York: Basic Books, 1977, 2000, p. 44.

without corresponding legal institutions. Can legal rules truly exist, and be violated, even though there are no institutions to affirm the breach and set penalties or punishments? In the next section I turn to 20th-century developments, especially to the "precedent" of Nuremberg.

II. The Nuremberg "Precedent"

The problem addressed in this chapter is well illustrated by the debate about the legitimacy of the International Military Tribunal at Nuremberg. Robert Jackson, one of the chief prosecutors at Nuremberg said: "It is high time that we act on the juridical principle that aggressive war-making is illegal and criminal."[12] The problem was to identify the source of this seemingly uncontroversial claim. The principal source of the supposed crime against peace was the Kellogg-Briand Pact, a multi-lateral treaty signed in 1928 by sixty-five States including Germany and Japan. Here is Article I of that treaty:

> The high contracting parties solemnly declare in the name of their respective peoples that they condemn recourse to war for the solution of international controversies, and renounce it as an instrument of national policy in their relations with one another.[13]

This is often cited as the central source of the norm against waging aggressive war. But notice that the language is hardly that of a criminal statute telling States, let alone individuals, what specifically they are proscribed from doing and what will be the penalties or punishments for breach.

The major problem is that not all States ratified this treaty, and some States, such as Nazi Germany, had seemingly "unsigned" it.[14] So it is not clear that Germany should be held liable for violating a treaty that Germany had rejected. There has been an enormous amount of

---

[12] International Conference on Military Trials, London, 1945, quoted in Cherif Bassiouni, *International Criminal Law*, 2nd ed., vol. 3, Ardsley, NY: Transaction, 1999,
[13] Treaty between the United States and Other Powers Providing for the Renunciation of War as an Instrument of National Policy, August 27, 1928, art. 1, 46 Stat. 2343, 2345–46, 94 L.N.T.S. 59, 63 (1929).
[14] I place the term "unsigned" in scare quotes for several reasons. First, the signing of a treaty is not the most important fact; rather, ratification is the key. Second, it is highly contentious that a State can unsign a treaty, let alone withdraw from that treaty. Third, there is a treaty that addresses these matters, the Vienna Treaty on Treaties, Article 18, but as one can glean from its title, there is also a question, raised recently by the George W. Bush administration, about whether a State can withdraw from the Vienna Treaty on Treaties.

controversy about this issue and I will not here take a side.[15] Throughout history there had been many declarations against war, and at least as many major wars that seemingly disregarded those declarations. It is undeniable, though, that a kind of normative consensus against the waging of aggressive war was arising in the early part of the 20th century and that the Axis powers flagrantly violated this normative consensus.

The much more difficult issue is that it was not Nazi Germany in the dock at Nuremberg, but individual political and military leaders. And there had been nothing equivalent to the Kellogg-Briand's condemnation of States for aggression that was directed at those individuals who were the leaders of these States. In addition, there had never been major international trials in which individual political or military leaders had been prosecuted for their roles in the waging of aggressive war.[16] So there is a serious question of what was the basis for the trials at Nuremberg against Nazi leaders. Here is how one strong supporter of these trials, Cherif Bassiouni, defends their legitimacy:

> The IMT [International Military Tribunal] made reference to many treaties which had outlawed war and cited many public declarations that aggressive war was an international crime. Although aggression had never been universally defined, it was clear to the court that the leaders of a state that deliberately and wantonly attacked its neutral neighbors without warning or just cause could not be exculpated. It would be a travesty of justice to allow them to escape merely because no one had previously been convicted of the crime against peace.... The time had come, as Jackson said, for the law to take a step forward.[17]

The question is, when the law takes a step forward should people be held liable for acts taken only after the announcement of this step? Or, before the change is announced, are individuals liable for what the changing standard requires of them?

The difficulty of trying to make sure that the principle against ex post facto legal proceedings, the so-called principle of legality, is upheld has haunted international criminal law since the trials at Nuremberg and perhaps has brought us a greater appreciation of the rights of the

---

[15] See the excellent article by Jan Klabbers, "How to Defeat a Treaty's Object and Purpose Pending Entry into Force: Toward Manifest Intent," *Vanderbilt Journal of Transnational Law*, vol. 34, no. 2, March 2001, pp. 283–331.

[16] One could debate whether the Leipzig trials after the First World War were directed at States or their political and military leaders. But in any event, no prosecutions of individuals ensued. I thank Jan Klabbers for this point.

[17] Bassiouni, *International Criminal Law*, p. 320.

defendants before international tribunals. The International Criminal Court has dealt with this issue by not prosecuting anyone for acts committed prior to the Court's Rome Charter coming into force. And in the area of international criminal law that concerns us in this chapter, there will be no prosecutions for the crime of aggression until there is an international agreement on what aggression means, and then only for those acts committed after that part of the Rome treaty comes into force.

In some respects all of these recent developments are surprising since there was a far simpler way to deal with the ex post facto problem, namely, to regard the trials at Nuremberg as having set a precedent both for what it means to wage aggressive war and for the idea that individuals could be held liable for planning or initiating such wars. I will address this issue in the remainder of this section. Let me begin by noting that there was also a kind of counter-precedent in that sixty years have gone by without any other trials of this sort. So, one would initially wonder which was the precedent: that it was an international crime for a person to plan or initiate aggressive war, or not a crime to do so?

Another thing to worry about is whether the trials at Nuremberg were a "precedent" for all aggressive wars or just for those that were waged on the scope and intensity of World War II. Many of the remarks by Justice Jackson and others at the time of the trials at Nuremberg focused on these unique factors, not on the more general point of whether leaders of States who wage aggressive war on far smaller scale than that waged by the Germans and Japanese would be prosecutable. Indeed, in striving hard to garner international acceptance of the Nuremberg and Tokyo verdicts, it was repeatedly stressed that it would be a travesty to let Nazi and Japanese leaders off the hook for the extraordinary horrors they had perpetrated. And in the German case in particular, there were many references to the concentration camps and the attempts to annihilate the Jewish people, issues that had little to do with the idea that State leaders should be prosecuted for waging aggressive war. What made the Nazi case stand out was the scale and viciousness with which it was fought, not that it was a case of aggression. So, the value of Nuremberg as a "precedent" for future trials of leaders for aggressive wars is here also unclear.

In defense of the "precedent," it could be said that the very fact that there were trials at Nuremberg for the crime of aggression should have put leaders on notice that they could indeed be prosecuted for waging aggressive war – after all, it only takes one trial to show that such trials could occur again. For this reason it can be said that the political and military leaders of States should realize that they also could be put on trial when their States wage aggressive war. The difficulty is that what counts as aggressive war was not well spelled out at Nuremberg. And who exactly is prosecutable for the crime of aggression was also muddied by the fact that leaders who planned or initiated aggressive acts of Allied States were not also prosecuted for similar acts to those committed by German leaders. This is why some people claim that the "precedent" is only that if you lose a war your leaders will be subject to prosecution. Of course, even this much could be "precedent," except that its deterrence value is unclear since when one decides to go to war it is normally very unclear whether one will be on the winning or losing side, and hence unclear whether one will ultimately be prosecutable or not, as vanquished rather than victor.

III. Rules in International Law

I wish next to get a good bit more abstract in asking how we should think about norms and rules in international law in trying to gain more insight into the debate about whether it is legitimate to prosecute State leaders for the crime of aggression. One interesting place to start is with H. L. A. Hart's famous treatment of international law in the final chapter of his seminal work, *The Concept of Law*. Hart regards international law as not conforming to his model, where law is understood as the intersection of primary and secondary rules, largely because there are no clear-cut secondary rules in international law. There certainly is no master rule, or rule of recognition, and there are barely even rudimentary rules concerning how to interpret and change international law. In this respect, international law and what Hart called primitive legal systems are quite similar. But Hart argued that little is lost by employing a wider conception of law in these cases, and then he tried to explain what features of international law are most like regular legal systems.

One of the central questions Hart addressed is how international law can be binding if there are no clear sanctioning institutions. Hart had earlier mounted one of the most significant challenges to the general idea that law's bindingness comes from fear of sanctions alone. He described this view as the "gunman" model and argued that one might be obliged to do something because of fear of sanctions, but obligations do not arise merely from fear of sanctions. Rather, what is crucial is the internal sense of feeling obligated by rules as a member of a society in which these rules define significant practices. In this respect, Hart argues that international law can be seen as strongly analogous to domestic law.

> [W]hat these rules require is thought and spoken of as obligatory; there is general pressure for conformity to the rules; claims and admissions are based on them and their breach is held to justify not only demands for compensation, but reprisals and counter-measures. When the rules are disregarded, it is not only on the footing that they are not binding; instead efforts are made to conceal the fact.[18]

In my view, this is consistent with the way that international lawyers talk about their field of law. For all practical purposes, they say, international law can be practiced and studied in the same way as municipal law: all of the same techniques for discovering what are the rules and how they have been interpreted apply to both domains.

Hart also takes the surprising position that it is not crucial that international law seems to lack a rule of recognition, or master rule, that would allow us to identify conclusively which are the rules of the system. He says:

> if the rules are in fact accepted as standards of conduct, and supported with appropriate forms of social pressure distinctive of obligatory rules, nothing more is required to show that they are binding rules, even though . . . we have not . . . a way of demonstrating the validity of individual rules by reference to some ultimate rule of the system.[19]

Indeed, Hart says that there is no "mystery as to why such rules of such a simple social structure are binding, which a basic rule, if only we could find it, would resolve." The rules are "binding if they are accepted and function as such."[20]

Hart then resets this debate in the following terms that will also be the point of departure for the rest of this chapter.

> once we emancipate ourselves from the assumption that international law *must* contain a basic rule, the question to be faced is one of fact. What is the actual character of the rules as they function in the relations between states.[21]

Hart's preliminary answer is that "the rules which are in fact operative" in international law "constitute not a system but a set of rules, among which are the rules providing for the binding force of treaties."[22] But, Hart argues, this set of rules still manages to operate analogously to municipal law, in content and function if not in form. As he says, "in this analogy

[18] H. L. A. Hart, *The Concept of Law*, 2nd ed., Oxford: Clarendon Press, 1961, 1997, p. 220.
[19] Ibid., p. 234.
[20] Ibid., p. 235.
[21] Ibid., p. 236.
[22] Ibid.

of content, no other social rules are so close to municipal law as those of international law."[23]

There remains the question of whether States are only bound by treaty law or also bound by customary law. Customary law is indeed often said to be the hallmark of the law concerning war, and hence an important subject for our main issue in this chapter – liability for States and their leaders who wage aggressive war. But despite the near consensus among international law scholars that customary law is binding on States, few have argued that State leaders can be prosecuted simply on the basis of customary international law. This is at least in part because of the concern about ex post facto prosecutions. In the United States, criminal law is almost solely based on statute rather than common law out of concern for the rights of defendants. Today, while there is still a major role for customary humanitarian law as providing background for the rules of war that are being enforced in international tribunals, the statutes that have codified much of that custom, rather than the customs themselves, are key in these prosecutions.

The Geneva and Hague Conventions have codified much of customary international law, and the trials that have gone forward in the last ten years have referred to these "statutes" rather than to customary law.[24] While there is a serious question of whether all of the people on this earth can be held accountable for statutes that do not clearly proscribe individual behavior, the more serious question is whether custom alone could be sufficient to ground prosecutions of individuals.[25] Customary norms are often slippery and unclear. For an individual to be prosecutable for violating a customary international norm, that norm would have to be shown to be transparent and public, in a way that people in distant parts of the globe could come to understand. For without such transparency and publicity, it is not clear why we would think that these norms constitute binding rules the violation of which would be subject to punishment.

In the end, I agree with Hart that this question is mainly a question of fact, namely, do States act as if there are binding rules against aggression, and do individual military and political leaders act as if they believe

---

[23] Ibid., p. 237.

[24] See the wonderful introduction to this issue written by Jean-Marie Henckaerts and Louise Doswald-Beck, *Customary International Law, Vol. I: Rules*, Cambridge: Cambridge University Press, 2005, pp. xxv–xlv.

[25] John Tasioulas raises the question of whether I have painted the picture too starkly here. Surely, it is not an either-or conundrum. A norm can first come into existence by means of a treaty and then eventually also become a custom. I partially address this problem later in the chapter.

there are rules against planning or initiating aggressive war? I will next begin to discuss an answer to the question of whether there is a clear set of international rules concerning what counts as State aggression and what elements must be proved by a prosecutor to convict individuals for the crime of aggression. I will be especially interested in the question of whether certain customs, as well as certain treaties, could come to constitute *jus cogens* norms in international law, that is, norms that are binding on States and perhaps also on individuals because they have achieved the status of nonderogable norms.[26]

IV. *Jus Cogens* Norms and the Crime of Aggression

The Vienna Convention on the Law of Treaties discusses what are called *jus cogens* norms, norms that cannot be overridden even by express treaty. Given their place in international law, *jus cogens* norms are sometimes equated with constitutional principles in a domestic legal system. Article 53 of the Vienna Convention provides that "a norm of *jus cogens* must satisfy three tests: the norm must be (a) 'accepted and recognized by the international community of States as a whole' as a norm from which (b) 'no derogation is permitted,' and which (c) 'can be modified only by a subsequent norm of general international law having the same character.'"[27] *Jus cogens* norms are norms from which no derogation is permitted, and hence seemingly norms that sit at the apogee of international norms, and for which there are obligations *erga omnes*, that is, obligations on everyone.

In the Barcelona Traction case, a case decided by the International Court of Justice in 1970, the first example of obligation *erga omnes* is the "outlawing of acts of aggression."[28] Some of the other *jus cogens* crimes include genocide and apartheid. So, one question to ask is why the crime of aggression is thought to be in this relatively uncontroversial category with other crimes that nearly everyone would recognize as wrong regardless of statute or treaty. One possible answer is similar to that given by the Nuremberg tribunal when it declared that the crime of aggression was the worst because it contained all of the others. Since this literally can't be true, what is most likely is that the tribunal meant that States that

---

[26] See chapter 2 of my book, *Crimes against Humanity: A Normative Account*, New York: Cambridge University Press, 2005.

[27] Quoted in Maurizio Ragazzi, *The Concept of International Obligations Erga Omnes*, Oxford: Clarendon Press, 1997, p. 51.

[28] See ibid., p. 74.

engage in aggression are likely also to engage in other crimes, or to have these other crimes as ancillary parts of the larger project of aggression.

One of the chief difficulties in using the idea of *jus cogens* norms to establish the criminality of acts of aggression is that there is another nonderogable principle that seems to be opposed to this, namely, the principle of legality, the principle against retroactive prosecutions, that we began to discuss earlier.[29] For no matter how obvious it is that certain acts should be criminalized, this doesn't make them criminal acts until there has been some clearly articulated rule that so criminalizes them. In a previous work I suggested that *jus cogens* norms were the backbone of international criminal law, insofar as *jus cogens* norms connected minimal principles of how people should behave toward each other with rudimentary legal norms. But even in that situation, it now seems to me, there are problems with prosecutions on the basis of uncodified *jus cogens* norms, of the same sort that affected criminal norms that are based solely on customs.

One might argue that there are some customs that anyone can be assumed to know, such as that genocide and apartheid are wrong and proscribed. But one wonders whether the social norms of a given community may not so blunt the obviousness of such norms that we still need explicit rules. Some theorists have argued that you could have customary norms alone constituting a set of primary rules for a given society. But even here this makes sense, it seems to me, only if the customary norms or rules were well known and widely disseminated. Even the proscription of apartheid and genocide cannot merely be assumed, since we know that some societies have seemingly found such practices acceptable.

Rules in international law take on a special importance when we are thinking of criminal liability. The reason for this has to do with the principle of legality for it is thought to be the hallmark of an unfair system of criminal jurisprudence for defendants to be held liable under a set of rules that were not promulgated or even widely known at the time that the defendant's putatively illicit behavior took place. We expect that the rules will be very clear and the conduct that is proscribed will be well known before it is fair to hold a person potentially subject to punishment for violating those rules. When loss of liberty is at stake, the rules have to be very clear, and not merely norms that are in some sense "in the air."

---

[29] See William Schabas, "Origins of the Criminalization of Aggression: How Crimes against Peace Became the 'Supreme International Crime,'" in *The International Criminal Court and the Crime of Aggression,* edited by Mauro Politi and Giusseppe Nesi, Aldershot, England: Ashgate, 2004, pp. 29–30.

Of course, violations of customary international law, especially those customs that are controversial, could trigger other sorts of reactions than criminal proceedings, which would be less problematical. Norm violators could be subject to shame or required to explain their behavior publicly, as is true of various so-called truth and reconciliation commissions. Or people could be required to contribute to a victim compensation fund as has also been attempted in the recent past.[30] But criminal punishments are different. They require a higher standard of publicity for the rules if the prosecutions are to be considered fair. In general this is because of the value placed on individual liberty that is put in jeopardy in such prosecutions. In what remains of this section, I wish to investigate reasons for thinking that criminal prosecutions for such things as the crime of aggression need to have quite explicit and public rules concerning what counts as aggression, and such rules must be applied only prospectively, not retrospectively.

Lon Fuller once said that a system of rules that were all retrospective was absurd since people would be required to conform to standards on Tuesday that were only articulated on Wednesday.[31] The same could be said about holding someone liable for violating rules that were unclear and only made clear after the person acted. In these cases, the problem is that it seems patently unfair to hold someone to a standard that the person couldn't have known about, or where it was unclear what exactly the person was required to do. When criminal penalties, including loss of liberty and even loss of life, are at stake, it is unfair to subject people to such jeopardy concerning standards that are anything other than crystal clear. Of course, we do not require that people actually know of these rules, but only that they could have found out about them and con-formed their behavior accordingly. This is what is meant by requiring clear "notice" of what is illegal, but still saying that ignorance of the law is no excuse.

Customary norms can be crystal clear, I suppose, although they are rarely so. This is because customs normally develop and change over time, and since they are not codified it is often unclear at any given time what precisely they proscribe. Let us return to the crime of aggression. While it may be true that there was a clear customary norm against waging aggressive war, what constituted aggressive war was not sufficiently clear,

[30] See Trudy Govier, *Taking Wrongs Seriously: Acknowledgement, Reconciliation, and the Politics of Sustainable Peace*, Amherst, NY: Humanity Books, 2006.

[31] Lon Fuller, *The Morality of Law*, New Haven, CT: Yale University Press, 1964, 1969.

and this is still true today.[32] In addition, while it makes some sense to think that those individuals who plan and initiate State aggression could commit a crime, this is merely a possible inference rather than a clear implication of the customary prohibition on waging aggressive war. As I indicated earlier, in part the problem develops because in the not too distant past – that is, the early part of the 20th century – it was relatively clear that only States, not individuals, could commit this crime. So, if the custom is said to have changed, there would have to be very clear indications for thinking so, and yet there were few if any such indications and quite a few counter-indications, such as that there had been no major prosecutions of individuals for this crime until Nuremberg and Tokyo, and none after.

If a political or military leader is trying to figure out what is required of him or her, and the custom seems to have been that he or she will not be held liable, then there really is a strong reason for a codification or other public statement that the rule has changed and these leaders will henceforth be held liable when they were not before. For there to be codified universal norms, the code must be one that is ratified by all States. One could claim that it should have been obvious that if States were proscribed from doing certain things, their leaders, who after all are the ones who act for the State, could not do them either. But here is where the counter-indication is so important. For it would not be obvious if other leaders were not held liable even as the States themselves were condemned for committing aggression.

As I have argued elsewhere, long-standing custom may be a very good *sign* that there is a *jus cogens* norm, but this custom does not itself *establish* such a *jus cogens* norm.[33] And in any event, *jus cogens* norms often do not themselves provide sufficient notice for criminal prosecution. For there is a kind of counter-norm at play here, namely, the principle of legality, which is itself on the same level as *jus cogens* norms. Let me just mention one reason for thinking that the principle of legality is the kind of principle that should not be breached. As Fuller has indicated, in minor matters where no penalties attach, the principle is not indefeasible. But in matters where punishments are at stake, even when the morality is clear-cut, we need a clear legal rule in place at the time the defendant supposedly committed a crime for that defendant to be treated as a fully

---

[32] For more reasons to think that even the case of Nazi aggression was not completely clear see the next two chapters, 8 and 9.

[33] Larry May, *Crimes against Humanity*, ch. 2.

mature person who will be held accountable for what he has chosen to do. If there is no sense that doing a certain thing is punishable, then there is no sense that the person chose to do what was legally proscribed and now deserves punishment. One might, though, try to take a conservative approach to what counts as custom, only recognizing customary norms or rules that appeared crystal clear. Such an approach seems directly to confront my approach and will be taken up in detail in the next section.

V. The Conservative Approach to Custom

In a recent article, Theodor Meron has argued strongly in favor of the use of customary international law in international criminal prosecutions, to which I raised significant objections earlier in this chapter. While not as carefully explained as one might want, the following elements of the conservative approach can be distilled from Meron's article in the October 2005 issue of AJIL.[34]

1. look only to those rules "which are beyond any doubt part of customary law;"[35]
2. use only those methods for establishing customary norms that are traditional;[36]
3. resolve any doubts about custom in favor of the defendant.[37]

Meron refers to the second principle as "methodological conservatism" and the third principle as "outcome conservatism." While he does not name the first principle, I shall refer to it as "epistemological conservatism." These three conservative principles then define Meron's conservative approach to the use of customary rules in international criminal proceedings. In this section, I will give reasons to oppose this proposal in light of what has been argued in the earlier sections of this chapter.

Initially, I wish to applaud Meron for his insistence that custom be appealed to in international criminal law only when "the legality principle does not bar its application." In particular, Meron argues against the attempt to stretch customs to fit new situations and fact patterns. What I am calling the "epistemological conservatism" principle is an overarching philosophical commitment to allow prosecutions only when at the time of

---

[34] Theodor Meron, "Editorial Comment: Revival of Customary Humanitarian Law," *American Journal of International Law*, vol. 99, no. 4, October 2005, pp. 817–834.
[35] Ibid., p. 821.
[36] Ibid., p. 822.
[37] Ibid., p. 823.

the offense it is beyond doubt that the defendant "could have identified the rule he was expected to obey."[38] Notice that this is not the same as saying that the defendant knew of the existence of such a rule. Meron has pointed out that in most areas of law we proceed on the basis of a "massive fiction" when we pretend that everyone has read and understood all of the relevant sources of law that are available to them. Given this legal fiction, it is not as odd as it might initially seem to think that custom as well as treaties can be valid sources of binding international criminal law.[39] The epistemological principle puts the burden squarely on the prosecutor to show, beyond a reasonable doubt, that the defendant violated a clear customary rule of international law. As long as the existence of the rule of custom is beyond reasonable doubt, why treat this source of law any differently from other sources of law?

The second principle, "methodological conservatism," is the one that, in my view, causes Meron's proposal the most potential difficulty. And here the chief problem is that the traditional methods of discovering custom are often very unclear. Meron himself dismisses, nearly out of hand, the idea that persistently objecting States can create a counter-custom to emerging custom. Indeed, he says that normally a State's objections, even if persistent and publicly proclaimed, will merely confirm the existence of the rule in question.[40] This is hardly the traditional approach, or if it is, it is hardly uncontroversial. For nearly as long as there has been debate about customary law there has been the view that States might be able to opt out of a customary regime by, from the beginning, consistently objecting to the customary rule. Otherwise, it would seem that a group of States could hold another State liable for violating a rule that that State had explicitly challenged and rejected.

At a certain point, Meron seems to admit that his methodological conservatism is not as conservative as even that widely employed by the International Court of Justice for non-criminal cases.[41] The problem is exacerbated by Meron's failure to give us a carefully delineated account of his own methodological approach. And concerning the third principle, his "outcome conservatism," it seems at times to amount to little more than an admonition "that criminal prosecutions be clear in their scope and application."[42] Finding one precedent might be sufficient, he suggests,

[38] Ibid., p. 821.
[39] Ibid.
[40] Ibid., p. 820.
[41] Ibid., p. 829.
[42] Ibid., p. 823.

as long as the precedent is itself clear. But as we saw in the case of the crime of aggression, there can be one clear precedent, with fifty-plus intervening years, that surely should raise considerable doubts about the supposed customary rule established by that one precedent.

The conservative approach is certainly better than the modern or loose approach, but the question on the table is whether Meron's conservative approach is really conservative enough to satisfy the legality principle and rule out ex post facto prosecutions. And part of my response has to do with how serious Meron is about "epistemological conservatism." If Meron is ready to require that it must be beyond doubt, or at least beyond reasonable doubt, that a customary rule existed at the time the defendant acted and that he or she could have known about it, and if he is more serious than he seems to be in saying that all doubts will be resolved in favor of the defendant, then I am not strongly opposed to what he proposes. But as he goes on to describe what his conservatism will allow, it becomes decreasingly clear that he is committed to those conservative principles.

Consider what Meron says about the main Nuremberg trial. He is forthright in noting that the Geneva and Hague Conventions, while setting out various proscriptions, "did not expressly *criminalize* their violation." And he admits that the International Military Tribunal "did not provide a very satisfactory explanation as to how aspects of the Geneva POW [Prisoner of War] Convention of 1929 and the Hague Convention No. IV of 1907 had so quickly metamorphosed into customary norms." Yet, Meron declares that "the tribunals' general approach was appropriate under the circumstances." And the rationale he then gives for thinking that the circumstances warranted what he calls "this loose approach" is simply that the crimes charged "were so clearly criminal under every domestic system in the world."[43]

Yet, surely Meron has not followed his own more conservative approach here and has not given much of an account for why he thinks that the looser approach is nonetheless justified. As I have argued in greater detail elsewhere, the question is not whether various crimes like rape and murder are recognized as domestic crimes at the time that the defendant acts, but whether these acts are recognized as instances of mass international crimes, such as persecution or ethnic cleansing. For when a defendant is in the international dock he or she is not being prosecuted for the domestic crime of rape or murder, but for an international mass crime

[43] Ibid., p. 830 following.

that the rape or murder is merely a part of.[44] The salient question is whether the defendant could have easily discovered that what he or she was about to do was proscribed as an international crime in order for the ensuing prosecution not to violate the legality principle.

Meron is more successful in adhering to his own conservative approach when he discuses command responsibility in non-international armed conflicts. He speaks supportively of several ICTY appeals chamber rulings. The cases concerned whether commanders could be held liable for crimes that "they had no reason to have known" about.[45] Meron here employs his conservative approach rather than the looser Nuremberg approach, and in my view he reaches the right result. The question for us is whether the use of Meron's approach, when properly employed by his own standards, will very often, if at all, support the use of customary norms in international criminal prosecutions. For, if we take seriously the overarching idea of the first principle that the criteria of adjudication must be beyond reasonable doubt, then custom, which is almost always reasonably doubtable, will not pass the test.

I am willing to allow that there might be a few cases that will pass this test, but the vast majority of cases would not, leaving us with the conclusion that even on Meron's conservative view custom will rarely be a firm basis for international criminal law. And it seems to me to be highly unlikely that trials for aggression could be based on custom, at least standing alone. This is because there has been so much controversy about how to understand aggression as a crime when individuals are in the dock, even as there has been, in my own view, a fair amount of agreement about what would justify condemning a State, rather than an individual, for aggression. In the next section, I briefly discuss each of the types of rules that international prosecutions for aggression could be based on and identify the problems that we have seen for each type of rule or norm.

VI. The Rules of the International Community

There are three main sources of rules in the international community. In this final section I will explore each of these sources of rule and say something about problems that are raised with each type in prosecuting the crime of aggression. Let us begin with one of the oldest and most explicit sources of international rules or norms, namely, treaties especially of the

---

[44] See Larry May, *Crimes against Humanity*, ch. 6.
[45] Meron, p. 827.

multilateral variety. Treaties are often said to be the statutes of international law. This is because once they are ratified then they operate much like black-letter law in that there are explicit proscriptions and sanctions for those who break the rules. There also is an explicit enforcement regimen that the ratifiers of the treaty agree to. For example, in recent times, most multilateral treaties concerning international criminal law or human rights law have the provision that ratifying States agree either to prosecute violators in their domestic courts or to extradite the violators to States that are willing to prosecute them. This is captured in the Latin phrase, *aut dedere aut judicare.*[46]

The major difficulty with treaties as a source of international rules is that they are binding on only those States that have ratified the treaties. Unless every State ratifies a given treaty it will not set rules for the entire international community, but only for those States that so ratify. There has also been the problem that even ratifying States have later "unsigned" certain important treaties, thereby undermining the stability that is normally achieved by getting States to ratify, and thereby self-bind, themselves in international law. So there are at least two problems with using treaties to ground international rules, and the second is the most important, since even if it were possible to get all States in the world to ratify a given treaty, there is nothing to prevent States from later "unsigning" the treaty whenever it suited their purposes and as a way to avoid sanctions.

The proposed solution to the problem of treaties has to do with the second main source of international rules: custom. Some have proposed that certain widespread multilateral treaties be considered binding on all States when those treaties have been in existence for a certain lengthy period of time and there has been a seeming acceptance of the treaty as having binding force on the non-ratifying States. This is a very complex issue and I do not have the space to explore it fully here. But it may be that multilateral treaties could be a strong basis for establishing a customary norm or rule, and that such a practice could solve one of the main infirmities of treaty-based international rules. And even if treaties are not a good source here, it may be that there are other sources of custom, especially long-standing and common practice among States and very little if any countervailing practice.

I have earlier rehearsed various objections to custom as establishing rules in international *criminal* law. Let me here remind the reader of three

---

[46] See M. Cherif Bassiouni and Edward W. Wise, *Aut Dedere Aut Judicare: The Duty to Prosecute or Extradite in International Law*, Ardsley, NY: Transnational, 1995.

of these criticisms. First, custom rarely provides a clear rule that would tell a State leader what precisely are his or her obligations in international criminal law. Second, customs change over time, and so it is often hard to predict whether a settled norm in one time period will remain so later, and hence hard to predict what rules one will be held to after one acts. Third, custom almost always exists alongside counter-customs, especially in international criminal law, and it is often hard to tell which customs are the ones that will be regarded as binding. For these and other reasons international criminal law does not have a firm footing in international custom.

Third, international rules could be grounded in international institutions that have themselves come to be accepted by the international community. If we ever find ourselves living under a world government, then there will be a ready source of international rules. Short of this, there are institutions like the United Nations or the International Court of Justice that perform some of the functions of a world government and may be the source of international norms and rules. Institutions create their own norms and rules, especially if those institutions operate under the color of law, as is true of both the UN and the ICJ.

The trials at Nuremberg were established on the basis of treaties and customs. As we have seen, the treaties that these trials were said to be based on were rejected by the Axis States whose leaders were tried by Nuremberg and Tokyo tribunals. So, the Judges in these tribunals tried to justify the trials in terms of custom. Yet it was hard to see exactly what the custom was, since so many States had engaged in aggressive war in the preceding decades. And the one attempt to create an international organization that could have legitimated these trials, the League of Nations, had foundered and died stillborn before the main crimes that the leaders of Germany and Japan were accused of committing. And unlike today, there was not a free-standing international criminal court, but only ad hoc tribunals, quickly established just for the purpose of trying the Nazi and Japanese leaders and established by the powers that had won the war, thus fueling the charge that these tribunals constituted merely victor's justice.

Short of the institution of world government it is not clear what would be the normative grounding of international institutional rules, other than treaties or customs. And to see the problems here one need only think about the International Criminal Court, the institution that should be providing rules and meting out sanctions for violations of the rules, if any international institution does so. And yet several major States, such as the United States, refuse to recognize the legitimacy of this institution and hence claim that they are not indeed bound by its rulings. Until there is a world government, rules or norms created by international institutions will remain infirm, although they will be better than nothing. Yet, in the field of international law, already heavily criticized for not being a proper field of law, such an infirm basis is disconcerting.

This discussion leads us back to our original topic: what to think of the source of prosecutions for violations of international rules in such areas as crimes against peace and the crime of aggression. In this chapter I have tried to indicate why there have been no significant international prosecutions for such crimes with the exception of the trials at Nuremberg and Tokyo sixty years ago. The inability for either multilateral treaty or international institutions to provide a codification of these crimes has been notorious. And many theorists, myself included, are very reluctant to rely on international customary rules to be the basis of such prosecutions. Such reluctance also opens a good window into the general problem of establishing and enforcing rules in international criminal law, where individuals rather than States are in the dock. In the next two chapters I will also look to a Nuremberg "precedent" for how to understand the *actus reus* and *mens rea* elements of the crime of aggression.

8

Prosecuting Military and Political Leaders

Obviously, no man may be condemned for fighting in what he believes is the defense of his native land, even though his belief be mistaken. Nor can he be expected to undertake an independent investigation to determine whether or not the cause for which he fights is the result of an aggressive act of his own government. One can be guilty only where knowledge of aggression in fact exists, and it is not sufficient that he have suspicions that the war is aggressive. Any other test of guilt would involve a standard of conduct both impracticable and unjust.

"The Ministries Case Judgment"[1]

In this and the next chapter, I will attempt to draw some lessons from an examination of several of the trials at Nuremberg for the crime of aggression. If we can get around the problems discussed in the previous chapter concerning the idea of precedent in international criminal law, the next question is what is the precedent-value of those trials. I am especially interested in how the elements of the crime of aggression, especially the element of *actus reus* was established and what defenses were recognized. I will examine cases of both military and political leaders tried at Nuremberg, drawing first on one of the seemingly easiest of cases and also one of the hardest. Throughout this chapter I try to provide some concrete detail to the rather abstract discussions of the previous part of this book, but I also will try to fill out and extend the abstract discussion as well, setting the stage for the reconceptualization of the main elements of the crime of aggression.

The first case I wish to consider in this chapter is the case of Admiral Karl Doenitz. There are two issues that will receive much attention here.

[1] *Trials of War Criminals before Nuremberg Military Tribunals under Control Council Law No. 10,* vol. 14, p. 337.

First is the issue of how to think of the *actus reus* element of the crime of aggression. Doenitz was ordered to attack neutral ships and gave orders to the U-boat captains under his command to do just this. He is accused of having participated in the war of aggression by directing these U-boats. Second is the issue of how to think about conspiracy theory in determining the *actus reus* element. Doenitz is accused of being part of a conspiracy to wage aggressive war because of his association with Hitler and other Nazi leaders as well as his acceptance, somewhat late in the war, of the appointment as commander in chief of the Navy. The prosecution at Nuremberg maintained that by accepting this appointment, Doenitz "ratified the previous happenings, all the endeavors of the Party since 1920."[2] I will take up each of these issues in the first two sections of this chapter.

The other case I wish to consider is the Ministries Case, a trial conducted by the American Military Tribunal under Control Council Law No. 10. This case concerned the prosecution of twenty-one relatively high-level political leaders in Germany. These individuals were also accused of crimes against peace largely on grounds of conspiracy, some as principals and some as accessories. In the third section of this chapter I will take up the complications of the conspiracy theory that prosecutors employed in Nuremberg to bring under its net these ministers of the German government for crimes against peace. In both the Ministries and Doenitz cases, the question raised concerning crimes against peace was whether the defendants played a sufficient role in participating in the war to make their individual acts guilty of the crime of aggression.

In the fourth section of this chapter I will discuss one of the main defenses that Doenitz employed, unsuccessfully, namely, that he did not know that the war he was participating in was an aggressive war, and it was not his place, even late in the war when he was made commander in chief of the Navy to question whether the war was aggressive or defensive. Doenitz in effect attempted to use a variation of the superior orders defense even though he was, by the end of the war if not earlier, one of the top members of Hitler's staff. In the fifth section, I will discuss a similar defense made on behalf of the Ministers, which was partially accepted by the American Military Tribunal sitting in Nuremberg. In general I argue that the Tribunals were correct to acquit Doenitz and also to acquit von Weizsaecker of all but one of the charges of the crime of aggression because of the prosecution's failure to establish the *actus*

---

[2] *Trial of the Major War Criminals before the International Military Tribunal*, Nuremberg, 1948, vol. XIII, p. 298.

reus element of the crime of aggression. Finally, I consider a successful prosecution for aggression at Nuremberg.

I. The Admiral Doenitz Case

I begin with a case that in many respects should have been an easy one for the Nuremberg prosecution team. That it turned out not to be easy at all will tell us quite a bit about whether and to what extent Nuremberg can be a precedent for the ICC if and when it starts prosecuting political and military leaders for the crime of aggression. Doenitz was, by the end of the war, the highest-ranking naval officer in the Third Reich, and he met regularly with Adolph Hitler to plan naval operations of the final years of the war. Doenitz never denied his role in the war effort and boasted that he shared with Hitler the goals of that war, including the subjugation of Germany's neighbors. I will focus on the act requirement of the crime of aggression as well as possible defenses to that element in what follows.

Doenitz and Admiral Erich Raeder were the only naval officers tried before the International Military Tribunal at Nuremberg. As was well documented, the Nazi regime used the Navy as an integral and essential element in waging aggressive war against its neighbors as well as against Great Britain and the United States. Indeed, the heads of the Navy were some of Hitler's closest advisors during the war. Doenitz was also responsible for one of the Nazis' most effective weapons during the war, the development of the U-boats, submarines designed with faster engines and better snorkels than in any other navy and that operated in packs in attacking military convoys and merchant fleets. Doenitz commanded the submarine division of the Nazi Navy at the outbreak of the war and played an integral part in the initiation and waging of that war.[3] But one of the central questions in the trial was whether this participation was sufficient to establish the *actus reus* element in his prosecution for the crime of waging aggressive war.

I wish to divide this question into two parts: first, what were the acts that Doenitz is accused of committing that contributed significantly to the war effort; and second, what considerations made these acts guilty ones? Doenitz's case is seemingly an easy one for the prosecution since there is little, if any, disagreement about what Doenitz did during the war. I here

---

[3] See the description of Karl Doenitz in Eugene Davidson, *The Trial of the Germans*, New York: Macmillan, 1966 [reprinted by University of Missouri Press, 1977], pp. 392–426.

confine myself to his acts of participation in the war of aggression rather than the alleged war crimes perpetrated by Admiral Doenitz.[4] Doenitz did not deny that he gave speeches regularly exhorting the men under his command to pursue the aims of war as vigilantly as they could and to do so to achieve the aims of the Third Reich. Doenitz did not deny that he had indeed sent U-boats to destroy military convoys and even merchant fleets in the Atlantic. And Doenitz did not deny that he continued to wage war long after it became clear that the war was hopeless and that Germany could not achieve its aims.[5]

There were three distinct acts that were thought to link Doenitz to the State aggression of the Nazi regime. First, the prosecution charged that Doenitz played a major role in directing the aggressive war by ordering U-boats to attack neutral ships. Second, the prosecution claimed that Doenitz acted in a way that participated in the war of aggression by accepting his appointment as commander in chief of the Navy. And third, the prosecution contended that Doenitz conspired with others to plan the aggressive war, at least after his commission as commander in chief. In all three charges, Doenitz's acts are characterized as satisfying the *actus reus* element of the crime against peace and the waging of aggressive war, and in all three charges, as we just briefly saw, Doenitz denies that his involvement constituted aggression. I will here, in this section, take up each of these charges and also give a bit more detail of Doenitz's responses to these charges. Throughout, we remain focused on *actus reus* but *mens rea* considerations will inevitably seep in.

Let us begin with the prosecution's claim that Doenitz committed guilty acts by ordering attacks on neutral ships and hence engaged in acts that directly participated in the waging of aggressive war. It was well known that using military ships to attack neutral ships was an act of war. And the prosecution claimed that Doenitz was actively engaged in "building up the U-boat arm"[6] so that "it can fight and strike."[7] There is also evidence presented that Doenitz ordered U-boats to move into proximity of England and to sink British ships and that the ships left their harbor long before war was declared. This evidence is supposedly meant to show that Doenitz was indeed directing his ships to sink British ships as part of the

---

[4] Doenitz was tried and convicted of war crimes, such as ordering German sailors not to rescue enemy sailors whose ships were sinking, and in some cases of ordering his sailors to fire on these enemy sailors in life rafts.

[5] Ibid., pp. 415–419.

[6] Vol. 4, p. 229.

[7] Ibid., p. 230.

very first stage of war against Great Britain in 1939.[8] The idea seems to be that Doenitz's forces were the very cutting edge of the first strike of the aggressive war against Great Britain, and that his commands were an essential component of that first strike.

The second charge was that Doenitz "took part in the planning and execution of aggressive war against Poland, Norway, and Denmark."[9] But what specific acts did Doenitz commit? According to the prosecution, Doenitz received an order from Admiral Raeder, then Commander in Chief of the Navy, for the invasion of Poland, the sixth copy of which was delivered to Doenitz. Doenitz is then accused of having issued an order to U-boats to carry out the general order for the invasion of Poland.[10] In addition, documents are presented to show that Doenitz sent memos to Raeder concerning the best way to invade Norway from the sea, which included flying the British flag on German U-boats until the boats had landed.[11] Here we have Doenitz seemingly actively engaged in the planning phase of the aggressive war against Norway as well as against Poland.

Third, there was a conspiracy charge that mainly concerned *mens rea* rather than *actus reus*. But there is a sense in which this charge also concerns *actus reus*, namely, that some of Doenitz's acts can be seen as sufficient participation in aggressive war to make him liable since he was aware that these acts, in conjunction with others, would constitute aggression. The chief evidence brought against Doenitz to establish the conspiracy charge was that he, along with other high-ranking members of Hitler's staff, met regularly and discussed plans to invade Poland and Norway, for instance. The prosecution contended that Doenitz not only knew about the plan to invade Norway but actually participated in that plan as well as in its execution.

Even if Doenitz was not part of the conspiracy that planned the illegal attack on Norway, it appeared that he was aware, or should have been aware, that his acts of ordering the invasion of Norway constituted a first-strike aggression against Norway. Why think that Doenitz could defend against this charge by repeating that he was just a military man following orders? He was head of the U-boat division and later head of the Navy. A person who holds such a rank appears to be not merely one of many military personnel but a military leader who should be held liable for his acts, not allowed to hide behind the orders he was given from someone slightly

[8] Ibid., p. 231.
[9] Ibid., p. 230.
[10] Ibid., p. 230.
[11] Ibid., p. 231.

higher up, even though as we will see, that person, Admiral Raeder, who was Doenitz's immediate supervisor, is convicted.

Before turning to Doenitz's defense, I wish to consider briefly the case of someone even higher in rank. At the top of the chain of military command there is someone who is giving orders, not following them. Such a person would not be able easily to offer the kind of defense we will shortly see Doenitz offer. In the case of Nazi Germany, Adolph Hitler was the person who was at the top of the chain of command. He did not follow orders but only issued them. Yet it is also true that some heads of State see themselves as taking orders from the people who put them in office. In a democracy there is a real sense that the head of State also takes orders from the people. Yet at some stage the excuse of following orders, especially at the top of the chain of command, must not be accepted. It is interesting that the Nuremberg Tribunal did accept, as we will see, Doenitz's claims that he was not the one ultimately in charge, the planner of the atrocities of the Third Reich. Future courts would do well to study Doenitz's successful defense.

II. Doenitz's Defense

Concerning the third of the prosecution's charges, Doenitz contended that he was not in on the planning of these unjustified attacks on Germany's neighbor States. Rather, as he repeated often in his own defense, he only learned about the plans after they were made. Here is his response to questions about the Norway invasion posed to him:

> Flottenrichter Krantzbuehler: I ask you, therefore, when, at what time, were you as Flag Officer of U-boats, and from 1939 as Commander of U-boats, informed about existing plans?

> Doenitz: I received information on plans from the Naval Operations Staff only after these plans had been completed; that is to say, only if I was to participate in some way in the carrying out of a plan, and then only at a time necessary for the prompt execution of my military task.

Flottenrichter Krantzbuehler, Doenitz's defense counsel, then asks specifically about a prosecution exhibit that indicates that the "Flag Officer of the U-Boats participates in a conference of the Chief of Staff of the Naval Operations Staff in Berlin" and where the "Object of the conference" was "Preparation of the occupation of Norway." Doenitz replies that "at that meeting I was instructed on the plan and my task."[12]

[12] Vol. XIII, p. 251.

The question then arises of whether Doenitz's obviously efficacious acts of participating in the war were also guilty. One simple answer is to determine objectively whether the war that he participated in was an aggressive and unlawful war and then merely to impute the guiltiness of the war to Doenitz's acts of participating in that war. The prosecution does not take this tack but instead argues that Doenitz meant for his acts to participate in the aggressive war. Doenitz responded, in part, that he did not concern himself with whether the war that Hitler was planning was an aggressive war. Consider this cross-examination of Doenitz by his defense counsel.

Flottenrichter Krantzbuehler: The prosecution has repeatedly termed the U-boat arm an aggressive weapon. What do you say to this?

Doenitz: Yes, that is correct. The U-boat has, of course, the assignment of approaching an enemy and attacking him with torpedoes. Therefore, in that respect, the U-boat is an aggressive weapon.

Flottenrichter Krantzbuehler: Do you mean to say by that that it is a weapon for an aggressive war?

Doenitz: Aggressive or defensive war is a political decision, and therefore it has nothing to do with military decisions. . . . If one should conclude that the navies which have U-boats are planning an aggressive war, then all nations – for all the navies of these nations had U-boats, in fact many had more than Germany, twice and three times as many – planned aggressive war.

Flottenrichter Krantzbuehler: In your capacity as Flag Officer of U-boats, did you yourself have anything to do with the planning of the war as such?

Doenitz: No, nothing at all. My task was to develop U-boats militarily and tactically for action, and to train my officers and men. . . . I received information on plans from the Naval Operations Staff only after these plans had been completed; that is to say, only if I was to participate in the carrying out of a plan, and then only at a time necessary for the prompt execution of my military task.

Flottenrichter Krantzbuehler: . . . did you have the opportunity to examine whether the tactical instructions you were to give to your U-boats led or were to lead to the waging of aggressive war?

Doenitz: No, I had neither the opportunity nor indeed the authority to do that. I should like to ask what soldier of what nation, who receives any military task whatsoever, has the right to approach his general staff and ask for examination or justification as to whether an aggressive war can evolve from this task.[13]

---

[13] *Trial of the Major War Criminals before the International Military Tribunal*, Nuremberg, 1948, vol. XIII, pp. 250–252.

Notice that Doenitz tries to make a firm distinction between what political leaders do, concerning the planning for war, and what military leaders do, even very high-ranking ones, concerning the tactical execution of those plans.

Doenitz presented himself, much as Adolf Eichmann did twenty years later as he stood trial in Jerusalem, as someone who simply did not question his orders despite how high-ranking he was in the German leadership. And Doenitz maintained that this was his view even when he was appointed head of the Navy on January 30, 1943.

> Flottenrichter Krantzbuehler: You know, Admiral, that the Prosecution draws very far-reaching conclusions from your acceptance of this appointment as Commander-in-Chief [of the Navy], especially with reference to the conspiracy. Were you aware of the significance of this foreign policy? Did you take this into consideration at all?

> Doenitz: The idea never entered my head. Nor do I believe that there is a soldier who, when he receives a military command, would entertain such thoughts or be conscious of such considerations. My appointment as Commander-in-Chief of the Navy represented for me an order which I of course had to obey, just as I had to obey every other military order. Unless for reasons of health I was unable to do so. Since I was in good health and believed that I could be of use to the Navy, I naturally also accepted this command with inner conviction. Anything else would have been desertion and disobedience.[14]

Doenitz remained steadfast in claiming that even as one of the most senior military leaders in Nazi Germany he did not know, and could not determine, whether he was participating in an aggressive or defensive war.

When asked whether he was a participant in planning meetings after he became head of the Navy, Doenitz also denied that he played a significant political role.

> Sir David Maxwell-Fyfe: . . . As Commander-in-Chief of the Navy you had the equivalent rank of Minister of the Third Reich; is that not so?

> Doenitz: Yes, that is correct.

> Sir David Maxwell-Fyfe: You had also the right to participate in meetings of the Reich cabinet; had any such meetings taken place?

> Doenitz: I was authorized to participate if such a meeting, or my participation in such a meeting, was ordered by the Fuehrer. That is the wording of the order. But I must say that no meeting of the Reich Cabinet took place at the time I was Commander-in-Chief from 1943 on.[15]

[14] Ibid., pp. 298–299.
[15] Ibid., p. 321.

Doenitz then explains that even though he met regularly with Hitler, fifty-seven times, those meetings were always strategic, not political.

> Doenitz: Adolph Hitler always saw in me only the first soldier of the Navy. He never asked me for advice in military matters which did not concern the Navy, either in regard to the Army or the Air Force, nor did I ever express my opinion about such matters concerning the Army or the Air Force, because basically I did not have knowledge of these matters. Of course, he never consulted me on political matters of a domestic or foreign nature.[16]

Doenitz denied that he engaged in any planning during the war, except that concerning the Navy, and only concerning tactical matters. The Court agreed with this argument and held that because Doenitz lacked the *actus reus* element of the crime of aggression he should be acquitted.

III. The Ministries Case

In the Ministries Case, the American Military Tribunal sitting in Nuremberg and operating under Control Council Law No. 10 explained its task in unmistakably clear terms:

> Our task is to determine which, if any, of the defendants, knowing there was an intent to so initiate and wage aggressive war, consciously participated in either plans, preparations, initiations of those wars, or so knowing, participated or aided in carrying them on.[17]

As is often true, the Tribunal here does not distinguish between *actus reus* and *mens rea*, but in what follows I will nonetheless try to maintain this distinction, focusing primarily on the *actus reus* of the ministers who were on trial in this case for crimes against peace.

When we shift from the previous sections where we discussed military leaders, to the case of political leaders we are far more likely to find individuals who participated in more than the tactical planning of how to carry out aggressive war. Typically, it is the political leaders who make the decision to launch a war, and it is these individuals who participate in the formation of the general plan that the military leaders are then merely told to implement. So it is here that we might expect to find a better case of those individuals who had the requisite *actus reus* of the crime of aggression and where we won't encounter the problems we found in the case of Admiral Doenitz.

[16] Ibid., p. 300.
[17] "The Ministries Case Judgment," *Trials of War Criminals before Nuremberg Military Tribunals under Control Council Law No, 10*, vol. 14, p. 337.

In this section I will set out the prosecution's charges and evidence in "The Ministries Case," and in the next section I will set out the defense. Let us begin with the case against von Weizsaecker, the first named defendant in "The Ministries Case." Ernst von Weizsaecker "was appointed Ministerial Director of the Political Division in 1937, and State Secretary in April 1938, serving in that capacity until the spring of 1943, when he was appointed German Ambassador to the Vatican. As State Secretary he was second only to Foreign Minister von Ribbentrop. All divisions of the Foreign Office were subordinate to him."[18] One could say, I believe, that von Weizsaecker was at an equivalent level within the political leadership to that held by Doenitz in the military leadership. But unlike Doenitz, von Weizsaecker appears to have been present in the meetings that planned the attacks on Germany's neighbors and not merely present for providing tactical advice. Here is a very high-ranking member of the political leadership who should provide a good test case for whether the Nuremberg precedent tells us how to prosecute leaders who are very high but not at the very top in a State's hierarchy.

The prosecution contended that von Weizsaecker met with various higher-ranking officials, sometimes in secret, from 1936 to 1938 and that during these meetings plans were drafted for the invasion of Austria. Interestingly, the Tribunal, in its Judgment, says the following about the prosecution's claims:

> These claims however do not establish guilt. The offense is the planning, preparation, and initiation of aggressive invasions. That such an invasion took place as a result of the planning, etc., is perfectly clear, but unless the defendant participated in them, he committed no offense under international law, and certainly not the one here charged.[19]

Specifically the Tribunal holds that "there is no evidence that von Weizsaecker at the time knew that Hitler intended to invade Austria." For all von Weizsaecker knew, Hitler could have been planning to achieve his aims "by means other than invasion by the German armed forces."[20] The Tribunal had similar things to say about all of the other cases of German aggression, except for the invasion of Czechoslovakia.

Concerning Czechoslovakia, the main evidence concerns statements that von Weizsaecker made to the French, British, and Czechoslovakian governments concerning the intentions of Nazi Germany as to whether

[18] Ibid., p. 340.
[19] Ibid., p. 343.
[20] Ibid.

Germany would respect the neutrality of Czechoslovakia, as it had agreed to do in the Munich Agreement. The statements seek to assure other States that Germany intended to respect Czechoslovakian neutrality, but von Weizsaecker knew that the statements he made as State secretary were in fact false. The acts of making false statements that facilitated the invasion of Czechoslovakia, even on the very day that German troops had crossed the Czechoslovakian border, were instrumental in Germany's invasion of Czechoslovakia.

Here is how the Tribunal characterizes von Weizsaecker role in the invasion of Czechoslovakia:

> He was not a mere bystander, but acted affirmatively, and himself conducted the diplomatic negotiations both with the victim and the interested powers, doing so with full knowledge of the facts. Silent disapproval is not a defense to action. While we appreciate the fact that von Weizsaecker did not originate this invasion, and that his part was not a controlling one, we find that it was real and a necessary implementation of the program.[21]

The Tribunal rules that von Weizsaecker was indeed guilty of crimes against peace concerning the invasion by Nazi Germany of Czechoslovakia.

Here is how the prosecution characterized some of the evidence in the case against von Weizsaecker concerning the preparations for the invasion of Czechoslovakia.

> At the very moment that Austria was forcibly embraced into the Reich, German diplomats were already looking eastward again, toward Czechoslovakia, a nation already marked for destruction on the German schedule of conquest. If perhaps it was Keppler who played the most important role in undermining Austrian resistance, this time it was Weizsaecker's turn. Weizsaecker was well trained and equipped for such a task: by virtue of his long experience as head of the Political Division of the German Foreign Office and of his close personal contacts with the highest ranking generals of the German Army he was in an excellent position to devise the ways and means to carry out, in the diplomatic field, the plans of the Third Reich.[22]

The prosecution then details statements that von Weizsaecker made that he must have known to be false that sought to assure the world that Germany would not invade Czechoslovakia.

In addition, the prosecution claimed that von Weizsaecker was instrumental in convincing Czechoslovakia that Germany intended to

---

[21] Ibid., p. 354.

[22] "The Ministries Case Judgment," *Trials of War Criminals before Nuremberg Military Tribunals under Control Council Law No. 10*, vol. 12, p. 152.

respect its neutrality as Germany had promised to do in the Munich Agreement.

> The assurances which Germany had given to Czechoslovakia at the time of the Anschluss of Austria gave way in a very few weeks to a different tone: as von Weizsaecker put it in a conversation with the Czechoslovakian Minister in Berlin on 2 April 1938 (*NG-3020, Pros. Ex. 61*), "If his country would take the necessary steps in favor of the Sudeten Germans, they would not have to worry about German-Czech relations." Even this assurance was a hypocritical falsehood. At this very time, von Weizsaecker and Woermann were increasing German subsidies to Henlein's Sudeten German party, and von Weizsaecker well knew that... Germany was prepared to use the threat of war, and, if necessary, war itself to gain her ends.... In this very same month of April 1938, in a top secret message to German diplomatic representatives abroad, von Weizsaecker informed them that Germany was making good progress in her mobilization, and that German diplomats should begin to organize their local affairs to meet a serious situation.[23]

The prosecution's case was surely the strongest concerning Germany's aggression against Czechoslovakia, compared to the other countries that were at war with Germany, and the Tribunal recognized this as it convicted von Weizsaecker for this instance of crimes against peace.

IV. Political Ministers and Waging War

In general, von Weizsaecker's main line of defense consisted in trying to show that he was opposed to, not in favor of, Germany's aggression against its neighbors and that he actively worked to thwart those in the Nazi government who wanted to advance these aggressive wars. One of the most interesting pieces of evidence comes from Lord Halifax, British Secretary of State for Foreign Affairs from 1938 to 1940.

> Baron von Weizsaecker... was frequently reported to me by my advisors at the Foreign Office... as being a convinced opponent of Nazi ideals and policies, and as using his official position in the Ministry of Foreign Affairs in Berlin to hinder, so far as lay in his power, the execution of the policy pursued by Herr Ribbentrop.[24]

There were several other prominent diplomats who also testified to the same effect, including Pope Pius XII, as well as a prominent Vatican official who spoke of von Weizsaecker as a deeply religious man who saw

[23] Ibid., p. 153.
[24] Ibid., p. 911.

himself as having little control over the absence of reason and order in his country.[25]

In his own defense, von Weizsaecker testified at length during his trial. He testified that he foresaw that the Treaty of Versailles that ended the First World War would only sow the seeds for the next war in Europe, and that he nonetheless had high hopes that the League of Nations would provide a place for Germany to interact with its European neighbors in the creation of a lasting peace, although he felt that without disarmament the League was not only likely to fail but was dangerous.[26] He described a split that arose between those like himself in the Foreign Office who favored peaceful diplomacy and those in the Nazi Party who favored the use of war to advance Germany's interests.[27] When von Weizsaecker joined the Foreign Office in 1936 he recalled that Hitler already referred to the diplomats in that office as "a club of defeatists."[28]

> Under normal circumstances an opinion is formed by the expert and is passed on up to the levels for decision. Instead of this, orders came to us out of the clear blue sky, from top to bottom as an accomplished fact. Our Foreign Service had sunk to the level of a technical apparatus. It was really only a façade, the façade of a firm which had undergone considerable internal rearrangements. There has sometimes been mention of the alleged omnipotence of our office. That was quite out of the question; it was quite the contrary.[29]

He thus claimed that his position was considerably weaker than the prosecution had claimed.

Von Weizsaecker thus tried to do two things in his general defense: first to establish that he did not have much if any input into the war plans of Germany, and second to suggest that what little role he did have he tried to use to stop Hitler from pursuing his aggressive aims. In this way, he tried to undercut the idea that he had played a major role in planning Germany's wars of aggression. Indeed, von Weizsaecker testified that he was not himself a Party member and that in his role as State Secretary he did not even have the right to attend cabinet meetings.[30] So, in general, von Weizsaecker denied that he acted affirmatively to advance the war effort, contrary to the prosecution's claims. Indeed, von Weizsaecker claimed,

[25] Ibid., p. 913.
[26] Ibid., pp. 915–916.
[27] Ibid., p. 918.
[28] Ibid., p. 920.
[29] Ibid.
[30] Ibid., p. 922.

and offered independent testimony to prove, that he was part of what he called "the resistance" to Hitler's plans.

The Tribunal recognized that von Weizsaecker had a history of disagreeing with the aggressive efforts of other officials in the Third Reich, but the Tribunal was not convinced that this was also true of his participation in the invasion of Czechoslovakia. Von Weizsaecker tried to defend himself about his role in this affair. In particular he claimed that

> I tried as hard as I could to learn as much as I could about what Hitler wanted and planned. However Hitler was really talented in camouflaging his real intentions. In the case of the Sudeten territory, he gave his instructions directly to a certain Henlein, a leader of the Sudeten-Germans. . . . Whether in the spring of 1938 Hitler already thought of expanding the German territory at the expense of Czechoslovakia, I don't know for certain even today.[31]

Because he didn't know what Hitler's intentions were and had no reason to think that Hitler was lying when he told von Neurath and others that he had no such expansionist intentions, von Weizsaecker says he felt he could give assurances that Germany was not planning to invade Czechoslovakia. In this way he tried to rebut the claim that he lied to try to deceive other State representatives about Germany's true intentions in dealing with its neighbors. Concerning the question of whether von Weizsaecker lied about troop movements right before and even during the invasion of Czechoslovakia, he said that he "secured information" that led him to think there was no invasion being planned and that is why he gave the assurances to Czech officials and others.[32]

Unfortunately for his defense, von Weizsaecker also admitted that he had serious worries that Germany would provoke a war with Czechoslovakia and when asked when he first learned about the planning of such a war, he says he does not remember.[33] And von Weizsaecker admits that he was present when Hitler planned the invasion, but he said he only performed "the role of a stagehand" during those discussions. He said he was ultimately asked to leave the meeting when the concrete planning and execution of the plan were discussed.[34] And when pressed by the prosecution in cross-examination about his exact role, von Weizsaecker

[31] Ibid., p. 926.
[32] Ibid., p. 927.
[33] Ibid., p. 930–931.
[34] Ibid., p. 932.

claimed a lack of memory; yet, during direct examination he had a nearly flawless memory.[35]

Ultimately, the Tribunal acquitted von Weizsaecker of all of the charges of crimes against peace except for that concerning Czechoslovakia. To restate part of the Tribunal's judgment: "Silent disapproval is not a defense to action. While we appreciate the fact that von Weizsaecker did not originate this invasion, and that his part was not a controlling one, we find that it was real and a necessary implementation of the program."[36] According to the Tribunal, the evidence proved that von Weizsaecker negotiated with various parties while realizing that diplomacy was only a smokescreen for the final preparations for war. These actions were sufficiently part of the initiation of an aggressive war as to make von Weizsaecker guilty. The Tribunal thus rejected von Weizsaecker's claim that he was merely a bystander to the crime of aggression concerning Czechoslovakia.

So we can learn two things from this case. First, leaders at the level of von Weizsaecker will be hard to convict, although not impossible. He was exonerated concerning his role in all other wars of aggression except for Czechoslovakia. And in the case of Czechoslovakia, he was convicted only because his acts were said to have played a necessary role in the implementation of the plan. Second, to convict even high-ranking political leaders, one needs to prove that they were not only present at planning meetings but that they played an active role in either the development or implementation of the plan. For the *actus reus* element of the crime of aggression, the precise role played will matter quite a bit and will be difficult to establish.

V. Roles and *Actus Reus*

In this section, I wish to raise the question of how one's role in the government or military affects one's guilt in terms of how we regard one's actions in a larger plan of initiating and waging aggressive war. In the cases of both Doenitz and von Weizsaecker, this was a crucial consideration and may form a lasting legacy, if not a "precedent," for future international prosecutions of the crime of aggression. As a first approximation, it seems clear that a person's role should affect how we regard that person's actions. Roles are "circumstances" in the sense to be

[35] See the text and note at ibid., p. 960.
[36] Vol. 14, p. 354.

discussed in Chapter 11, and as such they certainly will make a difference in how we regard someone's acts. And one of the central questions is how roles affect the *actus reus* element in criminal prosecutions for the crime of aggression.

If a person has the role of head of State, it will seemingly be much easier to show that this person played an important role in the planning and waging of a war of State aggression since this person's role was to be at the head of the State. Normally, anything that occurs that can be attributed to the State can more easily be attributed to the head of the State than to any other individual person. But this is not to say that everything the State does will allow us to find an *actus reus* of the head of State, only that it is easiest to do so with this person than anyone else in the State's political or military hierarchy. If we are looking for the ultimate act that sent a State into an aggressive war, we can do no better than look at the acts of the head of State immediately before that war began. Again, this is not to say that we will find "a smoking gun" in every case. Instead we may only find that the head of State didn't do anything to stop the war from starting. But even that act of omission, on the part of a head of State, will often be an *actus reus* in the crime of aggression as well.

In this chapter, I have not been considering heads of State but rather members of the military and political hierarchy who are very high ranking but not at the top. The reason for doing this is to begin to test the limits of the claim announced by the prosecutor's office that only State leaders will be prosecuted by the ICC. The question is whether it is feasible to prosecute leaders who are not actually the head of State in terms of establishing the *actus reus* element. And what is crucial is whether any of these high-ranking but not highest-ranking leaders played roles that were important in the waging of aggressive war. Here is the problem: in some respects it seems that the acts of the head of State made him guilty since only the head of State could declare war or issue the ultimate command to begin war, and all other acts were subsidiary to this act; or counter-intuitively, it seems that all of the acts of those who in some way facilitated the war effort are guilty acts. What we need is a middle ground – a principle that will allow us to determine when, if ever, non-heads of State can be said to have met the *actus reus* element of the crime of aggression.

This is where roles matter. If a person is commander in chief of the Navy or head of the State Department or Foreign Office, that person may very well be playing a role so similar to the head of State that conviction will be easier than otherwise. It is for this reason that the two cases we have examined in the current chapter are so interesting. Doenitz was head of the Navy and von Weizsaecker was head of the Foreign Office. Concerning the charge that they engaged in guilty acts in the crime of aggression, both Doenitz and von Weizsaecker said that they were either bystanders or mere technical facilitators of the war. Such claims of defense are more commonly found among those who are not so high ranking, but if it is true for these high-ranking officials, it should have the same efficacy for lower-ranking members too.

Let us consider the roles played by the two people discussed in this chapter. Doenitz said that even though he was head of the Navy, he was only consulted concerning the tactical considerations in the invasion of Norway and attacks against British shipping that drew Britain into war. Von Weizsaecker claimed that he tried to dissuade Hitler from waging war against Czechoslovakia and that when that failed he was only a bystander to the planning of that aggressive war. Normally the head of the Navy of a given State would be one of the chief people consulted by a head of State in planning for war. And the head of the Foreign Office would be similarly a crucial player, due to his or her role as head of the Foreign Service and as privy to information gleaned from the members of that service about foreign affairs. Yet, even though the people who often occupy these roles do play important roles in waging war, these particular people did not, or so they claimed, play such a part. In their view, the war was the responsibility of Adolph Hitler, either acting completely on his own, or acting in concert with only his closest advisors.

I wish now to return to the quotation by which I began this chapter. The American Military Tribunal sitting in Nuremberg in the Ministries Case, which had von Weizsaecker as one of its defendants, urged that we not convict individuals for crimes of aggression if they did not know that their government was waging an aggressive war. And the Court said it would be unjust to demand that defendants instigate an independent investigation to establish whether its government was acting illegally or issuing illegal orders to wage war. The cases we have been examining raise a related question about whether someone who is quite high up in the State hierarchy can say that he or she did not know that the acts in question were contributing to an aggressive war. Yet the leaders of a State normally have much greater knowledge than those lower down in the hierarchy, and it is much easier for them, often, to get information about the lawfulness of the State's practices. Of course, once again this raises questions of *mens rea* as well as *actus reus*. Keeping to *actus reus* for just several more pages before turning to *mens rea* in the next chapter, let me inquire about how the role played in the government might affect the

ability to say that one did not know that his or her act was contributing to
an aggressive war. Initially, it would seem obvious that if one held a role of
leadership that was quite high ranking, then this would normally block a
persons's ability to claim that he or she simply didn't know whether what
he or she was being asked to do was illegal. But the tribunals sitting at
Nuremberg seem to deny that this is the correct view to take, even for
very high-ranking leaders.

For an act to be guilty it must be unlawful. Was Admiral Doenitz's act
of ordering his U-boats into combat an unlawful act? Objectively it surely
was. But was it unlawful for him to order the boats in the first place? And
here is where the role comes into play. Doenitz was surely authorized and
even required to send his U-boats into combat if he had himself been
ordered to do so. So, the lawfulness of his issuing these orders turns itself
on the lawfulness of the orders issued to him. If he were a normal sailor,
we would not suppose him to know whether the order was lawful or not.
But as the head of the U-boat division of the Navy normally he would be
expected to have this knowledge. Yet surely, as Doenitz himself implies,
this is a rebuttable presumption. As indicated by the opening quotation
from the Ministries case, the Tribunal rejected the objective theory and
said that subjective knowledge of unlawfulness must be proved.[37] In my
view, this is one of the most important "Nuremberg precedents."

In the Ministries Case, the American Military Tribunal sitting in Nuremberg decided that evidence had to establish that von Weizsaecker knew
that Hitler was about to wage aggressive war against his neighbors – such
knowledge could not be merely assumed based on von Weizsaecker's position in the government. In the Doenitz case, the International Military
Tribunal likewise set a similar standard concerning whether Doenitz's act
of ordering ships and sailors into Norway's harbor was unlawful or merely
the exercise of his duty. In both cases, a very high bar was set for the prosecution concerning these high-ranking, although not the highest-ranking,
leaders of the Third Reich. One can challenge whether in these two cases
the leaders had the requisite knowledge or not. But the character of their
acts, whether or not those acts met the *actus reus* element of the crime
of aggression, was not merely judged against an objective standard of
unlawfulness.

I agree with this result. Fairness to these defendants dictates just this
result so that they are not held guilty merely by associating with leaders who do clearly plan and initiate aggressive war. I disagree with the

---

[37] Vol. 14, p. 336–337.

Ministries Case judgment, though, in that if high-ranking leaders intentionally shielded themselves from knowledge that the war they participated in was aggressive, prosecutors should be able to use a negligence standard to convict them. It is not enough for these leaders to say that they did not know, but rather that it was very difficult for them to find out. I agree that leaders should not be expected to undertake what the Tribunal calls "an independent investigation," for it certainly could be very dangerous to do so. But if these leaders have suspicions, they should not blind themselves to facts that would confirm their suspicions.

Purely objective standards of knowledge, in highly complex organizations such as States, can become merely a smokescreen for strict liability. This can sometimes be true of negligence standards as well. What one is assumed to know because of one's role, or what we think that one should have known, are often very hard to distinguish. I have written extensively about this problem elsewhere.[38] But there are obvious cases nonetheless. I do not think that Doenitz or Weizsaecker are obvious cases of high-ranking leaders who intentionally blinded themselves to the aggressiveness of the war they participated in. And hence it seems to me that we should indeed follow the Tribunals in not merely assuming that they had this knowledge, despite their high-ranking roles in the government.

VI. A Successful Prosecution: Admiral Raeder

I wish to end this chapter by looking briefly at a successful prosecution for the crime of aggression at Nuremberg: Admiral Erich Raeder, commander in chief of the German Navy prior to Admiral Doenitz, who was Doenitz's immediate superior for most of the war and the person mainly responsible for the invasion of Norway. Here is how Charles Dubost, France's Deputy Chief Prosecutor, summarizes the case against Raeder.

> Raeder was Commander-in-Chief of the German Navy before Doenitz. He was present at the conference at which Hitler revealed his plans, notes of which were taken at the time. He put the Navy at the service of the Nazi regime. He conducted clandestine rearmament activities and contributed to the preparation of aggression against Poland and Norway. His contempt for international law is well known.[39]

[38] See Larry May, *The Morality of Groups*, Notre Dame, IN: University of Notre Dame Press, 1987.

[39] *Trial of the Major War Criminals before the International Military Tribunal*, Nuremberg, 1948, vol. 19, p. 554.

Virtually the same charges were made against Doenitz, yet as we saw he was largely exonerated of the aggression crimes. Yet Raeder is convicted of the crime of aggression and sentenced to life imprisonment, whereas Doenitz gets only ten years' imprisonment.

One of the differences between Doenitz and Raeder is that Raeder was proven to be at the central meeting where Hitler laid out his plans to invade Norway – and the only other person present was Goering. Raeder also had been one of the very few ministers who were present when Goering and Hitler met to prepare their attack orders.[40] Doenitz was only proven to be present at much larger meetings. So when Doenitz claimed that he did not play a major role in the planning for aggressive war, he had a much easier time of it than did Raeder, who also tried to prove that he was only giving tactical advice, but apparently failed to be persuasive. The question to ask Raeder is why he did not try harder to find out more, given that he had much greater access to such knowledge than did Doenitz.

As with Doenitz, Raeder claimed that he was merely a soldier who was following orders. At the end of his summation, Dr. Walter Siemers, Raeder's defense counsel, said:

> Hitler...exercised an immense influence.... Accordingly, only the question remains: Is it ever a soldier's duty to revolt – to resort to open mutiny? This question will be denied by every commander all over the world and likewise by every other person with a sole exception, namely, if it concerns a dictator commanding the commission of a crime, the criminality of which is recognized by the commander himself. Accordingly, Raeder could be made responsible for a military crime only, but not a political one, because for the political crime the dictator himself must answer.... It must not be allowed to happen, that as a result of the deeds of a Hitler and his National Socialism, the officers and soldiers of this Navy be defamed by hearing their highest-ranking officer declared a criminal. From a historical viewpoint Raeder may be guilty, because he like many others within the country and abroad, did not recognize or see through Hitler and did not have the strength to resist the dynamic strength of a Hitler; but such is an omission not a crime. What Rader did or left undone in his life occurred in the belief that he was acting correctly and that as a dutiful soldier he had to act that way.[41]

[40] See the very interesting discussion of the differences between the Raeder and Doenitz cases in Bradley F. Smith, *Reaching Judgment at Nuremberg*, New York: Basic Books, 1977, pp. 241–242.

[41] *Trial of the Major War Criminals before the International Military Tribunal*, Nuremberg, 1948, vol. 18, p. 429–430.

The defense was very similar to that provided on behalf of Admiral Doenitz and von Weizsaecker. In the next few pages I will say a bit more about why such different results were achieved.

As I indicated, one of the most important differences between these cases was that Raeder was involved in very small, high-level meetings with Hitler where, apparently, major plans were made about the initiating of aggressive war against Germany's neighbors, whereas Doenitz was present only at rather large meetings where plans that had already been made were discussed. It is thus not difficult to infer that Raeder played a larger role than did Doenitz in the planning of aggressive war. On the other hand, Doenitz appears to have been much more of a supporter of Nazism than was Raeder. Nonetheless, on the specific question of what role each played, it was apparently quite important that Raeder was present at these very small meetings where planning of aggression took place and where Raeder either knew or could have known that it was aggression that was being planned.

Another interesting contrast is between Raeder and von Weizsaecker in terms of whether and to what extent they disagreed with Hitler or tried to stop him. As I indicated above, there was ample evidence that von Weizsaecker publicly expressed his disagreements with Hitler and with Nazism. In Raeder's case, his few disagreements with Hitler seem to have concerned the role of the Navy in the armed forces of Germany and occasionally matters of tactics, but not about the general direction of the wars of aggression, except for the case of invading the Soviet Union.[42] And even in this latter case, Raeder appears to have opposed Hitler also on general tactical grounds, worrying that such an invasion would expose German forces on too many fronts.

Raeder, Doenitz, and von Weizsaecker all held prominent roles in the Third Reich and all were at the equivalent rank of Cabinet Minister in Hitler's government. That Doenitz and von Weizsaecker were largely acquitted of the charges of aggression, and Raeder was convicted, means that one of the Nuremberg "precedents" is that fine-grained determinations will be made about whom to convict even among very high-ranking political and military leaders. Merely being a high-ranking leader who participated in the waging of aggressive war is not sufficient for conviction. In addition, one had to play a clear role in planning the aggression and not

---

[42] On this issue, see Eugene Davidson, *The Trial of the Germans*, Columbia: University of Missouri Press, 1966, pp. 371–374.

to have voiced at least public objections to the wars of aggression. This is a rather difficult standard to meet, but I support this approach. Aggression should be an international crime that can be successfully prosecuted against such leaders but not merely for passive participation. There must be more than lip service paid to traditional *mens rea* elements as well as the *actus reus* elements we have been investigating in this chapter.

An additional final point of comparison concerns the conspiracy charge, the proof of which sometimes seems to rely on mere participation and not on intention. Here is where I might disagree with the verdict against Raeder. It is not at all clear that he participated in a conspiracy just because he was present at very small meetings where aggression was planned. Yet the Tribunal seems to be properly attuned to what Raeder knew or could have known. I find it very hard, therefore, to understand why the same tribunals looked favorably on the conspiracy theory that the prosecution mounted at Nuremberg. Much more attention is needed to proving the actual mental states of the defendant than is normally called for when the substantive crime of conspiracy is charged. It is to an examination of that topic, along with the *mens rea* of civilians who collaborated with the war effort, to which we next turn.

9

Prosecuting Civilians for Complicity

The Krupp and I. G. Farben Cases

In this chapter I will examine the fascinating cases of those civilian leaders of companies that played such a large role in the war effort in Nazi
Germany: the Krupp works and the I. G. Farben works. I will use these
cases as a lens through which I examine the *mens rea* element of the crime
of aggression. And I will be especially interested in how to characterize
the idea of planning to wage a war of aggression. Both Krupp and I.
G. Farben were weapons manufacturers who may have lobbied for the
war but who were not directly involved in its planning. We will have reason to wonder about the idea of complicity in the crime of aggression.
In this respect, the opinion of Judge Paul M. Hebert will be crucial for
establishing a possible Nuremberg "precedent" in this domain.

In a war of aggression it is often true that all aspects of the society
contributed to the war effort. The question before us is whether civilian
leaders of major companies that supplied armaments and vital economic
products to the Army and Navy are to be seen as complicit in the waging
of aggressive war. In one sense, this is clear-cut – as a matter of causation,
the war effort, at least at the scale conducted by Nazi Germany, could
not have been undertaken without major industrial help. But in another
sense, there is the simple point that the Army and Navy were simply the
buyers and the munitions and chemical companies merely the sellers. Is
a company guilty of a crime when it sells material to those who actively
commit the crime? Are the members of these companies any less guilty
than the soldiers who are unwillingly drafted to serve as cannon fodder
for aggressive wars?

At the end of this chapter, I will turn to the question concerning what
standard of *mens rea* should be required if we are going to use a conspiracy
theory. I will also mount a major criticism of the use of the conspiracy

theory generally in criminal law, and especially in international criminal law. While it might make sense to argue that those who are complicit as well as those who actually conspire to wage aggressive war are morally responsible, it normally does not make sense to hold them criminally liable. Collective liability schemes make sense at the moral level but have a much more restricted use at the level of legal liability.

In this chapter, I will first set out the main facts in two of the chief cases that concerned the role of civilians in the war effort in Nazi Germany. In the first section, I will describe the case against Alfried Krupp, the head of the largest weapons manufacturer in Germany as well as the defense that he mounted against crimes against peace. In the second section, I will then present the case against I. G. Farben, the largest industrial corporation in Europe, especially its board chairman, Karl Krauch, and also his defense to the charges against him. Both companies supported the Nazi Party nearly from its beginnings. In the third section, I then turn to the proof advanced to show that Krupp and Krauch had the requisite *mens rea* for conspiracy to commit the crime of aggression, looking especially at the concurring opinion by Judge Hebert. In the fourth section, I discuss the use of the conspiracy theory to try to convict these defendants and why in the end that effort failed, drawing some lessons from that failure for the increasing use of the similar theory of joint criminal enterprise liability in international criminal law today. I end this chapter with some reflections on the difference between moral and legal liability, especially during wartime.

I. The Case against Krupp

I begin with the case against Alfried Krupp, who was prosecuted by the American Military Tribunal operating under Control Council Law No. 10 at Nuremberg. The case against Alfried Krupp and other members of the Krupp family munitions works for crimes against peace rested on the fact that Krupp had continued to manufacture armaments for Germany after the First World War, in violation of the treaty of Versailles. These weapons were crucial for sustaining Nazi Germany's various wars against its neighbors in the 1930s and 1940s. The prosecution brought forward a large number of documents to show that the Krupp Works contributed significantly to these aggressive wars and that it was rewarded in various ways for this contribution, thereby marking the Krupp Works as clearly a part of the Nazi war effort. In addition, the Krupp family and its business gave large sums of money to the Nazi Party in its fledgling years, allegedly making it possible for Hitler eventually to establish a dictatorship.

The prosecution's case turned on the idea that Krupp was aware of the central role played by the armaments it supplied for the war effort and that the leaders of the company were aware that the rearmament of Germany was contrary to international law. Here is how the prosecution characterized its case against Krupp for crimes against peace:

> From the First World War, the Krupp firm has conspired against the peace of Europe. Like the Nazi Party it has nurtured at all times the idea that Germany would rise to power through its military might. In 1933 it entered into an alliance with that Party for the realization of their common objectives. Its activities both before and after this alliance, contributed materially to Germany's ability to wage its wars of aggression. As new people came into positions of control in Krupp they continued the conspiracy which, starting in 1919, lasted at least until the defeat of Germany.[1]

Here we find two charges: that Krupp participated in the waging of aggressive war, and that Krupp participated in a conspiracy to wage aggressive war. I will take up the prosecution's case and the defense of each of these charges in what follows in this section.

The charge of participating in an aggressive war is grounded in two claims: first, that the Krupp Works supplied arms to the German government in violation of the Versailles Treaty; and second, that the Krupp works played an indispensable part in the ability of Germany to wage aggressive war against its neighbor States. The prosecution believed that the first claim was obvious if one looked at the Versailles Treaty and then observed how the Krupp Works operated after 1919. The second seemed obvious as well – the Krupp Works supplied the overwhelming majority of the arms that the German Army and Navy used to wage its various aggressive wars in the late 1930s and early 1940s. The prosecution claimed that the acts of the Krupp company and its officers, which constituted either preparation for or waging war, "is proved by their own acts and statements," and that their aims "were identical with Hitler's own."[2]

The American Military Tribunal, though, was highly skeptical, apparently from the beginning of the trial, about whether these claims by the prosecutor met the burden of showing that Krupp committed a *crime* against peace. The most significant question for the Tribunal was whether

---

[1] "The Krupp Case," *Trials of War Criminals before Nuremberg Military Tribunals under Control Council Law No. 10*, vol. 9, p. 369.
[2] Ibid., pp. 383–384.

Krupp contributed to the breaking of the Versailles Treaty and also to the waging of aggressive war. Here is a discussion of the issue between one of the judges and the prosecutor.

> Judge Anderson: Assuming that – without deciding or intimating a decision – the rearmament was actually in violation of the Versailles Treaty, unless it be further shown that it was for the purpose of waging not merely war but aggressive war, would that be a crime under international law?
>
> Mr. Kaufman: . . . Being a violation of an international treaty, it is a violation of international law.
>
> Judge Anderson: Yes, but is it a crime?
>
> Mr. Kaufman: As to whether or not it is a crime, that has to be answered as best we can, by the holding of the IMT that a violation of a treaty can be a crime even though not specified as a crime in the treaty.[3]

When the Tribunal eventually acquits Krupp on this charge it is because it finds no evidence that Krupp aimed at planning or participating in aggressive war just because Krupp aided in the rearmament of Germany, itself a violation of international law.

The prosecution had tried to save its case against Krupp by arguing that it was not merely the manufacture of weapons that made Krupp guilty of crimes against peace. In a telling analogy the prosecution argued as follows:

> It is an innocent and respectable tradition to be a locksmith; but it is nonetheless a crime, if the locksmith turns his talents to picking the locks of neighbors and looting their homes. The accusation in all of these cases where crimes against peace are charged is that in performing the functions of diplomats, politicians, soldiers, industrialists, or whatever the defendants happen to be, they prepared and waged wars of aggression. It is no defense for those who committed such crimes to plead that they practice a particular profession.[4]

As the prosecution recognized, the key to establishing their case was to show that the defendants manifested criminal intent, *mens rea*, just as it was key to the prosecution of the locksmith that he used his talents with the aim of stealing from his neighbors.

The prosecution sought to prove three things that would each establish Krupp's *mens rea*. First, the prosecution sought to prove that the "defendants intended, without regard to and without exact knowledge of Hitler's plans, that military power be used for the aggrandizement of Germany or

[3] Ibid., p. 355.
[4] Ibid., p. 376.

be used in violation of treaties." But the prosecution also alleged that "it is not necessary to show that defendants believed or intended that employment of Germany's military power would result in actual conflict. . . . If the military power of Germany was so overwhelming as to make resistance futile, there would be no war."[5] And the prosecution alleged that it did not have to prove that the defendants had as their aim that Germany would use its military might against a particular country either.[6] The prosecution then tried to prove that Krupp had the intent to break the Treaty of Versailles and to establish a "Greater Germany."[7]

The second part of the prosecution case alleged that Krupp participated in a conspiracy with other actors in German society to wage aggressive war. And by this conspiracy theory the prosecution sought to link the intent of Hitler to Krupp via the idea of "vicarious intent."[8] For vicarious intent to be imputed, all that was needed was to show that Krupp was part of a larger group that operated together and then to show what the shared intent of the group was. Hitler had an intent to wage aggressive war and Krupp, as a member of the conspiracy that Hitler was also a part of, was attributed whatever intent Hitler had. Here we can see how the use of a conspiracy theory weakens the normal conditions for *mens rea* in a criminal case. Vicarious intent is a significant weakening of what is normally thought of as criminal intent, as I will later argue.

Third, the prosecution claimed that mere knowledge of the existence of a crime in which Krupp was participating was enough to constitute intent on the part of Krupp. This is another widely disputed theory, namely, that knowledge that one is participating in a criminal endeavor is enough to ground *mens rea*. The IMT had soundly rejected that theory and it is rejected today in the ICC as well, as I will discuss in Chapter 12. The ICC requires both knowledge and intent; mere knowledge is not sufficient. The prosecution alleged that participation plus knowledge was nonetheless sufficient in the Krupp case. So this constituted the third part of the intent argument advanced by the prosecution, where it was said that any one of these theories could prove Krupp's criminal intent in the crime of aggression.

That the Tribunal rejected all three claims is as significant as nearly all of the other lasting "precedents" of Nuremberg. Here is the summary of

---

[5] Ibid., p. 382.
[6] Ibid., p. 383.
[7] Ibid., p. 384.
[8] Ibid., p. 382.

the ruling by the Tribunal, which occurred before the defense presented
any of its evidence.

> The prosecution has the burden of proving that these specific invasions and
> wars of aggression were the ones in connection with which the defendants
> either conspired ... or in which they participated. We concluded that the
> prosecution failed to prove any of the defendants guilty.[9]

The Tribunal did not accept the theory of the prosecution that a link
between the defendant's actions and the specific wars of aggression was
unnecessary for conviction.

The concurring opinion of Judge Anderson suggests that the "precedent" of this case may be even more in support of defendants than one
might have thought, especially concerning the conspiracy charge. Anderson says:

A conspiracy must meet at least three requirements:

1. There must be a concrete plan participated in by two or more per-
    sons
2. The plan must not only have a criminal purpose but that purpose
    must be clearly outlined
3. The plan must not be too far removed from the time of the decision
    and of action[10]

Anderson says that the prosecution failed to show that there was "a concrete plan to wage aggressive war clearly outlined in its criminal purpose." Instead, the prosecution only proved that in 1919 Krupp and others entered into a conspiracy to violate the Versailles Treaty by

> aiding the rearmament of Germany *if and when some future government
> embarked upon a rearmament program in support of a national policy of aggran-
> dizement.*[11]

Such a conspiracy is too distant from the actual waging of aggressive
war in 1930s Germany and hence does not link the defendant with the
contemporary wars of aggression that are the subject of these trials at
Nuremberg.

And concerning the non-conspiracy–based charge of participating in
the waging of aggressive war, Judge Anderson helpfully cites an authority,
Professor Quincy Wright, whose views he says are uncontroversial. What
the prosecution must show, but did not show, is the following:

[9] Ibid., p. 400.
[10] Ibid., p. 411.
[11] Ibid., p. 412, italics in original.

> The planning, preparation, initiation, and waging *must be related to an actual or concretely planned war which the individual believes has been or is about to be initiated for aggressive purposes.*[12]

This is the nail that seals the coffin against the prosecution case, since as we saw the prosecution maintained that Krupp did not participate in the planning of any specific aggressive war.

II. The Case against I. G. Farben

In the I. G. Farben case, another Control Council Law No. 10 case at Nuremberg, we have a more detailed treatment of the main conceptual issues in the Krupp case, especially concerning how to treat the conspiracy charge. According to the initial charges filed in the indictment against the leaders of I. G. Farben:

> All of the defendants, acting through the instrumentality of Farben and otherwise, with divers other persons, during a period of years preceding 8 May 1945, participated in the planning, preparation, initiation, and waging of wars of aggression and invasions of other countries, which wars of aggression and invasions were also in violation of international laws and treaties. All of the defendants held high positions in the financial, industrial, and economic life of Germany and committed these crimes . . . in that they were principals in, accessories to, ordered, abetted, took a consenting part in, were connected with plans and enterprises involving, and were members of organizations or groups, including Farben, which were connected with the commission of said offenses.[13]

The Statement of the Offense ends by declaring that the "life and happiness of all peoples of the world were adversely affected as the result of the invasions and wars of aggression."[14]

I will focus on the case against the main defendant in this case, Karl Krauch, chairman of the Supervisory Board of Directors of I. G. Farben. One of the central claims against Krauch is that under his direction the Nazi government formed very close ties with I. G. Farben, a giant German company involved in chemical production, synthetic fuels, and armaments. There were even closer ties forged between Krauch personally and the government.

> The defendant Krauch was appointed Chief of the Department for Research and Development in the [government's] Office of the Four Year Plan, the department responsible for preparing plans to make Germany self-sufficient

[12] Ibid., p. 427, emphasis supplied by Judge Anderson.
[13] *Trials of War Criminals before the Nuremberg Military Tribunals*, vol. 7, p. 14.
[14] Ibid., p. 15.

for war. Krauch participated in numerous conferences devoted to military planning at which Goering and other high officials of the third Reich were present. These meetings related to all phases of military mobilization and were not limited to the chemical field.[15]

Krauch effectively became both one of leaders at Farben and also at the government. This link was crucial for arguing that I. G. Farben in general, and Krauch in particular, merged with the German government, seeing their own success intimately tied to the success of the government in waging war against its neighbors.

One of the best pieces of evidence was that Krauch and Goering "worked out the so-called 'Karinhall Plan,' also called the 'Krauch Plan,'" which contained a new program for producing chemical warfare agents (poison gas), explosives, rubber, and gasoline." Krauch was rewarded by being made head of the government's Office of Economic Development. Indeed, Krauch "prepared special mobilization plans for the chemical industry, including an allocation and priority system for labor and building materials."[16]

Like Krupp, I. G. Farben played an essential role in providing material for the German war machine. Unlike Krupp, I. G. Farben executives like Krauch were incorporated into the German government, even as they still held positions in the industrial conglomerate. Indeed, Farben's "role in the government as a whole was so well known that Farben was considered by Albert Speer to have been 'promoted to governmental status' and was frequently referred to as 'the State within the State.'"[17]

It is largely unchallenged that Farben's testing and production of light metals, synthetic gasoline, and synthetic rubber as well as the secret production of poison gas made it possible for Germany to carry out its aggressive war effort earlier and for a longer period of time than would otherwise have been possible.

As in the Krupp case, the prosecution also charged Farben with being part of a larger common plan or conspiracy to commit crimes against peace. The job of linking Farben to that conspiracy was made considerably easier than in the Krupp case because Farben executives also held important positions in the German government. But as we will see, the stumbling block continued to be the problem of *mens rea*. There were also problems about *actus reus*, and these were not solved by the conspiracy

[15] Ibid., p. 23.
[16] Ibid., pp. 23–24.
[17] Ibid., p. 25.

theory. At the very outset of this trial, the defense counsel made this clear when it complained that the prosecution's "documents contain nothing about the participation of individual defendants."[18]

Some of the most damning evidence aimed at establishing Krauch's *mens rea* concerns a "work report" he wrote to Goering in his capacity as head of a committee addressing "Special Questions of Chemical Production":

> It is essential for Germany to strengthen its war potential as well as that of her allies to such an extent that the coalition is equal to the efforts of practically the rest of the world. This can be achieved only ... by expanding (and improving), peaceably at first, the greater economic domain corresponding to the raw material basis of the coalition.... If action does not follow upon these thoughts with the greatest possible speed, all sacrifices of blood in the next war will not spare us the bitter end which once before we have brought upon ourselves owing to lack of foresight and fixed purpose.[19]

This statement is set out to show that Krauch had the same intent, as did the top leaders of the German government. It is also meant to show that Krauch saw the German war effort as directly supporting his own company's profits.

But notice that Krauch does not necessarily call for aggressive war, but countenances the possibility that Germany's aims, as well as Farben's, can be advanced peaceably, at least initially. Indeed, just a few paragraphs earlier in his "work report" Krauch had called for defensive war to protect the emerging "military economic system,"[20] not for aggressive war. Even at the end of the passage above, Krauch does not advocate what the prosecution calls "the marshalling of the chemical industry of the continent of Europe, including Great Britain, to wage war against the world."[21]

The conspiracy charge is all the more important since there was no direct evidence that Krauch planned or even participated in the planning of the aggressive wars that Germany waged. Yet, it could be that perhaps Krauch was aware of this planning and aided it in various ways. Either he could then be an aider and abettor or a member of a conspiracy that planned and waged aggressive war. But the prosecution offered no additional evidence to show that there was indeed a conspiracy that included Krauch and the other defendants from I. G. Farben. And the

[18] Ibid., p. 86.
[19] Ibid., p. 175.
[20] Ibid., p. 174.
[21] Ibid., p. 176.

Tribunal held that one cannot prove conspiracy by "piling inference upon inference." There must be knowledge on the part of the defendant that there is such a conspiracy or common plan. According to the Tribunal, this was not established.

Even with the weakening of the *mens rea* conditions from intent to mere knowledge, the Tribunal held that in this case involving those who manufactured weapons there was not *mens rea* sufficient for conviction.[22] The businessmen were not part of the policy-making group and so their mental states were not intricately linked to the planning of aggressive war. These businessmen did participate in the plan to wage war by their actions, but their individual intentions were sufficiently removed from the criminal intentions of the leaders that they had to be acquitted. So, at least in this case from the subsequent trials at Nuremberg, those who participated were not treated as being agents for all of the others in the larger conspiracy.

III. Judge Hebert's Concurring Opinion

In one of the most detailed treatments of the idea of conspiracy in the crime against peace, Judge Hebert set out a 100-page concurring opinion in the I. G. Farben case. I will assess his opinion in this section. In particular, Hebert thinks that the majority opinion is too quick to acquit on the Tribunal's uncharitable reading of the evidence presented by the prosecution. While Hebert does indeed concur, he is deeply concerned that the

> issues of fact were so close as to cause genuine concern as to whether or not justice has actually been done because of the enormous and indispensable role that these defendants were shown to have played in the building of the war machine that made Hitler's aggressions possible.[23]

Hebert says: "That the defendants knew they were preparing for a possible war is certain. That their actions in this regard were not the normal activities of businessmen is equally clear."[24]

Yet Hebert also claims that "it has not been established beyond a reasonable doubt that there existed a well-defined conspiracy on the part of these defendants to crimes against peace as here alleged. The proof

[22] Vol. 8, p. 1128.
[23] Ibid., p. 1212.
[24] Ibid., p. 1213.

rather shows individual action by the defendants who utilized the instrumentality of Farben."[25] The problem is that it was not clear that any of the defendants ever agreed on a common plan. Hebert thus feels that he must agree with the majority that Krauch and the others should be acquitted on the charge of participation or conspiracy in a crime against peace.

As far as Hebert is concerned, the main issue concerns the *mens rea* of the defendants.

> We are thus brought to the central issue of the charges insofar as the aggressive war charges are concerned.... Does the evidence in this case establish beyond a reasonable doubt that the acts of the defendant in preparing Germany for war were done with the knowledge of Hitler's aggressive aims and with the criminal purpose of furthering those aims.[26]

Since it is not I. G. Farben in the dock but individual members of this corporation, since the intent necessary for the crime against peace is one of "specific" not general intent, and since the evidence must establish criminal intent beyond a reasonable doubt, the task for the prosecutor was a very difficult one, and one the prosecution in this case failed to meet, despite the fact that Krauch was not an ordinary businessperson.

One good example of both the problem of proof and Hebert's own reluctance to let Krauch and other high-ranking managers off the hook concerns I. G. Farben's production of mustard gas.

> There is in evidence a detailed "accelerated plan" dated 30 June 1938 outlining an acceleration of the expansion program for the production of many chemical products including chemical warfare agents.... Following his appointment by Goering ... Krauch in a communication ... urged the early completion of building projects for several chemical products, including mustard gas, "for which no postponement of the deadline set for the completion can be tolerated."[27]

Hebert says that this evidence makes it abundantly clear that I. G. Farben had the responsibility for production of chemical weapons for use in Germany's wars.

Another example concerns the way that Farben used its extensive business contacts throughout the world to disseminate information and seek intelligence that advanced the aims of the Third Reich.

[25] Ibid.
[26] Ibid., p. 1217.
[27] Ibid., p. 1268.

Thus it appears that Farben, through the energetic use of its foreign representatives and contacts and the power of its financial backing, was an active
instrument in furthering the Nazi propaganda program in a wide variety
of directions and willingly cooperated in various forms of Nazi intrigue. Of
even greater importance was the energetic initiative of Farben through the
use of its foreign connections in intelligence and espionage activities. Farben
worked closely with the intelligence of the Wehrmacht . . . the material thus
assembled probably surpassed that of any other institution in Germany in
extent and quality, and was made available to several agencies of the government regularly.[28]

Farben's foreign branches served as outposts of the German government
during the years leading up to the war.

Yet as Farben cooperated with, and indeed somewhat merged with the
German government, it was not clear that Farben's aim was to support
aggressive war. At least in part this was because "talk of war" and aid
toward the war effort did not mean that Farben supported a particular
kind of war, whether defensive or aggressive. And yet that is the difficulty.
Farben executives, like others in Germany, surely foresaw that aggressive
war could be on the horizon, but there was no evidence presented that
Farben intended to advance a specifically aggressive war. The evidence
showed only "a realistic appraisal of the foreign policy of Germany and
an understanding of the imminent possibility of war."[29]

In one of the clearest statements of Hebert's own mixed feelings about
the I. G. Farben case we have the following:

The irresponsible character of the Nazi regime, its constant emphasis upon
violence, and its oppressive policies as the regime gained in strength, did not
serve to deter the top leadership of Farben in supporting the regime, and
these factors represent how reprehensible was the course of action in which
Farben, through the acts of these principal defendants, was engaged. Such
action, however, is not criminal as constituting the crime against peace unless
it can be said to have been in violation of international law as recognized
by Control Council Law No. 10, the basic legal provision from which this
Tribunal draws its jurisdiction.[30]

As morally reprehensible as Farben's complicit activity was, it was not
clearly criminal.

Control Council Law No. 10 "draws no distinction between a private
citizen and a public official."[31] Anyone could commit an act that satisfied

[28] Ibid., p. 1284.
[29] Ibid.; see discussion of this point by Hebert at 1287.
[30] Ibid., p. 1298.
[31] Ibid., p. 1299.

the *actus reus* element of the crime against peace. But mere participation in aggressive war is not sufficient for *mens rea* concerning crimes against peace.

> In this regard, participation in the policies, planning and purposes of the Nazi regime, as such, does not of itself constitute the crime against peace. There must be participation after concrete plans for the waging of aggressive war have been arrived at and there must be in the mind of the individual sought to be charged a positive knowledge of the intention to resort to aggressive war.... Furthermore, at this stage of the development of international law denouncing the crime against peace it is preferable for a Tribunal to err on the side of liberality in the application of the rule of reasonable doubt.[32]

Hebert is thus, reluctantly, forced to draw the conclusion that "the evidence does not, however, establish beyond a reasonable doubt that the defendants actually knew or believed that force to the point of aggressive war would actually be resorted to if necessary."[33]

Hebert's very subtle analysis is worth quoting in some detail before we leave his opinion.

> In the case of Farben defendants, while they knew that acts of aggression had been and were being carried out in connection with Austria and Czechoslovakia, and, in fact, the defendants participated in acquiring industries resulting from acts of aggression mentioned, it cannot be concluded that such action necessarily amounts to the requisite knowledge or state of mind constituting plans to wage aggressive war. Activities of the defendants in this case, conceding that they were of material aid in bringing about territorial aggrandizement by use of threats of force, do not under the circumstances of this case constitute the crime of aggression. It is incumbent on the prosecution to go further with its evidence and to prove by specific evidence that the individual defendant sought to be charged was aware of a plan to resort to aggressive war if necessary to achieve the objective of territorial aggrandizement.[34]

Hebert's view, which amounts to another one of Nuremberg's lasting legacies, is that the *mens rea* of the crime of aggression requires that the defendant knew in advance of his or her participation that aggressive war would be waged on the basis, at least in part, of the defendant's participation. Only with evidence of this sort could it be said that the defendant's participation and knowledge was indeed sufficient to infer a criminal

[32] Ibid., p. 1302.
[33] Ibid., p. 1303.
[34] Ibid.

intent on the defendant's part for planning and preparation of aggressive war.

The key consideration here, it seems to me, is what is needed to infer that participation on the part of the defendant amounted to planning and preparation for aggressive war. If one participates after the aggressive war has already begun, the participation cannot be said to be planning or preparation of aggressive war since the aggressive war is already occurring. And if the participation occurs when it is still not clear that aggressive war, rather than mere threats, will be engaged in by the State, then again this participation is not planning and preparation of aggressive war since the aggressive war is not necessarily about to begin.

Hebert's position is that participation, by political and military leaders, becomes planning and preparation of aggressive war only when there is knowledge that aggressive war is imminent. This seems to me to be a good way to proceed if we are to allow that intent can be inferred from participation and knowledge. But I'm of two minds about the general strategy. It would be better to require evidence that the defendant actually intended to advance the aggressive war. Short of this, I agree that we need a very high burden on the prosecution. Such a burden, somewhat following Hebert, involves the following elements:

1. the defendant participated in the war effort
2. the defendant knew that the war being planned was to be an aggressive war

If we are not to insist on intent and are willing to settle for knowledge to establish *mens rea*, Hebert's conditions seem to me to be the best on offer. But if prosecutors today follow Judge Hebert, they will find that his condition is very difficult to meet. I next turn to the complications to this analysis that result when we also allow that conspiracy can affect the *mens rea* element in such cases.

IV. *Mens Rea* and Conspiracy

The first thing to note, especially given Hebert's concurring opinion, is that our loathing for what the defendant did should not unduly influence us. Conspiracy is both too easy a term to use and also one that is indeed often applied to collective enterprises that are truly noxious. Think again of Farben's production of mustard gas and other chemical weapons. It is of course hard to know what else this chemical was intended for except warfare, and indeed illegal warfare. But the illegality is not necessarily related to aggressive war rather than to war crimes. And while there may have been intent to produce these horrible weapons for the Nazi war machine, this does not necessarily constitute conspiracy to wage aggressive war.

The point about poison gases illustrates one of the main problems with the use of conspiracy theory. The production of poison gases may contribute to the waging of aggressive war. But it is hard to see the act of poison gas production as part of the planning, preparation, initiation, or waging of aggressive war. It is considerably easier to see this poison gas production as "participating in a common plan or conspiracy for the accomplishment" of waging aggressive war. Yet the problem is that once one starts down the conspiracy road, where most of the emphasis is placed on passive participation, it is hard to know where to stop. Here is how the I. G. Farben Tribunal put it:

> The defendants now before us were neither high-ranking public officials in the civil government nor high military officers. Their participation was that of followers and not leaders. If we lower the standard of participation to include them, it is difficult to find a logical place to draw the line between the guilty and the innocent among the great mass of German people. It is of course unthinkable that the majority of Germans should be condemned as guilty of committing crimes against peace. This would amount to a determination of collective guilt to which the corollary of mass punishment is the logical result for which there is no precedent in international law and no justification in human relations.[35]

Today, we may think that it is implausible to say that Krauch was merely one of the German masses. But the argument about the slippery slope still seems relevant.

In addition, it still seems plausible to follow the Krupp Tribunal in thinking that the only point of these trials was "to deter those capable of initiating that type of war from doing so,"[36] and this was a very small group. Krupp and I. G. Farben were not in a position to initiate aggressive war and hence were not those who could be properly convicted of the crime against peace. In the High Command trial, the point was put even more starkly as follows:

> It is not a person's rank or status, but his power to shape or influence the policy of his State, which is the relevant issue for determining his criminality under the charge of Crimes against Peace. International law condemns those

---

[35] Ibid., vol. 8, p. 1126.
[36] Quoted in *Law Reports of Trials of War Criminals*, vol. 15, p. 145, in the summary of the state of the law concerning crimes against peace.

who, due to their actual power to shape and influence the policy of their nation, prepare for, or lead their country into or in an aggressive war. But we do not find that, in the present stage of development, International Law declares as criminals those below that level who, in the execution of this war policy, act as the instruments of the policy-makers.[37]

The conspiracy charge merely muddied the waters by seemingly opening the door to convict those who could not either initiate aggressive war or be deterred from doing so. And for this reason, it seems to me that the use of the conspiracy charge is not apt for any but the top leadership.

The problem is that the conspiracy theory will normally be so elastic that it could support the conviction of businessmen and many other "minor players." As a recent article has noted:

> There appears to be no reason why the ICTR prosecution could not allege that the elimination of moderate Hutus and Tutsis in Rwanda was itself the object of a massive criminal enterprise. Through this charge the prosecution could argue that each ICTR defendant... should be found guilty for the murder of hundreds of thousands of people.[38]

For similar reasons, I think that the use of the conspiracy theory was not a good idea, and in any event the Tribunals sitting at Nuremberg did not allow the prosecution to employ that theory unless there was a clear-cut agreement among the leadership of a State to act in concert.

The Nuremberg "precedent" thus does not support a wide-ranging use of the idea of conspiracy, either as a substantive crime or on a collective liability model, despite the clear movement in that direction today. It is odd that the ICTY and ICTR have not appealed to the Nuremberg "precedent" for their increasing support for joint criminal enterprise responsibility. This might be a tacit recognition that the Nuremberg "precedent" actually won't support the new joint liability theory. Mark Osiel says, "Defense counsel have repeatedly pointed out that the ICTY's embrace of enterprise participation amounts to endorsing Anglo-American conspiracy doctrine."[39] Other commentators have noted the close connection between conspiracy theory developed at Nuremberg

---

[37] This quotation is also taken from ibid., p. 147.

[38] Allison Marston Danner and Jenny S. Martinez, "Guilty Associations: Joint Criminal Enterprise, Command Responsibility, and the Development of International Criminal Law," *California Law Review*, vol. 93, January 2005, p. 136.

[39] Mark Osiel, "Shared Responsibility for Mass Atrocity: Aligning the Incentives," unpublished paper in the possession of the author.

and joint criminal enterprise theory today.[40] While the substantive crime of conspiracy appears to be dead in international law, joint liability theories abound. My view is that if closer attention is paid to the Nuremberg "precedent" courts and commentators will see more difficulties for the joint liability theories than are currently recognized.[41]

We can take some lessons from the Nuremberg trials in understanding how to approach collective liability theories now and in the future in international criminal law. We should realize that the Nuremberg "precedent" here is rather straightforward and not especially supportive of collective liability theories. As the United Nations War Crimes Commission put it, summarizing the cases of Krupp and I. G. Farben heard under Control Council Law No. 10:

> On the facts before them, the Military Tribunals held all accused charged of crimes against peace to be not guilty of such offenses on the grounds either of lack of knowledge or lack of ability to influence policy.[42]

If there is a group that decides to join together to influence policy in a State it might make sense to use a collective liability theory. But if the people who join this group are all themselves very high-ranking political or military leaders, the question is why we should not simply try them individually rather than for what they decided to do together.

The ICC has in my view rightly rejected establishing jurisdiction over the crime of aggression merely by appealing to the jurisdictional "precedent" of Nuremberg as customary international law. The ICC rightly waits for a firmer treaty-based grounding for this jurisdiction. The Court also waits for a treaty-based grounding for the elements of this crime. If there is such an amendment to the ICC treaty, the Court should then be mindful of the other lessons of Nuremberg. In particular, the ICC should set a high bar for the prosecution concerning the *actus reus* and *mens rea* elements of the crime of aggression. If the ICC follows this latter Nuremberg "precedent" it will find itself on much firmer normative grounds than if it follows the ICTY and ICTR in weakening the *actus reus* and *mens rea* elements of the crime of aggression by reference to a collective liability theory.

---

[40] See Richard Barrett and Laura Little, "Lessons of Yugoslav Rape Trials: A Role for Conspiracy Law in International Tribunals," *Minnesota Law Review*, vol. 88, November 2003, p. 3085.

[41] See *Hamdan v. Rumsfeld*, 126 S.Ct. 2749 (2006), plurality opinion of Judge Stevens, where it is held that conspiracy to commit war crimes is not prosecutable because it is not part of customary or conventional international law.

[42] *Law Reports of Trials of War Criminals*, vol. 15, p. 149.

I will end this section with an extended discussion about the Nuremberg "precedent" for the role of *mens rea* in prosecutions for mass crimes of the sort we have been examining, namely concerning the crime of aggression or crimes against peace. As we have seen, participation in an aggressive war is not enough to establish criminal liability. The question that the I. G. Farben Tribunal considered was whether knowledge of the aggressive war, along with participation, is sufficient for criminal liability. My interpretation of what the Tribunal said is that only a certain fairly restricted type of knowledge would work, namely, knowledge that one is participating in the preparation for an aggressive war that is about to be launched. It is not enough that one learns later that one's participation had played a role in what became an aggressive war, and it is not enough that one merely suspects that one's participation might be part of the preparation for an aggressive war. It must be established that the defendant knew that his or her participation was preparation for an aggressive war.

My view is that normatively this requirement is potentially too weak, even though it did allow for many of the defendants at Nuremberg to be acquitted. As I understand this strategy, if the prosecution has established knowledge and participation, criminal intent can then be inferred. But I think there is reason to doubt such an inference. One's intention could be to contribute to the objectives established by one's country, where the knowledge that these objectives could constitute aggression is indeed quite minor and not part of one's intention. Think of the Krupp case in this respect. The Krupp executives seemed to think that it was their patriotic duty, as weapons manufacturers, to supply weapons to their own military. Let us say that it had been established that the Krupp executives knew that the war they were contributing to was an aggressive war. Does that mean that it was their intention to contribute to the preparation of an aggressive war? Not necessarily.

It is certainly possible that a person could have the knowledge that what one was doing contributed to a certain result without intending that result. I will discuss an example of such a possibility in Chapter 13. Here in the Krupp case, the Krupp executives did express that their only intention was to do what they believed to be their patriotic duty. On the assumption that they are telling the truth, or that someone else could be telling the truth in alleging this defense to the *mens rea* element of this crime, then it appears that we should not allow a straightforward inference from the knowledge and participation to the intention. Of course, we could merely assert that we will constructively infer such an intention. But such a move would be contrary to the important role that actual intent plays in the determination of *mens rea* in criminal law generally and international criminal law in particular.

Employing constructive intention is in effect to apply a strict liability standard in place of a proper *mens rea* standard. And strict liability standards are often quite problematic, as I have tried to show elsewhere.[43] In any event, knowledge is not the same as intention, and the inference from knowledge to intention is not conceptually sound. The addition of the element of participation helps but does not make the inference sound either. By knowingly participating in an event that has a certain result I do not necessarily aim at that result; indeed, I may legitimately say that it is not my intent at all. Rather, my intent is merely to advance the interests of my country by doing what my country has asked me to do. I may greatly regret that doing my duty meant that I also contributed to an unjust war and would try to show this by pointing out that if there was some way that I could have done my duty and not contributed to such a war I would have chosen that path instead. This is the classic way to understand the doctrine of double effect, as we will see in greater detail in Chapter 13.

As we saw earlier in this chapter, one way to get around this problem is to employ a conspiracy theory. The intent dimension is reduced to an intent to join the conspiracy, rather than an intent to participate in an aggressive war. And while this sounds a bit better than relying on knowledge plus participation, it is at least as problematic as I indicated earlier. One way to think about it is that at least the conspiracy theory requires some kind of actual intent, rather than a mere constructive intent – namely, the intent to join a group that has as its stated aim to wage aggressive war. So, in this one respect, the conspiracy theory may have a certain advantage. But this is only true if we are comparing it with the knowledge plus participation view, rather than with the actual intent plus participation view.

In this chapter, I have suggested that the best strategy is to look for actual intent to participate in bringing about an aggressive war, plus participation, rather than the knowledge plus participation. And the conspiracy model is often as problematic as the latter for such trials. More needs to be said, though, about conspiracy theories, as well as collective liability schemes, and I will indeed do so in a subsequent chapter, Chapter 12. But first, I want to address the most important element of the crime of

---

[43] See my discussion of this issue in chapter 12 of my book *War Crimes and Just War*, New York: Cambridge University Press, 2007.

aggression, the element of State aggression. And the first major task in that respect is to reconceptualize the very idea of aggression in light of what has been said about *jus ad bellum* principles so far. For, as we will see, there are problems with the State aggression element just as there are serious problems with the *mens rea* and *actus reus* elements of the crime of aggression.

CONCEPTUALIZING THE CRIME OF AGGRESSION

10

Defining State Aggression

That monarchs and States, at least those that consider themselves civilized, have for centuries recognized that aggressive wars and invasions violated the law of nations is evident from the fact that invariably he who started his troops on the march or his fleets over the seas to wage war has endeavored to explain and justify the act by asserting that there was no desire or intent to infringe upon the lawful rights of the attacked nations or to engage in cold-blooded conquest, but on the contrary that the hostile acts became necessary because of the enemy's disregard of its obligations; that it had violated treaties; that it held provinces or cities which in fact belonged to the attacker; or that it had mistreated or discriminated against his peaceful citizens.

"The Ministries Case Judgment"[1]

The primary purpose of the International Military Tribunal's prosecution at Nuremberg and the subsequent proceedings under Control Council Law No. 10 at Nuremberg was to prosecute Nazi leaders for crimes against peace and waging aggressive war, what was there called the "supreme international crime."[2] There have been no successful major international prosecutions for crimes against peace since the trials at Nuremberg and Tokyo, just as there were none before Nuremberg, because of a failure to agree about what aggression means.[3] This history hardly seems consistent with calling the crime of aggression, or crime against peace, the supreme

---

[1] *Trials of War Criminals before Nuremberg Military Tribunals under Control Council Law No. 10,* vol. 14, p. 318.

[2] *Trial of the Major War Criminals before the International Military Tribunal,* 1948, vol. 22, p. 427.

[3] The authors of a leading textbook, *International Criminal Law: Cases and Materials,* 2nd ed., edited by Jordan J. Paust, M. Cherif Bassiouni, Michael Scharf, Jimmy Gurule, Leila Sadat, Bruce Zagaris, and Sharon A. Williams, Durham, NC: Carolina Academic Press, 2000, p. 717, begin their section on crimes against peace by saying: "Some have assumed wrongly that crimes against peace were not recognizable violations of international law until the post–World War II trials at Nuremberg and Tokyo." I do not dispute this point

international crime. In this chapter, my main task is to try to set out a plausible set of factors that I believe could garner international support concerning what constitutes a State's aggression, based on our previous discussions.

In my view, State aggression should be defined as the first use of violent force by one State against another State that jeopardizes basic human rights, which has not been initiated in self-defense or defense of other innocent states, is not provoked, and has not been authorized by the United Nations. I will spend considerable time defending each aspect of this definition. Each part of this definition involves complex normative considerations, but I believe that this definition could achieve widespread acceptance in the international community. As so defined, State aggression is always prima facie wrong and can form the basis of the first element of the crime of aggression.

I leave to the other chapters in this section, Chapters 11 and 12, to examine what other elements must be proved to establish an individual's criminal liability for the crime of aggression. As I indicated earlier, this is an especially relevant topic since a special committee drafting a definition of aggression for the International Criminal Court is supposed to issue its report by 2009. At the moment, while the crime of aggression is listed as one of the four crimes that the ICC will prosecute, no elements of the crime are listed and no prosecutions are allowed until there is an agreement about what constitutes the crime of aggression.[4] I try to provide a beginning understanding of the elements of this crime in the chapters that follow.

In this chapter I will also try to explain what is the harm or wrong of State aggression. The Nuremberg judges held that the crime of aggression was the supreme international crime because it differs "only from other war crimes in that it contains within itself the accumulated evil of the whole."[5] But is this right? Why cannot non-aggressing States also commit horrendous war crimes, crimes against humanity, and even genocide? And if this is so, then what makes the crime of aggression so terrible? And if the crime of aggression is the supreme crime, then in order to deter this supremely important crime shouldn't even individual soldiers be held criminally liable if they have committed this crime, as well as the

---

but only point out that there were no successful prosecutions for crimes against peace nonetheless until Nuremberg and Tokyo.

[4] The Rome Statute of the International Criminal Court, Art. 5.

[5] *Trial of the Major War Criminals before the International Military Tribunal*, 1948, vol. 22, p. 427.

leaders of highly aggressive States, like Slobodon Milosevic of Yugoslavia and Saddam Hussein of Iraq?

In the first section of this chapter, I discuss what aggression means when it is not necessarily connected to the acts of a State. In the second section, I relate the idea of aggression to State aggression looking primarily at the older Just War tradition, especially the 16th- and 17th-century theorists normally thought to be the founders of international law today. In the third section, I discuss definitions of State aggression that have been proposed in international law including an important UN resolution. In the fourth section, I briefly discuss what is so terrible about aggression and I also then begin to address the hard question of whether humanitarian wars can count as aggressive wars, and if so under what conditions, a discussion that is continued in Chapter 13. In the fifth section, I say a bit about individual liability, returning to the trials at Nuremberg for inspiration and end with some thoughts about how best to conceptualize State aggression in crimes against peace and the crime of waging aggressive war.

I. What Is Aggression?

The term "aggression" has many different meanings and is certainly not restricted to what States do when they wage unjust war. I begin this chapter by discussing some of the other meanings of this term in a way that should help us in later discussions when we turn back to the idea of State aggression. *The Oxford English Dictionary* (*OED*) gives a seemingly simple but conceptually quite complex definition of aggression, namely, "An unprovoked attack, the first attack in a quarrel, an assault, an inroad."[6] There are arguably four distinct meanings of aggression listed here, and it is not clear how they are all related to each other. As in so many other cases, the *OED* gives us instances of the usage of the term, not a definition. Nonetheless, it is a place, indeed an interesting place, to start to understand aggression.

When we say that someone is acting aggressively we normally mean that the person is acting in a threatening or hostile manner, perhaps calling to mind the "assault" component of the *OED*'s definition. When we say that someone has aggressed into my space, perhaps by leaning over into what is clearly marked as my airline seat, we get the sense of "an inroad." But

---

[6] *The Compact Edition of the Oxford English Dictionary*, vol. I: A-O, Oxford: Oxford University Press, 1971, p. 46.

the place where aggression has its most obvious use is either in discussions of law or perhaps psychiatry, where the question is whether a person acts inappropriately by starting a fight. Yet there are two quite different things that the *OED* points to in this respect, namely "an unprovoked attack" and "the first attack in a quarrel." The first attack is not necessarily the attack that is unprovoked, unless we stipulate that an attack that is provoked is not a "first" attack. I will say more about this strategy later in the chapter, but merely note how odd this use of the term "first" initially sounds, as we saw in Chapter 4.

Think of a barroom brawl. When the police finally arrive and try to sort out who should be arrested for disturbing the peace, they typically ask who was the aggressor. Sometimes all they are trying to determine is who started the brawl. This can mean who threw the first punch, or it can mean who provoked the first punch by hurling verbal insults, or it can mean who acted in a threatening way, or it can mean who reacted angrily when undue attention was paid to a girlfriend or boyfriend. Aggression can take the form of physical acts, verbal acts, hostile gestures, or mere angry responses. It is often hard to sort out which of these acts was "the" act of aggression in a barroom brawl, especially when all seem to be present nearly at once.

Psychologists who study aggression in individual humans have tried to separate and define these four types of aggression as well as to measure these forms of aggression in the general population and to understand their causes. In the psychology literature, "aggression has been generally defined by most authors as behaviors that are intended to hurt or harm others."[7] Arnold Buss and Mark Perry have designed what they call an "Aggression Questionnaire" to measure on a scale the four factors that contribute to a person's overall aggression: physical aggression, verbal aggression, anger, and hostility.[8] And Buss and Durkee had earlier developed a Hostility inventory that measured hostility in terms of seven other factors: assault, indirect aggression, irritability, negativism, resentment, suspicion, and verbal aggression.[9] Other psychologists divide the aggression landscape into two rather large domains: overt aggression (including physical as well as verbal aggression) and relational aggression (subtle

---

[7] Nicki R. Crick and Jennifer K. Grotpeter, "Relational Aggression, Gender, and Social-Psychological Adjustment," *Child Development*, vol. 66, 1995, p. 710.

[8] Arnold Buss and Mark Perry, "The Aggression Questionnaire," *Journal of Personality and Social Psychology*, vol. 63, no. 3, 1992, pp. 452–459.

[9] Arnold Buss and A. Durkee, "An Inventory for Assessing Different Kinds of Hostility," *Journal of Consulting Psychology*, vol. 21, 1957, pp. 343–349.

attempts to hurt or harm by means of exclusion, spreading rumors, with-drawal of friendship, etc.).[10] All of these measures could be useful to a certain extent in our search to understand State aggression, since they indicate the various factors that could go into a seemingly straightforward assessment of individual aggression.

One of the most prominent psychologists to study aggression, Leonard Berkowitz, begins a 1990 essay as follows:

> Most people, psychologists and non-psychologists alike, are fairly confident about when people will be prompted to become angry and attack an avail-able target. Anger arises and aggression occurs, it is widely assumed, as a result of a perceived threat or the belief that one has been intentionally mis-treated or even because of some frustration. However, there may be more to the origin of aggression than is commonly supposed. Mounting evidence indicates that aggression can also be produced by a remarkably broad range of unpleasant occurrences that are not intentionally or unfairly produced by a human agent. Foul odors, high temperatures, exposure to painfully cold water, or even disgusting scenes can also heighten hostility displayed, or the aggression that is displayed toward another person, even when that individ-ual cannot possibly be blamed for the unpleasantness, and the aggression cannot alleviate the negative state of affairs.[11]

Berkowitz concludes his study by saying that people "can restrain their hostile and aggressive tendencies, as a result of becoming aware of their feelings and seeing clearly that it is wrong for them to blame or attack others."[12] What is true of the relations among human persons is probably also true of the relations among the members of States, although perhaps not of States themselves since States lack a conscious life.

This all presents us with a rather complex landscape of aggression. Yet the overriding idea seems to be that aggression in individual humans is a behavior that is meant to harm another human who is perceived as a rival, a threat, or an annoyance. The difficulty is to sort out whether the person who is perceived as the rival, threat, or annoyance has already acted aggressively in a way, for instance, that causes the annoyance and triggers the aggressive behavior that we observe. This is especially prob-lematic, as we will see, if one is trying to assess blame or possible punish-ment for aggression since it will matter quite a bit whether the aggressive

[10] Nicki R. Crick and Jennifer K. Grotpeter, "Relational Aggression, Gender, and Social-Psychological Adjustment," pp. 711–712.
[11] Leonard Berkowitz, "On the Formation and Regulation of Anger and Aggression: A Cognitive-Neoassociationist Analysis," *American Psychologist*, vol. 45, no. 4, April 1990, p. 494.
[12] Ibid., p. 502.

behavior was intentionally provoked by a person who could have chosen not to provoke, or whether the aggressor was not so provoked and could have decided to do the right thing and not act aggressively. Of course, it is also possible that both parties could have done something differently and thereby avoided the confrontation. But as Berkowitz points out, the interesting cases are those where aggression is not provoked by the intentional acts of another person and where the aggression could have been stopped if the aggressor decided to do the right thing.

Assessments of aggression are thus, even for empirically minded psychologists, both descriptive and normative. Aggression is the name of a behavior, but it is also an evaluation of that behavior as deserving some kind of blame or punishment. As the *OED* definition indicates, the aggressor is the one who attacks and is unprovoked. Following Berkowitz, we can say that provocation does not have to be by the intentional acts of others. What is crucial is that the one labeled the aggressor could have avoided acting aggressively, and no one else is more at fault than he or she is. Such a characterization will be a good start for understanding State aggression, where many of the same issues arise about provocation, and where the term "aggression" is used both as a descriptive and a normative term of art.

II. Historical Roots of the Idea of State Aggression

If there are going to be trials for those who initiate or perpetrate an aggressive war, we need to be able to say what constitutes an aggressive war, or an act of State aggression generally. Indeed, if individuals are going to be prosecuted and their liberty put in serious jeopardy for allegedly committing this crime, it is incumbent on the international community to have a very clear understanding of what State aggression is. Philosophers, diplomats, and lawyers have debated this topic for hundreds of years and have not all agreed. In this section I wish to discuss several ideas about which we might reach consensus, even if much of the terrain of aggression remains mired in political and ideological squabbles. And to try to accomplish this moderate objective, I will first turn to the 16th- and 17th-century debates on the morality of war.

There is a relatively modern-sounding translation of Thomas More's work that I find quite useful as a starting point for understanding State aggression. Here is part of More's discussion of Just Wars in Book II, "Military Affairs," of his famous work, *Utopia*:

Utopians "go to war only for good reasons: [1] to protect their own land, [2] to drive invading armies from the territories of their friends, or [3] to liberate an oppressed people in the name of humanity, from tyranny and servitude."[13]

We can begin to understand what aggressive war is by first thinking about what it is not. And I would think that today many would agree that wars waged for the three reasons given by More would not be considered aggressive wars. Indeed, it is interesting that as far back as Augustine, as I discussed earlier, theorists held that war was most surely justified when undertaken on behalf of those who were innocently attacked, which included wars waged in defense of others as well as self-defensive wars.[14]

One could challenge this beginning idea, taken from Thomas More, by arguing that protecting State territory is not sufficient to warrant the taking of human life that is nearly inevitably a part of war. Invasion of territory does not necessarily mean that innocent people are attacked. Indeed, territory can be uninhabited, for instance, as in the case of certain small islands. If one State claims these islands and another State captures them, is this enough to justify initiating a war when it is highly likely that people, both combatants and noncombatants, will be killed? It can also be true that some islands claimed as part of a State's territory provide no particular military or economic advantages for the State that claims them. If these islands are captured by another State, it would be unclear that the interests of the State, such as its ability to defend the populated mainland or to have economic self-sufficiency for the populated mainland, would also be adversely affected. So, it is not initially clear why simple invasion of one State's territory by another State is aggression that warrants prosecution.

As I argued in Chapter 5, I would be willing to countenance a wider scope for what counts as *State* aggression when we are not considering

---

[13] Thomas More, *Utopia* (1516), edited by George M. Logan and Robert M. Adams, Cambridge: Cambridge University Press, 1989, pp. 89–90. See the discussion of this passage in Richard Tuck, *The Rights of War and Peace*, Oxford: Oxford University Press, 1999, p. 42. The standard translation of *Utopia* is that edited by Edward Surtz, S. J. as the second volume of the *Selected Works of St. Thomas More*, New Haven, CT: Yale University Press, 1964. The Yale edition translates the passage, on p. 118, as follows: "Yet they do not lightly go to war. They do so only to protect their own territory or to drive an invading enemy out of their friends' lands or, in pity, for a people oppressed by tyranny, to deliver them by force of arms from the yoke and slavery of the tyrant, a course prompted by human sympathy."

[14] Augustine, *The City of God* (c. 420), translated by Henry Bettenson, New York: Penguin Books, 1984, Book XIX, ch. 1, 7, and 12, pp. 843, 861–862, and 866–867.

State aggression as one of the elements of the *crime* of aggression.[15] If we wonder whether a State should be condemned rather than that one of its leaders should be prosecuted, we might allow for a simple "violation of territorial integrity" criterion to suffice, especially since there is a long history of using this criterion in international law.[16] But what I am contending here is that more than this should be needed for demonstrating State aggression as the first hurdle in establishing the elements of the crime of aggression. And this is because when we put an individual's liberty in jeopardy by a trial for such a crime, we need to make sure that the individual has indeed done something of commensurate harm to the loss of liberty he or she is now forced to risk in the trial.[17]

Self-defense should also not be identified with merely repelling invasion. The contrary position is supported by an analogy between States and individual human persons. The self of the human person is the person's body and the corresponding self of the State is its territory. If a person's body is attacked, this is the kind of aggression that will trigger a criminal trial. If a State's territory is attacked, this is also supposed to be the kind of aggression that could trigger an international criminal trial. But there is a significant disanalogy. If a physical attack occurs on a person's body there are serious repercussions for the rest of the body – any attack will cause bruising or bleeding that will adversely affect the functions or stability of the rest of the body. But as I indicated above, States can have as part of their territories land that is not contiguous with the mainland, or in any event land that when attacked will not necessarily affect the rest of the State's territory or "body."

One could object to this proposal that a State is more than a mere population within a territory. A State is also a territorial jurisdiction in which it has a monopoly of enforcement power.[18] Insofar as a State's enforcement jurisdiction is limited by an occupation of part of its territory, the State becomes less of a State than it was before. Indeed, the traditional way of understanding aggression was to see it as merely involving a violation of territorial integrity or political sovereignty, and this characterization survived in the drafting of the United Nations Charter. This "Statist" way

---

[15] See Elizabeth Wilmshurst, "Definition of the Crime of Aggression: State Responsibility or Individual Criminal Responsibility?" in *The International Criminal Court and the Crime of Aggression*, edited by Mauro Politi and Giuseppe Nesi, Burlington, VT: Ashgate, 2004, p. 94.

[16] I thank Simon Cabulea May for helping me clarify this point.

[17] See my discussion of a similar matter in prosecutions for crimes against humanity in my book, *Crimes against Humanity: A Normative Account*, New York: Cambridge University Press, 2005.

[18] I thank an anonymous journal referee for this objection.

to understand aggression has been dominant for a very long time, but I think it is wrongheaded.

One could accept the traditional way of understanding aggression if one were interested in a merely stipulative legal meaning of the term. But if one is interested in a definition of aggression that was normatively persuasive, more is needed than merely a reference to violating territorial integrity or political sovereignty. At the very least, a normative defense of territory or sovereignty would be needed. And in addition, one would have to give some normative rationale for thinking that continuing as a State is indeed always worthwhile. My view is that this cannot be done in general but only by reference to a State's protection of human rights.[19] I have argued for this conclusion in earlier chapters and will continue to provide additional arguments as the current chapter proceeds.

Another objection could be made on similar grounds – namely, to the idea that aggression can involve the repelling of a State that has invaded the territory of a friendly State. Again, since the friendly State's territory is not analogous to a human person's body, it is not clear why invasion per se should count as aggression that warrants retaliation and that is not itself considered aggression. We will later, in Chapter 13, consider serious objections to the third rationale that I have taken from Thomas More, namely, that it is not aggression to liberate an oppressed people in the name of humanity. As we will see, humanitarian wars pose an especially difficult problem for an account like More's. The general presumption in favor of a State's not being attacked if it has not attacked other States is in need of a normative rationale, which is generally lacking in the literature on aggression.

There is an initial way to get out of some of these traditional problems and still save the main idea behind More's account. My initial proposal is that defense of self or others that aims to protect the core of the State – that is, its human population and essential economic and political institutions that protect this population – should not count as aggression. In addition, military action that involves self-defense of a State's core population and the institutions that support that population should also not constitute aggression.[20] Whenever another State acts in a way that

---

[19] See David Rodin's book, *War and Self-Defense*, New York: Oxford University Press, 2002, for an extended argument in support of the view that something other than State self-defense is necessary for understanding the wrongness of aggression, which I here endorse.

[20] My idea of defining legitimate State self-defense in terms of protecting the core population of a State is similar to Michael Walzer's discussion of "the survival and freedom of political communities" in his book, *Just and Unjust Wars*, New York: Basic Books, 1977, 2000, p. 254 and elsewhere.

threatens a given population or its supporting institutions, then rising to defend that State from such assaults is not itself a form of aggression. And the main rationale here is drawn in terms of the value of, and need for protection of, the human rights of members of a population. But defense of a population is not the same as defense of a territory, as I have been arguing throughout this book.

It is seemingly even harder to say what constitutes aggressive war than what does not. But here we can also draw some inspiration from 16th-century philosophers. For we could say, following Francisco Vitoria, that "Assuming that a Prince has authority to make war, he should first of all not go seeking occasions and causes of war."[21] In Vitoria's view, in most situations sovereigns act aggressively when they initiate war. War is prima facie aggressive if the first State to use violent force does so for reasons other than the three mentioned earlier, namely, for self-defense, defense of an ally, or to liberate an oppressed people, insofar as those are linked to human rights protection. The first strike element of aggression is not alone sufficient but it does seem to be necessary for a prima facie showing of aggression.

The first strike element is meant to separate those who initiate violence and those who merely respond or retaliate. Again the idea is intuitively related to the case of human persons. In a barroom brawl, one of the first questions on the table is who threw the first punch. Of course, this can sometimes be countered by the claim that the first person to act was not the one who threw the punch but the one who provoked the first punch, perhaps by the use of insults. So the first strike element should not be understood literally as the first State to use violence. The first strike element is an attempt to get people to try to see which State *wrongly* started a causal chain that resulted in a war, and hence which State is normatively prima facie the aggressor.

My amendment to, or clarification of, the traditional Just War way of understanding aggression is that "first strike" should be seen as shorthand for "first wronging" rather than about which State literally engaged in physical assault first. It may seem odd to say that the State that provokes is an aggressor rather than the State that launches an attack. But history has shown many examples of States that try to start wars stealthily by provoking another State to use violence that can then be countered by supposedly

---

[21] Francisco Vitoria, *De Indis et de Jure Belli Reflectiones* (Reflections on Indians and on the Laws of War) (1557), edited by Ernest Nys and translated by John Pawley Bate, Washington: Carnegie Institution, 1917, p. 187.

self-defensive violence. Think of a state that menacingly moves its troops to the border of another State thereby provoking that other State to attack first. For my idea not to be quite so odd, we simply need to think of "strike" as a metaphor for the one to act first in a seriously wrongful way in a chain of events that leads to war. The State that "strikes" first then has a kind of burden since it is on the face of it (prima facie) the aggressor unless it can prove that the first strike should not be regarded as wrongful. On the view taken over from More and Vitoria, only certain wrongs can warrant initiation of war. This would help make things much clearer than they often were in the Just War tradition, especially in the writings of those like Augustine, who said that war is unjust unless initiated to right a wrong or avenge an injustice.[22]

Engaging in acts that start a war also should not count as aggression when we are under something like "compulsion." The wrongs that should compel us to wage war are only those that concern the defense of human rights of one's own or another people.[23] As I argued in Chapter 3, a State may be compelled to go to the aid of another State or group within another State as well as to act in self-defense. And as the 17th-century founder of international law, Hugo Grotius, says, war is justified only if it is done to ward off a clear danger to life, not just to property, that is "immediate and imminent in point of time."[24] Grotius makes this point to counter those, like Alberico Gentili, who contended that mere fear of any sort was sufficient to justify what Grotius called "anticipatory slaying." Grotius argued that the danger must not be merely assumed but must be shown to require immediate action because of the impending harm that would result to the victim, as we saw in Chapter 4. If an assailant seizes weapons and acts in a menacing manner, this may be enough to justify anticipatory violence as long as there is a necessity that one strike the first blow to avoid the imminent danger.

So first strike will only be a prima facie, not an all things considered, determination of which State is the aggressor. The State that defends self or other against an imminent and unjustified attack may be compelled to strike first, but it is not the aggressor. Indeed, another way to characterize this situation is to say that the State that is threatening to attack has already in effect been the one to "strike" first. Of course, if the "threatening" State is only beginning to plan for a possible attack or if its leaders are merely

---

[22] Augustine, *The City of God*, p. 862.
[23] See Vitoria, *De Indis et de Jure Belli Reflectiones*, p. 187.
[24] Hugo Grotius, *De Jure Belli Ac Pacis* (On the Law of War and Peace) (1625), translated by Francis W. Kelsey, Oxford: Clarendon Press, 1925, p. 173.

making bellicose speeches, the attack is not imminent and the State that attacks to prevent the threat from being actualized is still the first to strike and as a result the prima facie aggressor.

While still somewhat preliminary, we could follow the ideas of the Just War theorists, especially the highly plausible ideas of More, Vitoria, and Grotius. We could think of the prima facie case for proving State aggression as involving the first use of armed force by one State that wrongs another State not justified by self-defense, the defense of an innocent State being attacked, or the liberation of an oppressed people in the name of humanity. For simplicity I shall collapse these three latter reasons into one, namely, "self defense or defense of others"; but when I use this phrase I do not mean to include anything more than what Thomas More meant, with the changes I indicated, most importantly the reference to human rights. And in any event some preemptive wars will be justified by this criterion since when one State has menacingly built up its armies on the border of another State, self-defense or defense of others may call for the first use of armed force rather than to wait for a first strike attack by another State, as we saw in Chapter 5. Yet in this case, not all such threats will do, but only those that are serious, immediate, and imminent. In the next section I will explain how this historically based understanding of State aggression can shed light on contemporary debates in international law.

III. Waging Aggressive War

The canonical contemporary treatment of aggression comes from the United Nations General Assembly Resolution 3314 on the definition of aggression. This 1974 Resolution, adopted by consensus but not binding, declared that the "first use of armed force by a State shall constitute prima facie evidence of an act of aggression."[25] And as I indicated above, I believe that this is indeed a highly plausible way to approach the idea of aggression in war, although as I argued, "first strike" is probably better understood as "first wrong." Just as in the case of deciding which of two persons is the aggressor, we can normally do little better than to ask which State struck first or acted to provoke. This is only a prima facie determination to be sure, but as we have seen, it is a very good place to start, and

---

[25] Resolution on the Definition of Aggression, December 14, 1974, U.N.G.A. Res. 3314, 29 U.N.GAOR, Supp. (No. 31) 142, U.N. Doc. A/9631, Annex (1975). Also see Theodor Meron, "Defining Aggression for the International Criminal Court," *Suffolk Transnational Law Review*, vol. 25, Winter 2001, p. 7.

many other attempted definitions of aggression at the international level have also started in this way.

So if we are going to attempt to give an abstract, as opposed to a stipulative, definition of State aggression in international criminal law, we can start with the one that the General Assembly came up with. Here the first element is that a State was the first to initiate war by wronging another State, normally by the use of violent force in invading or firing across the border in a way that jeopardized human rights. As I have indicated, the first "strike" might also include doing things that provoke retaliatory violence. So in the hope of keeping the factors of prima facie aggression relatively uncontroversial, let's leave the idea of first strike in its clearest form, where first strike means first wrong and where this normally means the first use of force by one State against another State not provoked by that State.

Before going further we might try to enumerate the various uses of force as first strikes that States commit. Turning back to slightly earlier times, here is an attempt to stipulate the forms of aggressive war that I also find initially highly useful, provided by the Soviet Union in 1933, and often cited today:

The aggressor in an international conflict shall be considered that state which is the first to take any of the following actions:

a. Declaration of war against another state.
b. The invasion by its armed forces of the territory of another state, without declaration of war.
c. Bombarding the territory of another state by land, naval, or air forces.
d. The landing in, or introduction within the frontiers of another state, of land, naval, or air forces without the permission of the government of such a state....
e. The establishment of a naval blockade of the coasts or ports of another state.[26]

And while this is surely not an exhaustive list, it may very well become the basis of an emerging consensus about which acts of States constitute the prima facie initiation of aggressive war, as long as these actions did indeed jeopardize human rights.

---

[26] See Evgeny Nasinovsky, "The Impact of 50 Years of Soviet Theory and Practice on International Law," *American Journal of International Law*, vol. 62, 1968, p. 189.

This list is very helpful for it gives us relatively uncontroversial examples of a first wrong, although we would need to qualify (b), the second action on the Soviet list. Notice that at least one of the acts, the first (a) concerning declaring war, is actually not properly a use of violent force at all. In fact, this first form of first "strike" is more like the controversial case of provocation that we have been discussing, and this seems to be true of the last act on the list (e) as well. In general, what this kind of list does is to focus our attention on the kinds of preliminary questions that we would need to ask to discover whether one State had indeed engaged in a first wrong against another as the first element in the prima facie case for liability for crimes against peace.

Calling an action on the list an act of State aggression in the prima facie case for the crime of aggression is meant to say that making the case that a State did act in this way is the initial hurdle that must be crossed by a prosecutor to prevent the dismissal of a case against an individual for crimes against peace. In addition, calling it a prima facie case is meant to indicate that it could be rebutted by other considerations. I would propose that we have a reasonable likelihood of reaching agreement on the following:

A State is engaged in illegal aggression when that State

1. has been the first to use violent force in a confrontation against another State that jeopardizes basic human rights;
2. has not been provoked, or, if provoked, the provocation did not constitute an imminent and immediate threat to it;
3. has not acted in self-defense or defense of other States or subgroups of a State;
4. has not been authorized by the UN to use violent force against another State.

This establishes the prima facie case for the first element of the crime of aggression. Other elements having to do with objective and subjective states of the accused individuals will also have to be established and defenses will have to be considered as well. While these criteria have never been listed in just this way in international criminal law, I think it is a fair reflection of the way that tradition is being plausibly interpreted by some legal scholars today, as well as of a certain important strain in the Just War tradition that I discussed in previous chapters.

I make this proposal as a way to get us past the roadblock that has been in place for the past sixty years preventing international prosecutions for waging aggressive war.[27] What I propose is that we simply scale back our expectations to include under the rubric of aggressive war only those acts and events that are relatively uncontroversial. Of course, one could say that pacifists and others would not regard even my very modest proposal to be uncontroversial. But I am working with the assumption that there is widespread interest, especially by pacifists, in being able to mount prosecutions for crimes against peace and the waging of aggressive war. So even principled as well as contingent pacifists might be willing to allow that some wars have prima facie justifiability so as to allow us to get on with the business of mounting prosecutions against the most blatant warmongers in the international community.

Theodor Meron is right to think that we need a definition that satisfies the principle of legality in that it has been agreed to by all, or virtually all, States or perhaps that it tracks custom, and then is only applied prospectively.[28] And this would be a major undertaking indeed unless we greatly restrict the scope of the term "aggression." I have tried to do this by looking only to what is prima facie needed to prove that a State was waging aggressive war. What is controversial is what will subsequently count as excusing or justifying conditions, such as whether and to what extent a history of bellicose acts by one State might be a basis to justify the use of force. So at least in this chapter, I will leave this matter largely unexplored. Yet it seems to me there is a long-standing moral and legal tradition that holds that first use of armed force by one State against another State, not based on self-defense or defense of others, is prima facie evidence that a State is waging aggressive war. In addition, the prosecution will also have to prove that the defendant had both objective and subjective elements of the crime. I will discuss these elements in Chapters 11 and 12.

Meron is also right to worry about the problem of ex post facto prosecutions. We cannot assume, especially given the controversy about what constitutes aggression, that there is a clear customary or common law basis for aggression that all States must conform to at the moment. Even in the relatively uncontroversial way that I have been proceeding, we need to have a multilateral treaty or a clear statement from the Security Council or the ICC about what will henceforth be punishable as the crime against peace or waging aggressive war. Prosecutions cannot occur until this matter is definitively settled. But while I share Meron's worries,

---

[27] See Jennifer Trahan, "Defining 'Aggression': Why the Preparatory Commission for the International Criminal Court Has Faced Such a Conundrum," *Loyola University of Los Angeles International and Comparative Law Review*, vol. 24, August 2002, pp. 439–466.

[28] Meron, p. 7.

I am not quite as pessimistic as he is about the likelihood of having a codification of at least the prima facie case for the first element of the crime of aggression, namely, State aggression, given my historical and contemporary discussion of the moral and legal proposal I have been outlining.

Regardless of how we define aggressive war, even in a prima facie way, we will need rather precise mental and physical elements of the crime of aggression if there are to be justified prosecutions of individuals for committing this crime. In addition to proving that there was an aggressive war, it needs to be shown that an individual had both a guilty act and a guilty mind in participating in that war. Before turning to the objective and subjective elements, I will return to the trials at Nuremberg and current practice in the International Criminal Court to get some guidance on how best to understand, and what problems arise in understanding, what is the wrong of aggression.

IV. The Wrong of Aggression

Now that we have an understanding of the element of State aggression, I wish to spend some time speculating on why the Nuremberg court thought that the crime of aggression was the worst of all crimes, even worse than genocide or crimes against humanity such as ethnic cleansing. I also wish to explain why the drafters of the Rome Statute of the ICC took a somewhat similar position in their Preamble, in which this crime is said to be one of "the most serious crimes of concern to the international community as a whole."[29] As a preliminary matter, it is important to note that the idea of State aggression is very hard to make sense of without a strong presumption in favor of State sovereignty. If States are not, or are only weakly, sovereign, then it does not seem to make much difference whether one of them invades or attacks another State. Indeed, in a world without States the idea of aggression might still exist but it would be completely different from what we have seen so far. This doesn't yet help explain why aggression is sometimes thought to be the worst, or one of the worst, of crimes but it does locate where we should look if this idea is to be rendered plausible.

In a world without sovereign States, it is often much harder for human rights to be protected than without sovereign States. Of course, this is

---

[29] Rome statute of the International Criminal Court, Preamble, entered into force July 2002.

an empirical claim and not one that I can defend in this current work. While there have certainly been States that did not protect the human rights of their citizens, virtually all states have this capability. Sovereign States are able to promote the peace and to protect individuals, especially the basic human rights of their members, and hence when one State attacks another, which had been protecting the basic rights of its citizens, a serious harm has been committed.[30]

The Nuremberg Tribunal held, implausibly, that the crime of aggression contained all other international crimes, but perhaps what the Tribunal meant was that it was more likely that the leaders of a State would commit other crimes if their State was acting aggressively toward its neighbors. I'm not at all sure of the empirical claim that aggressive States are more likely to commit other crimes than non-aggressive States. Indeed, I doubt that such a thesis could be supported by empirical research. Of course, one could say that when aggression is linked to other crimes, especially crimes against humanity and genocide, then things are worse than when these crimes occur outside of State aggression. This claim seems plausible but doesn't establish that aggression is the worst of crimes.

It seems to me that a more productive direction to take is to see the crime of aggression not as the supreme crime but nonetheless as a very serious crime because of its link to the horrors of war. If the crime of aggression is epitomized by the idea that its perpetrators strike first, or wrong first, and initiate an unprovoked war with another State, then the simplest thing to say is that its wrongness comes from just this initiation of war with all of its attendant horrors. Wars are normally horrible, and anyone who initiates them has normally engaged in a very serious wrong. But not all wars are equally horrible. Some wars, what in previous centuries were called just wars, may seemingly have overall positive effects. But could some just wars also be aggressive wars?

One war that could be aggressive and yet have overall positive effects might be a war waged to protect or confront an insurgency group. We can see this problem in a recent case when one State claimed that it was engaging in a justified war and the State that it was attacking claimed that it was defending against a war of aggression. In the *Democratic Republic of the Congo v. Uganda*, the Congo alleged that Uganda illegally maintained troops in the Congo from August 1998 until 2003. Prior to August of 1998, the Ugandan troops had been welcomed by the Congo's then

---

[30] I here rely on arguments advanced by Allen Buchanan in his important book, *Justice, Legitimacy, and Self-Determination*, New York: Oxford University Press, 2004.

president Laurent Kabila to help with security problems on one of the Congo's borders. The troops from Uganda were waging war against an insurgency group that threatened to topple the Congolese government and to broaden their insurgency movement into neighboring States.

In August 1998, President Kabila ordered Rwandan troops, who were also fighting the insurgents, to leave his country, and by implication this included all foreign troops fighting the insurgents. After troops were asked to leave, the Ugandan troops remained, supposedly on grounds of self-defense. The self-defense issue concerned the security problems at the border where an insurgency group seemingly threatened not only Congolese security but also Ugandan security. Uganda in effect argued that it had the right to wage war against the insurgents within the Congo to stop them from attacking Uganda, even though the Ugandan troops' presence in the Congo constituted a violation of the territorial integrity of the Congo, and the Congolese government did not want Ugandan troops in its country.

In the case of *Congo v. Uganda*, the International Court of Justice (ICJ) relied on its earlier ruling in the Nicaragua case, when it had ruled that States could not intervene in the affairs of other States to support or confront an insurgency effort. The ICJ ruled in December 2005 that Uganda could not claim self-defense or defense of others and avoid the charge of aggression simply because it crossed the border of the Congo to confront a guerilla group fighting an insurgency in the Congo.[31] The ICJ acknowledged that it might make a difference if Uganda's troops were responding to the wishes of the Congolese government. If the troops were waging war on the insurgents at the behest or under the direction of the Congolese government, it wasn't aggressive war. But if the troops were effectively an occupying force, then this did constitute an act of waging aggressive war.

Increasing the likelihood of the horrors of war is what constitutes the primary harm or wrong of the crime of aggression. But is this sufficient to mark the crime of aggression as more significant than genocide or crimes against humanity? The *Congo v. Uganda* case helps us see how complex things can become. Uganda's actions may very well have been destabilizing, but giving a certain benefit of the doubt to Uganda, they may also have helped with security in the region and hence

---

[31] See "Case Concerning Armed Activities on the Territory of the Congo: The ICJ Finds Uganda Acted Unlawfully and Orders Reparations," Margaret E. McGuiness, *Newsletter of the American Society of International Law*, January/February 2006, p. 6.

probably also with human rights protection. Indeed, there were going to be horrors of war regardless of whether Uganda sent troops across the Congolese border, since the insurgency was already highly violent. So it remains unclear what marks off State aggression as the worst of all crimes.

State aggression, and the crime of aggression that corresponds to it, is not clearly the worst of all crimes. But this does not mean that State aggression, as I have defined it, does not constitute a wrong or harm that should be prevented and sanctioned, and that the leaders who are responsible for the aggressive war should not be prosecuted for the international crime of aggression. All that I have been suggesting in this section is that State aggression is not clearly the worst of crimes. State aggression will itself always constitute a serious wrong, but in some cases, the State aggression is a lesser evil.

Perhaps for reasons related to the problems that arose in the *Congo v. Uganda* case, it might make sense to amend our analysis taken from Thomas More and greatly restrict what counts as defense of others so that only wanted and needed defense is allowed. Nonetheless, I would urge that we follow Thomas More's lead and think that some wars waged for the defense of others, especially wars waged to stop genocide, can be justified as non-aggressive, for the wrongness of State aggression will vary quite a bit based on what that aggression is aimed at accomplishing. State aggression is not the supreme crime, but it is normally quite a serious crime that sometimes can warrant prosecutions and serious punishments for those responsible for it.

V. Who Decides? Another Lesson from Nuremberg

At the main Nuremberg trial, it was maintained that there was no serious definitional hurdle to begin prosecuting Nazi leaders. Germany had clearly struck first when it invaded Poland and other countries, and Germany's first strikes at least seemed not to be grounded in self-defense or defense of others. This fact was thought to be sufficient to establish that Nazi Germany had waged aggressive war. It is not clear whether the prosecutors at Nuremberg thought that Nazi Germany's seemingly blatant first use of armed force, not in self-defense or defense of others, was sufficient merely for the prima facie case or also for establishing this element for ultimate conviction. I am inclined to think that it was only the former since as the trial proceeded quite a bit of time was spent addressing the defense claims that Nazi Germany was provoked into attacking, or that Nazi Germany attacked in order to protect those who could not protect themselves.

Yet it was thought to be sufficient to get the trial under way that Nazi Germany's invasions of the population groups in its neighbor States was prima facie the waging of aggressive war. This is another clear lesson from Nuremberg. At Nuremberg it was thought to be not that difficult to determine, at least prima facie, that a State has indeed initiated a war of aggression. This is not yet to say anything, of course, about whether what is true prima facie is also true all things considered. And as I have indicated, there was a serious discussion of whether Nazi Germany was provoked or in some other way not itself fully liable for its first strikes against its neighbors. But because so little time was spent establishing that Nazi Germany committed the first wrong, and because that seemed sufficient, I am inclined to think that sometimes this part of the prima facie case is clear-cut.

It could be argued that the Nazi case was unique in that in modern times we have not seen such a clearly aggressive State as this, when the State attacked all of its neighbors and this was done as a first strike in each case. If the case is truly unique then it might be a bad idea to try to draw any lessons from that case. I will leave the discussion of whether this was a unique case to the historians. But I would note that there certainly have been many examples since the Second World War when States have indeed attacked their neighbors in a seemingly unprovoked way. In this sense, we could say that the Nazi case provides some help in deciding how to proceed, namely, by having the determination of State aggression be made at trial on the basis of something like the factors I have proposed, on the assumption that the world community does come to accept my proposal about what constitutes the prima facie case for the crime of aggression.

There is a very serious question, though, about whether any proposed test for what constitutes State aggression should be administered by a court or by some more explicitly political body. One strategy is to take out of the hands of the Prosecutor of the International Criminal Court any case concerning the crime of aggression that has not been referred by the Security Council of the United Nations. Article 13 of the Rome Statute lists three ways that a case can come to the Court: (a) referral from a State party, (b) referral from the Security Council, and (c) direct initiation from the Prosecutor of the ICC. It might make sense to restrict jurisdiction of the Court concerning crimes of aggression only to (b) as a way of shielding the Court from getting involved in making decisions that will be seen as highly political.

The drawback is that the Court is then, at least concerning this matter, subordinate to the Security Council, not independent of it. And given the history of the Security Council, there are very good reasons to think that it will become embroiled in political controversy about whether a member State has engaged in aggression. Indeed, even in otherwise clear-cut cases, it may be that a State that has a veto on the Security Council will stop a referral to the ICC. The Security Council is not like normal legislatures in that it gives more power, many would say too much power, to certain States that may have vested interests in blocking prosecutions that come from certain parts of the world where those States also reside.

My view is that it will be better, although far from problem-free, to let the ICC decide whether State aggression has occurred rather than to let the Security Council make this determination. The ICC will be somewhat tainted by making these political decisions, but at least it will retain its independence from the Security Council, which would be likely either not to issue many referrals or to issue them for the wrong reasons. Independent judges are, in my view, better able to make these often highly politically charged decisions than is the Security Council. Of course, if there were major changes to the Security Council in the future, or if a true international legislature were to arise that had the power of referral, I might change this assessment.

In any event, the crime of aggression surely can be defined in a way that could garner widespread international support given how much convergence there is between the historical Just War tradition and contemporary international legal documents about the international use of force and the initiation of war. I have argued for a particularly intuitive idea of what counts as the prima facie element of State aggression. Here the main factor is whether a State has been the one to strike first in a way that is not justified by reference to provocation, self-defense, or defense of others. I have characterized this view as the "first wrong" rather than the "first strike" view. That each of these factors may themselves be debated further is no reason not to recognize that they can be supported by an international consensus. Nearly every element of every crime can be debated, and here also this is no reason not to recognize these elements as legitimate bases for establishing prima facie criminal liability.

As far as the State aggression element goes, I have agreed with the Nuremberg judges that in some cases acts of hostility are so grave and obvious, such as when unprovoked invasions into populated areas occur, that trials can proceed beyond the first stage without acceptance of more fine-grained definitions of aggression.[32] Whitney Harris, one of the Nuremberg prosecutors, puts the point this way:

> No fair-minded person could read the record of the Nazi regime and fail to conclude that the attacks commencing with the assault upon Poland were clear cases of aggression.[33]

This is a reasonable approach to the first of the prima facie elements of the crime of aggression.

In my view, defining aggression as a crime and setting out its elements is a manageable task and certainly should not cause the international community to shy away from prosecuting this important crime. The United Nations and nearly all international organizations are committed to the promotion of peace and protection of human rights across the globe. Surely such goals must start with outlawing wars of aggression, and intuitively there seems to be no reason not to follow the Nuremberg "precedent" and common sense in setting the stage for prosecutions against those who initiate or plan such wars by setting out the elements of such a crime. To fail to do so because we failed to reach such an agreement during the Cold War years is to disregard what has been emerging as a consensus for many years now within the Just War and international communities. In this chapter I provided a sketch of how we might solve some of the most difficult conceptual problems in this area of international criminal law. But to convict individuals for the crime of aggression, more is needed than to show that the State of which these individuals are members engaged in a war of aggression. This is indeed a start and an important start at establishing the case against these individuals. In the next two chapters I will examine the objective and subjective elements that must also be proved, in addition to State aggression, for successful prosecutions of individuals for the crime of aggression.

---

[32] But as I argued above, an explicit form of acceptance will be necessary to satisfy the principle of legality.

[33] Whitney R. Harris, *Tyranny on Trial*, Dallas, TX: Southern Methodist University Press, 1954, 1999, p. 515.

11

Act and Circumstance in the Crime of Aggression

In this chapter and the next, I will discuss conceptual and normative problems in the additional elements, other than State aggression, that must be proved to hold individuals liable for the crime of aggression. The central concern will be with the objective and subjective elements that the prosecution needs to prove to link an individual defendant's act and state of mind to the State aggression and therefore to make the individual person liable for what the State has done in waging aggressive war. In international criminal law it is individuals, not States, who are in the dock, and yet the crimes that are alleged are those that only States or other groups can commit. Concerning the crime of aggression, there are even larger problems than in other international crimes in order for trials to proceed. In the crime of aggression, the acts that individuals commit are not themselves criminal: they are only criminal because they are part of the initiation of illegal war. In the current chapter, I attempt to solve this problem, but along the way I indicate how difficult the problem is and why it will often be very hard for individual prosecutions to go forward except against the highest-ranking State leaders.

There is both a conceptual and normative question about how we link the act of an individual person to State aggression in a criminal trial. The conceptual difficulty taken up in this chapter is that one individual cannot wage war. An individual's act is always only one of many acts that constitute waging war. The conceptual question is why this individual's act is singled out among so many other acts, and why this individual's act is called the *actus reus*, the guilty act, of the crime of aggression. The normative question follows closely on the heels of the conceptual question. Why should we think that an individual's act is sufficient to establish criminal liability for the crime of aggression? Even if we think that an individual's act could be conceptually called an *actus reus* of some kind of crime, why think that this is normatively sufficient for establishing liability for something as enormous as the crime of waging aggressive war? Of course, in answering these questions, it will be significant that we will almost always be looking at the acts of leaders rather than mere followers.

The chapter proceeds as follows. In the first section, I consider some additional lessons to be learned from the trials at Nuremberg, the only significant trials that we have had for the crime of aggression. Here I highlight one of the more interesting findings of these trials concerning the *actus reus* of individuals. In the second section, I explore an idea put forward by Roger Clark that the key to *actus reus* in this type of crime is to think of how the act relates to the circumstance or context of the overall war. Ultimately I agree with Clark that this is the right question to ask but disagree with his proposed answer to the conceptual question posed earlier. In the third section, I examine two of the main candidate acts, commanding and planning, that seem to be the best at linking individuals to the larger State aggression. In the fourth section, I argue that merely taking part in an aggressive war is not sufficient to establish the *actus reus* of the crime of aggression. In the final section, I discuss one important defense that is open to some State leaders, the defense of superior orders. Throughout this chapter, I try to find the most plausible basis for holding State leaders criminally liable when State aggression occurs. I argue that the *actus reus* element can be met by some individual military or political leaders but that it is far harder to do so than is normally thought.

I. The Problem of Acts

Not all acts committed during war, or even as contributions to the war effort, are guilty acts that satisfy the act or objective element of the crime of aggression. For an act to be an *actus reus*, it must be both an act and in some sense a violation of a legal duty. As we will see in greater detail later in this chapter, there is a controversy about how to understand acts in legal theory. One way initially to understand an act is as having three constituent parts:

1. its origin, such as bodily activity
2. certain surrounding circumstances
3. certain consequences

LaFave and Scott give the following example: "in a situation where A shoots and kills B, this 'act' might be said to include the muscular contraction by which the trigger was pulled, the circumstances that the weapon was loaded and that B was in the line of fire, and the consequence of B's death."[1]

What makes the act criminal is that to do that act is in some sense illegal or wrongful. So one question to ask is whether every act that in some sense contributes to a war of aggression should be an illegal or wrongful act. Consider the act of growing the wheat that contributes to the making of the soldier's mess. It is odd indeed to think that such an act should be illegal, especially if we strip it from its corresponding mental element and leave open the possibility that the farmer is unaware that a war is occurring at all. Why does the fact that a war is being waged, and that the act of the farmer contributes to the war effort, make his act so different from growing wheat just yesterday before the war was begun? It looks like it is the mental element, knowing about the war or intending to contribute to it, that should make the act illegal rather than that the act of growing wheat is itself illegal or wrongful.

And where would the farmer go to find out that his act of growing wheat is now proscribed and satisfies the *actus reus*, objective, element of the crime of aggression? It certainly is not reasonable to expect the farmer, in some remote section of the country, to know that his government has initiated a war of aggression and to realize that continuing to farm will make the farmer's actions complicit in that war. And what of the farmer who knows that a war has broken out and that his produce will support the troops but also believes that the war is just rather than unjust? As we saw in Chapter 8, an American Military Tribunal sitting in Nuremberg ruled in the Ministries case that it is not appropriate to hold someone like our farmer liable for doing what he thought was his patriotic duty. But we are also asking the question of whether there is a sense that his act might be guilty regardless of what he thought he was doing, as long as his act did indeed contribute to the waging of aggressive–that is, illegal–war.

There are two strategies that could be proposed but that have rather obvious problems. First, one could try to infer that the farmer did have knowledge of the State aggression as a constructive knowledge that emanated from the farmer's behavior. Such a strategy merely begs the question of whether there is anything about the behavior to distinguish what this farmer is doing from what any farmer would normally do in times when there was no illegal war. Second, one could look to the political role of the farmer to see if the farmer had been authorized to act

---

[1] Wayne R. LaFave and Austin W. Scott, Jr., *Criminal Law*, 2nd ed., St. Paul, MN: West, 1986, p. 195.

for the State and hence was complicit in the waging of aggressive war. Yet here, too, farmers don't generally play political roles of this sort, and this is true of soldiers and most leaders within a State as well, except for the highest-ranking leaders.

The Charter of the International Military Tribunal laid out the general principles and jurisdiction that would govern the trial at Nuremberg. Importantly it listed, among the acts within its jurisdiction, the following:

> Crimes against peace: namely, planning, preparation, initiation or waging of a war of aggression, or a war in violation of international treaties, agreements or assurances, or participation in a common plan or conspiracy for the accomplishment of any of the foregoing.[2]

The prosecution then divided this crime into two charges: "Count one of the Nuremberg indictment charged the defendants with conspiring or having a common plan to commit crimes against peace. Count two alleged that the defendants were responsible for specific crimes against peace by planning, preparing, initiating, and waging wars of aggression."[3] For our purposes this division makes it clear that the defendants were being tried either for having initiated aggressive war by planning or preparing for it, or for conspiracy to do these acts.

Here is the conceptual puzzle that will consume the rest of this chapter. Crimes against peace, unlike war crimes, for instance, are crimes committed by States, yet criminal trials do not have States in the dock. The most obvious person to put in the dock when States commit crimes would be the State's head. But even this person, the president of a State for instance, typically does not act as an individual but as a representative of the people or of the ruling elite. Even the head of a State is not clearly responsible, as an individual, for waging aggressive war. Things are even more difficult when we are thinking of lower-ranking individuals within a hierarchical State structure. How, if at all, can these individuals be linked to the State's responsibility? The theory of conspiracy was advanced at Nuremberg to try to solve this conceptual problem, but there remain significant difficulties with this proposed solution, as we have seen earlier and will see again in the next chapter.

At Nuremberg, some of these problems already were evident. One question is whether one needs to show that a single plan was *developed by all* of the members of a single set of conspirators for the initiation

[2] Charter of the International Military Tribunal at Nuremberg, Annex to the London Agreement (August 8, 1945), 82 U.N.T.S. 279, Article 6 (a).

[3] Matthew Lippman, "The History, Development, and Decline of Crimes against Peace," *George Washington University International Law Review*, vol. 36, 2004, p. 992.

of the war or whether the plan was to be thought of as mainly that of one person with lots of others *merely following* the plan. The Nuremberg Tribunal displayed a somewhat cavalier attitude toward these important issues. Concerning the first alternative, the Tribunal held, "It is immaterial to consider whether a single conspiracy to the extent and over the time set out in the Indictment has been conclusively proved. Continued planning, with aggressive war as the objective, has been established beyond doubt." And concerning the second alternative, the Tribunal held that

> A plan in the execution of which a number of persons participate is still a plan, even though conceived by only one of them; and those who execute the plan do not avoid responsibility by showing that they acted under the man who conceived it. Hitler could not make aggressive war by himself. He had to have the cooperation of statesmen, military leaders, diplomats, and businessmen.... That they were assigned to their tasks by a dictator does not absolve them from responsibility here any more than it does in the comparable tyranny of organized domestic crime.[4]

On this basis the International Military Tribunal at Nuremberg convicted some of the very top leaders of the Third Reich for crimes against peace and waging aggressive war.

In a subsequent case before the American Military Tribunal sitting at Nuremberg under Control Council Law No. 10, the Tribunal ruled:

> If and as long as a member of the armed forces does not participate in the preparation, planning, initiation, or waging of aggressive war on a policy level, his war activities do not fall under the definition of crimes against peace.... The crime denounced by the law is the use of war as an instrument of national policy. Those who commit the crime are those who participate at the policy making level in planning, preparation, or in initiating war.[5]

And here, in this subsequent case that tried high-ranking but not policy-making members of the Third Reich, all of the defendants were acquitted of crimes against peace because they were not thought to be at a sufficiently high policy-making level.

The conclusion that I will support is two-part. First, we should not regard acts as illegal or wrongful by linking the act element to the mental element. But second, if we do not link the act element to the mental element then it will be very difficult to say that the act should indeed be illegal or wrongful, and hence difficult to say that the *actus reus* element has been satisfied. Acts, such as growing wheat or marching while carrying

[4] Opinion and Judgment, International Military Tribunal at Nuremberg, 1946, quoted in Jordan Paust, et al., *International Criminal Law: Cases and Materials*, pp. 759–760.
[5] United States v. von Loeb (The High Command Case), American Military Tribunal, 1948; *Trials of War Criminals*, 1950, p. 462, quoted in Paust, ibid., pp. 764–765.

guns, should rarely in themselves be seen as illegal or wrongful. This is because acts of this sort, the acts that mainly constitute participation in war, are not wrong outside of the circumstances of war. And these acts are really only wrong because of the intent to do them to advance an illegal war objective. Of course, it is possible to finesse this issue by looking to the circumstance component of the act as a way of differentiating acts without bringing in mental states. Such a strategy has an enormous amount of merit but there are also significant hurdles nonetheless. I will next examine an important conceptual question about the act element and how it relates to the State aggression element.

II. State Aggression as a Circumstance

State aggression is an element in the crime of aggression of an individual. We need to distinguish acts of State aggression from individual acts of participating in the crime of aggression. We then need to recognize that there will be elements concerning the individual defendant other than State aggression and these elements will need to be linked to the State aggression. In 2002, the last Coordinator of the Preparatory Commission's (PrepCom's) Working Group on the Crime of Aggression issued a discussion paper setting out various alternatives in trying to reach a final proposal on the crime of aggression in the ICC statute.[6] In this working group paper it remains somewhat unclear how the ICC will understand the element of State aggression in the individual crime of aggression. This is, at least in part, because the drafters of this document do not seem to have a firm grasp on the distinction between act, consequence, and circumstance.

A political or military leader cannot engage in an "act" of State aggression since this is a collective act, an act of a State or State-like entity that has the ability to make war on another collective entity.[7] This is not to say that prosecutors do not need to prove that political or military leaders acted,

[6] Discussion paper proposed by the Coordinator; Part I, Definition of the crime of aggression and conditions for the exercise of jurisdiction; Part II, Elements of the crime of aggression (as defined in the Rome Statute of the International Criminal Court), UN Doc. PCNICC/WGCA/RT.1 (2002). See the excellent discussion of this document in Roger Clark's "The Crime of Aggression and the International Criminal Court," forthcoming in Jose Doria, Hans-Peter Gasser, and M. Cherif Bassiouni, editors, *The Legal Regime of the International Criminal Court*, 2006.

[7] There is a sense in which State leaders, in their role as representing the State, can initiate aggressive war. But there remains a good question as to whether these leaders, as individuals, should be prosecuted on this basis alone. I would contend that individuals, not representatives, are in the dock and should be treated accordingly. I am grateful to Andy Altman for pressing me on this point.

but only that the *actus reus* in question cannot be called State aggression. It might be that the act of the leader is to give the order to go to war, and so aggression would be the consequence of the acts of the leader. This seems plausible until one realizes that typically there are many other acts that feed into the consequence of initiating war, so it is rare if ever that the acts of a leader are the sole basis for aggressive war.

Waging war is a collective action, that is, a combination of individual acts that are organized in a certain way. As in collective action generally, the organization of the individual acts cannot itself be reduced to the acts and states of mind of the individual actors. I have previously defended this analysis by arguing that collective action is the action of a group, and a group is best understood as individuals in various relationships, where the relationships cannot be reduced to features of those individuals.[8] Collective action is not the same as aggregated individual action since there is something about the organizational structure or relationships that at least partially transforms the individual actions into something more than merely their sum.

Metaphysically, waging war cannot be reduced to what a leader does in declaring war and then adding in what his or her troops do in attacking the troops of an enemy. Rather, any account of waging war would have to mention the acts of leaders and soldiers as well as the way these various acts are coordinated so as to be able to produce various consequences. And when we come to sort out who is morally responsible or legally liable for which consequences, we will not be able to focus only on the acts of one or another person whose collective acts constituted waging war. Waging war is a collective action and yet trials put discrete individuals in the dock, most likely the political or military leaders of the State that is judged to have acted aggressively. Waging war is not *merely* a consequence of the acts of a military or political leader, or a soldier for that matter. A more promising approach would be to see State aggression as a circumstance of the acts of the leader who is being prosecuted. This would mean that State aggression is not seen implausibly as what these leaders do, but as one of the elements that needs to be proved as a surrounding factor in what the leader did.

One could object that some leaders engage in acts that come very close to constituting war, such as when a State's leader issues a declaration of war. Such an act of declaration does not appear to be part of a circumstance of war rather than a constitution of war. Earlier, in Chapter 10, I rejected the idea that merely issuing a declaration of war should count

[8] Larry May, *The Morality of Groups*, Notre Dame, IN: University of Notre Dame Press, 1987.

as an act of aggression. Indeed, I would add that if all we have is such a declaration, and there are no other actions by members of the State, then there certainly isn't aggressive war, let alone war at all. The act of declaring war is only an act of war when it is issued in the circumstances where troops are ready to attack or missiles are ready to be launched, and so on. The leader normally plays a very significant role here, but his or her acts are only acts of war when in the midst of the circumstances of war.

To see what the individual leader did as a part of the waging of aggressive war, it is crucial to look at the role played by that individual. The individual should not be held responsible for the role, but for what was accomplished by the individual acting in that role. Indeed, we should probably discount the individual's responsibility by what is added by others who have established or facilitated the performance of that role. But an individual could indeed be prosecuted for what that individual did, without diminishing the idea that the crime is largely a collective crime, if what the individual did can be significantly linked to the aggressive war. I suggest that the way to make this linkage is by considering the circumstances of that individual's act.

Circumstances are conditions or events surrounding an act that give the act a special character that the act would not necessarily have otherwise. If I try to strike you, this is normally a wrong. But if I do so in the circumstance or context of a boxing match things are quite different. Similarly, if I say "charge," it normally has little significance. But if I do so when the soldiers under my command are waiting for my signal to begin attacking the enemy, there is quite a lot of significance to my act. Bentham saw circumstances as background conditions that added sense to the meaning of acts and allowed certain acts to be seen as discrete actions. It seems to me that the category of circumstances has a special relationship to the acts of leaders in aggressive wars.

According to the 18th-century philosopher Jeremy Bentham, circumstances "must necessarily be taken into account before any assessment can be determined relative to the consequences. In some circumstances, even to kill a man may be beneficial."[9] Bentham says:

> the etymology of the word *circumstance* is perfectly characteristic of its import: *circum stantia*, things standing around . . . the field of circumstances, belonging to any act, may be defined a circle, of which the circumference is no where, but of which the act in question is the center. Now then, as any act

[9] Jeremy Bentham, *An Introduction to the Principles of Morals and Legislation*, 1789, edited by J. H. Burns and H. L. A. Hart, Oxford: Oxford University Press, 1970, p. 79.

may, for the purpose of discourse, be considered as a center, any other act or object whatsoever may be considered as of the number of those that are standing around it.[10]

Bentham thought that there were many ways to characterize acts in circumstances. Indeed, for Bentham, there is a cone of circumstance that corresponds to the famous cone of causation surrounding any act, and we can slice this cone many different ways and get distinctly different actions that contain the act in question.[11]

Circumstances also determine which consequences will be considered related to a particular action. Bentham divides circumstances into four classes: criminative, exculpative, extenuative, and aggravative. Depending on which circumstance we focus on, an action may be considered criminal or not. Indeed, most crimes fix a specific circumstance to the elements of a crime. If I kill someone accidentally but while in the circumstance of committing a robbery, my action will be seen as the criminal offense of murder, whereas in most other circumstances, an act of accidentally killing is not considered murder. Similarly, if the circumstance of my killing is that there was a threat to my own life that could be eliminated in no other way than by killing, this is at the very least an extenuating circumstance that will mitigate, if not relieve, me from punishment.

Roger Clark gives an account of how to understand the relation between State and individual acts in various international crimes by reference to the idea of "contextual circumstances":

> In practice the sub-category included only three items in the Elements: a manifest pattern of similar conduct, in the case of genocide; a widespread or systematic attack against a civilian population, in the case of crimes against humanity; and an armed conflict, in the case of war crimes. Perhaps the act of aggression by a State which … is an element of the crime of aggression by an individual, as currently defined in the negotiations, can be classified as a 'contextual circumstance.'[12]

I will spend the rest of this section assessing Clark's proposal, which I initially find to be quite plausible.

Let us expand on Clark's observations about some of the differences between the crime of aggression and other international crimes concerning acts and circumstances. In crimes against humanity, the prosecutor

[10] Ibid., note l, pp. 79–80.
[11] Ibid., p. 81.
[12] Roger Clark, "The Crime of Aggression and the International Criminal Court," draft p. 13.

must prove that the defendant's acts were part of a widespread or systematic attack on a civilian population. To put the element this way construes the widespread or systematic attack as the whole of which the defendant's act, for instance of torture or murder, was a part. It is a bit misleading to say that an ethnic cleansing campaign was merely a contextual circumstance. For then it could be that the acts of torture or murder need not have played any role at all in the ethnic cleansing campaign, but only that there was such a campaign occurring at the same time that the defendant acted. One could then try to link the act and circumstance by way of the mental element, that is, by requiring a showing that the defendant was aware of the larger circumstance or even intended that his act be part of it. But even doing this opens the door rather far to the possibility that a defendant's act could have no *significant* role in a larger enterprise, and yet the defendant could be found guilty of the crime of perpetrating the larger harm.

Things get even more problematic when we are talking of crimes of aggression or crimes against peace rather than crimes against humanity. In crimes of aggression, the defendants will be high-ranking political and military leaders. It would be problematic indeed for a leader to stand trial for acts taken in the circumstances of aggressive war but where there was no clear-cut connection between the leader's acts and the aggressive war. Perhaps there won't be too many cases of this sort, but this will depend on how high in rank the defendants are. It seems odd to think that a person could be prosecuted for the crime of aggression when the acts he is accused of having committed bear no significant connection to the waging of aggressive war, except that they had the war as a contextual circumstance.

The plausible idea that lies behind Clark's suggestion is to tie the acts of a leader to the circumstances of State aggression by requiring that it be proved that the leader participates in the plan to wage aggressive war. Such participation need not be causally efficacious, or at least not if causation is understood in a but-for way. For leaders, like soldiers, are often replaceable, so we could not say that but for the participation of the leader the war would not have occurred. This is further evidence for thinking that the right relationship between acts of leaders and State aggression is not one of act and consequence. Rather, the participation is indeed part, although not a significant part, of the planning and initiating of war.[13]

---

[13] It may be that ultimately it makes more sense simply to say that the acts of the leader must be a part of the war as a whole. I thank Michael Zimmerman for suggesting this point to me.

Clark may mean to avoid some of the problems I have identified by adding the term "context" to circumstance, even though he only says that this makes a subcategory of circumstances. I would urge that Clark's proposal be amended so that instead of "contextual" we use the term "overarching" as a way to indicate that there is a relationship between the act and the circumstance. I am in general agreement with Clark that State aggression is more like a circumstance than an act or a consequence in the elements of the individual crime of aggression or the crime against peace, for what we want to rule out is the possibility that a leader could be convicted for this crime even though his acts were not significantly related to State aggression occurring around him or her. I leave out of consideration whether this will happen very often but merely propose this amendment to make sure that defendants are indeed properly protected from this sort of occurrence.

The element of State aggression is, in my view, best understood as a type of circumstance that must be proven by the prosecutor in order to establish the prima facie case against an individual leader for committing a crime against peace or a crime of aggression. Aggression is both the name of a type of war, a type of crime, and also an element of a crime. This can be ripe for confusion unless we keep all of these senses of aggression separate. I have tried to keep these different senses of aggression separate in this section, although only in a preliminary way. More good conceptual work needs to be done if this type of international crime is going to be as well defined as the other three types of crime (crimes against humanity, war crimes, and genocide) that the ICC is beginning to prosecute individuals for having committed. I next turn to an examination of some of the specific acts that a State leader could commit that would link him or her to State aggression and establish the objective element in the crime of aggression in international criminal law.

III. Participating and Being Liable

In this section I wish to indicate why I think that the individual act component cannot best be understood as merely a part of the overall waging of aggressive war without being connected to the circumstance of the State aggression. I will be especially interested in examining the theory advanced by Christopher Kutz about how best to understand acts of complicity. In a very clear manner, Kutz sets out three competing principles that can be used to understand which acts of individuals who participate in groups make those individuals responsible for what the group does.

1. Individual Difference Principle: I am accountable for a harm only if what I have done made a difference to the harm's occurrence.
2. Control Principle: I am responsible for a harm only if I could control its occurrence, by producing or preventing it.
3. Complicity Principle: I am accountable for a harm of others only if I intentionally participate in the wrong they do or the harm they cause.[14]

The first two principles lead to the result that I am accountable only for the difference my action has made in the overall group effort or for what I had control over in that effort. But the third principle results in a very different notion of accountability: "I am accountable for the harm we do together, independently of the actual difference I make."[15]

Kutz rightly points out that the first two principles are best understood in light of third-party understanding of collective action, that is, those looking at the collective action who do not participate in it. These first two principles are also most in line with consequentialist and deontological accounts of ethics. In a crucial section of his book, Kurtz argues that traditional ethical theory has difficulty making sense of collective action. The argument is largely intuitive: complicity seems to make sense and yet individualistic normative theories cannot account for these intuitions. As a remedy for this failure, Kutz develops the idea that participation is the key to determining whether an individual's act should be counted as sufficiently part of the group action to make the individual accountable for what the group did. I agree that participation is key but disagree with Kutz about which type of participation is key.

Kutz distinguishes between accountability and blameworthiness. He argues that the "intentional participation in the collective endeavor does not make them blameworthy." But if the group in question cannot be blamed or cannot compensate for the harm done, it may be that the individual is "accountable in the domain of repair" when the group "cannot meet its warranted claims."[16] So it seems that accountability can be transformed into blameworthiness for Kutz in certain kinds of circumstance. I agree that this may appear to be warranted but I remain unconvinced that such accountability is morally or legally significant.

---

[14] Christopher Kutz, *Complicity: Ethics and Law for a Collective Age*, New York: Cambridge University Press, 2000.
[15] Ibid., p. 122.
[16] Ibid., p. 246.

I believe that a control principle rather than a complicity principle should remain the cornerstone of our assessments of individual acts in collective action cases. Mere participation is not sufficient for moral or legal accountability or responsibility. And this can be made especially clear, I think, by looking at the acts of even the members of a group that are most identifiable with the group: its leaders. The issue is whether those who participate in aggressive war, but whose participation really didn't make a difference in the sense that the war would have gone on even without their participation, should be held liable for the crime of aggression.

This raises a difficult issue of causation. In legal theory one traditional way to think about an act is that it plays a causal role in a result if "but for" the act's existence, the result would not have taken place. Such a view of causation has been recently thought to be inadequate for several reasons I will outline. However, it is not clear what theory of causation should replace the discredited "but for" theory. I will propose a replacement, in outline form, and then argue that the replacement theory will solve some of the problems of how we should view the act component of the crime of aggression or other international crimes that were left unsolved when the strict but-for test is used.

The main problem with "but for" causation is that it extends back so far in time that an enormous number of acts, quite counter-intuitively, turn out to satisfy the causation condition. Think again of the farmer whose growing of wheat causally contributes to the making of bread that is then included in the soldier's mess and the soldier then takes part in a war of aggression. The farmer's act might be a remote cause of the waging of the war, if "but for" the farmer's growing of wheat the war could not be waged. But the "but for" approach to causation does not stop there. It is also true that the farmer's father who got the farm in inheritance, and the farmer's grandfather who bought the farm, and the original seller who had diverted the stream to create the farm, and on back we can go, all might be causally necessary in the soldier's waging aggressive war. Yet, now we are talking about acts that are so remote from the waging of war that it is ridiculous to think that the illegality of the war makes those acts themselves illegal or wrongful due to their causal contribution to the waging of that war. What we need is a mechanism for eliminating the remote causes and focusing us on the proximate ones.

The famous cone of causation, where causation extends back in time in ever widening directions, was designed to illustrate the conceptual problems in thinking of causation according to the "but for" model. If we had sufficient information, we could trace back in the "but for" way each of our own acts to the acts of Adam and Eve, or whoever the first humans were. Surely, it makes little sense to think of participation in the "but for" way. But it is hard to figure out a good alternative to this strategy. One possibility, which I began to explore earlier in this chapter, is to use the circumstances surrounding the physical act as a limiting condition for the "but for" test. We will get an enormous boost by being able to disregard acts that were remote in time to the event in question.

If the growing of wheat is done in the circumstances of war in the sense that contemporaneous to the growing of wheat the war is being waged, then we can greatly reduce the number of acts that would be causally related to the war. Unfortunately, we still have the problem that the wrongness of the act needs to be linked to the wrongfulness of the war. And the fact that the act is causally linked to the wrongful war, as a consequence, does not yet show that the act is itself wrongful for similar reasons to what we rehearsed earlier in this chapter when we discussed the relation between acts and consequences.

IV. Participating in the Circumstances of War

In the wonderful film about Robert S. McNamara, "The Fog of War," we get some insight into how to understand the circumstances of war and why it is often so hard to figure out who, if anyone, should be held liable when wars go astray. During the lead-up to war, and certainly during wartime, the focus of attention of most of the people in leadership roles is simply on winning the war, not on whether it was initiated properly or whether it is being waged justly. As the title of the movie indicates, the circumstances of war cause a fog to spread over all of the people who participate in war rendering the morality and legality of the war nearly invisible.

In this section of the chapter, I begin to explore a possible defense to the charge of aggression that is based on a parallel consideration to the "fog of war" illustrated in the McNamara film. Earlier we discussed the problem of the farmer who simply does not realize that yesterday a war was initiated that made his act of growing wheat a potentially wrongful act as part of the waging of aggressive war. We can also think about a commander who, in training his or her troops, is in a similar predicament to that of the farmer. The commander may be blinded by the fog of war in that he or she is unable to tell whether the war he or she is participating in is a war of aggression, and hence unable to tell that his or her acts are wrongful. We can perhaps go straight up the line to all of the military and civilian leaders in a country, stopping only at the top leader who did an act that initiated the waging of aggressive war. If the farmer's act does not meet the *actus reus* requirement for criminal liability, why think that anyone else's act, with the exception of the top leader's acts does as well? Even if the commander, like the farmer, knows that war has just broken out, it is far from clear that the commander and the farmer know that that war is a war of aggression. Once again, their acts seem to be the same as they were before the war broke out. There is some sense in saying that their acts are not clearly wrongful, and hence that they didn't meet the *actus reus* element of a crime. But there are problems with the attempt to assimilate the role of commanders to that of farmers.

Commanders and other military and political leaders are different from farmers in that they normally not only know about plans of war but also often have participated in the planning of the war. Unlike the farmer, military and political leaders are sometimes in a position to be able to stop a war from being initiated or waged. And unlike the farmer, the military or political leaders of especially non-democratic States may themselves issue commands that cause the war to come into being. There is nothing like the issuing of commands that farmers or other civilians typically do in a war. This is one of the main reasons that it will make sense for the ICC to prosecute only the top State leaders for the crime of aggression, as we saw in Chapter 8.

When we come to examine the standard kinds of acts thought to satisfy the *actus reus* component of the crime of aggression, many of the issues we discussed earlier in this chapter come to a head. If a commander issues an order to place the state's troops and aim their weapons at troops on the other side of the border, in the circumstances of heightened tensions between two States, such an order could constitute the commander's *actus reus* in a crime of aggression. By so acting, the commander could participate in waging aggressive war and may do so as clearly as if the commander were the one who planned the invasion. Based on our earlier analysis, the command is a link to liability. We look to the circumstances that surround the act of the commander and ask whether those circumstances were such that war was likely to occur if the commander did what she was about to do.

If a commander fails to issue an order to restrain the State's soldiers from shooting across a border in the circumstances of heightened tensions between two States, such failure to act could also constitute the commander's *actus reus* in a crime of aggression. Similar to our earlier analysis, the key here is whether the failure to act made a difference in the sense that if the failure had not occurred the war would not have been initiated. And we begin by looking at the circumstances that surrounded the failure to act. But ascertaining the circumstances surrounding a failure to act is even more difficult than making this assessment for acts that are positive rather than negative, to use the terminology often employed to distinguish acting from failing to act. This is because it is much more difficult to predict what would have happened in the counter-factual than what is likely to happen in the real case.

Whether the act in question is positive or negative, it may constitute the *actus reus* component of the crime of aggression, but a number of defenses can be brought forward even in the case of military or political leaders. A defense can be drawn in terms of knowledge or intent, which I will explore in the following chapter. But in this chapter I wish to examine a defense against the *actus reus* element of the crime of aggression. And here one of the first things to think about is that even very high-ranking leaders may still be merely in the chain of command, that is, their actions are taken because they have been ordered to act in certain ways. If one person commits an act, or fails to act, because she has been ordered so to act, or not to act, it is hard to see that act as the salient act that initiated war, at least in the sense that it is wrongful. This raises the thorny issue of whether there could be State aggression without some acts of individuals that count as crimes of aggression. Georgio Gaja has contended that a finding of State aggression "necessarily implies that at least some leaders of the aggressor State are criminally responsible."[17] I do not agree that there is a necessary connection here, but I do agree that normally someone is criminally responsible, yet the question is who in the chain of command would indeed count here.

Mere participation by an individual in State aggression is obviously not enough to count as satisfying the *actus reus* element of the crime of aggression, as the example of the farmer was meant to show. We can also see this point by differentiating between a commander who, on her own initiative, issues an order to place her troops and aim their weapons at troops on the other side of the border during circumstances of heightened tensions between two States, and a commander who does this because she has herself been ordered to issue this order. Do both acts of issuing orders

[17] Georgio Gaja, "The Respective Roles of the ICC and the Security Council in Determining the Existence of Aggression," in *The International Criminal Court and the Crime of Aggression*, edited by Mauro Politi and Giuseppe Nesi, Burlington, VT: Ashgate, 2004, p. 124.

count as significant participation in aggressive war? In one respect the answer is surely yes since both acts are important ingredients in initiating war, and if either act had failed to happen the war might very well not have occurred. But when we ask the further question of whether both acts satisfy the *actus reus* element of the crime of aggression, the answer gets murkier.

The problem can be seen by reference to another comparison. If one soldier tortures a prisoner of war on his own initiative and another soldier tortures because he has been so ordered, both of these acts seem to satisfy the *actus reus* element of the war crime of torture of a prisoner of war. Torture is wrongful, and it doesn't matter who does it. But in the case of issuing an order to place her troops and aim their weapons at troops on the other side of the border, it is unclear that such an act is always wrongful, since this may be a self-defensive response, as was indicated in Chapter 4 as well as in Chapter 10. Of course, in the context of heightened tensions, the act could be thought of as initiating war, which is surely wrongful in many circumstances. But we would need to know whether the current circumstances of heightened tensions are indeed wrong-making circumstances, and we will also need to know more than this since the ordering of troops to move from one point to another, and even to aim their weapons at other troops, is not itself proscribed by international law. The act that the second commander is ordered to perform is not like the act of torture, namely, an act that is always wrongful.

Indeed, the act of ordering troops to move from point A to point B is rarely a wrongful act, and whether it is wrongful will depend on a large number of factors, many of which may be unknown and even unknowable by the person issuing the order. If an act is unknowably wrongful, it seems odd indeed to say of that act that it is *actus reus*, that is, a guilty act. Guilty acts seem to be ones that a person could have known to be wrongful, even if we don't require that the person actually knew this. We can accept the idea that lies behind the truism that ignorance of the law is no excuse and still think that an act that couldn't be known to be wrongful should not count as *actus reus*. For *actus reus* is all about doing that which is illegal or wrongful, and it seems odd indeed to make this a kind of strict liability, where we only look to see whether the act was performed and then independently ask whether such an act is illegal or wrongful.

Of course, what this does is to ask whether *actus reus* can be completely separated from *mens rea*, since awareness or knowledge is here seen as crucial to the very assessment of the character of the act. As we will see, one of the hallmarks of the superior orders defense is that the person did not know that an order was indeed wrongful. For this reason we may very well want to let the commander have the defense that his act was not proscribed and hence not an *actus reus*, or we might at least give the commander a defense, such as the superior orders defense in such cases, despite the fact that since Nuremberg superior orders defenses have not fared well. I will take up this latter issue in more detail in the final section of this chapter.

V. Revisiting the Superior Orders Defense

The fact that a commander was given an order to do something does not always affect the character of the act that is then performed in conformity with the order. The circumstances are not affected, for instance, nor often are the consequences of the act. In torture cases this will not be true. But the kinds of acts that constitute participation in aggressive war are often quite different from torture in that they are not themselves wrongful but only wrongful as they are part of something else. If a person has been ordered to do something that is wrongful in all circumstances, it may make sense to deny that person the superior orders defense. But when the act, such as ordering troops to move from point A to point B, and even to point their guns at other troops, is not itself wrongful, we may wish to reopen the defense of superior orders since the thing that makes the act of issuing these orders wrongful is something else that may not be any part of the plan of the commander who is ordered to issue this command. Of course, there is always someone at the top of the chain who cannot claim superior orders, but my point is that it may only be one person, while all of the others are in a sense merely following that order. Superior orders defenses are generally not much in favor these days,[18] but it is my contention that if there are to be prosecutions for crimes of aggression such defenses should come back on the table. In this section I will provide conceptual and normative support for such a claim.

Since the trials at Nuremberg, the superior orders defense has been under attack. The Rome Statute of the ICC devoted Article 33 to superior orders:

1. The fact that a crime within the jurisdiction of the Court has been committed by a person pursuant to an order of a Government or of

---

[18] See my discussion of this issue concerning crimes against humanity in *Crimes against Humanity: A Normative Account*, New York: Cambridge University Press, 2005, ch. 10.

a superior, whether military or civilian, shall not relieve that person
of criminal responsibility unless:

  (a) The person was under a legal obligation to obey orders of the
      Government or the superior in question;
  (b) The person did not know that the order was unlawful; and
  (c) The order was not manifestly unlawful.

  2. For the purposes of this article, orders to commit genocide or
     crimes against humanity are manifestly illegal.

Notice that the third condition (c) is probably satisfied in the crime of
aggression, since only genocide and crimes against humanity are explicitly ruled out. And the first condition (a) will be satisfied in most situations
as well. The second condition (b) may sometimes be a sticking point in
crimes of aggression and will need to be discussed in relation to *mens rea*
rather than *actus reus* in any event.

The issue I wish to discuss is whether superior orders should sometimes
be a defense against the *actus reus* element of the crime of aggression.
This issue does not arise in the case of acts that are manifestly unlawful,
since the order does not change what the commanded person knows, or
should have known, about the act in question, since the act is manifestly
wrong. Acts of genocide, or crimes against humanity, are patently illegal
or wrongful whether ordered or not and regardless of the circumstances.
But if the act is not manifestly unlawful, such as the acts involved in
the crime of aggression, then there are good conceptual and normative
questions about how to regard an act that has itself been ordered by a
superior.

Conceptually, the act is often more appropriately attributed to the one
who ordered the act than the one who was ordered to do it. Ordering can
sometimes have the same effect as pushing. If I push you and you fall into
another person, injuring that person, we normally assign responsibility
for the injury to me not to you. You are seen as my instrument. When
I order you to do something, especially when I have the power to sanction you significantly for non-compliance, sometimes we would also not
assign responsibility to you, but only to me. The superior is sometimes
like a pusher in the way that orders are issued. Conceptually, in such
cases the soldier could be seen as merely the instrument of the superior. Normatively, we would want to take this into account in assigning
responsibility.

If responsibility is connected to control and choice, as I think it should
be and as most thinkers have also thought at least since Aristotle, then

there is a sense that we should not exonerate those who chose to follow orders.[19] Of course, if the followers are indeed like those pushed, then choice is reduced or eliminated by fear of the consequences of nonconformity. But perhaps there is still enough choice to make us think that the followers, especially those who are fairly high up the chain of command, should still be held responsible. I wouldn't deny this possibility. But I think that there is still something to the defense of superior orders that will hold true even for the seemingly high-ranking officials in a government. We might consider the Nuremberg case of Admiral Doenitz as well as the Ministries case, where very high-ranking Nazi military and political officials were acquitted of the crime of aggression because the defense counsel could show that they did not engage in the planning of the war and were only following orders from Hitler, as we saw in Chapter 8.

So there are two issues. One concerns whether the very status or quality of an act is conceptually affected when that act is in response to an order that has been given by someone higher up. The second concerns whether the responsibility for the act is affected by the superior orders. The second issue depends on what we think about the general idea of holding people morally responsible for doing wrongful acts, along with the corresponding idea of holding them legally liable. We might want to separate the moral from the legal ascription since so much more normally rides on the legal than the moral ascription. We might say that the soldier, or even the lower-ranking leader, is still morally responsible for following orders, but that legally we will let the person mount a defense based on superior orders.

Morally, we might want to assess people based on whether their conduct was objectively wrong in that we make this assessment independently of what the person knew or even could have known. I myself would not follow this strategy and have argued against it in several places previously.[20] But the idea certainly has more appeal than the idea that *actus reus* should be understood objectively in *legal* proceedings. In legal proceedings, we hold people liable and punish them for doing what is proscribed. It is virtually the same as prosecuting people for an ex post facto law violation as to punish people for violating a law that either they couldn't know to be unlawful or when it was extremely difficult to make this determination.

---

[19] For my account of how choice is related to responsibility, see my book *Sharing Responsibility*, Chicago: University of Chicago Press, 1992.

[20] See especially May, *War Crimes and Just War*, ch. 13.

In both cases, the people did not know, or found it very hard to know, at the time they were deciding to act that so to act was unlawful

If in some circumstances the fog of war makes it virtually impossible for soldiers and even some commanders to know that the orders they are given are unlawful, then it seems to me that these individuals should be exonerated on the grounds that they did not manifest an *actus reus*. Of course, this understanding of the fog of war probably affects *mens rea* more than *actus reus*. And the case for commanders using the superior orders defense is admittedly not quite as strong as it is for soldiers who use this defense. But of course how one reacts to the difference will have a lot to do with how thick the fog of war is. If commanders in the field cannot, or would have grave difficulty to, know that the war they are participating in is an unlawful war, then even some commanders are in the same boat as the soldiers and farmers in terms of whether they should be held responsible for having participated in an aggressive war.

In this chapter I have argued that it will be difficult to establish the *actus reus* element of the crime of aggression, if this crime is indeed prosecuted by the International Criminal Court in the future. But I have also argued that reference to the circumstances of the acts of the defendant can help to prove that especially high-ranking leaders have met the *actus reus* element of the crime of aggression. Even though the waging of aggressive war is a collective crime, some individuals can be prosecuted for the role or part they play if their acts are indeed significantly connected to the war. In this respect, farmers and line-soldiers generally do not play roles that are significant, but military and political leaders may sometimes play the kind of role that would satisfy the *actus reus* element of criminal liability. The idea of circumstance, rather than consequence, is the key consideration in determining when an individual participates in State aggression and should be prosecuted for the crime of aggression. In the next section I turn to the *mens rea* element for the crime of aggression, paying special attention to how that element has changed since the introduction of collective liability schemes.

12

Individual *Mens Rea* and Collective Liability

Contrary to what many people think, the trials at Nuremberg did not primarily concern the prosecution of Nazi leaders for perpetrating the Holocaust as a genocide or crime against humanity, or even for various war crimes, such as the fire bombing of Coventry. Rather, the primary purpose of the Nuremberg trials was to prosecute Nazi leaders for crimes against peace and waging aggressive war. As the International Military Tribunal noted, aggression "is not only an international crime; it is the supreme international crime."[1] The Nazi leaders who were executed at Nuremberg were convicted primarily of crimes against peace, eight of them convicted for "participation in a common plan or conspiracy" to wage aggressive war.[2] Today, however, while the International Criminal Court lists the crime of aggression as falling under its jurisdiction, there can be no prosecutions for this crime today because there has been no agreement about what it means to wage aggressive war and what are the elements of this crime.[3]

The main question taken up in this chapter is when, if ever, it makes sense to hold individuals criminally liable for starting or perpetuating an aggressive war in terms of their mental states. While it seems to have made sense to hold Nazi leaders responsible for the Holocaust, did it also make sense to hold individuals criminally liable for invading Poland, for example? What would link their individual intentions to the collective intentions of the State? Does it make sense to prosecute military and political leaders for this crime as members of a conspiracy? The key in this chapter will be the *mens rea* of the defendant. I ask whether it makes sense

---

[1] *Trial of the Major War Criminals before the International Military Tribunal,* 1948, vol. 22, p. 427.
[2] Charter of the International Military Tribunal at Nuremberg, Annex to the London Agreement (August 8, 1945), 82 U.N.T.S. 279, Article 6 (a).
[3] Rome Statute of the International Criminal Court, Article 5 , sec. 1 (d) and sec. 2.

to lower the *mens rea* requirement by reference to the idea of conspiracy theory, as was done in Nuremberg, or as the International Tribunals for Yugoslavia and Rwanda are increasingly doing today with their joint criminal enterprise theory. I contend that collective intent schemes, such as those involved in conspiracy theories or joint criminal enterprise theories, are insufficient to link an individual to State aggression for purposes of establishing individual criminal liability.

In the first section of this chapter, I focus on the element of "participation in a common plan or conspiracy" being especially attuned to what *mens rea* means in this context. In the second section, I attempt to explain how the *mens rea* of a State can be linked to the *mens rea* of individual human persons. In the third section I explain why conspiracy theory was used at Nuremberg and distinguish two intent elements in conspiracy theory. And in the fourth section, I complete my criticism of conspiracy theory and offer some preliminary suggestions about what mental element should be used in prosecutions for the crime of waging aggressive war. Throughout, I reject the idea that the *mens rea* elements for this crime should be diminished by reference to the idea of conspiracy. I argue that conspiracy theory makes good normative sense only if *mens rea* elements are not weakened. But then it will almost always make sense to charge the defendant with what he or she actually did and intended rather than with conspiracy. While useful for the prosecution, the conspiracy charge is not good for justice and the rule of law.

I. Conspiracy at Nuremberg

One of the main lessons from Nuremberg concerns the *actus reus* and *mens rea* elements of crimes against peace and waging aggressive war. In a case involving the mid-level Nazi leadership, the so-called Ministries Case, the American Military Tribunal declared:

> Obviously, no man may be condemned for fighting in what he believes is the defense of his native land, even though his belief be mistaken. Nor can he be expected to undertake an independent investigation to determine whether or not the cause for which he fights is the result of an aggressive act of his own government. One can be guilty only where knowledge of aggression in fact exists, and it is not sufficient that he have suspicions that the war is aggressive.[4]

[4] *US v. Weizsaecker and Others*, Nuremberg Military Tribunal IV, Judgment, April 11–13, 1949, *Trials of War Criminals before Nuremberg Military Tribunals under Control Council Law No. 10*, vol. 14, p. 337.

As was discussed in Chapter 9, I regard this to be one of the most signifi-cant "precedents" of the trials at Nuremberg.

At Nuremberg, the conspiracy charge was one of the key components of nearly all of the prosecutions, and the main reason was the difficulty of showing that the people in the dock did the planning, since the main person to have clearly done that, Adolph Hitler, had killed himself at the end of the war and could not be questioned. To prosecute Hitler, the charge of conspiracy would not have been needed since he was the one who clearly planned, prepared, and initiated the aggressive wars against Austria, Czechoslovakia, and Poland, among others. Those in the dock were other high-ranking officials, but not the leader who seem-ingly planned it all, that is, not Hitler. And the U.S. prosecution team convinced the other prosecution teams that the best way to link these officials to what Hitler did was in terms of a larger conspiracy to commit these crimes that all of the defendants participated in. As Justice Jackson, a U.S. Supreme Court justice assigned to be the chief U.S. prosecutor at Nuremberg, put it, war broke out in 1939 as a result of a "conspiratorial premeditation."[5]

As in conspiracy law in United States jurisprudence, at Nuremberg employing the conspiracy charge treated the members of the Nazi lead-ership as a kind of gangster mob operating as a unit. In such cases, each person who participated is held responsible for what every member of the group did. Sidney Alderman, Justice Jackson's assistant, said, "All the parties to a Common Plan or Conspiracy are the agents of each other and each is responsible as principal for the acts of all the others as his agents."[6] In this way, the Nuremberg prosecutors believed they were able to bring these Nazi leaders to justice for what Nazi Germany did during the war.

In some respects, it made good practical sense for the prosecution to introduce conspiracy theory into the case against the Nazi leaders. The war was not produced by the acts of one or two individuals, but only by the coordinated efforts of many people. Otherwise, no one would have been held liable for the true horrors of the Nazi reign of terror. With Hitler dead, it seemed that someone should be held accountable so that there was not impunity for one of the gravest horrors of the 20th century.

---

[5] *Trial of the Major War Criminals before the International Military Tribunal, Nuremberg, 14 November 1945 – October 1946*, 1947, vol. 2, p. 131.

[6] Sidney Alderman, "Address to the Tribunal," November 23, 1945. Quoted in Michael Marrus, *The Nuremberg War Crimes Trial of 1945–46: A Documentary History*, Boston: Bedford Books, 1997, p. 124.

There were rooms filled with documents establishing these horrors and there were conveniently many high-ranking leaders held in captivity by the Allied victors. It seemed to many that the world deserved a trial to set the record straight and to mete out appropriate punishment to someone for the seemingly wrongful wars that were waged. So thinking of the Nazi wars as having been the product of a kind of conspiracy initially makes sense. The question is whether what the Nazi leaders did was enough like a conspiracy to use the legal theory of conspiracy to convict them and sentence them to death or life imprisonment.

At Nuremberg, the idea was put forth, and is well accepted also today, that merely participating in a war of aggression is not sufficient for individual liability. And in addition, merely suspecting that the war is aggressive rather than defensive is also not sufficient. What this illustrates is that there is a need to get into the state of mind of the individual who is in the dock and accused of the crime of aggression. We have delayed this inquiry from the last chapter. In the current chapter we will try to examine the mental element. But, to say the least, separating mental from physical elements of a crime is not an easy matter, yet at least for analytical purposes such an effort is often worthwhile.

In the I. G. Farben case before the American Military Tribunal sitting at Nuremberg, Judge Hebert addressed the objective and the subjective elements quite well.

> Acts of substantial participation by certain defendants are established by the overwhelming proof [of the historical record]. The only real issue of fact is whether it was accompanied by the state of mind requisite in law to establish individual and personal guilt. Does the evidence in this case establish beyond reasonable doubt that the acts of the defendants in preparing Germany for war were done with knowledge of Hitler's aggressive aims and with the criminal purpose of furthering those aims.[7]

According to Hebert, each co-conspirator should be held responsible for what the State accomplished as long as there was a group within the State that acted in concert and a given individual had knowledge of the criminal enterprise and some aim to pursue those purposes. One did not have to do the act of planning oneself; and one did not have to intend all that was planned. Thus both the act and the intent requirements were weakened from what is normally required for criminal liability with the use of a

---

[7] *Trials of War Criminals before the Nuremberg Military Tribunals*, vol. 8, p. 1217, concurring opinion of Judge Hebert in the I. G. Farben case.

conspiracy theory at Nuremberg, despite the fact that the conspiracy charge was greeted with quite a bit of skepticism at Nuremberg.

The *actus reus* and *mens rea* elements need to link the defendant, the political or military leader, to the war. And the simplest way to do that is to require the prosecutor to show that the leader intended for his or her acts to contribute to the planning or initiating of the war. Mere knowledge is not enough; the leader must aim at advancing the war by what he or she chooses to do. Without this element there will be insufficient connection between what the individual defendant chose to do and the perpetration of the aggressive war, and hence it will be unfair so to prosecute him or her for the crime of aggression. In this section I will try to portray the mental element as an important element in the crime of aggression, and more important than the act element.

One of the reasons the act element may be of diminished importance is that nearly every adult does some act that adds to the war effort in a given society. Unless we are prepared to think of every person living in a given State as potentially liable for the crime of aggression, we should not regard the act element as being the most important element. Put another way, since nearly every adult in the society does some act that contributes to the war effort, it would follow that anyone in that society has met the act element of the crime of aggression. However, this way to think about the act element in the crime of aggression is wrongheaded, as I argued in the previous chapter.

But should even higher-ranking officials have been convicted for conspiring to wage aggressive war on the basis of their *mens rea*? One of the central problems is that using conspiracy theory seems to diminish *mens rea* by not requiring criminal intent to do the wrongful act, but substituting for it mere knowledge of the existence or likelihood of criminal actions by other members of the conspiracy. This is because the Nuremberg conspiracy theory only required intent to join a criminal group, with some knowledge that the group might commit criminal acts, not the intent to do what the group does. This gives to prosecutors such latitude that they can catch in their net individuals who were somewhat remote from the actual planning or instigating of crimes.

And yet nearly everyone agrees that criminal prosecutions should succeed only if they can establish that the accused had more than mere knowledge of the possibility of contributing to a criminal act. In the Krupp Trial, another trial conducted after the main Nuremberg trial that I examined in Chapter 9 in some detail, Judge Anderson put the point quite straightforwardly:

> In the individual crime of aggressive war or conspiracy to that end as con-
> tradistinguished to international delinquency of a state in resorting to hos-
> tilities, the individual intention is of major importance.[8]

But it is often very unclear whether anyone, except perhaps the highest-
ranking official, would meet the requirements of *mens rea* concerning
waging of aggressive war.

The 1998 ICC Statute, to its credit, distinguishes carefully between
intention and mere knowledge. Here is Article 30 of the Rome Statute:

1. Unless otherwise provided, a person shall be criminally responsible
   and liable for punishment for a crime within the jurisdiction of the
   Court only if the material elements are committed with intent and
   knowledge.
2. For the purposes of this article, a person has intent where:
   (a) In relation to conduct, that person means to engage in the
       conduct;
   (b) In relation to a consequence, that person means to cause that
       consequence or is aware that it will occur in the ordinary
       course of events.[9]

I would quibble with the very last remark in (b), but the Charter is otherwise to be praised for not confusing knowledge and intention. My quibble
concerns allowing mere awareness – that is, merely a form of knowledge –
to substitute for active intent. My reasons for this quibble will become
clear as the chapter progresses.

The ICC Statute drafters were seemingly aware that intent and knowledge are different and that both need to be proven for conviction. There
is a difference, even at just the behavioral level, between knowing and
intending, and such a distinction remains crucial for criminal prosecutions. And despite the increasing reliance on conspiracy-like theories
today, I think we should continue to separate knowledge from intent,
even if it means that it will be harder to convict State leaders.[10] In the

---

[8] *Trials of War Criminals before the Nuremberg Military Tribunals*, vol. 9, p. 382, quoted in The
United Nations War Crimes Commission, *Law Reports of Trials of War Criminals*, vol. X,
London: His Majesty's Stationery Office, 1949 [reprinted by William S. Hein, Buffalo,
1997], p. 123.

[9] Rome Statute of the International Criminal Court, Article 30.

[10] See William Schabas, "*Mens Rea* and the International Criminal Tribunal for the Former
Yugoslavia," *New England Law Review*, vol. 37, Summer 2003, pp. 1015–1036. Mark Drumbl
has also recently written about this issue in ways I find helpful. See Mark A. Drumbl,
"Pluralizing International Criminal Justice," *Michigan Law Review*, vol. 103, no. 6, May
2005, pp. 1295–1328.

next section I will provide a negative critique of the idea of intent in conspiracy theory, and in the following section I will begin to develop a positive theory about how we should think of intention in crimes against peace and waging aggressive war.

II. Intent to Wage War

In considering crimes against humanity one of the central conceptual problems is how to link individuals to what were really mass crimes.[11] Ethnic cleansing, for instance, was not something a given individual person did alone, or often even intended to do alone, so how could individuals be put on trial for such a crime? In the discussion of waging aggressive war, a similar, although even harder, problem emerges. The problem with crimes against peace and waging aggressive war is that it is States, or State-like entities, that wage war and so how could individual human persons be prosecuted for such crimes? This problem is even harder than that concerning crimes against humanity. In crimes against humanity, an individual human person cannot commit the mass crime – the mass murder, for instance, only lots of such persons can do so by their acts of murder. But then the problem is merely an aggregation problem. The individuals act wrongly, by murdering, say, and the conceptual problem is how to link these already wrongful acts to the larger wrongs, which are only the aggregated wrongful acts of lots of people. Aggressive war does not involve merely aggregated acts, since the acts that constitute aggressive war are coordinated.

In crimes against peace and waging aggressive war, there are two additional problems. First, the actions of individuals are sometimes not themselves wrong independent of what is going on at the State level; rather, they are things that could be neutral, such as strategic planning for how to win various battles, or even justified killing. And second, it is not individual human persons, even lots of them, who initiate the waging of aggressive war. A war is initiated and waged by a State, a collectivity, not by an individual or even lots of individuals. So it is not clear that individuals should be personally prosecuted at all if they have not done anything wrong personally, as opposed to what they have done in their roles in the State structure. As Mohammed Gomaa has said:

---

[11] See Larry May, *Crimes against Humanity*, New York: Cambridge University Press, 2005. Also see Mark A. Drumbl, "Collective Violence and Individual Punishment," *Northwestern University Law Review*, vol. 99, no. 2, Winter 2005, pp. 539–610.

Aggression has particular features which distinguish it from other crimes under the [ICC] statute. It is not a crime committed by individuals. It is an unlawful act which could only be committed by a collectivity.

Gomaa argues that the International Criminal Court has jurisdiction only over individual persons and hence "aggression per se cannot be entertained directly by the ICC."[12] And while I do not share Gomaa's strong view, I agree that it will be sometimes very difficult to link individuals to what the State has done.

Julius Stone raised the question in a slightly different way by asking how, if at all, individual *mens rea* is to be related to State *mens rea* in the crime of aggression.

> The question whether imputation of *mens rea* to a State is possible . . . is not easily answerable, at any rate by juristic techniques. Certainly we cannot dispose of the matter of State *mens rea* merely by insisting that both the *factum* and *mens rea* of State "aggression" are those of human beings who act for the State. For how are we to fix the *animus aggressiones* of the human beings themselves, except by reference to the notion of "aggression," which in turn refers us to State conduct and State objectives?[13]

If we are ultimately to link the *mens rea* of individuals with the *mens rea* of the State, or with a conspiracy within the State, there remains the question of how these two different subjective elements relate to each other. If there are going to be prosecutions for crimes against peace, we cannot avoid taking a stand on how collective and individual intentions relate to each other.

Animus aggressiones, the guilty intent of aggression, is indeed at the hub of the controversy. For it would seem initially that it is only a State, or State-like entity, that could form the intent unjustifiably to invade another State. It could be claimed that to intend to go to war one would have to have the capacity to initiate and wage war, and only States seemingly have that capacity. If waging aggressive war is nonetheless waging war, then it seems that States primarily, if not exclusively, are the ones who would have the intent to wage aggressive war. Of course, there is always a problem about figuring out the intent of organizations and groups, but it rarely makes sense *simply* to think that the individuals who hold the decision-making power in the State "decide" or "intend" what the State

---

[12] Mohammed M. Gomaa, "The Definition of the Crime of Aggression and the ICC Jurisdiction over that Crime," in *The International Criminal Court and the Crime of Aggression*, edited by Mauro Politi and Guiseppe Nesi, Burlington, VT: Ashgate, 2003, p. 58.

[13] Julius Stone, *Aggression and World Order*, Berkeley: University of California Press, 1958, p. 141.

"decides" or "intends." In this view, the State is more than the mere sum of its component parts.

Insofar as a particular head of State is identified with the State itself, we can begin to see how one individual could also be thought to have the intent to wage aggressive war. But even this individual, such as a president, normally does not form intentions personally that then become the intentions of the State. Rather, it is when this individual is forming intentions within a certain role that this occurs. So even if Hitler had been in the dock at Nuremberg, there would still have been serious questions about whether it was Hitler, qua individual human person, who had the criminal intent to engage in aggressive war, or whether it was Hitler as Head of State who had that intention. Indeed, this was the thought behind the traditional legal idea that there is Head of State immunity from criminal prosecutions. The idea was that a Head of State acted on behalf of the State, not on his or her own behalf. For States to be able to function at all, their heads needed to be immunized from personal liability. The now partially discredited idea of Head of State immunity highlights the conceptual problem in a particularly graphic way. If it makes some sense to wonder whether heads of State, who are often so closely associated with State behavior, can be prosecuted for what the State does, then it is much more problematic to think that individuals lower down the planning chain should be prosecuted for what are State crimes.[14]

One could claim, now arguing from an individualist perspective quite different from the collectivist perspective that inspired the previous paragraphs, that we should not reify States and think that they could actually form criminal intentions on their own without individuals who were forming intentions. So maybe the idea of *animus aggressiones* is itself a kind of reification. States don't really have the guilty intent to wage aggressive war. Indeed States don't even really wage aggressive war. Rather, it is collections of individuals who do both of these things. And if this is right, then we can return to the idea that individuals are the ones who can be prosecuted since they have both the *actus reus* and *mens rea*, if anyone has these at all.

Animus aggressiones would simply be the individual intentions of those who participate in the decision to wage aggressive war. And it is here

---

[14] See Sheldon Glueck, *The Nuremberg Trial and Aggressive War*, New York: Alfred A. Knopf, 1946, ch. 4. Also see Hersh Lauterpacht, "The Grotian Tradition in International Law, *British Year Book of International Law*, vol. 23, 1946, pp. 30–35.

that the idea of conspiracies and other forms of collective liability is so appealing since on either a collectivist or individualistic account of how to conceptualize States it isn't solitary individuals, but groups of individuals acting together, in concert, which wage aggressive war and have the guilty mind to do so. Yet we cannot merely use conspiracy theory to pierce the corporate shield of formal organizations like States. Conspiracy theory only helps us see how individuals can be linked to each other on the basis of an agreement. But conspiracy theory does not explain why these individuals who have reached some kind of agreement should be held liable for what States intend to do.

As Gomaa has said, "the attribution of a wrongful act to a State is the attribution of a conduct by an individual to that State."[15] And in any event, the question we are asking is a different kind of question since we are asking about mental and not physical elements. We are asking when we can attribute to individuals what seem to be the intentions of States. It is as if we say that based on what individual persons intend we are entitled to redescribe this as what the State intends to do. And then later, we feel entitled to reverse the process and say that based on what the State intends we are entitled to redescribe this as what the individual persons intended to do. Yet in the intervening time, something important has transpired that may block the attribution of what the State intended to do to what the individual intended to do. Such redescriptive legal projects are fraught with peril, although I have defended them in the moral domain in some of my previous writings.[16]

Of course, it may be that the talk of the intentions of States is merely a convenient linguistic placeholder for talk of individuals. It may be convenient, as a kind of shorthand, to talk of the State intending to initiate aggressive war instead of individuals doing so. And at other times it may be convenient to drop this fiction and go back to talking about individuals. These practices may be acceptable linguistic conventions or perhaps even acceptable metaphysics, but there are still legal problems nonetheless. It is States that are proscribed from intending to initiate aggressive war, not individual persons. So even if we think that talk of States is a mere convenient shorthand for talk of individual human persons, we still have a problem of how to move back from the intentions of States to the intentions of individuals in international law.

[15] Gomaa, "The Definition of the Crime of Aggression . . . ," p. 65.
[16] I take up these issues of redescription in the first two chapters of my book, *The Morality of Groups*, Notre Dame, IN: University of Notre Dame Press, 1987.

III. Two Intentions

It is important to distinguish the various mental states that could constitute *mens rea* in conspiracies to wage aggressive war. In its most basic form, a conspiracy is merely an agreement between two or more persons to pursue an illegal objective, or to pursue a legal objective by illegal means. On this understanding, there are at least two mental states that are elements in a conspiracy: (a) the intent to agree and (b) the intent to pursue the illegal objective or to use the illegal means. To get a sense of how quickly conspiracy theory could turn into a muddle, one needs to realize that the *actus reus* of the conspiracy is mainly the agreement, with some minimal action toward carrying it out. So, if the *mens rea* is mainly the intent to agree, the two main elements of a conspiracy, *actus reus* and *mens rea*, would be virtually indistinguishable from one another. We must "separate the mental state requirement from the agreement which constitutes the act,"[17] and to do so we need to focus on the intent to attain a particular objective, which "has been characterized as a special intent."[18]

In at least U.S. domestic law, conspiracy is often thought to be a special intent crime because it requires more than the intent to agree. There must also be the intent to commit a particular offense. For our purposes this has three important implications for international law. First, when people agree to form a group they are not yet involved in a conspiracy until they also settle on particular objectives to be accomplished by the group and those objectives, or the means to achieve them, are illegal. If Hitler's inner circle did agree to work together to achieve a stronger Germany, this is not yet a conspiracy unless "achieving a stronger Germany" was a specific objective and it was also illegal or involved illegal means. It is not enough that there be a kind of hortatory goal; there had to be specific things they agreed to do. And those things had to be illegal or to involve illegal means.

Second, even if there is a conspiracy, it would not make sense to say that all the members are responsible for everything that some members do or strive to do. If Hitler's inner circle agreed to advance the objective of creating a thousand-year Reich, this does not mean that all the members were part of a conspiracy to invade Poland, even though some members saw invading Poland as the means to achieve the thousand-year Reich.

[17] Wayne R. LaFave and Austin W. Scott, Jr., *Criminal Law*, 2nd ed., St. Paul, MN: West, 1986, p. 535.
[18] Ibid., p. 536.

Some of the other members could have thought that the thousand-year Reich could be established without invading Poland, and in agreeing to establish the Reich they may not have agreed to a common plan that involved invading Poland. The agreement must involve a common plan to which all "sign on," although they need not have the same reasons to do so. Of course, there can be good questions raised here about whether people who agreed to a plan also agreed to the obvious consequences of carrying out the plan. But things get very tricky as we try to figure out what was the implication of agreeing to a specific plan.

Third, merely because individuals have acted in concert to commit a certain crime does not yet mean that they committed a conspiracy, since there must be an intent to achieve specific illegal things or a particular illegal objective. The acting in concert probably required some kind of agreement, but what the group members agreed to may not have been what the group in fact accomplished. Again things get very dicey here very quickly. And various theorists disagree about how best to understand conspiracies. But it is interesting for our purposes that the drafters of the U.S. Model Penal Code provide the following example as a kind of cautionary tale.

> Assume that two persons plan to destroy a building by detonating a bomb, though they know and believe that there are inhabitants in the building who will be killed by the explosion. If they do destroy the building and persons are killed, they are guilty of murder, but this is because murder may be committed other than with an intent-to-kill mental state. Their plan constitutes a conspiracy to destroy the building, but not a conspiracy to kill the inhabitants for they did not intend the latter.[19]

This example highlights just how conceptually problematical conspiracy theory can be.

I imagine that some might well wonder whether the drafters of the Model Penal Code are right here. If a person intends to do x, and knows that doing x will necessarily mean doing y, then it seems that the person also intends to do y, or intends to allow y to occur. But there are indeed at least two different kinds of case. If I intend to stand here and turn off the lights, and the only way to do this is to flick a switch, and I know this, then it certainly seems that I also intend to flick the switch. In this kind of case, flicking the switch is pretty much the same thing as turning off the lights. The plan to turn off the lights could be accomplished by other means, such as throwing the circuit breaker in the basement. Yet

[19] Model Penal Code, Sec. 5.03, Comment at 407-08 (1985), paraphrased in ibid., p. 537.

my intent to stand here and turn off the lights is intimately connected to my intent to flick the switch on the wall next to me. It seems very hard to separate the two intentions here.

But there are other cases, perhaps epitomized in the example from the Model Penal Code drafters, that are not so clear-cut. Indeed, there is a whole literature that has grown up since the Middle Ages, that ushers in what is often called the "doctrine of double effect,"[20] a doctrine I will examine in Chapter 13 in connection to humanitarian interventions. Here there is a foreseen consequence, y, that will result from doing x, but y is not itself part of the doing of x. Since at least Aquinas,[21] philosophers have thought, similarly to what the Model Penal Code drafters thought, that in this case the intent to do x does not entail the intent to do y. Think of the example of someone who intends to turn off the lights but also knows that by doing so the carpet will no longer be visible. It may be that he could have the intent to turn off the lights without also having the intent to make the carpet no longer visible. This is supposedly because, unlike the first case, making the carpet no longer visible is not a necessary means to turning the lights off but rather merely the foreseen consequence of doing so.

I am not convinced that there is a major difference between the two above cases since I am not at all sure that we could give a clear account of the difference between the cases in terms of means and consequences of an act. Nonetheless, I raise this issue as a way of indicating how incredibly messy the very idea of conspiracy is when one focuses on the intent requirement. What is apparent is that the use of conspiracy theory makes it possible for prosecutors to be unclear in answering the question of what it is that defendants intend. This is because, in conspiracy theory, conspirators are thought to intend whatever any member does as long as the members are following the common plan that all had initially agreed to.

My view is that if we are going to use conspiracy theory in international criminal law, then we should be scrupulous in insisting that prosecutors must prove two intent elements to conspiracies: the intent to agree, and the intent to plan to do a specific illegal act. And I think it is also very important that mere knowledge of the illegal plan, or mere awareness of

---

[20] See the essays in Part II.B of *The Morality of War: Classical and Contemporary Readings*, edited by Larry May, Eric Rovie, and Steve Viner, Upper Saddle River, NJ: Prentice-Hall, 2006, pp. 160–200.

[21] Thomas Aquinas, *Summa Theologica*, Pt. II-II, Qu. 64, Art. 7, trans. by Fathers of the English Dominican Province, London: Burns, Oates and Washburn, 1936. The Aquinas passages are reprinted in ibid., p. 32.

it, not be allowed to suffice here. If we follow this advice, then in many cases conspiracy theory should not be used at all. For if there is evidence of an individual's intent to plan to wage aggressive war, then it does not seem to matter that there was also an intent to agree with others to do this. And yet the latter is the core of the conspiracy charge.

The Tokyo Tribunal took another tack: it saw the two Nuremberg charges as "duplicative" and prosecuted the Japanese leaders only on the conspiracy count. But to do so, the Tokyo Tribunal focused only on the intent to join part of conspiracy *mens rea*, thereby weakening the intent requirement and allowing the prosecutor to prove the planning element by looking to the actions and intentions of those other than the defendant.[22] I think that this was wrongheaded. It is true that the two charges overlapped, at least on my construal of conspiracies. The conspiracy charge required showing that each individual engaged in the proscribed planning and preparation of waging aggressive war. But that is a reason to drop the conspiracy charge rather than the planning charge.

Unlike in Tokyo, at Nuremberg there was a very narrow reading of what conspiracy meant, closer to what I am advocating. This is seen when the International Military Tribunal in Nuremberg declared:

> In the opinion of the Tribunal the conspiracy must be clearly outlined in its criminal purpose. It must not be too far removed from the time of decision and action. The planning, to be criminal, must not rest merely on the declarations of a party program.[23]

I will next argue that using conspiracy theory at all was ill advised at Nuremberg.

IV. Conspiring to Wage Aggressive War

The same debate about the merits and limits of conspiracy theory in domestic U.S. law also exists in the international debates on this topic. Yoram Dinstein, for instance, says that perhaps only a "criminal conscious-ness" may suffice instead of a full-blown criminal intent in conspiracy cases at international law.[24] So the next thing to ask is what he might have in mind and whether it is sufficiently like real criminal intent still to provide

---

[22] See Matthew Lippman, "The History, Development, and Decline of Crimes against Peace," pp. 1010–1015.

[23] *Trial of the Major War Criminals before the International Military Tribunal*, 1948, vol. 22, pp. 467–468.

[24] Yoram Dinstein, *War, Self-Defense, and Aggression*, 3rd ed., Cambridge: Cambridge University Press, 2001, p. 124.

a ground for international criminal prosecutions. And we should ask whether such a subjective element will indeed link the individual human persons to the conspiratorial *mens rea*. And then we should ask whether conspiracy theory should be used at all.

It is interesting that Justice Jackson, the chief American prosecutor at Nuremberg, upon returning home after the main Nuremberg trial, wrote a scathing concurring opinion in a conspiracy case while he sat on the United States Supreme Court. In that opinion, Justice Jackson claimed that conspiracy was an "elastic, sprawling and pervasive doctrine...so vague that it almost defies definition."[25] The twenty-two Nuremberg defendants had all been tried together as co-conspirators, and it is especially telling that Justice Jackson, after Nuremberg, identified as one of the main faults of conspiracy prosecutions that the individual defendant "occupies an uneasy seat":

> There generally will be wrongdoing by somebody. It is difficult for the individual to make his own case stand on its own merits in the minds of jurors who are ready to believe that birds of a feather are flocked together. If he is silent, he is taken to admit it, and if, as often happens, confederates can be prodded into accusing or contradicting each other, they convict each other.[26]

Surprisingly, Justice Jackson did not convey the same worries when he was employing the theory of conspiracy to convict Nazi leaders in Nuremberg. Jackson did not worry that the twenty-two individuals in the dock at Nuremberg would "occupy uneasy seats" because they would be confused with each other, and yet in my view, that is precisely what he should have been worried about, and what his later opinions written when he was back on the U.S. Supreme Court commit him to.

Instead, Jackson worried only about making sure that someone was convicted. Justice Jackson addressed this issue in his "Closing Address" at the Nuremberg Trials.

> In conspiracy we do not punish one man for another man's crime. We seek to punish each for his own crime of joining a common criminal plan in which others also participated. The measure of the criminality of the plan and therefore of the guilt of each participant, is of course the sum total of crimes committed by all in executing the plan. But the gist of the offense is participation in the formulation or execution of the plan. These are rules

[25] *Krulewitch v. United States*, 336 U.S. 440, 69 S.Ct. 716, 93 L.Ed. 790 (1949).
[26] Ibid.

which every society has found necessary in order to reach men, like these defendants, who never get blood on their own hands but who lay plans that result in the shedding of blood. All over Germany today, in every zone of occupation, little men who carried out the orders are being convicted and punished. It would present a vast and unforgivable caricature of justice if the men who planned these policies and directed these little men should escape all penalty.[27]

Here Jackson, who we saw was highly critical of conspiracy theory in U.S. domestic law, defends the use of the conspiracy charge in international law as the best way to get at the perpetrators of Nazi aggression.

I do not dispute Jackson's claim that if those who followed orders are to be punished, surely those who issued the orders deserve to be punished. But convicting the order-issuers of conspiracy "as an elastic, sprawling and pervasive doctrine" seems to me to be an odd way to make sure that justice is done. In my view, it makes much more sense to do what Jackson himself proposes in U.S. domestic law, namely, to attempt to prove that each member of the Nazi leadership is responsible for "participation in the formulation or execution of the plan" that is attributable to each. And if there are joint ventures, then hold each participant responsible for the role that each played. But none of this need involve the use of a broadly construed conspiracy charge.

My proposal is that leaders should be prosecuted for crimes against peace and waging aggressive war based on their own acts and intentions in planning, or participating in the planning, of that war. Applying that thesis, I would say that the second of the charges at Nuremberg, namely, "planning, preparing, initiating and waging aggressive war," seems to have been the right charge against the Nazi leaders in the dock at Nuremberg. But the first of the charges, namely, "conspiring or having a common plan," seems merely to muddy the waters at best, and at worst to violate the rule of law. If there was a true common criminal enterprise that each participated in, then each should be held guilty for having agreed to the common plan and for his or her specific role and specific intent, not for what others intended to do and did.

There may be special circumstances when a group of leaders acted truly in concert with one another, when it would make sense to treat them as a unit. But it seems to me that such occasions typically are quite

[27] Robert H. Jackson, "Closing Address for the United States of America," in *Nazi Conspiracy and Aggression*, Supplement A, edited by Charles A. Horskey et al., Washington, DC: United States Government Printing Office, 1947, p. 37.

limited and concern only those cases when there really is coordinated activity toward a specific goal. And even in such cases, it makes sense to contemplate the use of conspiracy theory only when it is difficult to tell who did what. In such situations there may indeed be a use for conspiracy theory, especially if it appears that criminal activity is intensified by the existence of cabals in the upper leadership in a State. Conspiracy theory may be legitimately used to reduce in significance the *actus reus* element, but I do not think it should be used also to reduce in significance the normal *mens rea* element as well. This would seem to be more in keeping with standard conceptions of justice.

Conspiracy theory is normally used to weaken the act element of criminal liability since all individuals are held liable for what any member of the group did. If conspiracy theory is also used in a way that weakens the intent element of criminal liability, we move dangerously close to something like guilt by association, since merely agreeing to join makes one guilty of what the group one is now associated with does and intends. My view is that it is always better to hold people criminally liable for what they themselves did and intended rather than for what others did and intended, given what is at stake in criminal prosecutions. It is not sufficient to show that people knew that others intended to do wrong, even if one also joined with those others in a single group. Unlike in noncriminal contexts, where it might make sense to hold people collectively responsible because the penalties are relatively light, things change dramatically when what is at stake is loss of freedom and even loss of life in criminal prosecutions. And yet the conspiracy legacy of Nuremberg is still, at least partially, with us.

V. Collective Liability Schemes

Talk of collective liability has resurfaced some sixty years after Nuremberg in several high-profile crimes against humanity judgments at the International Criminal Tribunal for the Former Yugoslavia.[28] The most

---

[28] See Mark Osiel, "The Banality of Good: Aligning the Incentives against Mass Atrocity," *Columbia Law Review*, vol. 105, October 2005, pp. 1773–1804, where Osiel says, "Defense counsel asserting the ICTY's embrace of enterprise liability amounts to an endorsing of Anglo-American conspiracy doctrine, even liability for membership in a criminal organization." Also see "ICTR: The MRND Trial Goes Adrift," *International Justice Tribune*, no. 31, 12 September 2005, p. 3: "Prosecutor Lombardi said that the prosecution's key task was to prove that the accused had been part of a common criminal enterprise. This, he says, justifies why there is no mention in the indictment of circumstances in which the rapes occur."

conspicuous case in which it was used concerns the establishment of con-centration camps in Bosnia.[29] Camps are indeed run as joint enterprises, although I am still not convinced that there is enough of a collectivity here to hold a person involved responsible for what every other person involved did. It is better to hold each responsible for what he or she did and intended, although I admit that the act side of things is often especially difficult to establish in such cases. Indeed, I am less critical of the weakening of the act element in such cases than I am of the weak-ening of the intent element. Those who plan do not often commit acts that are abhorrent, yet the act of planning is indeed often crucial for the subsequent commission of horrible acts by others, especially when concentration camps have been established.

Regardless of which types of international crime we are considering, crimes against humanity or crimes against peace, my view is that we should not weaken the intent element. It may be justifiable to weaken the act element when looking at high-ranking officials, and perhaps joint crim-inal enterprise theory is one of the acceptable ways to do that. For it is not these leaders who do the torturing or murdering on their own. As Justice Jackson said, the leaders do not have blood on their hands. So we should look at what they did, such as giving orders, making plans, or instigating action. But if we have already weakened the act element of criminal liability, it seems an especially bad idea also to weaken the intent element. As I said earlier, if we weaken both act and intent elements then we run the risk of moving toward mere guilt by association for these leaders.

We could now revisit the question of superior orders in the context of the somewhat discredited conspiracy theory employed in Nuremberg and the increasingly used joint criminal enterprise theory. If the mental element is not weakened by the joint liability models, then it will be harder to show that there was a sense that all of the people who participated did know that what they were doing was indeed unlawful. Recall that this is the sticking point for many superior order defenses, namely, to try to show that the defendant did not know that following an order was unlawful. Once we eliminate the constructed knowledge that flows from a collective liability theory, then acting on superior orders becomes somewhat easier to prove as a defense to the crime of aggression, as I

---

[29] Here the case to examine is that of *Prosecutor v. Kvocka*. See Judgment of the Trial Chamber of the International Criminal Tribunal for the Former Yugoslavia, Case No. IT-98–30/1T, T.C. I, 2 November 2001.

indicated in the previous chapter. In the context of the superior orders defense it becomes even clearer that it is normatively not a good idea to weaken the mental requirement by use of a collective liability theory. To do so is effectively to eliminate a serious discussion on whether the defendant did indeed know or realize that the order he was following was unlawful.

I here offer a final caveat to the various attempts in this discussion to provide ways for a defendant to avoid prosecution concerning the *mens rea* element of the crime of aggression. I do not dispute that the waging of aggressive war is a terrible thing, nor do I dispute that individuals could be prosecuted for crimes against peace. Indeed, my own pacifist leanings, contingent but not in-principle pacifist leanings though they be, certainly lead me to condemn aggressive war as well as to condemn those who plan, prepare, initiate, and wage these wars. What I have tried to do in this chapter is to offer some strong normative cautions about how prosecutions for these crimes should be conducted. And once again my proposal might be regarded as disappointing by its refusal to move from my previous support for the assignment of collective *moral* responsibility to collective *criminal* responsibility in these cases.[30] But given the overwhelming advantages that prosecutors already have, I am very reluctant to give them any more advantages, especially when so much is at stake. It is for this reason that I have taken a defendant-oriented approach throughout this book.

Crimes against peace and the crime of waging aggressive war are very serious crimes, even if they are not the supreme international crimes. It makes sense to prosecute the Saddams and Milosevics of the world for the way they have initiated and planned aggressive war on their neighbors, since they have thereby made the world so unsafe for all of us. But if we drop below the top leadership of a State, very serious problems arise about what level of *mens rea* should have to be proved in order to gain convictions. In this chapter, I have mainly provided negative arguments against attempts to prosecute such leaders, although at the end I did provide the beginnings of a positive thesis about what to require prosecutors to prove in cases of crimes against peace and waging aggressive war. Undoubtedly prosecutors won't like my proposal, since it will make their jobs much harder. But in such cases we should not weaken the normally required individual *mens rea* to get a better chance of convictions. The rule of law

---

[30] See especially my book, *Sharing Responsibility*, Chicago: University of Chicago Press, 1992.

will be the victim of such weakening, and in the end we all will suffer. In the final part of the book, I will address two hard cases for a theory of how to prosecute the crime of aggression, namely, the cases of humanitarian war and terrorist violence. And in the last chapter I will also respond to a very serious conceptual assault on the very idea of holding international trials for crimes such as the crime of aggression.

PART E

HARD CASES AND CONCLUDING THOUGHTS

13

Humanitarian Intervention

In this chapter, I take up the difficult question of whether humanitarian wars are wars of aggression, as well as the related question of who, if anyone, should be prosecuted for initiating and waging such wars. In taking up this topic, I will indicate how it is that questions of tactics play into the determination of whether a war is aggressive, that is, how *jus in bello* considerations affect *jus ad bellum* judgments. Humanitarian intervention raises the issues we have been exploring in this book in especially poignant ways since civilian deaths, even targeted civilian deaths, have become a commonplace of the waging of these wars. Nonetheless, many theorists today see humanitarian wars as clearly justified wars. In this chapter I will also continue the discussion begun earlier about what moral priority to give to sovereign States. Humanitarian crises make it all the more important to think of basic human rights abuses and their prevention as much more important than territory or borders, although in some cases protecting borders also dovetails with protecting human rights.

Humanitarian intervention has replaced self-defensive war and become the new favored example of those who think there are clear cases of morally justified wars. Surely if there are morally justified wars, then wars fought to stop a genocide or to curtail crimes against humanity are more likely to be the ones, rather than wars fought to gain territory or convert heathens. Wars fought in self-defense look less justifiable than wars fought to save innocent parties from being slaughtered – even Augustine, the founder of the Just War tradition, thought that wars fought for defense of others were more justifiable, because more selfless, than wars fought in self-defense.[1] But there is an unfortunate part of most wars

---

[1] See Chapter 3, Section 1, where I discuss Augustine's views.

fought for humanitarian reasons: innocent people will be killed. This is the inevitable result of all wars and is even more likely to occur in humanitarian wars since there is often no clear military target that needs to be destroyed, such as a supply depot. Indeed, recent humanitarian wars have been waged in such a way as to be directed against civilian targets to get the civilian population to put political pressure on a government to stop a genocide. Or as in the recent case of Rwanda, where the civilian population was involved in massive killing, it looks like it would take attacks on that civilian population to stop the genocide.

To win most humanitarian wars, one must try to break the will of a part of a population that is oppressing another part of a population rather than merely to defeat the enemy army in certain military campaigns.[2] And to break a people's will, infrastructure and population centers often must be attacked. Yet if it is true that a large part of a population is complicit in causing, or allowing, a genocidal campaign, perhaps a war that must target that civilian population is not so difficult to justify after all.[3] Humanitarian intervention raises other issues involving collective responsibility, including how to understand the responsibility of States for rescuing distant peoples and whether individual human persons should be held liable for what their States do.

I wish to consider criticisms of so-called humanitarian wars, such as NATO's war to stop Serbs from engaging in ethnic cleansing against Kosovar Albanians. In the first section, I will set the stage for our discussion by briefly assessing the current state of international law regarding humanitarian intervention today. I will then examine two arguments often used to justify humanitarian wars. In the second section, I will look at the argument based on collective liability of those otherwise innocent people who will die in a humanitarian war. In the third section, I will look at the arguments based on the doctrine of double effect for discounting the deaths to innocent members of a society in a humanitarian war. In the fourth section, I will discuss several other problems of collective responsibility, especially how to reconcile obligations of States with obligations of the world community. In the fifth section, I will then provide

---

[2] I am thinking primarily of humanitarian wars aimed at ending genocidal campaigns rather than those aimed at ending a civil war. As Brook Sadler has pointed out to me, the latter are easier to justify since the sovereign State may welcome intervention and in addition there are clear-cut military targets. But such wars are not unproblematic since one needs to side with one party over another, whereas in the case of stopping genocide it is easy to see which side has the moral high ground.

[3] See Deen K. Chatterjee and Don E. Scheid, *Ethics and Foreign Intervention,* New York: Cambridge University Press, 2003.

a brief defense of humanitarian wars. In the final section, I will address the problem of who if anyone should be prosecuted for humanitarian wars. In general, I argue that theorists today are too quick to replace self-defensive wars with humanitarian wars as paradigmatically justified wars, and that attention to collective responsibility issues makes this clear.

I. Humanitarian Intervention in International Law

Consider the state of international law today regarding the case of human-itarian interventions. In the 1986 Nicaragua case, the International Court of Justice points to a problem with humanitarian intervention. The case concerned the mining of Nicaragua's harbors by the U.S. Central Intelli-gence Agency (CIA) and by "contras," who were merely paid operatives of the United States. The United States tried to topple the Nicaraguan government in the early 1980s to prevent what it predicted would be mas-sive human rights violations by the communist government of Nicaragua in the region. Here is part of the Court's judgment:

> In any event, while the United States might form its own appraisal of the situation as to respect for human rights, the use of force could not be the appropriate method to monitor or ensure such respect. With regard to the steps actually taken, the protection of human rights, a strictly human-itarian objective, cannot be compatible with mining of ports...which is based on the right of collective self-defense.[4]

This ICJ opinion seems to see humanitarian intervention to prevent human rights abuses as just one form of aggression. Yet there has been a controversy about how to interpret this ICJ opinion, some reading it narrowly as applying only to the unusual factual circumstances of this case, and others seeing in it a broad condemnation of humanitarian intervention.

Ian Brownlie, writing in 1963, says this of the doctrine of humanitarian intervention:

> The state practice justifies the conclusion that no genuine case of humanitar-ian intervention has occurred with the ... embarrassing exception provided by Germany [by its claim to be going to the aid of oppressed Germans in Czechoslovakia]; the institution has disappeared from modern state prac-tice. As a matter of legal international policy this is a beneficial develop-ment. The institution did not conspicuously enhance state relations and

---

[4] See Case Concerning Military and Paramilitary Activities in and against Nicaragua (*Nicaragua v. United States*), 1986, International Court of Justice Advisory Opinion, para-graph 268.

was applied only against weak states. It belongs to an era of unequal relations. Many modern authorities either ignore humanitarian intervention or expressly deny that such a right to intervene exists.[5]

Brownlie points to the fact that even when discussions "in the Sixth Committee of the General Assembly" in the 1960s considered "whether action taken by a state to prevent genocide against a racially related minority in a neighboring state" would be aggression, many of the delegates said that it would.[6] And if stopping genocide was not then considered to be sufficient to justify the initiation war, it is hard to imagine any other humanitarian goal that could have done so.

One reason for the reluctance of the international legal community to accept the legitimacy of humanitarian intervention is that there have been so many cases of mixed motives on the part of governments who have claimed to be engaging solely in humanitarian efforts. Brownlie's reference to Nazi Germany is a case in point. Hitler claimed to be engaged in a humanitarian war to stop atrocities against native German peoples in the Sudetenland portion of Czechoslovakia. Yet it was also clear that Hitler was engaged in a power grab in Eastern Europe that had nothing to do with humanitarian motives.

From 1960 to the present day, sentiments have changed, but it is probably fair to say that the vast majority of international law scholars still find wars waged for humanitarian reasons to be illegal as of this writing in 2007. Indeed, most of the authorities today continue to think of humanitarian intervention as a form of aggression. Nonetheless, wars waged for humanitarian reasons, such as NATO's attempt to stop ethnic cleansing in Kosovo by its brief war against Serbia, are sometimes described as paradigmatically justified wars. Two UN Security Council Resolutions, concerning the terrorist attacks against the United States on September 11, 2001, seem to open the door to a broader right of self-defense of States than had previously been acknowledged in international law.[7] Yet this is a very recent movement, although one that is often strongly represented in the media and in moral and political theory. And there has been a counter-movement, spurred by an International Court of Justice ruling about the U.S. bombing of Iranian oil platforms, that seemed to attempt

---

[5] Ian Brownlie, *International Law and the Use of Force by States*, Oxford: Oxford University Press, 1963, pp. 340–341.
[6] Ibid.
[7] See United Nations Security Council Resolution 1368, adopted on September 12, 2001; and United Nations Security Council Resolution 1373, adopted on September 28, 2001.

to close the door of broadening self-defense that the Security Council resolutions had opened.[8]

Some legal scholars have recently supported the idea that some humanitarian wars can be legally fought. Article 2 (4) of the UN Charter declares:

> All members shall refrain in their international relations from the threat or use of force against the territorial integrity or political independence of any state, or in any other manner inconsistent with the purposes of the United Nations.

Michael Reisman argues that humanitarian wars are not straightforward violations of Article 2 (4) of the UN Charter.[9]

> Since a humanitarian intervention seeks neither a territorial change nor a challenge to the political independence of the State involved and is not only not inconsistent with the purposes of the United Nations but is rather in conformity with the most fundamental peremptory norms of the charter, it is a distortion to argue that it is precluded by Article 2 (4).[10]

If the intent is to save a people from annihilation, it is possible that there was no additional intent to change the territorial boundaries or political independence of a State.

Critics of this legal argument respond that any humanitarian war will cross borders and this is surely a violation of the territorial integrity of the State. Here is one common response, provided by Oscar Schachter:

> The idea that wars waged in a good cause such as democracy and human rights would not involve a violation of territorial integrity or political independence demands an Orwellian construction of those terms.[11]

And this view seems reasonable if we just look at the wording of the UN Charter.

While a growing number of scholars in moral and political theory argue that some humanitarian wars are justified,[12] the majority of legal scholars

---

[8] See Case Concerning Oil Platforms (*Islamic Republic of Iran v. United States of America*), International Court of Justice, November 6, 2003, General List No. 90.

[9] Charter of the United Nations, Article 2, Section 4.

[10] W. Michael Reisman with the collaboration of Myres McDougal, "Humanitarian Intervention to Protect the Ibos," in Richard Lillich, editor, *Humanitarian Intervention and the United Nations*, Charlottesville: University Press of Virginia, 1973, p. 177.

[11] Oscar Schachter, "The Legality of Pro-democratic Invasion," *American Journal of International Law*, vol. 78, 1984, p. 649. This quotation and the previous one are taken from the excellent article on this topic by J. L. Holzgrefe, "The Humanitarian Intervention Debate," in J. L. Holzgrefe and Robert O. Keohane, editors, *Humanitarian Intervention*, New York: Cambridge University Press, 2003, pp. 15–52.

[12] The most prominent scholar to argue in this vein is Allen Buchanan.

continue to follow Schachter here, and the Nicaragua case continues to be cited as the main precedent in international law, despite the failure of the international community to condemn NATO's humanitarian war against Serbia to stop the persecution of the Kosovar Albanians.[13] In general, while international law may be in flux about humanitarian intervention, legal scholars have not followed their colleagues in political and moral philosophy in urging wholesale changes in what appear to be straightforward applications of *jus ad bellum* concepts.

II. Immunity, Complicity, and Collective Liability

Despite a growing support from moral and political theorists, humanitarian intervention is not morally unproblematic, especially since large loss of civilian life is a nearly inevitable result of such wars. One strategy for dealing with the inevitable loss of innocent lives in a humanitarian war is to argue that the members of a society engaged in oppression of its own citizens have lost their immunity and hence ceased to be innocent. Perhaps the otherwise innocent members of a political society that engages in such abhorrent practices as ethnic cleansing have lost their immunity from attack, even though these people may not straightforwardly deserve to be attacked. Some, like Erin Kelly, as well as Seumas Miller,[14] have recently argued that the people who will inevitably lose their lives in humanitarian wars may not suffer injustice since they are collectively liable for such things as ethnic cleansing that have precipitated the need for the humanitarian wars in the first place. Since I have also defended the idea of collective responsibility in the past, and since I find the application of these arguments to the justifiability of humanitarian war to be unsettling, I will take this subtle issue up in some detail.

Kelly contends that "the liability of the perpetrators allows us to focus primarily on the needs of the victims, even at serious costs to the perpetrators."[15] And she has an expansive view of who is liable for an injustice. As she says, "It is not necessary that members of a liable group should

---

[13] The Congo case, discussed in chapter 10, has also raised the question of whether a State that is being attacked for humanitarian reasons can justifiably defend itself. The ICJ has not given a clear answer to this question, although I have given reasons to think that a State can provoke humanitarian force by other States and then legitimately claim that it acts in self-defense to repel that force.

[14] See Seumas Miller, "Civilian Immunity, Forcing the Choice, and Collective Responsibility," in I. Primoratz, editor, *Civilian Immunity*, Oxford: Oxford University Press, forthcoming.

[15] Erin Kelly, "The Burdens of Collective Liability," in Deen K. Chatterjee and Don E. Scheid, *Ethics and Foreign Intervention*, New York: Cambridge University Press, 2003, p. 132.

each have acted with the intention of causing the result that they together in fact caused. Nor is it necessary that they knew the result would ensue. But it is important that they could have foreseen that unjust harms would occur."[16] While I have written in a similar vein concerning collective moral responsibility, I am not willing to follow Kelly in thinking that such considerations translate into liability of the sort that could result in a person's losing his or her immunity to be attacked. Shared or collective moral responsibility does not translate well into such legal or quasi-legal notions of liability.

Employing a concept of distributive collective liability, Kelly argues that individuals are liable for injustices as long as they are part of a collective agent for which the following are true:

1. The group or some of its members are causally responsible for an injustice via the political and social arrangements they impose or perpetuate.
2. Passive members of the group, that is, members who do not actively promote the offending result, benefit from the injustice and could together have played a role in preventing it.
3. Members of the group could have foreseen the possibility that some injustice or other could result.
4. Members of the group have had an opportunity, weakly construed, to exit the group, to take political action to combat the injustice, or to refuse the benefits that accrue to them as a result of the injustice.[17]

I have no trouble accepting these conditions for assigning shared or distributive collective *moral* responsibility. Indeed, Kelly claims to be indebted to me for just such an argument. But I worry when such conditions are employed to justify, quoting Kelly again, "loosening moral prohibitions on the use of violence in response to injustice."[18]

Shared or distributive collective moral responsibility is a strong tool – indeed one that many people find counter-intuitive. I have employed it in the past as a way to get people to take more responsibility for their actions as well as their omissions. I have also suggested that such considerations may warrant the instilling of shame, but I have been very reluctant to think that legal guilt or liability follows from the ascription of shared

[16] Ibid., p. 127
[17] Ibid., pp. 131–132.
[18] Ibid., p. 133.

or distributive collective moral responsibility. For me, this would create an undue burden. Things come to a head when ascriptions of collective agency are said to lead to collective liability and then to a weakening of the immunity from attack and death that we all normally have.

In U.S. domestic criminal law, merely having foreseen the possibility that an injustice could occur, in conjunction with being able when acting with many others to have prevented the injustice, would not count to make one liable for punishment. One could argue that suffering injury or death in a just war is not equivalent to punishment. In the next section I examine in more detail the relationship between punishment and humanitarian intervention. Suffice it here to say that with the possible exception of conspiracy laws, punishment is not justified on such weak grounds of liability as those proposed by Kelly to justify loss of life during war. And even in conspiracies in domestic criminal law, there has to be some wrongful act on the part of the defendant for him or her to be subject to punishment.

Yet Kelly argues that there is no such act component required on the part of previously innocent people for them to lose their immunity from attack in societies where serious injustice is occurring. On her view, it is sufficient that a passive member of a group benefit from the injustice that other members of the group are actively perpetrating for the passive member to be liable in a way that loses her immunity from attack. Such benefiting seemingly makes the individual complicit in the injustices and thereby makes her liable in a way that would affect her status as "innocent" as well as her corresponding immunity from attack.

There is an interesting question of what one who is complicit is liable for. I have been proceeding as if the liability is a liability to be attacked. This is in part because some humanitarian wars have indeed been waged by attacking civilians, some of whom are instigating a genocide. It may be, though, that one defends a weaker claim, namely, that the complicity of some makes them liable to be put at risk of harm as a merely foreseen effect.[19] I will address this second possibility in the next section of this chapter. At the moment, I am mainly interested in justifications for direct attacks on a population when members of that population are at least passively complicit in an atrocity and where the attack is said to be justified because of the passive complicity.

Yet the idea that people are immune from attack unless they have actively done something wrong is a cornerstone of liberal moral and political theory, as far back at least as Grotius in the early 17th century.

---

[19] I am grateful to Steven Lee for this point.

We do not hold someone liable for merely having thoughts of a certain kind and we do not typically hold a person liable merely because he or she benefited from a wrongful act. Liability to be punished or attacked is such a serious matter that we look for much more than merely having had immoral thoughts or having benefited. Having immoral thoughts might warrant moral criticism of various sorts, but it does not warrant criminal punishment or other forms of sanctioned violence. And while having benefited from a wrong is often quite a serious matter, typically it triggers some kind of monetary or civil liability rather than liability to punishment or attack, if it triggers a legal response at all – think of unjust enrichment cases. Of course, this statement of how things are is only mentioned to give a beginning intuitive basis for an argument, not a replacement for that argument.

The argument against Kelly's view begins with the idea that there is a division of labor in the moral domain. We reserve the most strongly condemnatory responses for the worst of wrongs committed by individuals. If one individual intentionally and inexcusably harms another, criminal sanction is the appropriate response. If one conspires with others intentionally and inexcusably to cause harm, I am willing to agree with Kelly that punishment or some forms of force – or in rare cases, violence – might be justified as a response here as well. But the conspiring must involve some explicit act on the part of the agent in question. From all I can tell, Kelly would disagree with this point since she seems to require only that one not have exited from a group that one could have predicted would cause harm. This is, as she recognizes, to make passive participation a basis for the most serious of responses, and this seemingly denies that there is a division of labor in the moral domain concerning proper responses.

One of the main reasons to preserve a division of labor in the moral domain is to deter the worst of wrongs: the intentional decision directly to cause harm to another. While it is surely true that great harm in the world is indeed caused by those who participate passively, the passive actors would not cause nearly as much harm if it were not for the active participators. Most people simply go along; and while it would be good to get people to be more active in the prevention of harm, surely the more important thing is to get the active participators to stop. Holding passive members of groups to the same standards as those who are active sends the wrong message[20] and seems unfair as in many instances the passive

---

[20] I do not mean here to restrict myself to consequentialist arguments, as we will see in the next section where I also discuss the intentions of the agent.

participants could have chosen to be more active in the perpetration of the harm but did not so choose. So while their choice – not to try to prevent the harm or not to distance themselves from the group causing harm – may be morally wrong, treating them as if they did the same as those active members of the group fails to take morally relevant factors into account and hence is unfair.

Another problem with the argument by Kelly and others we have been considering is that humanitarian wars do not only kill adult civilians who might be complicit in genocide or ethnic cleansing. Humanitarian wars also kill children. Young children – that is, those who are under the age of seven – cannot possibly be said to be complicit in the genocide or ethnic cleansing campaigns, and so they will be innocent deaths regardless of the arguments we have been considering. Hugh LaFollette and I have made a similar point about those who try to argue that the poor and starving of the world are not owed help because they should have helped themselves. The case of children makes this and the arguments about humanitarian war not seem very plausible after all.[21]

Kelly and others who employ collective liability strategies to justify the killing of the innocent in humanitarian wars fail to distinguish between criminal sanctions and the sanctions of war. One could agree that being a passive member of a group that causes harm makes one subject to criminal sanctions, perhaps on the basis of a conspiracy theory. But criminal sanctions and war sanctions should not be treated the same. Criminal sanctions are only meted out after extensive consideration of the facts, with attention paid to mitigating circumstances and various excuses that the agent has. There is in the end a determination of guilt by an independent fact-finder: the judge or jury.

In war, there is no such determination of the guilt or liability of a particular person. At best there is a non-independent determination of such guilt, but more often there is no serious attempt to make this determination at all. Rather, bombing campaigns are launched with little regard for the particular liability of an otherwise innocent person who is likely to be killed. Because of this, even if one agreed that collective liability schemes could be used to eliminate the immunity from criminal punishment we all normally have, more would be needed before similar arguments could justify the loss of immunity from attack in war.

---

[21] Larry May and Hugh LaFollette, "Suffer the Little Children," in *World Hunger and Morality*, edited by William Aiken and Hugh LaFollette, Englewood Cliffs, NJ: Prentice Hall, 1996, pp. 70–84.

III. The Applicability of the Doctrine of Double Effect

Even if it turns out that the otherwise innocent members of society that engage in such practices as ethnic cleansing have not lost their immunity from attack by being complicit in the violence, there is another strategy one could employ to justify the loss of innocent life by the bombing of cities, for instance, in humanitarian wars. One could argue that the taking of these innocent lives was not the intended result of the humanitarian bombing, for as the name implies, the primary intent of such bombing was to stop the atrocities from taking place. One could claim that the killing of the innocents was merely the unintended, if foreseen, result of the war to stop the atrocities. But as Henry Shue has pointed out, this strategy hits a major hurdle if fear is also part of the war strategy. There is a major problem if part of the war strategy is that civilians be killed so that enough fear is generated that the larger population rises up and demands an end to the atrocities.[22]

Humanitarian wars can be fought in conventional ways involving military targets, and in hitting these targets innocent civilians may be killed. The doctrine of double effect can seemingly be used to provide a non-consequentialist justification of these deaths if it can be shown that the primary objective was to take out the military targets and that the civilian casualties were only the unintended effects. But some humanitarian wars today are increasingly being fought by another means, namely, by hitting civilian targets, such as electricity plants or apartment buildings, to get the members of a society to become so fearful that they capitulate and force their government to stop the atrocities. In such cases, as Shue demonstrates, one cannot easily distinguish the military objective from the targeting of civilians. Because the two are causally so closely linked, there is no clear "double" effect; there is only one effect, namely, the killing of civilians. In such cases, if there are two effects, both of them must name the killing of civilians and yet this is unjustified despite the attempt to use the doctrine of double effect here. Shue concludes:

> NATO's bombing of Serbia flagrantly violated the principle of discrimination by intentionally causing civilian distress as a means to producing acceptance by Milosevic of NATO's terms (by way of his hypothesized worry about losing political power to an aroused public unwilling to endure further misery, especially perhaps loss of electricity during the winter to come).[23]

[22] Henry Shue, "Bombing to Rescue: NATO'S 1999 Bombing of Serbia," in *Ethics and Foreign Intervention*, edited by Chatterjee and Sheid, pp. 97–117.

[23] Ibid., p. 114.

I agree with Shue, but I think that his criticisms raise a more fundamental problem with the application of the doctrine of double effect than he realized and perhaps than he would be willing to accept.

Think of one of the first uses of the doctrine of double effect: Aquinas's attempt to justify the killing of the innocent in war. Aquinas explains how killing in self-defense is justified:

> Nothing hinders one act from having two effects, only one of which is intended, while the other is *beside* the intention. Now moral acts take their species according to what is intended and not according to what is beside the intention, since this is accidental as explained above. Accordingly, the act of self-defense may have two effects, one is the saving of one's life, the other is the slaying of the aggressor. Therefore this act, since one's intention is to save one's life, is not unlawful.[24]

Aquinas here first develops the idea of double effect. But in the very same paragraph he also sets a serious limit on this doctrine.

> But as it is unlawful to take a man's life, except for the public authority acting for the common good, as stated above, it is not lawful for a man to intend killing a man in self-defense, except for such as have public authority . . . as in the case of a soldier fighting against the foe.[25]

The key here is that one can intend to defend one's life. In executing this intention, one may find that the only avenue open may be to kill. As long as the killing is not intended, then the act that brings about death may be justified. The death must be an unintended side effect of defending oneself for the killing to be *beside* rather than a *part of* the intention.

Notice that Aquinas allows for some intentional killing of the innocent in self-defense but only by those who have public authority and act for the common good. This is not the same argument as the double effect argument. The double effect argument is independent of the public authority and common good argument. Rather, the double effect argument is about the morality of anyone's act that has unintended but otherwise prohibited consequences. But how is the argument supposed to proceed? It looks like it will come into effect only in rare cases when the killing of the innocent is not aimed at. What we will explore is whether such an argument can help us out of the difficulties posed by humanitarian intervention when many innocent people will be killed.

---

[24] Thomas Aquinas, *Summa Theologica*, I, II, Q. 64. A., in *The Morality of War*, edited by May, Rovie, and Viner, p. 32. My italics.
[25] Ibid.

In the NATO bombing of Serbia, the civilian casualties were not the unintended side effects of the bombing but rather the intended effects – since the idea was to startle the civilian population by these deaths. Yet if this is true, then there are also other cases when the doctrine of double effect would seem to be applicable but where it will turn out not to be. Take the classic case of a bombing campaign aimed at a supply depot in a heavily populated part of a city. Seemingly, we intend to bomb the supply depot but not to kill the civilians even as we recognize that civilians will nearly inevitably be killed. But the intended act is probably better described as the bombing of a certain part of a city where it is hard to disconnect the bombing of the supply depot from the bombing of the civilians. If this is right, then it isn't true that the bombing of the civilians is truly unintended, in the way it would be if one did not know there were any civilians in that part of town.

I would make the somewhat controversial claim that we cannot easily say that we do not intend to do that which we foresee to be the nearly inevitable result of what we are intentionally doing. Say we intend to shoot at a target and at the last minute a person walks in front of us. It seems odd to say that when we shoot anyway we are only intending to hit the target, not to hit the person. In such cases, we cannot avoid having our act described as intending to kill. And except in special circumstances, such killing will not be justified even though the doctrine of double effect appears to apply. Even if one does not agree with my conception of intentionality here, another route to the same result is to see that the killing of a person that is a nearly inevitable result of what one is doing is at least gross negligence, even if not intentional killing, assuming that there are no other reasons to defend such killing.[26] This weakened version of my view still makes the case that it will be hard to justify humanitarian wars when killing innocent persons is the nearly inevitable result of such wars.

The crucial premise in my argument above was that if something is foreseen as an effect and one chooses to do what is foreseen, one cannot normally say that one has not intended that effect. One could argue that some acts that do not normally have certain effects may be intended without also intending the effects even if the effects in this case are foreseen. But what is at issue here is the case of an effect that is intended and where there is nearly always a second effect as well whenever the first effect is

---

[26] I am grateful to Marilyn Friedman for suggesting this variation of my argument that might be more plausible to those who do not share my intuitions about how to think about intentionality.

brought about. In such cases, it seems hard to separate the intention to do the one effect from the intention to do the second. And as I just said, even if one still insists that one has not intended to kill, it looks like something nearly as bad has occurred – namely, the knowing risk of civilian death as a kind of gross negligence or recklessness.[27]

In the bombing case, it seems odd indeed to say that even though dropping bombs in cities is nearly always to risk civilian casualties, intentionally bombing cities is not intentionally to risk civilian casualties. Here the idea is that foreseeability alone is not the problem but that a certain effect nearly always accompanies the achievement of a certain objective. The problem with the bombing case is that it would be downright perverse to say that of course bombing cities nearly always causes civilian deaths but that intentionally deciding to bomb cities is not intentionally to risk such civilian casualties. It is beyond the scope of this chapter, but I would argue that intentionality cannot be sensibly carved up in this manner.

It will not be easy to show, by the use of the doctrine of double effect, that the normal, and foreseeable, civilian casualties of a bombing campaign are justified in a humanitarian war. Indeed, I have given some reasons to doubt that this can be accomplished. We are left then without the two most obvious nonconsequentialist ways to justify such campaigns: the liability and the double effect grounds. One can still fall back on the old consequentialist argument that the consequences of liberating a people or stopping genocide simply outweigh whatever civilian casualties result in waging humanitarian war. Such an argument will be explored in a subsequent section, but first I will say something more about collective responsibility and States.

IV. Collective Responsibility of States

As we saw in previous chapters, humanitarian intervention is a difficult case for *jus ad bellum* considerations because it involves a State initiating war against a State that has not attacked or even threatened it. No invasion is imminent and no population group of the attacking state has been

---

[27] One might also simply want to say that a person can be responsible for things that one has not explicitly aimed at, thereby avoiding altogether the problem of reconstruing the doctrine of double effect. I am not unsympathetic to this position, but as I say, my intuitions about intentionality allow for a somewhat more robust view, although I will have problems with cases where the side effect is not a normally occurring part of the act in question. I thank Brook Sadler for this point.

jeopardized. To be sure, people are being attacked or threatened, but they reside normally within the confines of a sovereign State that has not by and large acted in a hostile manner toward its neighbors. And yet, if the only way to prevent large-scale harm to a population is for one State to wage war against the State that so threatens this population, it seems that this is indeed a just cause for war. But as we will see, there will be problems of proportionality as well as other serious problems that make this case a very difficult one indeed.

Central to the questions raised in this chapter is how we are to understand the collective responsibility of States. We could proceed, as I have suggested in some of my earlier writings, to treat the collective responsibility of a State in a non-distributive way. This strategy is attractive especially when considering questions of responsibility for waging aggressive war. I would contend that war is one of the best examples of something that collectivities do rather than what individuals do – at least, individuals acting in isolation from one another. And humanitarian wars raise the issue of what States are responsible for in particularly graphic ways.

There is of course a serious debate about whether States or other collectivities can have non-distributive responsibilities. In my earlier writings I said that this issue turns on whether States can act in a non-distributive way, or at least can have actions attributed to them in this way.[28] Waging war is the kind of action that makes sense to attribute, if anything does, to a collectivity, and specifically to a State. For war to be waged there must be highly coordinated actions of many individual human persons, and these actions must be occurring in the midst of certain circumstances. War is not best seen as a duel writ large unless by the phrase "writ large" we mean that it is best seen as a duel among States.

If it makes sense to attribute actions to States, such as the action of waging aggressive or humanitarian war, then it also makes sense to blame or praise these States and in general to talk of these States being responsible for waging war. The only other person or entity that it might make sense to blame for waging aggressive war is the individual human person who is often most associated with the State: the head of State. I will address this point in the final section of this chapter. Aside from this person, there is really no one else who is responsible for the highly coordinated action that constitutes war. And this perhaps explains why for so many

[28] See Larry May, *The Morality of Groups*, Notre Dame, IN: University of Notre Dame Press, 1987; Larry May, *Sharing Responsibility*, Chicago, IL: University of Chicago Press, 1992; Larry May, *The Socially Responsive Self*, Chicago, IL: University of Chicago Press, 1996.

centuries discussion of war has almost always focused on the actions and responsibilities of States rather than on the members of States. Indeed, it is very hard even to talk about war as a function of what individual human persons do without elliptical language. The idea that States have responsibilities for waging war is not a difficult one conceptually if we are receptive to the idea of collectivities acting at all.

Let us return to the issue of collective liability that we discussed in Section II. If a State could but did not go to the aid of a State or sub-group of that State to stop oppression or aggression, there is a sense in which that State as well as other similarly placed States, and even the international community, could be collectively liable for failing to supply such aid. When the aid in question is providing military force to stop aggressive troops from carrying out oppression, it still seems as if it would be wrong not to do so, and the collective failure to aid people in such places as Darfur is a collective liability of the State or other institution that could help. We must not allow another Holocaust to occur because States and other institutions do not understand their collective respon-sibilities.

So, as one can see, the idea of collective responsibility has been used on both sides of the debate concerning humanitarian intervention. For there are at least two collectivities in play: the State, as we have just seen, and the international community. If there is anything like an international community, the members of this community have both collective respon-sibilities for what they do toward one another and collective responsi-bilities if they fail to do what they should do. And for our purposes this raises two questions: first, are States the proper members of the inter-national community; and second, are the members of the international community implicated in the moral responsibilities of the international community? International law is premised on international enforcement of rules at the international level. Those who support humanitarian intervention see it as one source of enforcement of international law. Those who oppose humanitarian intervention see that States have a col-lective responsibility not to violate the UN Charter and jeopardize the sovereignty of fellow States.

In addition to the issues of non-distributive collective responsibility raised by humanitarian intervention, there are also distributive collective responsibility issues as well. I will here address moral issues and leave legal issues until the final section of this chapter. Morally, we need to ascertain whether the responsibility of a State for waging aggressive or humani-tarian war gives rise to moral responsibility for the members of States, that is, individual human persons. And here we face one of the greatest challenges, namely, to explain why every member of a State does not share responsibility, and to the same extent, for the State's actions. My view, defended elsewhere, is that the better approach is to talk about differential moral responsibility based on the different roles that the members of a State played, where greater participation normally means greater moral responsibility.[29]

Individual human persons will share moral responsibility for what their States do not merely because of group membership but also because of participation in what the State does. This thesis is easy to accept when we talk of shared individual moral responsibility for war. In some wars, all of the members of a State participate; in other wars, only a small number of people participate. But participation is the key component that links the individual human person to the State in moral terms and perhaps also in legal terms, as we will explore later. Since State action is only the coordinated action of the State's members, and since the action of its members is best understood as participation, when we move from non-distributive to distributive responsibility, the best strategy is to do so by reference to individual participation. [30]

V. Defending Humanitarian Wars

I wish to mount a limited defense of humanitarian wars based on some of the ideas of the 18th-century theorist Emer de Vattel and in light of what we learned in earlier sections of this book as well. Perhaps humanitarian wars can be justified by reference to Vattel's principle of humanity, namely, when it is in a State's power to help other States without risking greater harm to itself, it is permissible (perhaps even obligatory) to do so.[31] Vattel worried about how the application of this principle could disrupt sovereignty. And we have also wondered about the risk of civilian casualties from humanitarian war. One way to modify the Vattelian principle to respond to such worries is to stipulate that one has a responsibility to act only if one does not risk greater harm to self *or others*. We should

---

[29] See my discussion of this issue in my book, *Sharing Responsibility*, Chicago: University of Chicago Press, 1992.

[30] For a similar strategy, see Christopher Kutz, *Complicity*, New York: Cambridge University Press, 2000. Also see *Individual and Collective Responsibility*, edited by Peter French, New York: Schenkman, 1972.

[31] Emer de Vattel, *Le Droit des Gens, ou Principes de la Loi Naturelle* (The Laws of Nations or the Principles of Natural Law) (1758), Washington, DC: Carnegie Institution, 1916, p. 130.

also stipulate that the States must have very good grounds for thinking that the State or people to be rescued are truly in need of, and desire, rescue.

Vattel worried that humanitarian wars would often jeopardize whatever good there is from having stable sovereign States. I would agree with his analysis. But Vattel also said that the most obvious case in which such worries were not clearly overriding concerned those situations involving a civil war or those in which there was confusion about where sovereignty resided. We could expand on his idea, extrapolating to emergency situations generally, and say that humanitarian wars should be allowed only where what is to be gained is not overridden by the negative effects on sovereignty that occur from such intervention. Such considerations would naturally fall under the category of potential harm to others by the waging of humanitarian wars. Only when the risks from intrusion on sovereignty are less than the gains from such intrusion can humanitarian wars be justified on this reconstruction of Vattel's position. Proportionality considerations would be key here.

When discussing Kelly's arguments about collective liability, we encountered a worry about the loss of life to civilians in humanitarian wars. I tried to show that Kelly's argument did not work to justify such civilian losses. But these losses may nonetheless be justified, yet only in very few cases, if the sheer extent of the humanitarian crisis is so large as to outweigh considerations of the lives of the innocent that are risked by the attempt to stop the crisis through military means. If innocent lives are on both sides of the balance sheet, there is no reason to think that greater saving of lives cannot justify lesser loss of lives, assuming that there is no other way to save the greater number of lives than by war.

When discussing the doctrine of double effect we also saw how some, although again very few, humanitarian wars might be justified by reference to this doctrine. When the war is aimed at civilian targets, the doctrine of double effect will not help much. But we might be able to justify even the targeting of civilians if it could be shown that this was necessary to save many more lives than those that were risked by the targeting. It is sometimes said that the intentional targeting of civilians can never be justified. But I follow Vattel in thinking that there can be emergency situations when what is normally banned may sometimes be allowed, as when a large number of innocent people are threatened by the actions of a State or there is much potential harm to the world community, such as by a genocidal campaign. Of course, emergency situations do not have much precedent, but that is just to reaffirm what has been thought at least since Augustine: namely, that all war, even humanitarian war, can be justified, if at all, in only the most extreme cases of harm that can be prevented in no other way.

Humanitarian intervention has been so controversial because of the difficulty in characterizing the acts by the State that caused the humanitarian crisis as threatening either the State that intervenes or the world community. And for this reason it is hard to see that the offending State has engaged in a first strike or otherwise provoked the attack by the intervening State. And without any provocation – at least based on the traditional elements of what constitutes State aggression – where unprovoked first strikes are paradigmatically cases of State aggression – it looks like the State that has engaged in humanitarian intervention has itself engaged in an act of aggression.

Of course, since the State has gone to war to defend the rights of others, in my view of what counts as aggression, it is not clearly an example of State aggression. Yet the question is whether this kind of defense of others, where the other in question is not itself a State that is being attacked, can justify intervention. It is odd indeed to call the humanitarian actions of a State by the name "aggression" since that implies that there is some hostility behind the intervention. If the intervention is truly motivated by humanitarian concerns, then calling it aggression and therefore also hostile seems out of place.

It is also hard to see that humanitarian interventions constitute wrongs at all, let alone the most important of wrongs in the international arena, and hence we have reason to think that crossing State borders is not always wrong. Humanitarian intervention may indeed often be ill advised since anything that contributes to the horrors of war is to be avoided at nearly all costs. But if the motivation for the humanitarian intervention is to stop genocide, then the war may not be ill advised even though there is a serious risk of the major loss of civilian life that occurs in most wars. Here we might do some rudimentary utilitarian calculation to see that stopping genocide by means of a war could be justified.

I would be hard pressed, though, to see humanitarian intervention that risks the horrors of war as a paradigmatically good thing to do or as an example of a paradigmatically justified war. Anything that increases the likelihood of major loss of civilian life must at best be a necessary evil, surely not a paradigmatically justified war. The morally ambiguous character of humanitarian intervention is made even more clear when one realizes, as we have seen, that humanitarian wars are more likely than other wars to involve massive civilian casualties. Such considerations contribute to the continuing debate today about how to regard humanitarian intervention.

We see that it is next to impossible to justify all humanitarian wars, but at least some may be justified, and even strongly so. Many humanitarian wars will violate the proportionality principle by bringing more harm than good to the civilian population or to the security of the region. But some humanitarian wars will not run afoul of the proportionality principle since they will confront genocides and other mass crimes with less loss of life through the conduct of the war itself. In addition, many humanitarian wars do not meet the last resort principle since war has rarely been able to stop, at least not for very long, mass crimes like genocide in ways that diplomacy often can. But there surely are some humanitarian wars that seem to satisfy the last resort principle and are likely to have some efficacy. And the justification of such wars will indeed be best grounded in collective responsibility principles.

Think of a war waged to stop the genocide in the Darfur region of the Sudan. The Sudanese government, if we can even refer to the near anarchy in the Sudan as having a government, has shown itself unwilling or unable to stop the slaughter. Diplomatic efforts have been tried and have all failed miserably. The attempts by the United Nations to put peacekeeping troops in place have met with strong resistance and the death of many peacekeepers. Threats of economic boycotts and incentives of economic aid have similarly failed to stop the carnage in the refugee camps. In this kind of case, war might be the last resort to ending the genocide and doing what the international community has a collective responsibility to do.

Indeed, it seems that the failure to go to war to end genocides of the sort that are occurring in Darfur would indicate a failure of the international community to enforce its most widely praised multilateral treaty, the Genocide Convention, and hence a serious failure of international law itself. As we saw in earlier chapters, if law is not enforced it ceases to have any claim to be called law. In international law – an area of law already thought of as controversially labeled "law" at best – there is an especially pressing reason to demonstrate that there is enforcement of its most widely accepted provisions. Failure to intervene in places like Darfur to stop the flagrant violation of the Genocide Convention is also a major failure of international law.

Humanitarian wars can at least be prima facie defended in such circumstances as the genocide in Darfur. Such wars might be technically aggressive – at least, according to traditional doctrine – in that they involve invasion by one State against another State that is resisting rather than consenting to the invasion. Yet, since no "hostility" motivates the invading State and the international community in effect consents to allow the invasion, it seems as if the designation of aggression is the kind of technical characterization that doesn't bear much normative weight. Aggression, as traditionally understood, is not itself a trigger of normative disapproval; some aggression, such as that form that stops worse aggression, could be a very good thing indeed, as theorists from the Just War tradition and contemporary international law have claimed. This is one reason I urged that we abandon the traditional way of understanding aggression.

The major problem with humanitarian intervention wars is that despite their lofty aims they are still wars. And because they are wars often with no clear military targets, there will be innocent civilians who will be killed, perhaps in very large numbers. And the horrors of war do not stop just with the killing of the innocent, no matter how unintended, but extend to massive injuries and infrastructure damage that may take a generation to overcome. Because of the likelihood of the civilian casualties involved, wars of humanitarian intervention remain morally and legally problematical. Yet when it really does seem like the last hope for saving many lives, saving wide-scale injury, and saving property from mass destruction, then sometimes such wars seem worth it. And those who initiate and wage such wars have not clearly done wrong when they pursue humanitarian intervention as a strategy for the promotion of international law.

VI. Should Anyone Be Prosecuted for Humanitarian Wars?

Despite the difficulty of condemning or justifying all humanitarian wars, I wish to argue that it is not difficult to say whether anyone should be prosecuted for waging such wars. In my view, it is very rare that an individual, even a political or military leader of a State, should be prosecuted for initiating and waging a humanitarian war regardless of the fact that at least some of these wars could be characterized as aggressive. In Chapter 5, I argued that we should think of the principle of just cause and the corresponding idea of State aggression as a bifurcated principle. We should prosecute individuals for only clear-cut cases of aggressive war, and from what we have seen in this chapter, humanitarian war is anything but clear-cut. While we might want to condemn and even sanction States for waging humanitarian wars, it is rarely justified to prosecute even the State's top leaders for the crime of aggression.

In contemporary international law, the elements of the crime of aggression are not well settled. But there seems to be agreement that there are at least three elements of this crime. First, the prosecution must show that there is State aggression. This is often highly contentious, especially when considering wars waged for humanitarian reasons. To repeat a point made earlier, State aggression is an element of the crime of aggression, meaning that to convict an individual for the crime of participating in an aggressive war one must first prove that the war in question was indeed a war that a State was waging aggressively. Second, there is the matter of *actus reus*, and normally this means that one had a fairly high level of participation in waging the war of aggression. Third, one must also prove that the individual in question had *mens rea*: he or she intended to participate in a war of aggression. And while any individual human person could be prosecuted for such a crime, the ICC has made it clear that only State leaders will be so prosecuted, if anyone is.

One of the main reasons to think that we should rarely prosecute even State leaders for waging humanitarian war comes from considerations of *mens rea*. For most wars this is the stumbling block for individual prosecutions. State leaders are often doing what they think is in the best interest of their country, or are doing their patriotic duty, or merely following orders from those who are even higher up the chain of command. These intentions and motives make it hard to show that State leaders had a guilty mind when they participated in initiating or waging aggressive war. And this is especially true since it is often hard for State leaders to figure out whether a given war is indeed a war of aggression and hence difficult to tell whether these leaders meant to be participating in an aggressive war.

When humanitarian war is being initiated or waged, it is even harder than it normally is to prove *mens rea* of State leaders. At the very least there will be mixed intentions or motives, as the State leader seeks to aid another State or a subpopulation within a State. Coming to the aid of others is certainly not a straightforwardly guilt-making act. Indeed, given the rich tradition about the Good Samaritan, many would find humanitarian intervention to be the opposite of something for which an individual should be judged guilty. And when we add to this the extreme difficulty of telling whether a given war of humanitarian intervention is also a war of aggression, proving *mens rea* of State leaders will be very difficult indeed. Of course, one could contend that we won't know what the true intentions or motives were unless some kind of trial is undertaken. I would agree to a certain extent, and for this reason one could read this section of my text as perhaps only establishing the weaker view that State leaders should rarely be convicted rather than the stronger view that they should rarely be prosecuted.

The *actus reus* component also now looks very difficult to prove as well in humanitarian wars. Participation in such wars will be no harder to prove than normal, I suppose, but that only means that the act part is no more difficult than normal. Establishing that the act was guilty depends on the circumstances even more in humanitarian intervention than in other types of war, for it is very unclear what exactly are the illegal circumstances within which individual acts of participation are to be located. Specifically, it will matter quite a bit whether the individual human person in question saw his or her participation as part of an aggressive war, and this will indeed turn on the state of mind of this individual human person.

The circumstances of humanitarian intervention concern such things as an ongoing genocide or ethnic cleansing campaign as well as the normal circumstances of planning for war. So we could see the acts of State leaders either as participating in stopping genocide or ethnic cleansing, or as participating in the preparation for war. The first set of circumstances may not imply anything guilty about the acts while the second set of circumstances may do so. But if the war is clearly waged purely for humanitarian reasons, then it is hard not to see the second colored by the first. Because of these mixed considerations, it is especially hard to convict State leaders in such cases, even though the consensus in international law remains in favor of the illegality of humanitarian intervention.

The State aggression element is of course also very hard to prove in cases of humanitarian intervention. And because humanitarian intervention does not look like normal cases of State aggression, it will be harder for the prosecution to prove the State aggression element in such cases, just as it is also harder than normal to prove *mens rea* and *actus reus*. One might argue that prosecutions of individuals for participating in humanitarian wars should take place even if it is unlikely that convictions can be secured so as to make a statement about the wrongness of such wars. It is surely not a good normative reason to fail to prosecute just because conviction is unlikely. On pragmatic grounds, most prosecutors do take likelihood of conviction into account, but that is normally because the prosecutors have too many other possible cases to prosecute waiting in the wings. But at the international level, this may not be as big a practical problem as in the domestic sphere, since at least for the foreseeable future few cases will be referred to the ICC. Nonetheless, it is normatively odd to urge that prosecutions not take place because they will be hard to bring to convictions. Shouldn't prosecutions for crimes of aggression be undertaken so as to deter individual leaders from waging war?

My view is that the answer to this question would normally be yes, but that there is a countervailing consideration in the case of humanitarian wars. Yes, it is true that we want to discourage States from waging wars, but it is also true that we want to encourage States to go to the aid of other States or subgroups within States that are experiencing serious and sustained oppression. Morally, it would be a mistake to discourage individuals from going to the aid of other individuals who are in serious trouble and are unlikely to extricate themselves on their own. Indeed, encouraging State leaders to be good Samaritans seems like just the kind of thing that international law should aim at, just as it also should aim at minimizing use of force. And legally there are also similar reasons to worry about such counter-vailing considerations, especially considerations tied to deterrence.

In this chapter, I have tried to explain how difficult a case humanitarian intervention is when we are considering the crime of aggression. For all three elements, humanitarian intervention is problematic. Yet I argued that it makes sense to think that some wars of humanitarian intervention can be justified. I also argued that on similar grounds it rarely makes sense to prosecute State leaders for participating in such wars. Humanitarian intervention will remain very controversial at the level of asking about whether States should be condemned and sanctioned for engaging in them. But it is less controversial concerning prosecutions, since there are many reasons to think that State leaders and other individual human persons should not be convicted in humanitarian intervention cases, even when aggressive, more than in other cases of aggressive war. The participation is less likely to be guilty as it is so hard to tell whether the war that one participates in is aggressive, and the motives and intentions are more likely to be admirable than in other types of war. For these reasons, it will be rare indeed that prosecutions for humanitarian interventions should go forward. In the next chapter, I will turn to the equally hard case of how to regard war waged against terrorism. As we will see, some of the same issues arise concerning terrorist wars as concern humanitarian wars.

14

Terrorist Aggression

There is no reason to think that only States can wage aggressive wars. In contemporary times, we have seen non-State actors, including terrorist groups, wage war against States and against other non-State actors. I will adopt an amended version of a definition offered by Andrew Valls and define terrorism as violence committed by State or non-State actors directed against civilians or their property for political purposes.[1] In Just War theory, wars by non-State actors were not generally contemplated because the legitimate authority to wage war resided only in States. There is an interesting exception, which I will explore, concerning piracy as a form of aggression by non-State actors. Throughout, I will argue that the *jus ad bellum* principles we have been discussing in this book apply to some terrorist groups and that when the leaders of such groups wage aggressive war they should be confronted by international legal institutions. I will also argue that when terrorists are confronted and prosecuted they should be afforded the same rights as State leaders when the latter are similarly confronted and prosecuted.

The strategy I adopt, of allowing that some terrorist groups can wage war and that terrorist leaders can be prosecuted for waging aggressive war as long as such prosecutions are subject to the rule of law, recognizes the reality of the contemporary situation where there are multiple types of actors on the world stage. Non-State actors have increasingly become dominant players especially in a world where many States are quite weak and where groups that have not been elected can operate in a State's territory unhindered by even the authorities that have been designated

---

[1] Andrew Valls, "Can Terrorism be Justified?" in *Ethics and International Affairs*, edited by Andrew Valls, Lanham, MD: Rowman and Littlefield, 2000, pp. 65–79; reprinted in *The Morality of War*, edited by Larry May, Eric Rovie, and Steve Viner, Upper Saddle River, NJ: Prentice-Hall, 2006, p. 318.

to serve all of the people of that State. My strategy does not maintain the fiction that only State leaders can operate in State territories and wage war against other States or peoples.

There is an interesting initial question of whether some terrorist groups can ever resemble sovereign States in the world. For if the answer is no, then it makes little sense to talk of terrorist groups waging aggressive war or any kind of war. This is an especially hard case for a theory of aggression and a consideration of *jus ad bellum* principles, which has been the subject of this book. Like humanitarian intervention, terrorist aggression pushes the limit of the conceptual and normative categories we have been developing. In particular, the idea of terrorist aggression calls into question the idea that the world is composed largely of State actors and that the *ad bellum* rules of war are primarily a matter of regulating State behavior. When non-State actors are added into the mix, the central categories are disrupted.

In general, my strategy is to treat non-State actors like States when non-State actors act like States. The chapter thus confronts the idea of terrorist aggression initially through several levels. In the first section, I revisit the 17th-century debates about how to treat pirates, especially concerning the ability of pirates to wage naval battles and seize State ships. In the second section, I examine the causal role that terrorist organizations play today in employing force to attack States or peoples. In the third section, I argue that there is a sense in which some terrorist groups can count as legitimate authorities waging war. Then in the fourth section, I provide my positive argument for thinking that terrorist groups can be guilty of waging aggressive war and their members can be prosecuted for those acts of aggression. And in the fifth section I discuss the special human rights concerns involved in prosecuting terrorists and how best to maintain the rule of law even in the face of terrorist aggression. Finally, I ask how these human rights concerns have changed, if at all, since September 11, 2001.

I. Piracy and Terrorism

Alberico Gentili, writing at the end of the 16th century, provides us with a good place to begin. He argues that the laws of war do not apply to pirates since they stand outside the system of rules that governs States during times of war.

> There is another reason why such men do not come under the law of war, namely, because that law is derived from the law of nations, and malefactors do not enjoy the privileges of a law to which they are foes. How can the law,

which is nothing but an agreement and a compact, extend to those who have withdrawn from the agreement and broken the treaty of the human race as Florus puts it?

Pirates are the common enemies of all mankind [*hostes humani generis*].[2]

This is representative of 16th- and 17th-century thinkers on the topic but not of thinkers who wrote in earlier centuries of the Just War tradition.

The early Just War theorists were not as committed to the idea that only States can justly wage war. At least part of the explanation is that until the 16th century there was not as clear a divide between States and other political entities and similarly, it was not clear that non-State actors were always illegitimate. Unincorporated non-State actors were much more plentiful in these early eras, and it was not out of the question that they could wage just wars in self-defense. There is also an old tradition of thinking that everyone is entitled to humane treatment, even those who are our worst enemies. Indeed, as we will see there was somewhat of a debate in the early 17th century about whether even pirates should be treated humanely, although it should be clear that thinkers like Gentili were on the side of the majority of theorists who denied this thesis.

Before leaving Gentili, I wish to comment on the idea of *hostes humani generis*, common enemies of humanity, a term that today is sometimes also applied to terrorists. This term, or an equivalent, was probably first used by Cicero in his *De Officiis*.[3] But while the term appears to be used in both more ancient sources as well as in 17th-century debates, it is not at all clear that the term has always had the same meaning.[4] Indeed, it seems to me that there are several distinct meanings of *hostes humani generis* that are not necessarily related to each other.

1. One of the earliest examples of the idea behind this term relates simply to people who had rejected the rules of how States are to be formed and lived without a centralized authority.
2. The term also seems sometimes to have been applied to those political associations, even States, that failed to follow the rules that other States had established concerning property or preservation of life.

---

[2] Alberico Gentili, *De Jure Belli* (The Law of War) (1598), Book I, ch. 4, translated by John Rolfe, Oxford: Clarendon Press, 1933, p. 22.

[3] See Alfred P. Rubin, *The Law of Piracy*, 2nd ed., Irvington-on-Hudson, NY: Transnational 1995, pp. 15–17.

[4] Ibid., pp. 90–95.

3. The term seems to have been most often used for bands of robbers who operated on the high seas and recognized no rules of property or preservation of life.

It is interesting to speculate why these very different examples came to be captured with the same term and what made people think that each case is truly a threat to humanity, not merely to those States in the region where they operated.

The rationale for seeing the groups in the first category as enemies of humanity is merely that they reject the model of State formation as the way to organize political society. One can think of examples today of unincorporated groups that manage to function well and not to threaten their neighbors unduly. Not organizing as States is only the loosest of threats to humanity and is really a threat only if one thinks that States are the best form of political organization. Indeed, one could see the pro-liferation of forms of political organization as a healthy, indeed perhaps necessary, means to promote the development of humanity.

The second category is also not obviously a group that poses a threat to humanity. At least in part it depends on whether the rules that most States live by are better than the rules that the non-State actors, or "rogue" States, subscribe to. Here there are three distinct possibilities: the rules of the rogue State are worse than, better than, or no worse than those of the other States. Only in the first case is there cause for alarm, as is true today when some terrorist groups seem to have completely different rules of engagement that put civilians at much greater risk than would be true if they followed the traditional rules of engagement of States and their armies. Humanity would not be harmed if there were merely different rules that one State, or non-State actor, followed than were followed by other States. There is often some loss in predictability or efficiency when there is no conformity of rule following, but such a situation hardly places humanity in jeopardy.

The third category is the worrisome one, since here the non-State actor simply doesn't play by the rules at all and is seemingly unrestrained in its behavior toward all with whom it comes into contact. The pirates who flew the skull and crossbones might have been signaling that anyone was at risk of death who happened to come into contact with these pirates. This category seems most clearly to be an enemy of humanity. But even here, it depends on whether the non-State actor does in fact have much interaction with the rest of the world. If this lawless group kept to itself, such as a White supremacist, separatist group in Montana, it is not at all clear that it poses a threat to humanity merely by its existence. How they conduct their societies may be reprehensible, but if the members are there uncoerced, interference may be unjustified.

This third category may also include some contemporary terrorist groups. Indeed, what makes some terrorist groups morally and legally problematic is that they do not recognize the legitimacy of the rules of war, especially the rule against targeting civilians. In this sense, many terrorist groups do not play by the rules. But unlike some pirates of old, terrorists normally play by other rules than those rules that would be recognized by States around the world. Indeed, many terrorist groups see themselves not as enemies of humanity but as insurgents fighting repressive regimes. There is a sense in which some terrorist groups see themselves as acting much as some States see themselves acting in situations of humanitarian intervention. In this sense, some terrorist groups not only mainly play by the rules but also see themselves as the ultimate protector of those for whom the rules are not providing protection.

One could argue that the mere fact that terrorist groups do not play by the same rules as most States makes them a threat to the international rules. If there are two alternative sets of rules that one can adhere to, it may seem that no one is held to any particular rules at all, thereby undermining the continued existence of any rules at all.[5] I'm not convinced that having alternative rules weakens or jeopardizes any rules. Think of the alternative ways of computing U.S. taxes or the alternative ways of doing double entry accounting. While cumbersome, and ripe for unfairness, having alternative sets of rules between which one can choose does not necessarily undermine the rules.

The situation of pirates and their treatment in ancient times may still provide valuable lessons for how to regard some terrorists. As Alfred Rubin points out, in Roman times some pirate groups were treated as no different from small States: some of these non-State groups were the proper subject of war on the part of Rome and others were simply given no moral or legal status since they were enemies of humanity.[6] Today, one could similarly divide "terrorist" groups into those that behaved more in State-like ways than others. Some pirates were treated like brigands and others were given quasi-State status. Today, similarly, we could think of

---

[5] I am grateful to Cindy Holder for suggesting this objection to me and for generally an excellent set of comments on a paper of mine that was an ancestor to this chapter. Also see Mark Osiel's unpublished paper, "Reciprocity and Anti-Reciprocity in International Law."

[6] Ibid., p. 13–17.

terrorist groups like the Bader Meinhoff group as more like criminal gangs and brigands, and groups like Hamas, which in fact won a significant election in Palestine in 2006, as sufficiently State-like to be given a different status.

Before we leave this topic, I wish to say a bit about Grotius who generally opposed Gentili's views in early international legal theory. Grotius claims that pirates are beyond the moral pale in the sense that they are "banded together for wrongdoing,"[7] yet he thinks that pirates should be treated in a moral way. According to Grotius, pirates must have their rights protected, not for their own sake, but for the sake of God or other parties. If we fail to take the rights of pirates seriously, there is a sense in which rights themselves are jeopardized since we share in common with all other humans this protection of rights.[8] There is a difference between asking whether the life of a pirate is to be condemned and asking how the rights of pirates should be treated, especially in war. I will follow Grotius here in thinking that we can see pirates as *hostes humani generis* and yet still as having rights that need to be protected. Even as they are common enemies of humanity they are also members of humanity.

My view of terrorists is similar to Grotius's view of pirates. As I said above, it does make a difference what kind of terrorist we are talking about for some considerations. But in general, I will maintain that we can see even those terrorists who are common enemies of humanity as nonetheless also members of humanity. As members of humanity, terrorists are owed the same human rights considerations as any other member of humanity, since human rights attach merely to membership not to what the person otherwise deserves.

II. Legitimate Authority and Non-State Actors

Regardless of whether one admits that terrorist groups and other non-State actors can be efficacious actors during war and elsewhere, there is first a significant question about whether terrorist groups can ever meet the legitimate authority test of traditional Just War theory. In Chapter , I voiced skepticism about the contemporary relevance of this principle. Here I will assume that the principle has at least a bit of relevance and begin by asking whether terrorist groups could attain legitimate authority

---

[7] Hugo Grotius, *De Jure Belli ac Pacis* (On the Law of War and Peace) (1625), translated by Francis W. Kelsey, Oxford: Clarendon Press, 1925, p. 631.

[8] Ibid., pp. 373–374. I have argued for a similar conclusion about what a Grotian position would look like concerning terrorists in the final chapter of *War Crimes and Just War*, New York: Cambridge University Press, 2007.

to wage war. But I wish to leave open the question of whether and to what extent we should continue to think of legitimate authority as central to *jus ad bellum* normative principles.

Legitimate authority was employed in the past to help explain who in a State can declare that the State is initiating war. At least in part this comes from historical worries about the State being highjacked by a rump element that tries to drag the State into war or to set the State up for being attacked by seemingly being the first to declare war. It is indeed useful to think about whether the State is initiating war or whether there is merely some faction within the State that is trying to make it seem as if the State has initiated war. And in the context of terrorism today, it is especially interesting whether a weak State has declared war or whether strong factions within the State have done so with no particular authorization from the people, as in the case of Hezbollah's attack on Israel in 2006. One of the problems though is that legitimacy does not come only from the people's consent. It also comes merely from following the right procedures in a way that has routinely been recognized as a sign of legitimate State action.[9]

With a terrorist group we will normally have to think a bit beyond the standard range of cases of legitimate authority. Since many terrorist groups do not have a democratic process that establishes its leadership, we must recognize other mechanisms for establishing who can speak and act for the group, or we must think of all the acts of terrorist groups as failing to have legitimate authority. The latter option does not make much sense since many States are considered to act with legitimate authority even though they are not democracies. Perhaps we can make some progress by thinking about States that have been granted legitimacy even though they are not democracies. Think of a small State, like Saudi Arabia, where the government is run as an extended family. Many terrorist groups do not have structures that are all that different from that of Saudi Arabia.

Douglas Lackey summarizes three criteria of competent authority that have survived through the centuries and remain important considerations today.

1. There must be a controlled use of force,
2. directed through a chain of command, and
3. aimed at a political purpose.[10]

[9] See H. L. A. Hart, *The Concept of Law*, Oxford: Clarendon Press, 1960.
[10] Douglas P. Lackey, *The Ethics of War and Peace*, Upper Saddle River, NJ: Prentice Hall, 1989, p. 30.

I find this framework quite useful and also see no reason in principle why some terrorist groups could not be thought to operate under legitimate authority. While in the past this condition was meant to rule out all non-State actors from being able legitimately to wage war, today there is no good reason to exclude these groups unless they really are closer to criminal gangs or even mere perpetrators of random violence.

Many terrorist groups exert controlled rather than random violence. Today, Jihadist suicide bombers do not strike at random. There have been some terrorist groups that strike at random, but normally only for a short period of time and only for a very particular objective. Fidel Castro apparently orchestrated nearly random attacks in Cuba as a way to make the citizenry increasingly hostile to the Batista government that could not regain control. But even this campaign of uncontrolled violence, due to its short duration, still looks like a kind of controlled violence in that the very randomness of the violence was itself planned to begin at a certain time and end at another time. To instill terror in the population, acts that appear to be random actually are normally very well planned and controlled.

It is contentious, however, whether terrorist groups also meet the chain of command requirement. On the one hand, without some kind of organizational structure it would be difficult for terrorist groups to accomplish much at all. Al Qaeda, for example, seems to have an elaborate chain of command that survives even when major figures are killed or captured. The same could seemingly be said of many of the terrorist groups currently operating in the Middle East. On the other hand, this issue is dependent on the strength of the links in the chain of command. If a terrorist group operates by semi-autonomous terrorist cells that only occasionally take orders from a central authority, or perhaps where there is no clear central authority at all, can there still be a chain of command? Perhaps there is a chain of command within each cell, but then it would be odd to think that the overarching terrorist group could decide much of anything as a group that would be representative of its members or in some other way be legitimate.

Perhaps the most difficult requirement to meet is the political objective condition. But at least in part this is made easier or harder by how broadly or narrowly one defines "political." Terrorist groups always have objectives, and those objectives often connect to some political situation, such as the overthrow of an existing government. Here it is important to ask whether a terrorist group must "represent" a people to claim to be protecting them. We do not impose this requirement on a State, so initially we might wonder why such a condition should be imposed on non-State actors. Non-democratic States can protect their citizens and even do a good job of protecting their basic human rights and yet not "represent" those citizens. Of course, there must be a group of people that in some sense the terrorist group is protecting for its use of force to be potentially justified. And there may be few terrorist groups that meet this requirement.[11] But my point in this chapter is to inquire about what may be true of some terrorist groups, not all of them, as a way to explore possible non-State actors and waging aggressive war.

There is an interesting question of whether the violent overthrow of a duly authorized political regime can itself be called a political objective. I'm inclined to think that this is also a political objective, since revolutionaries over the centuries have certainly understood their own mission in political terms. Many terrorist groups claim that their objective is to end various types of oppression. Is this a political goal? Again, I would say yes especially since some political authority normally imposes the kind of oppression that some terrorist groups oppose. It is true that most terrorist groups do not see themselves as defending territory, but the goals of many terrorist groups do not seem merely to kill as many people as possible. Instead there often is a political point to these killings, even if not normally one that involves territory.

Terrorist groups rarely elect their leadership, but the same can be said of most States throughout history and continuing into the modern era. If we move beyond the narrow conception of political legitimacy that connects to democratic elections, then some terrorist groups seem able to meet the legitimate authority test as well as many non-democratic States can. And for that reason we can say that some terrorist groups can wage war, whether aggressive or defensive. Of course, it still isn't clear that legitimate authority is doing much work anymore in contemporary debates about *jus ad bellum* norms. It could do so, especially if we employ a narrow conception of legitimate authority and argue, as some theorists seem inclined to do, that democracy is crucial for legitimacy. But at the moment, as long as a somewhat wider conception of legitimacy is employed I do not see why some terrorist groups could not attain legitimate authority and then be said properly to wage war and to have war waged against them. This proposal does not necessarily provide terrorist

---

[11] How many terrorist groups meet this requirement will in part be determined by whether we distinguish between insurgent and terrorist groups. The definition of terrorism I provided at the beginning of the chapter does not explicitly draw this distinction. Steve Lee is to be thanked for pointing this out to me.

groups with increased moral credibility. Legitimate authority is merely a technical designation recognizing that when terrorist groups act like States they can be held accountable like States as well.

III. Similarities between State and Non-State Actors

The central question of these early sections of the chapter is whether terrorists can wage aggressive war and whether terrorists can rightfully be prosecuted for such international crimes. This issue arises because today it has become common to say that terrorists can only be confronted as common enemies of humanity, and if they wage war it is always illegitimate war. But those who take this view do not wish to grant to terrorists even the idea that their wars can be assessed as defensive or aggressive because the group itself is without moral or legal legitimacy. I addressed the question of legitimacy straightforwardly in the previous section. In the current section, I will address how we should think about terrorist groups in terms of their causal agency and other factors that might allow us to compare them favorably to States.

The central insight, elementary though it may be, that I wish to bring to this issue is merely that some terrorist groups are able to act in ways so similar to some States that there is little practical reason to distinguish between them. In fact, some States are not able to act on the world stage with nearly the efficacy of some terrorist groups. The events of September 11, 2001, cited so many times recently for the wrong reasons, can here be cited just to affirm the fact of the efficacious power of some terrorist groups – no State had previously managed a successful attack on the American mainland prior to the September 11, 2001, attacks. That these attacks were not carried out by another State but by a terrorist group is truly significant. Also consider Hamas, a powerful terrorist group that managed to capture the government in Palestine.

In my view, the most important question is whether a terrorist group acts as an effective State-like agent – if it does so, then it can be held responsible as if it were a State. Indeed, if the terrorist group acts, or fails to act, in a way that constitutes an omission, this may trigger its responsibility, both moral and legal. Today, few people would argue that some terrorist groups are not effective actors on the world stage. But the question will nonetheless arise about whether we should count what terrorist groups do as "war." The U.S. administration has said that it is at war with Al Qaeda, and talks as if this is a real war, not merely a metaphor for real war.

One of the questions about whether a terrorist group like Al Qaeda could wage a war at all concerns whether it sees itself as playing by the normal rules of war. If not, then it is an "outlaw" group, and as such, its members may also fall outside the realm of law, including international criminal law, the way some pirates were once regarded. The only solution to piracy was to kill them all, or so it seemed to many 16th- and 17th-century thinkers. Similarly, today we non-terrorists could kill all terrorists with impunity because we needn't worry about the rules of war since neither did they. I will return to this issue in the final section of this chapter. Here I wish merely to indicate that if terrorist groups are not seen as even being able to wage war, whether defensively or even aggressively, then there are certain things that follow from this, one of them being that terrorists do not need to be treated according to the normal restraints we recognize even when we are dealing with people who are waging aggressive – that is, unjustified – war. There are worse things than waging aggressive war, and one of those things is the choice to be outside all law and rules, regardless of how efficacious and State-like a terrorist group might otherwise appear.

But I wish to suggest that one of the tests for whether to think that a group can wage war and be subject to, and demand others to restrain themselves by, the rules of war, is whether the group in question is able to act like a State. Such a claim needs defense and I will try to provide it in the remainder of this section. The first thing to note is that being able to act like a State is already a pretty high bar to cross. Individuals, and even many groups of individuals, lack the coordination to be able to do anything even vaguely State-like. The idea is that States are the paradigm case of entities that can wage war, but if there are other entities that can act like States, then perhaps they too can wage war. Waging war actually provides one with a kind of legal framework within which one operates. If one can not be said to wage war, then one is outside this set of laws and rules.

Yet some terrorist groups, and other non-state actors, can indeed do all of the things that normally are thought to constitute waging war. Perhaps one of the best contemporary examples is Al Qaeda. Al Qaeda sees itself as being at war with the United States and its Western allies. It has training camps throughout the world to create a group of people who will be the frontline "soldiers" in such a war. There are "ministers" who are in charge of various aspects of the international armed conflict that Al Qaeda is waging against Western powers. There are also elaborate although secret chains of command that link all of the far-flung members to a kind of central authority – with Osama bin Laden at its head. Most significantly,

Al Qaeda is highly successful at its operations and has for a number of years battled the Pakistani army to a near standstill. Even though Al Qaeda does not occupy a territory or have a normal governmental structure it is able to do what, if done by a State, we would call the waging of war.

We can also think of insurgent groups – the Tamil Tigers, for instance – that similarly operate quite an effective paramilitary operation that stalemates the armed forces of a government in the State where they operate their insurgency. Indeed, most civil wars these days are truly wars in every sense indistinguishable from non–civil wars in the world. The civil war is a struggle for control of the territory of a State, not a struggle among States. But in every other respect, the sides of the struggle employ the same tactics, the same command structure, and the same efficacy of waging and winning, or likelihood of winning, battles. Civil wars are not misnamed but should truly be seen as wars. And this is one of the best reasons for thinking that non-State actors can wage war.

The issue is whether we have an in principle reason for treating States and State-like entities differently even if they can do most of the same things during armed struggles. Once we have dispensed with the legitimate authority objection considered in the previous section, it is not clear what else can be said other than that non-State actors cannot do those things that States can do. Yet in the current section I have given strong reasons to doubt that this other reason is true. Indeed, especially in a civil war when the insurgents are nearing the end of their campaign and about to seize control of the government, the State actor seems actually weaker than the non-State actor, that is, the State actor is capable of less than the non-State actor in terms of the waging of war. For this reason it does not appear that it will be easy to show that there is an in principle reason to distinguish State actors from non-State actors in terms of the waging of either defensive or aggressive war. The conclusion to reach, in considering the arguments of the previous two sections, is that some terrorist groups can be said to wage war, and if the war that is waged is aggressive war, then those terrorist groups should be subject to sanction by the international community, just as is true when a State engages in aggressive war.

IV. Prosecuting Terrorist Aggression

Terrorist aggression can be sanctioned either by sanctioning the States that had allowed violence to occur, or that had facilitated it,[12] or by

---

[12] A good treatment of this option is Tal Becker's book, *Terrorism and the State, Rethinking the Rules of State Responsibility*, Oxford: Hart 2006.

sanctioning the terrorist group itself, perhaps by prosecuting its leaders. Just as it is today rare that we should grant a head of State immunity, similarly it is rare that we should grant immunity to heads of terrorist groups and other non-State actors that act like States. For terrorist groups to be prosecuted by international tribunals they only have to have members who satisfy the elements of the crimes that fall under the jurisdiction of those courts. As currently conceptualized, there is no bar to terrorist leaders being prosecuted by the International Criminal Court. But if it turned out that terrorist groups couldn't wage war, then their leaders couldn't be prosecuted for the crime of aggression. Having given reasons to reject this option, at least concerning some terrorist groups, we now turn to the question of sanctioning a terrorist group that wages aggressive war. And given the subject of this volume, I will focus on the prosecution of the leaders of a terrorist group for the crime of aggression.

Given the somewhat looser structure of terrorist groups than of some States, it might be harder to identify who exactly are the leaders, and we might be tempted to think that prosecution of each member of the group for terrorist aggression is the better strategy to employ. I will attempt to refute this suggestion. In general, I think it is a bad idea to prosecute anyone other than political or military leaders for the crime of aggression, as I have tried to indicate at various points earlier in the book. In this section I will discuss some of the potential problems in prosecuting leaders of terrorist groups for the crime of aggression.

The first difficulty is the secretive nature of the chain of command in many terrorist groups. While this is largely a practical problem, there are normative issues as well that are associated with it. A similar problem would result if the leadership of a State was secretive in terms of who was responsible for what. The Nuremberg trials were successful largely because the Nazis were unashamed in disclosing, in their own record keeping and public accounting, who played what role in the aggressive wars they waged. If instead, the Nazi State had been more secretive, the trials at Nuremberg would have been much more difficult to run, and even fewer defendants would have been convicted. The same sort of difficulty confronts most terrorist groups that must remain highly secretive to operate effectively in a world of States that seek to eliminate them.

The normative side to this practical problem concerns whether in conditions of uncertainty it is fair to single out some of the members of a terrorist group for prosecution while letting others remain untried due to lack of knowledge on our part of who did what. Of course, there is always an element of selective prosecution in most cases – those for whom there is more evidence are tried and those who probably did the same things are often left untried. But it would be considerably worse to prosecute those who are lower ranking and then leave others who are higher ranking as not prosecuted. And yet this seems to be nearly an inevitable result of the practical problem of identifying who did what in a highly secretive organization.

The second difficulty is that terrorist groups come into existence and go out of existence with much greater rapidity than do States. It is much harder to tell whether a given terrorist group is retaliating for past aggression against it than it is for a State, since the history of most terrorist groups is often shrouded not only in mystery but also in uncertainty about when the group first came onto the scene and what its goals are. Normatively, it is also not nearly as clear why a terrorist group should have the right to preserve itself when its existence is threatened, and hence harder to defend its right of self-defense, than it is for a State. Indeed, when the leaders of a terrorist group say that their otherwise aggressive acts are justified by self-defense of the terrorist group, we are much more interested in the goals of that group, that is, whether there are any legitimate goals, in order to assess whether we think the self-defense claim can be legitimate, than we are in the case of a State's leaders that make similar claims.

The relatively unstable nature and purpose of many terrorist groups, compared to that of most states, makes the possible defenses against the charge that the terrorist group engaged in aggressive war very hard to assess. If a State engages in aerial bombing of a terrorist training facility by warplanes that are launched from ships at sea, and the terrorist group retaliates by placing bombs on those ships, is the terrorist group engaging in aggression or self-defense? If a terrorist leader is assassinated by a State, and suicide bombing missions are launched against the leaders of that State, is the terrorist group launching a first strike or a retaliatory strike? Such questions are difficult to answer, and more difficult than if we are dealing with two States, because of the difficulty in ascertaining whether the terrorist group has enough legitimacy to think that it has a claim to continued existence unhindered by other international actors. Of course, respect for the sovereignty of States is often misplaced and questionable, but things look much more difficult normatively in the case of terrorist groups than in the case of States, especially since many States have by and large protected the rights of their members, whereas the same cannot be said of many non-State actors.

A third difficulty concerns the tactics often employed by terrorist groups as compared to States. In Chapter 2, I argued that *jus ad bellum* considerations should include one *jus in bello* consideration as well. For war to be initiated and waged justly there must be a high likelihood that the war could be conducted justly in terms of tactics. If the only way to be successful in a war is to use nuclear weapons and such weapons are immoral, then the war itself cannot be initiated justly. In this respect, we may wonder whether some terrorists can wage war justly, given that their tactics seem to be unjust in that they target civilians. Of course this does not prove that some terrorists cannot wage war but only that they cannot wage a just war. Terrorists could still be prosecuted, and indeed this would be true in every case since the terrorist tactics violated *jus in bello* norms and then also adversely affected *jus ad bellum* norms.

Not all terrorists target civilians indiscriminately, and indeed not all terrorists target civilians at all. It is certainly possible for terrorists to target civilian sites and then either notify the occupants in advance or plan their destructive efforts for times when civilians will not be present. This seems to be the case of the Irish Republican Army at least in the early years of its existence.[13] So it isn't even true that terrorist groups can never wage just war because of considerations of tactics. But it is true that on tactical grounds, many terrorist groups will find it harder to justify the wars they initiate than States would. But this does not mean that some terrorist groups cannot initiate wars and be prosecuted for those wars when they are not defensive but aggressive.

In general, I see no significant conceptual or normative bar to thinking that some terrorist groups can initiate and wage aggressive war and no strong reasons to think that some of the leaders of terrorist groups should not be prosecuted for the crime of aggression.[14] The normative and practical problems do not bar in principle the prosecution of terrorist leaders. Instead, the different structure of terrorist groups when compared with States will sometimes make it harder, but other times make it easier, to prosecute terrorist leaders for the crime of aggression. And it is the latter cases that matter most and give us reason to think that prosecutions for the crime of aggression would not be redundant when there might also

[13] See Carolyn Kennedy-Pipe, "Torture, Rights, Rules, and Wars: From Northern Ireland to Iraq," unpublished paper prepared for Rethinking the Rules Conference at St. Andrews University, June 2006.
[14] There is a jurisdictional problem, though. At the moment the ICC can only prosecute individuals if their States of nationality are parties to the Rome Statute of the ICC or their crimes are committed within the territory of a State party to the ICC. I am grateful to Mark Drumbl for this point. It is not easy to solve this problem. I would merely note that the same jurisdictional problem exists at the moment for State leaders as well as for non-State leaders.

be prosecutions of terrorist leaders for other international crimes that are harder to prove. But as we will next see, when criminal law is used to deal with terrorists there are rights issues that kick in and make it harder to employ other kinds of tactics against terrorists, especially assassination.

V. Terrorists and Due Process Rights

The main question asked about whether terrorists who are being tried for horrendous crimes should receive a full panoply of due process rights is why the international community should extend to terrorists what those terrorists clearly were unwilling to extend to their victims. Of course a similar question can be asked about any of those who waged aggressive war or who waged war in a way that failed to respect the rules of war. Indeed, in most wars, when one side is victorious there is a clamor that the "war criminals" simply be executed rather than treated as defendants and prosecuted for what they did. In those situations as well the question is why we should treat these people any better than they treated their victims. And the main answer that I will give concerns the effects on us, not them, if we withhold such rights-recognition and protection from even terrorist defendants.[15]

In trials for aggression, if we get to the point that the ICC does engage in this endeavor, the rights of leaders of terrorist groups will be difficult to take seriously since victor's justice has always been the fall-back position anyway, and in this case it is so much easier merely to kill the leaders as a means to end the terrorist insurgency. Unlike the case of States, when it was thought that State leaders had a vested interest in not executing fellow State leaders lest the same be done to them if the tables were turned, there seems to be no clear disincentive merely to execute terrorist leaders rather than to put them on trial. With no clear disincentives, State leaders will try to execute terrorist leaders with seeming impunity, just as the terrorist leaders themselves seemed once also to kill with near impunity.

But there is a major counterweight to the failure to take the rights of terrorist leaders seriously once they have been captured – namely, the

---

[15] If, for instance, the United States grants extensive due process rights to Rwandans and Serbs but does not grant these same rights to those held prisoner in Guantanamo, it undermines the value of such rights, and our own credibility, since it appears that the United States grants such rights only to those who are not our enemies. On this point, see Mark Drumbl, "Victimhood in Our Neighborhood: Terrorist Crime, Taliban Guilt, and the Asymmetries of the International Legal Order," *North Carolina Law Review*, vol. 81, 2002, pp. 1–113.

rule of law will be adversely affected by such actions. Once we start down the road of criminal prosecutions, certain other alternatives are ruled out by the rule of law. And the most basic is that one not be allowed to circumvent the criminal justice system by assassinating the defendant or depriving the defendant of rights that are crucial for fair trials. Trials cannot proceed when there is also the possibility that defendants, or their attorneys, will be executed at crucial stages in the proceedings. There is no incompatibility between waging war against a State or State-like entity and then later using the criminal justice system to deal with the defeated leaders.

There is also no incompatibility between waging war and then before the war is over pursuing criminal justice measures against some leaders of the enemy group, although this will take a bit of explanation and defense. There are serious impediments to prosecuting leaders before hostilities have ended, namely, that captured leaders are supposed to be considered prisoners of war and not captured criminals who can be brought to trial. The rights of prisoners of war are more stringent than the rights of defendants. Prisoners of war are to be treated as one would treat one's own troops who pose a risk of injury to others. Defendants who have not yet been convicted are supposed to be treated relatively well also, but after conviction they may be treated punitively. Prisoners of war are not supposed to be treated punitively at all unless the POWs become defendants and are convicted of war crimes, as I have previously argued.[16]

Despite the strong temptation to dehumanize them, prisoners of war and criminal defendants do share at least one major thing in common: namely, they are human beings whose rights as humans must be respected. And while I subscribe to a minimalist interpretation of human rights, even this can be a substantial impediment to abuse of terrorists held in captivity, whether they are prisoners of war or criminal defendants awaiting trial. Assassination, or just plain killing, is not acceptable regardless of how we regard terrorists who are held in captivity. Torture is also ruled out, as are other forms of cruel, degrading, or dehumanizing treatment. Human beings are, at a minimum, not supposed to treat fellow human beings in these ways, no matter what these people have done.

In the criminal justice system, as well as in the rules of war concerning POWs, most of the rights concern proper procedures. Due process rights

---

[16] See chapter 7 of my book, *War Crimes and Just War*, New York: Cambridge University Press, 2007.

are crucial to respecting human rights. Summary execution is perhaps the most egregious violation of due process rights in that the term "summary" indicates that no particular procedures were followed but that what is done is done without delay and at most with a minimal attempt to prove that the defendant did that of which he is accused. Summary executions are like assassinations in that there is no attempt to follow due process and no attempt to provide for the rights of the person in custody or who is being targeted. And yet this seems to be one of the preferred methods of dealing with terrorists today, as both the United States and Israel, to name only those States that seem to employ assassination most frequently, simply drop bombs on those they believe to be terrorists.

The second most important normative idea connected to the rule of law is the principle of legality, that is, the principle that prosecutions should take place only for violations of the rules of law that were clear-cut at the time the defendant acted. Despite its seeming banality, this principle has proven to be one of the most important hurdles to overcome in prosecutions at the international level. I discussed some of these issues in Chapter 11. Since much of international law is customary, and since customs are generally vague at best, it is difficult to say that a defendant violated a rule that was clear-cut at the time he or she acted. Retrospective prosecution and punishment has come to be seen as the hallmark of unfairness, and in virtually every international prosecution this issue is one of the first that must be addressed before the trial can go forward.

A third consideration, also very important in possible trials of terrorists for the crime of aggression, concerns selectivity of prosecution and proportionality of punishment. Often terrorism from one side breeds terrorist responses. We must try to be fair and prosecute terrorism in all of its many guises, not merely when it manifests itself on one side of a war. In addition, we must not be overly influenced by the often gruesome forms of terrorist violence in assigning punishments, and we should certainly not provide stiffer punishments just because we are dealing with terrorist leaders as opposed to other political or military leaders who are couched within States. Indeed, punishments must be meted out evenhandedly, where similar punishments are given for the same, or virtually the same, criminal behavior.

While there are certainly other due process rights that we could discuss, I hope that these brief words give a sense of which rights are the most important for possible prosecutions of terrorists for the crime of aggression. Terrorist leaders should generally not be treated as outlaws who deserve whatever fate comes to them. In my view they should not be targeted for assassination any more than State leaders on the enemy side of a war should be targeted for such treatment. Terrorist leaders should be captured and given the benefit of either POW status or full due process rights of defendants who will stand trial for what they allegedly did.

At least in part, I think we have been led down the wrong path by the emotive meaning that is attached to the term "terrorist." Are suicide bombers that strike in cities so much worse than aerial bombers that also strike in cities to make us think that one should be treated as outlaws and the other as full members of the international community? It is true that the international community condemns some of the tactics employed by terrorists, but the international community has also condemned some tactics used by States in most major wars. The use of such weapons might very well make us think that the war was less justifiable, or not justifiable at all, but it should not make us think that so-called terrorists are to be treated outside the law, especially when we generally think that State leaders should always be treated within the domain of international law and human rights.

Throughout this book I have tried to indicate what would be acceptable normative principles to employ in prosecuting individuals for the crime of aggression as an international crime. I have expressed my qualified support for adding such crimes and prosecutions to the jurisdiction of the International Criminal Court. I have also indicated the serious conceptual and normative problems that such trials must overcome. In the current chapter I have addressed the very difficult case of how to treat terrorists who wage war and have once again expressed support for criminal trials rather than treating terrorists like outlaws. Just as some 17th-century theorists like Grotius came to see that even pirates should not be treated as mere outlaws, so we today should see that terrorists should not be treated as mere outlaws, but instead be subjected to, and be subjects of, the rule of law.

VI. Human Rights after September 11, 2001

How are human rights affected when we think of the world as involving not merely States and human persons but also non-State actors such as terrorist groups? To begin to answer this question I want first to ask what it would mean for the rule of law if there were truly outlaws on the international stage. Could we still talk about human rights meaningfully if there was one group of people, the members of non-State actors such as terrorist groups, who were excluded from the rule of law? And what rule, if any, would they be subject to? Would it be the "rule of the jungle" or the "state of nature"? I will argue that even if there are outlaws, self-imposed though they are, it is a mistake to think of them as if they are outside of the rule of law, despite the tragedies of September 11, 2001.

One of the most often discussed differences between Hobbes and Locke is that Hobbes seemed to think that there were only two options: either one was a member of a State or one was in the state of nature, whereas Locke seemed to recognize a third alternative: where one could be in civil society yet neither a member of a State nor in the state of nature. Think of the stories from the "Wild West" of the 19th century in the United States. The town of Tombstone was supposedly a town for outlaws and at least initially, or so the folk history of the town goes, there were literally no laws or law enforcement officers. But over time, the residents of this town found such lawlessness intolerable and so even the outlaws found it necessary to create and enforce rudimentary laws. Such laws were still outside of the legal framework of the surrounding territory, but they resembled a rudimentary civil society nonetheless, no longer the state of nature that had existed initially. Pirates and some terrorists seem also to slip between the cracks – they are not truly in the state of nature and yet they are also not members of States.

One of the difficulties is that many terrorist groups lack a stable political and social structure of the sort found in most States. This is a problem for several reasons. First, a terrorist group like Al Qaeda can change, seemingly quite rapidly, from a hierarchically structured group, as it apparently was in the mid-1990s, to a highly decentered group, or group of groups, in the mid-2000s.[17] Second, it is not clear whether the group has enough coherence to be a party to international treaties and other agreements that limit their tactics, at least not in the way that most States can be counted on to remain sufficiently the same over time to hold themselves accountable, and be held accountable, for keeping their treaties and other agreements.

Since September 11, 2001, there has been an increasing role on the international stage played by non-State actors such as terrorist groups. Given the instability of many such groups, it is not at all clear how the international community should treat these actors vis-à-vis State actors. One possibility is to deny the members of these groups even the most basic human rights protections, since human rights protections are premised

---

[17] See Scott Shane, "Terrorist Experts Cast Doubt on Qaeda Ties to London Arrests," *New York Times*, Sunday, August 13, 2006, p. A8.

on a kind of mutuality of recognition and respect. But we might also think about this on the model that Aristotle first proposed about how virtue is learned. Aristotle suggested that we first learn virtue by watching the virtuous behavior of others and then mimicking this behavior on our own. The more we mimic this virtuous behavior, the more we develop the virtues, which are largely a matter of habits that are formed from repetition. Similarly, we might think that State and non-State actors, or at least their members, could also learn to be virtuous by observation and mimicry. It would then be important that non-State actors, such as terrorist groups, not be treated as outlaws but as within the framework of the rule of law in the anticipation that these terrorist groups could develop certain virtues even if they are largely absent to begin with.

We don't have to hold to an Aristotelian picture of moral development, for there is also an alternative route to the same result that has to do with recognition of what is a matter of mutual self-interest. Seeing the value of respecting human rights is not merely a matter of learning the virtues but also of recognizing what promotes mutual self-interest. And one of the main values of human rights is that they afford protection for everyone regardless of what one has done and hence regardless of what one deserves. In what follows I will attempt to explain why continuing to think about human rights protection as highly valuable, even in the face of atrocities, is advantageous.

One of the chief advantages of continued attention to human rights, even after September 11, 2001, is that peace is more easily achieved and sustained. We can see this most clearly when we consider, as we have in this volume, the human rights protections that result from a recognition that aggression is to be deterred. The warring factions in the world are divided into camps. This is no more apparent than in the face of the continued terrorism that emanates from the developing countries, especially the religiously inspired Muslim world that sees itself at war with the secular capitalist world. If Islamic terrorists see themselves primarily as fellow humans instead of enemies of those in the West, terrorist violence will likely be diminished, and all peoples will gain in security. Focusing on human rights would have that effect, especially if the human rights were seen as truly universal.

Attention to human rights remains crucial, especially when the world appears to be fracturing into global units as has seemed to be true since the terrorist attacks on the United States on September 11, 2001. To talk instead of a clash of grand political ideologies is permanently to consign the "one world" thesis to the dustbin. Talk of human rights does not necessarily commit one to a utopian belief in cosmopolitanism, although it doesn't rule out such ideas either. But talk of human rights diminishes the importance of grand ideological struggles among humans since the very idea that there are rights that attach to each and every human being accentuates what joins us rather than what divides us. And one of the best places to start such a conversation concerns the human rights discourse that grounds the prohibition on State aggression and that sets the stage for the deterrence effects of having criminal trials for political and military leaders who wage aggressive war.

Pirates were once thought to be *hostes humani generis* just as terrorists are today. But surely this is the wrong approach. To describe some humans as the enemies of humanity dehumanizes them and also causes them to think of themselves as different from, and enemies of, the rest of us rather than as all part of the same family. To be sure, there will be some humans who are dangerous for the rest of us. And those individuals should be incarcerated if for no other reason than for the protection of those other humans put at risk. But to label an entire group of people, containing thousands of members, as the enemies of humanity is also to risk the undermining of what has been the foundation of universal human rights protections, namely, that we are all much more alike than different and that all are subject to the same rule of law. Those terrorist leaders that cause harm, especially by the waging of aggressive wars, should be prosecuted and also given full rights under the umbrella of the international rule of law, not pushed outside the protection of that umbrella where they are far more likely to be true enemies of humanity.

15

Defending International Criminal Trials for Aggression

International criminal law is under assault from both realists and communitarians.[1] International law generally is often portrayed as a pipe dream at best and a dangerous distraction at worst. Such criticisms will have an effect on whether there are to be international trials for the crime of aggression. To defend international criminal trials diverse authors have proposed various normative rationales: some proposing deterrence, some proposing retribution, and others proposing truth and reconciliation. Yet each of these theories has been shown to fall short of defending the entirety of international criminal law. In this final chapter, I will provide a limited defense of international criminal trials conducted in a neutral locale such as The Hague, not by reference to a single normative principle, such as deterrence or retribution or truth and reconciliation, but by reference to a combination of principles applicable differently for different contexts. I do not claim that the sum of these defenses is larger than its parts but only that it may be possible to construct a partial defense on the basis of each that overlaps sufficiently to justify most of international criminal law.

Throughout this book and the two previous books I have written on the moral foundations of international criminal law, I have also voiced many criticisms of the movement toward the increasing use of criminal trials at the international level. But I have nonetheless tried to construct a limited defense of these trials. Most of this defense is normative, as this chapter will rehearse. But there is also a very practical part of the defense as well, namely that there are no good alternatives to such trials. Impunity

---

[1] I do not subscribe to either communitarianism or realism. I suppose my own view comes closest to what Simon Caney has called "the 'society of states' approach." See his book, *Justice Beyond Borders*, Oxford: Oxford University Press, 2005, pp. 10–13.

is not an option that can be justified morally. And I remain resistant to the idea that there should be a kind of international vigilante justice as well, where any State prosecutor can claim to bring to justice any putative perpetrator anywhere in the world. More localized alternatives may have merit, but they will not accomplish what the high-profile international criminal trials aspire to do. In this final chapter, I will try to explain my practical as well as positive normative reasons on behalf of international criminal trials.

The task of defending international criminal trials for the crime of aggression is made more difficult by the fact that there has been only one significant set of trials for this crime, namely, the trials at Nuremberg. And today, there are no trials even planned since the members of the international community cannot seem to agree about what constitutes State aggression or about what entity should make the decision about whether a State has indeed engaged in aggression in a particular case. I believe that such trials should be held much less frequently than those for crimes against humanity and for war crimes. Nonetheless, international criminal trials for aggression and crimes against peace can be defended in a limited way. In this final chapter I will bring together various arguments from previous chapters and add a few new ones to support the view that some international criminal trials for aggression can be justified.

The chapter is divided into five parts. In the first section, I will summarize the arguments advanced by Martti Koskenniemi concerning the seeming inability to find a normative ground for international criminal trials. In the second section, I will attempt to respond to Koskenniemi, agreeing with him about the difficulty of providing such a normative grounding but disagreeing that the task cannot succeed. In the third section, I will consider the nuanced arguments of Mark Drumbl on these themes and try to respond to him as well. I am sympathetic to both Koskenniemi's and Drumbl's critiques.

In the fourth section, I consider the challenge of trying to make international criminal trials less prone to the charge that they are politicized. And in the final section, I will mount a limited defense of international trials for aggression while recognizing that these trials pose the most difficult problems of all. I will also provide a summary of the main conclusions that I have established in the book.

I. Koskenniemi's Critique of International Criminal Law

The distinguished Finnish legal scholar Martti Koskenniemi has mounted a significant critique of the project of international criminal law in his essay, "Between Impunity and Show Trials."[2] There are two parts to his challenging and rigorous exposition. First, he argues that the standard normative groundings offered in defense of international criminal law – deterrence, retribution, and truth – are each seriously flawed as bases of international criminal law. Second, he argues that political leaders brought before international tribunals, as was true of Slobodon Milosevic brought before the ICTY, will try to politicize the trials even more than they already are. The only alternative seems to be to silence these leaders by not allowing them to defend themselves. And yet this alternative will also merely point up the political nature of these trials and make them look even more like show trials. In this section I will summarize Koskenniemi's important objections to the project of international criminal law.

Let me take up the issue of retribution first. Koskenniemi claims to agree with Hannah Arendt that "punishing an individual does not come close to measuring up" to the tragedies, such as crimes against humanity, for which the individuals are charged.[3] Koskenniemi also cites Karl Jaspers, who held that "something other than law [was] at stake here – and to address it in legal terms was a mistake."[4] Koskenniemi agrees, calling Jaspers's insight "plainly evident" and then arguing that this is also true today:

> it seems clear that whether or not Milosevic goes to prison is in no way an "adequate" response to the fact that over 200,000 people lost their lives – while millions more were affected – by the succession of wars in the former Yugoslavia. If the trial has significance, then that significance must lie elsewhere than in the punishment handed down.[5]

For Koskenniemi, the crimes are too enormous, or at least the tragedies that the crimes are based on are too enormous, to be adequately dealt with in retributive terms by the punishment of just one person or even a group of people.

Koskenniemi says little else about retribution in his essay, leading me to think that this is not the main basis of his critique of international criminal law. One can imagine a more concerted effort to buttress the claims advanced by Koskenniemi. It could be claimed that putting one, or even

---

[2] Martti Koskenniemi, "Between Impunity and Show Trials," *Max Planck Yearbook of United Nations Law*, vol. 6, 2002, pp. 1–35.

[3] Ibid., p. 2.

[4] Lotte Kohler and Hans Kohler, editors, *Hannah Arendt – Karl Jaspers. Correspondence 1926–1969*, 1996, p. 410, quoted in ibid., p. 2, note 3.

[5] Koskenniemi, "Between Impunity and Show Trials," p. 3.

several people, in prison pales by comparison with the number of those killed in mass atrocity. Even if the trials could employ capital punishment, how many times would the person in the dock have to be killed to make up for the deaths and suffering of so many victims? Standard international prison terms of ten years seem not to do justice to crimes involving mass atrocity. Such an argument, which seeks to establish that standard punishments cannot adequately reflect what perpetrators of mass atrocity deserve, might buttress Koskenniemi's case against seeing international criminal trials grounded in the moral principle of retribution.

Another matter that is treated briefly is that of deterrence. Koskenniemi argues that deterrence is unlikely if the crimes in question "emerge from what Kant labeled 'radical evil,' an evil that exceeds the bounds of instrumental rationality."[6] And even if this "metaphysical" idea of radical evil is not accepted, says Koskenniemi, "the deterrence argument would still fail to convince inasmuch as the atrocities of the 20th century have not emerged from criminal intent but as offshoots from a desire to do good."[7] Koskenniemi makes the point crystal clear when he says:

> As criminal lawyers know well, fitting crimes against humanity or other massive human rights violations into the deterrence frame requires some rather implausible psychological generalizations. Either the crimes are aspects of political normality – Arendt's "banality of evil" – in which case there is no *mens rea*, or they take place in exceptional situations of massive destruction and personal anger when there is little liberty of action.... [I]t is implausible to believe that criminal law is able to teach people to become heroes, not the least because what "heroism" might mean in particular situations is often at the heart of the confrontation between political values underlying the criminal justice system (perhaps seen as victor's justice) and the system that is on trial.[8]

If the locals see the trials held so far from home as "mere propaganda," those trials and the ensuing punishments will be highly unlikely to deter anyone.

Koskenniemi's argument against grounding international criminal trials in the normative principle of deterrence is more subtle than his argument against grounding such trials in retribution. But to defend such a view persuasively one would have to devote much attention to the actual "facts on the ground" in order to show that such trials have not and are unlikely to have deterrent effects. Others have attempted to provide

[6] Ibid., p. 8.
[7] Ibid.
[8] Ibid., pp. 8–9.

reasons to doubt the deterrent effects of international criminal trials,[9] but the main problem is that there have not been enough of these trials for a statistically significant sample in any study that did more than speculate about deterrent effects. For all we know, the ICC may very well have a strong deterrent effect. In any event, Koskenniemi seems to be more interested in another rationale, to which we now turn.

In my view, Koskenniemi's most important critique concerns the inability of supporters of international criminal trials to defend these trials by reference to the search for truth and reconciliation. And here we need to distinguish several distinct strains in his argument: there is the question of whether international criminal trials do or are likely to get at the truth, and then there is the symbolic argument that in any event people may feel better, perhaps reconciling somewhat with their attackers, for having made the effort to get at the truth even if the truth was elusive or impossible to ascertain by means of criminal trials. Both arguments dovetail nicely but since in the next section I will insist on separating them, I will also keep them separate in this expository discussion. Once again appealing to the common knowledge of lawyers, Koskenniemi offers the following set of claims:

> As criminal lawyers have always known, legal and historical truth are far from identical. The wider the context in which individual guilt has to be understood, and the more such understanding defers to the contingencies of historical interpretation, the more evident the limits of criminal procedure for reaching the "truth."[10]

The argument behind these claims is that in domestic law all we need to do is to answer the question: "did the accused do it?" Beyond that question, no "further question about how to understand what he did, how to place his behavior in relation to the overall behavior of those around him, emerges."[11] Thus, according to Koskenniemi, the truth of domestic trials is "relatively uncontested."[12]

But, Koskenniemi argues, in trials for mass atrocity crimes, "there are many truths and many stakeholders. In the Milosevic trial, for instance, the narrative of 'Greater Serbia' collides head on with the self-determination stories of the seceding population while political assessments of 'socialism' and 'nationalism' compete with long-term historical

---

[9] See Mark Drumbl. *Atrocity, Punishment, and International Law*, New York: Cambridge University Press, 2007. I address Drumbl's arguments in Section Three of this chapter.

[10] Koskenniemi, p. 12.

[11] Ibid.

[12] Ibid.

and even religious frames of explanation."[13] Criminal trials privilege the individual over the contextual, and yet at the international level neither can "a priori override the other" and the individual frame may not "enact a lesson of historical truth."[14] Trials would need to pay as much attention to contexts as to individuals if they were to stand any likelihood of getting at the truth.

In addition, the victims will not necessarily feel better because trials are ongoing since the symbolism of international trials is so hard to divorce from "victor's justice" or even from political "show trials." Indeed, to turn the tide of "symbolism" well-schooled defendants will attack the legal system itself or will attempt to fix the blame on other institutions, especially Western institutions like the United Nations that are responsible for forcing the trial to be waged concerning such politically charged matters. It is not at all clear which symbolic message will be received by the often highly nationalistic audience back home: the message that the defendants committed horrible acts that have now received their comeuppance or that the defendants were mere scapegoats in a show trial. The symbolic value of trials may be just the reverse of what is hoped for when such trials are planned.

This final point relates to Koskenniemi's worries about having especially heads of State defend themselves. Either these leaders will be allowed to play to the audience back home or they will have to be silenced, pointing out that these really were "show trials" after all. There is a very serious problem of establishing that international criminal trials are fair if the defendant is not allowed to speak in his or her own defense. It is rather like the Chicago Seven trial where Bobby Seale was strapped to a chair and gagged, a perfect symbol of a trial that had no more positive symbolic value than if Seale had been subjected to summary justice. The higher ranking the official in the dock, the greater is the likelihood that he or she will be a skilled rhetorician, able to transform the trial into an indictment of Western institutions that are conspiring against nationalist movements at home. The only option other than to set oneself up for a show trial is to allow impunity. In neither case, argues Koskenniemi, does it look good for the normative grounding of international criminal law.

II. The Diversity of Norms Defense

One way to respond to Koskenniemi is to agree that no one norm is able to justify the project of international criminal law but that different

[13] Ibid.
[14] Ibid., p. 15.

aspects of that project may be justified by different norms, allowing an overarching justification that utilizes a diversity of norms. In this section I will sketch this response. The idea is that a partial defense of international criminal law can be constructed from a combination of the norms of retribution, deterrence, and reconciliation but not by any one of these norms alone. As will become evident, I agree with many of the points that Koskenniemi has made, but I disagree that he has provided a devastating critique of the project of international criminal law. I leave to a later section of this chapter a discussion of the symbolic argument and the problem of having political leaders in the dock defending themselves.

Koskenniemi makes a good case for thinking that the enormity of the harms and wrongs that mass atrocity involves do not translate well into individual criminal sentences. Retribution directed at individuals cannot fully make amends for such atrocities as are involved in ethnic cleansing or waging aggressive war. I do not dispute this point, but what criminal trials can sometimes do is to punish individuals for their roles in such atrocities. And here I would also agree with Koskenniemi that the roles that are played are not as important as are the contexts, or circumstances, within which those who played the roles acted. As I have argued, mass atrocities occur due to the coordinated efforts of many individuals. It is patently unfair to hold one of these individuals responsible for the entire atrocity. Indeed, it is normatively unjustified to do so.

What an individual can be held responsible for is that person's participation in a mass atrocity. I am skeptical of the importance of retribution in criminal law generally, but I do agree that there is a sense in which individuals who participate in wrongdoing should have their comeuppance. And in this respect, I think that international criminal trials can be partially justified in that sometimes these trials can accomplish this objective. It is important that individuals pay for the harms and wrongs they have participated in. By this I mean that a retributive model can justify some international trials insofar as the part played by individuals in the dock can match the punishment they are sentenced to. Since individuals did not, and generally cannot, cause mass atrocities on their own, international courts should look only to the part each individual played – and standard punishments can sometimes be adequate retribution for those parts. But this is only a partial grounding for international trials since, as Jan Klabbers has pointed out,[15] sometimes international atrocities do not divide up neatly. It is often difficult to say which part each person played in the atrocity and in any event it is normally not practicable to

---

[15] Private correspondence.

prosecute all of the individuals who so participated. Hence there is a gap between the horror of the crime and the extent of punishment. I return to this point in the next section.

Deterrence is similarly problematical in international trials since normally not all of even the major participants can be prosecuted. But this is a problem in all of criminal law. Inevitably, many people who participate in crimes will not be prosecuted or punished. Surely this fact will diminish the deterrent effects of criminal law. But deterrence is, in my view, primarily about increasing the risks that a perpetrator has of suffering a serious consequence for committing a harm or wrong. And in this sense, there can be some deterrence that results from international criminal trials. Even if the population that one wishes to deter does not recognize the legitimacy of the tribunal, the punishments handed down can still deter. We are all motivated, at least to a certain extent, by fear of adverse consequences. There are also conflicting motivations that may offset the adverse consequences threatened by punishment and hence block the deterrent effect. But this is true of all criminal law. In the end, whether international criminal law deters less than domestic law is an empirical question that can only be answered after there is enough evidence. At the moment, there have been so few international trials and so few sentences that it is mere speculation whether there is a robust deterrent effect here.

So we need to look to the similarities and differences between domestic and international criminal law to see whether there are likely to be impediments to deterrence in the international setting. The major difference, Jan Klabbers argues, is that many international crimes are not committed from evil but from good motives, whereas domestic criminals act from evil motives.[16] But I would argue that there are important similarities as well. Human rights violators may still have *mens rea* insofar as they realize that what they are doing is wrong and they nonetheless aim at violating the law. Criminality is established by looking at intentions, not motives. And deterrence can still sometimes operate to stop people from intentionally violating the law, either domestic or international, regardless of whether their motives were good or evil. Even those who act from what they believe to be good motives can be deterred from so acting by threat of punishment.

Deterrence is only a partial grounding for international criminal law since motives do affect how deterrence operates. If one's motives and

[16] See Jan Klabbers, "Just Revenge? The Deterrence Argument in International Criminal Law," *Finnish Yearbook of International Law*, vol. XII, 2001, pp. 249–267, especially p. 253.

intentions are bad, then deterrence has the most efficacy. The deterrence effects will likely be diminished when people are motivated by patriotism or nationalism, even as they recognize that their actions violate a law. But I don't see any reason to think that people cannot sometimes be deterred nonetheless from breaking the law if they recognize that they may still be subject to punishment. Liability to punishment changes the weights of people's reasons to act in various ways. Those who are otherwise strongly motivated to break the law may still pause to do so if the risk of punishment is great enough. Deterrence, like retribution, can give us a partial defense of international criminal law as in many cases the threat of punishment will have an effect on behavior, at least lessening the likelihood of harmful behavior if not completely eliminating it. Deterrence is less likely in certain situations than others to have a dramatic effect on the incidence of international crime, but there are situations nonetheless where it is likely to have such an effect, giving us a partial justification for international criminal trials. Just as retribution will succeed in some cases, so deterrence is likely to succeed in some cases as well.

I next turn to the truth and reconciliation norm. Koskenniemi is surely right there as well, at least partially, since trials are sometimes not the best or even a particularly good way to get at the truth. This looks to be even more of a problem when trials are highly politicized, as sometimes happens in international criminal trials. It will not be possible to give a complete normative grounding for these trials by reference to such norms. But if we are only looking for partial grounding things look different. For some trials, at both the domestic and international level, surely do allow for the truth to be told, that is, for some victims to feel reconciled with perpetrators and for some perpetrators to prove their innocence. It is true that the "truth" of the matter may indeed be skewed by ideological differences among the principal parties in any given war. But this need not block all truth and reconciliation.

Some of the standard procedures in criminal trials may need to be adjusted or changed to make it more likely that truth will be achieved in some international criminal trials. Let us think about this matter from the standpoint of the defendant. In highly politicized trials, the procedures should give defendants ample opportunity to prove that they have been set up or scapegoated. Prosecutorial overreaching should be curtailed, as should attempts to block, by procedural maneuvering, the introduction of exculpatory evidence. I have argued for similar procedural changes in U.S. domestic law, especially in highly publicized criminal cases when it will be otherwise hard for the defendant to tell his or her story in a way that brings out the defendant's innocence.[17] Of course, procedural safeguards will not always prevent the manipulation rather than the accurate telling of the truth, just as procedural safeguards cannot always prevent miscarriages of justice.

The truth that I have in mind here is not what victims' families often most desire. International trials are limited affairs – they can try to tell us whether a given defendant did in fact participate in an atrocity and to what extent. Criminal trials serve the limited task of allowing victims and their families to confront particular people who are believed to be the ones who perpetrated horrible acts. But of course, there is often a larger story to be told about what brought about an atrocity and some victims want that story to be told. Trials have only limited value in disclosing these larger truths, but sometimes the combination of smaller truths will add up to something significant for the victims and their families nonetheless. And in at least one sense, concerning the defendants, the small-scale truth of innocence is highly important.

One must ask what alternatives are likely to do a better job of uncovering some of the truth and providing for some reconciliation between the parties. I have elsewhere admitted that trials sometimes are not the best venues for obtaining truth and securing reconciliation.[18] Sometimes amnesty for truth programs are better at securing truth and even better at achieving reconciliation. But these proceedings must be initiated internally and hence are not always an alternative to international criminal trials. And in any event, amnesty for truth programs are not always better than criminal trials at ferreting out the truth. Indeed, there are circumstances when trials are clearly better, such as when a society has been so oppressed that people will speak out about the truth only if their identities are hidden in the way that witnesses have been protected in trials for several centuries. Whether considerations of truth and reconciliation will normatively ground international trials depends on the alternatives available and on whether these alternatives are likely to be any better at uncovering the truth and achieving reconciliation than are the trials in question, especially to get this evidence made public in a timely manner.

Sometimes historians are better at getting at the larger truth of atrocities, while historians are often not as good as lawyers in getting at particular truths. In many cases, historians cannot get access to the relevant

---

[17] Larry May and Nancy Viner, "Actual Innocence and Manifest Injustice," *St. Louis University Law Journal*, vol. 49, no. 2, 2004, pp. 481–497.

[18] See Larry May, *Crimes against Humanity: A Normative Account*, New York: Cambridge University Press, 2005, ch. 13.

specific facts about who did what. In a trial, both parties have the ability to demand that evidence be produced that may have been intentionally hidden. Historians are unlikely to get access to that information for many years if not generations. The system that allows both sides, through their lawyers, to confront witnesses and subject evidence to careful scrutiny, in real time, is not available to historians. So there is a kind of truth that historians are not necessarily better at, and there is no good reason to think that the goal of ferreting out the truth is generally better served by historians than by trials.

International trials are sometimes the only way, or at least the only practicable way, for victims to be able to tell their stories and for alleged perpetrators also to tell their stories. Indeed, it seems to me that the best normative grounding for international criminal trials comes in these last resort cases, where for various reasons no other reasonable alternatives are open to allow for the truth, or at least some of it, to be disclosed, and for reconciliation between the parties, or at least some of the parties, to be achieved. And here we have one more partial normative grounding for international criminal trials.

While I agree with Koskenniemi that there is no single grounding norm for international criminal law, I think that a combination of diverse norms, including retribution, deterrence, and reconciliation, can provide such a grounding in enough cases to constitute enough of a normative grounding nonetheless. And I'm not sure why anyone would think it likely that there would be such a single grounding norm for any criminal trial. For there have been centuries, if not millennia, of criticism of retribution and deterrence models for justifying punishment. We should not expect things to be any better in the international domain. My proposal is that if we consider the partial normative grounding offered by each of these norms, something approaching an overlapping good-enough rationale for such trials can be constructed. Of course, it will always be possible to criticize specific international trials on each of these counts, but the consideration of each of these norms makes the ground under international criminal law considerably firmer than Koskenniemi has led us to believe. I next examine a very recent attempt to provide a nuanced critique of the normative underpinnings of international criminal law by Mark Drumbl.

III. Drumbl's Arguments about Retribution and Deterrence

Mark Drumbl has written an excellent book-length treatment of these topics in which he develops some of the arguments we have been considering in very interesting directions.[19] Specifically, I find his arguments about selectivity of prosecution and the rational capacity of those to be deterred to warrant special consideration in my ultimate attempt to provide a limited defense of international criminal trials for aggression and other international crimes. Drumbl also develops an expressivist argument in favor of those trials that I partially endorse, as will become clear in the next section of this chapter.

Drumbl argues that selectivity and leniency of punishment undermine the retributive goals of international criminal law by creating what he calls "a retributive shortfall." The selectivity argument is that not all of the worst of international criminal acts are punished, and this underscores "the difficulty of ascribing retributive purposes to international criminal law as a whole when a 'confluence of political concerns,' and not the inherent gravity of the crimes, prods the punishment of offenders."[20] Since "too few people or entities receive just deserts," there is "a retributive shortfall" that results.[21] The "tiny subset of alleged perpetrators" calls attention to the fact that retributive goals are not well served by international criminal law. At least in part this is because prosecutors make decisions about who to prosecute on such factors as the cooperation of States, utility of convicting low-level perpetrators for strategic purposes, and availability of material resources rather than on who is most deserving of prosecution.[22]

Drumbl also argues that lenient sentences undermine the retributive goals of international criminal law. On the assumption that international crimes are supposed to be the worst of crimes because they involve multiple or mass criminal acts, one would expect the sentences to match the gravity of the crimes. Yet international sentences fall far short of what one would expect for the worst of crimes. As Drumbl argues, "the data reveal that at both the national and international levels, sentences for multiple international crimes are generally not lengthier than what national jurisdictions award for a single serious ordinary crime."[23] Drumbl also argues that even if one does not see quantity of sentence as definitive of sanctions and looks also to conditions of imprisonment and stigma associated with sentence, international criminal sanctions do not exceed those of national tribunals.[24]

---

[19] Mark Drumbl, *Atrocity, Punishment, and International Law.*
[20] Ibid., p. 151.
[21] Ibid., p. 153.
[22] Ibid., p. 152.
[23] Ibid., p. 155.
[24] See ibid., p. 157.

I would grant that there is a retributive shortfall in international criminal law today and that it is unlikely to get much better in the near future. But it is not clear to me that because international criminal law cannot now convict and punish all wrongdoers this means that one important function, and rationale, for international criminal law is not retribution. To say that there is a retributive shortfall is to commit one only to say that more needs to be done in this area of law than is currently being done. Prosecutors always face limited material resources and can hence not bring to trial all of those who deserve to be punished for their crimes. And while this is worrisome, it need not undercut the retributive rationale of the prosecutions that do take place. If two people deserve to be punished and only one of them is caught, this does not change the fact that the one who is caught deserves to be prosecuted, and if convicted, punished. The retributive rationale of the trial of the second person is not undermined by the failure to catch the first person.

A more serious worry is that political decisions are made that allow those who are not the worst offenders to be put in the dock. If there are harsher sentences administered for lesser than for graver crimes, retribution is seriously undermined as well. This raises fairness issues and can cut into the retributive rationale of international criminal law. But as far as I can tell, there is nothing endemic to international criminal law that would not allow for such political interference, or unfairness, to be diminished if not eliminated in the future. Similarly, the wide variation in sentences and the seeming lightness of sentences given in international, as opposed to national, tribunals is also not endemic to international criminal law. Until the passage of the federal sentencing guidelines in the United States, a similar disparity of punishments as well as a comparative lightness of sentence in certain jurisdictions existed. But the uniform guidelines solved many of these problems. There is no structural impediment to stiffer sentences or to uniformity of sentencing in international law just as there is no structural impediment to it in national legal systems. There are and will continue to be limited resources guaranteeing that not all who are guilty can be prosecuted – but that is true in all of criminal law, not merely in international criminal law.

Drumbl also offers a very powerful argument against the deterrence rationale of international criminal law. He forces us to consider a more subtle argument here than considered in the previous sections of this chapter. Drumbl argues that those who perpetrate atrocities are not as likely to be deterred as common criminals because there are factors that undermine their rationality; specifically, their calculations about gratification and survival are undermined by the context of atrocity. Since the perpetrators of atrocities are not fully rational, they will not be as easily deterred as common criminals are. In the remainder of this section I will set out and respond to Drumbl's powerful arguments.

Drumbl first points out that many perpetrators of atrocities find solidarity in being members of violent groups. As Drumbl says: "They are captured by angry social norms, or at least, are captivated by them."[25] And based on this motivation, these perpetrators of atrocities come to believe that they are acting for a collective cause. Drumbl then makes two points. First, it is unlikely that rational choice can occur during the violence that surrounds them. Second, "the value of living or dying for a cause" exceeds the worries about being punished. In addition, the circumstances of mass violence make individuals feel that they could not have made a difference in any event. These considerations make it much less likely that these perpetrators can be deterred in the way in which common criminals are.[26]

The other consideration that Drumbl focuses on is survival. Many people join violent groups because they feel they don't have any choice in the matter. Drumbl says, "Even those individuals for whom violence is not gratifying may willingly join, insofar as participating in massacre can guarantee survival to the next morning."[27] When a person's own survival is in jeopardy, it seems unlikely that he or she would be deterred by "the prospect that some distant international 'institution' might punish them" several years from now.[28] In Drumbl's view, deterrence theory "leaves the masses unaccountable."[29] It isn't just leaders but "broad public participation" that perpetuates mass violence, and the public is unlikely to be deterred by international criminal sanctions.

Again, while I share Drumbl's concerns, I do not find them to show that international criminal law cannot be partially justified by reference to deterrence. First, I would note that Drumbl has not addressed the political or military leaders who will be the overwhelming majority of people brought before the ICC. Those people are not typically rendered less rational by considerations of gratification or survival. And despite what Drumbl says, it is the leaders who are most in need of being deterred if atrocities are to be diminished, especially those related to the crime of

[25] Ibid., p. 171.
[26] Ibid., pp. 171–172.
[27] Ibid., p. 172.
[28] Ibid.
[29] Ibid.

aggression, since it is the leaders who plan, initiate, and motivate most atrocities. It is hard to say whether such leaders have been deterred in the past, but there is no evidence that I am aware of that shows that threat of international punishment has not had a deterrent effect, and good reasons to think that it will have such an effect. For leaders like Pinochet, Milosevic, and Saddam seem quite resistant to serving prison sentences, going to great lengths to avoid being captured and tried. This seems to indicate that they are rational and care about potential loss of freedom.

The minor actors also play a crucial role in atrocities, and I am not unsympathetic to some of the worries Drumbl voices about the chances of deterring them. It is certainly true that many small fry are influenced by gratification or fear, although I don't see why Drumbl thinks that these factors, which after all affect nearly all humans, affect these small fry to such an extent that they lose their rational capacities.

I agree that the small fry are harder to deter, but for my argument to go through, international criminal law does not have to have strongly deterrent effects on everyone, since deterrence is only a partial justification. In any event, as we will next see, there are also good reasons to support international criminal law in terms of what Drumbl calls expressivism. Even if there were no deterrent effects of international criminal sanctions, the sanctions may be justifiable for the condemnation expressed to the world.

IV. Political Leaders Defending Themselves

I now turn to symbolic issues, especially to the way those issues are affected when we have political leaders who choose to defend themselves before international tribunals, or at least when such leaders are allowed to speak in their own behalf. The positive symbolic value of international criminal trials is indeed often offset by the countervailing message that a political leader in the dock is able to deliver to his or her fellow citizens back home. I wish to discuss the problem of having a political leader defend himself or herself, and like Milosevic, turn the trial into a mechanism for challenging the legitimacy of international tribunals. I will also address an alternative to having to muzzle a leader who tries to disrupt the trial making it difficult to get the evidence presented and weighed objectively, or as objectively as commonly happens in criminal trials.

David Luban has argued that the normative point of international criminal trials is norm projection, namely, "International public trials declare, in the most public way possible, that the condemned deeds are serious transgressions . . . through the dramaturgy of the trial process, not through treatises or speeches."[30] I have been assuming so far that the point of international criminal trials was pretty much the same as that of any other form of criminal law, namely, deterrence, retribution, and truth. But I actually agree with Luban that norm projection can also be a goal of international criminal law, although I disagree that this is primarily accomplished through the dramaturgy of the trial process. Rather, there are book-length treatises being written as the judgments from these courts – indeed, the first few judgments of the ICTY were considerably longer than the book of which this current chapter is a part.

Similar to Luban, Drumbl has argued that the best strategy of justifying international criminal law concerns its expressive dimension, although he also notes various problems with such a rationale. Drumbl worries that the kind of narrative that trials can provide is often adversely affected by the nature of trials themselves, namely, that trials can only selectively expose the facts that are relevant to the case against a particular defendant. This is certainly true, but even the selective telling of the story of a narrative has some expressive value and can contribute to the overall diversity of norms defense of international criminal law. Plea bargaining and the death of a defendant can disrupt the telling of a narrative, as well, argues Drumbl.[31] Perhaps plea bargaining should be disallowed in high-profile international criminal trials – there certainly is nothing structural to prevent such a prohibition.[32] The death of a defendant cannot be so easily addressed, although the telling of the narrative is often able to proceed with some other defendant in the dock, just as was true when Hitler killed himself before he could be put on trial. Drumbl also worries that trials can get highjacked, as they were by Milosevic, a topic I will return to later.

The problem is that individuals are being put in prison as a result of these international trials. I agree with Koskenniemi that these trials are not and should not be thought of as "show trials" in which the international community merely makes a scapegoat of certain people. So if there is a dramaturgy of international criminal law, it will have to be one that does not merely use defendants as part of the drama, thereby disregarding their rights. Nonetheless, I agree with Luban and Drumbl that some

[30] David Luban, "Beyond Moral Minimalism," *Ethics & International Affairs*, vol. 20, no. 3, 2006, pp. 354–355.

[31] Drumbl, *Atrocity, Punishment, and International Law*, pp. 187–194.

[32] See Nancy Combs's excellent book on this topic, *Guilty Pleas in International Criminal Law*, Stanford, CA: Stanford University Press, 2007.

international criminal trials can be justified morally as norm projection, although perhaps with less dramaturgy than they allow.

The Milosevic and Saddam Hussein trials are good illustrations of what the International Criminal Court is likely to face in the future when strong political leaders are put in the dock and charged with mass atrocities. Koskenniemi is right to think that such leaders will be highly motivated to change the nature of the trial, and to try to indict the tribunal, or the Western powers that back the tribunal, rather than to address the evidence within the confines of the rules established for international criminal trials. Milosevic managed to drag the trial out for so long that he eventually died before the trial concluded. And in any event, his standing with the people back home rose rather than fell as the trial progressed. He was seen as a martyr who stood up for his people rather than as the butcher that the prosecutors hoped to portray him. Of course, the truth probably was somewhere in the middle, and it is a shame that prosecutors feel compelled to overstate the case against defendants, thereby making it more likely that defendants will then overstate the case against the tribunal back home.

Yet over time such a problem may dissipate as more and more States ratify the Rome Statute of the ICC and as clearer rules against prosecutorial overreaching are put in place. As more States and defendants see the Court as a fair forum to help solve various problems with their neighbors, it will be harder to indict the Court as if it is one more instance of Western colonialism or hegemony. In my view, the International Criminal Court needs to gain widespread acceptance, especially in non-Western countries, to best thwart the specter of political leaders in the dock continuously indicting the ICC itself instead of being forced to respond to the evidence of their putative misdeeds. Political leaders know better than most others when it makes sense to play certain emotionally charged cards and when to hold them back. One of the best long-term strategies to confront the truly daunting problem of what to do about the grandstanding of such leaders is for the ICC to garner the broadest of public support. Since over one hundred States have ratified the Rome Treaty of the ICC, this process seems to be well along already.

Some, like Koskenniemi, will claim that highly politicized trials will never appear fair to both sides. If hegemony and colonialism remain strong in the world, then it is indeed likely that the ICC will merely reflect the dominant powers in the world. But neither the strong critics of the ICC, like Koskenniemi, nor the much weaker critics, like me, can predict the future with any certainty. Courts always reflect, to a certain extent, the reigning political powers of the time. Yet if there are conflicting powers, courts have a fighting chance to escape the influence of just one power and to attain a modicum of fairness, or at least be perceived so by both parties to a dispute. In the long run, my hope is that the ICC will emerge from under the influence of strong powers and be perceived by victims and defendants alike, although not necessarily all of them, as a fair tribunal that it would be pointless to vilify.

In the short run, the problems addressed at the beginning of this section remain of pressing importance. One strategy, again only a partial strategy, is to appoint backup counsel for those political leaders who demand to represent themselves. Such a strategy is likely to be partially effective at restraining the more bellicose of leaders, since backup counsel will be in a position to point out the countervailing effects of bad behavior by these leaders. But the behavior that is truly problematic – behavior that is not clearly bad but is aimed at making a geopolitical point – will still be hard to deal with. We must recognize that sometimes the geopolitics of the trial may be relevant to proving that the trial is indeed a show trial. We must distinguish the mere cynical playing to the home audience's virulent nationalism from the serious attempt to show the people back home that the trial is indeed a setup. For this reason, muzzling defendants should never be countenanced. Nonetheless, it may be necessary in some cases to try temporarily to keep the political speech making of the defendant to a minimum and allow the backup counsel to act in his or her stead, until the defendant, or the prosecutor for that matter, is then willing to address the relevant evidence being brought before the Court.[33]

My proposal will no doubt be seen as unsatisfactory to those who are generally opposed to international criminal law in particular and international law in general. They will find such trials to be political through-and-through and will regard even my attempt to restrict one or both sides from politicizing the trials as merely a heavy-handed bias in favor of another type of politicizing that routinely goes on in international law. I am indeed bothered by such criticisms. I would be equally worried about such criticisms voiced against domestic trials. But to give voice to criticisms is not to establish the legitimacy of those criticisms. We must examine whether it is true that international trials are merely, or primarily, the reflection

---

[33] The ICTY's Judge Richard May was a master of controlling the microphones, temporarily cutting off both defendants and prosecutors who strayed too far from the consideration of the evidence in their speech making. I am uncomfortable with this form of censorship, but it may be a temporary solution that is worth considering.

of political bias. And in any event we must look closely at each trial to see whether there is evidence of political bias. In some cases this task will be easier than in others, although in no cases at the moment do trials seem to be completely free from the charge of some political bias. The key consideration, in my opinion, is to resist the temptation to make the proceedings into "show trials" for publicizing what seems to be political extremism of one State or one party.

To try to portray the trials as having at least the appearance of fairness, these trials must minimize the politicizing of the trials by either the defendants or the prosecutors. Specifically, I advocate not allowing the joining of defendants together, especially that type of joining that was done at the main Nuremberg trial at which all of the major defendants were tried together, making it seem as if what any one defendant did was not the main point at issue. In addition, I advocate not allowing the joining of charges together, as was done in the Milosevic trial when it then took years to present the prosecution's case, potentially frustrating the defendant, who had to wait so long to present his side of the story.

In many cases, politics can be kept to a minimum if the number of defendants and the number of charges are kept to a minimum, allowing the focus of the trial to be on very specific acts of just one party and not giving the appearance that the trial is really about what the whole society has done over a very long period of time. It is true, though, that accepting my proposals will make the pursuit of the truth of the causes of the larger atrocity harder to ascertain by means of trials. There will be truths nonetheless that will emerge, and the kind of truth that is less prone to be challenged as blatantly political, namely, that truth concerning whether a given defendant did participate in an atrocity and to what extent. But those victims looking for trials to provide a broader truth about these atrocities will sometimes have to give ground to maintain a respect for the defendants' rights and the rule of law.

There is a sense in which many of the criticisms of international trials I have been considering are even more apt in cases of the crime of aggression. The idea that one State has acted aggressively and another State has acted only defensively, especially in situations where two States have been feuding for decades, is extremely hard to ascertain without at least the appearance of bias toward one of the parties. It is for this reason, among others, that I have advocated caution in proceeding against State leaders for the crime of aggression. And the caution should be greater than that exercised for crimes against humanity or war crimes trials. Yet I continue to believe that some criminal trials for the crime of aggression should be conducted so that whatever the retributive, deterrent, or expressivist effects had by such a trial can manifest themselves. But here even more restrictions on scope must be implemented to make sure that we do not fall prey to the charge of conducting "show trials" that will, for instance, often further widen the divide between Western and non-Western societies.

V. International Criminal Trials and Aggression

The first three volumes of my multi-volume project track the three crimes that were charged at Nuremberg, surely the most significant international criminal trial: first, crimes against humanity, the new category of crimes that were designed to cover the holocaust – that is, an attack on a population that does not necessarily occur in wars and where the crime may be committed by a State against its own people; second, war crimes – that is, the violations of the rules and customs of war by those who are fighting in armed conflicts; and third, crimes against peace – that is, the crime of initiating and waging aggressive war.

In all three books I take a moral minimalist approach to understanding international crime. The moral minimalist methodology seeks the best principles already embedded "in the standing political arrangements of" our communities whether or not we think "these the best principles from a utopian standpoint."[34] On my construal of this methodology, I also look for the least controversial and least far-reaching principles that will nonetheless justify what practices are thought to be intuitively appealing. In addition, I take a defendant-oriented approach. It is curious that groups like Human Rights Watch and Amnesty International take a defendant-oriented approach in domestic law settings but are often victim-oriented in international law. Indeed, the overwhelming majority of the literature in international criminal law is victim-oriented. My books seek to correct this imbalance.

In this volume, *Aggression and Crimes against Peace*, I discussed the idea of waging aggressive war as well as the more recent idea that individuals can be prosecuted by international tribunals for waging such wars. At the moment, there are no trials for this crime since the international community cannot agree on what constitutes aggressive war and what are the elements of the crime of aggression. I argued for the very limited use of such trials by the ICC.

[34] Ronald Dworkin, *Law's Empire*, Cambridge, MA: Harvard University Press, 1986, p. 213.

This volume dealt with the correlate in international criminal law to the *jus ad bellum* tradition in philosophy. In Part A, I began by explaining that war is a horrible thing and that only in the most extreme cases can it be justified. Given the likelihood that innocent people will be killed in war there remains a strong contingent presumption that all wars are unjustified. I also explained that war is nonetheless needed in certain cases since international solidarity seems to require that a State be willing to go to war to aid victim States or prevent harm to individuals and hence to preserve the peace.

One of the normative difficulties is that if what makes war immoral is the killing of people, then all wars are immoral and there is no relevant moral distinction between aggressive wars and defensive wars. If one wants to punish people for waging aggressive but not defensive wars, focusing on killing alone will not work. One strategy is to show that some wars destabilize a sovereign State and other wars do not; indeed, purely defensive wars shore up rather than destabilize. The difficulty is that today not all sovereign States deserve to be morally supported, in the sense that the international community grants to those States exclusive jurisdiction in criminal matters, since some States are the worst human rights abusers. Aggression is wrong morally because of its destabilizing effect on particular States that generally have a record of protecting the basic human rights of their citizens.

In Part B, I examined three of the most important normative principles thought to be crucial for *jus ad bellum* considerations in justifying war, in light of my understanding of what is morally wrong with aggression. I began by rethinking the idea of first strikes, sometimes called the priority principle, and argued that it is better understood as the State that engages in "first wrongs." I then reexamined the idea of what constitutes a just cause for waging war. Causes must be significantly linked to defense of a State's people and their basic human rights, not merely the protection of territory. This idea is crucial to determining which wars are aggressive and which are defensive. In addition, I tried to reframe the idea of proportionality, a normative principle crucial for both *jus ad bellum* and *jus in bello* branches of the Just War tradition and for the establishment of a legitimate basis for international criminal trials. Proportionality was of key concern in Israel's 2006 war in Lebanon against Hezbollah. While it may be justified to confront violations of State sovereignty with war-like means, the response must not exceed what is necessary for that objective, and civilian injuries must be kept to a minimum, even in wars fought against non-State groups that hide in civilian centers.

In Part C, I discussed some of the case law from Nuremberg. I spent time on each of three different kinds of defendants prosecuted at Nuremberg: top military leaders (the Admiral Doenitz and Admiral Raeder cases), middle-level political leaders (the Ministries case), and civilians whose businesses strongly supported the war effort (the Krupp and I. G. Farben cases). I directly addressed the main conceptual puzzle I find in this area of law: how can we prosecute individuals for a crime, waging aggressive war, that is committed by States, or State-like entities? And how do we link the State plan to the criminal intent of the defendants?

In Part D, I tried to pull things together to form a coherent set of elements of the crime of aggression. I tried to understand aggression as any war waged by a State that was in the wrong in the sense that it was waging war not for self-defense or to prevent oppression or other humanitarian crises. I provided an understanding of *actus reus* in terms of significant participation in the circumstances of an aggressive war. And I provided an understanding of *mens rea* as involving intent to participate in a significant way in such a war effort. I ended this section by arguing against the use of collective liability schemes to diminish the *mens rea* element in the crime of aggression.

In Part E of the book, I discussed two very hard cases. I looked at humanitarian intervention, which is especially problematic because the justification or excuse of waging war is the protection of innocent life and yet wars also threaten the loss of innocent life. Humanitarian wars are in one sense the easiest to understand since they are aimed at stopping human rights atrocities. On the other hand they are the hardest to understand since they do not involve a self-defensive response to State aggression and they risk doing even more harm than they seek to prevent. Specifically, I pointed out that humanitarian wars often require attacking a group that is abusing another, where both are civilian groups. Bombing civilian centers to stop humanitarian wars does not clearly result in fewer civilian deaths. I also looked at terrorist wars, arguing that they are very much like pirate wars of old. But like the situation with pirate wars, it does not make sense to treat the terrorists as outlaws, since some are more State-like than actual States today.

In this chapter, I argued that prosecutions of leaders who initiate such wars should occur, although prosecutions of lower-ranking military and political leaders should proceed more cautiously. I defended such trials, and international criminal trials generally, not by reference to a single normative principle, such as deterrence or retribution or reconciliation, but by reference to a combination of principles applicable differently for different contexts. I also recognized that trials are not likely to satisfy all of the parties, for they are compromises of a sort, where both parties have to settle for a more limited truth, namely, whether a given defendant did participate in an atrocity and to what extent. For some international criminal trials, it may be best that the defendant goes free even though there remains some evidence that he or she did participate in some atrocities, especially the waging of aggressive war, when it is so hard to figure out who did what. For such trials to be defended against the critics from various diverse political persuasions, they must be greatly restricted in scope.

We stand at a crossroads in the movement for international law and justice. I see myself as squarely in the middle of the debate about which direction to take. On one side are those who argue for cosmopolitan justice; on the other side are those realists who urge that we retreat from any kind of morally grounded international interference in the affairs of sovereign States. I defend a limited scope for international trials. One of the most important limitations is that we respect the international rule of law and not merely prosecute on the basis of our heartfelt moral outrage in the face of mass atrocities. Human rights are indeed important and need to be protected, especially when it is a State that seeks to abridge these rights. But it is not as clear as it might seem that individuals should be held legally accountable in international proceedings for each and every human rights abuse committed by a State. If we limit our scope, we will have a better chance of defending international trials for the most egregious of human rights abuses.

Bibliography

Alderman, Sidney. "Address to the Tribunal," November 23, 1945, quoted in Michael Marrus, *The Nuremberg War Crimes Trial of 1945–46: A Documentary History*, Boston: Bedford Books, 1997, p. 124.

Aquinas, Thomas. *Summa Theologica (1265–1273)*, translated by Fathers of the English Dominican Province, London: Burns, Oates and Washburn, 1936.

Arendt, Hannah. *Eichmann in Jerusalem*, New York: Viking Press, 1963.

Augustine. *The City of God* (c. 420), translated by Henry Bettenson, New York: Penguin Books, 1984.

Barrett, Richard, and Laura Little. "Lessons of Yugoslav Rape Trials: A Role for Conspiracy Law in International Tribunals," *Minnesota Law Review*, vol. 88, November 2003, pp. 30–85.

Bassiouni, M. Cherif, and Edward W. Wise. *Aut Dedere Aut Judicare: The Duty to Prosecute or Extradite in International Law*, Ardsley, NY: Transnational, 1995.

Becker, Tal. *Terrorism and the State, Rethinking the Rules of State Responsibility*, Oxford: Hart, 2006.

Bentham, Jeremy. *An Introduction to the Principles of Morals and Legislation* (1789), edited by J. H. Burns and H. L. A. Hart, Oxford: Oxford University Press, 1970.

Berkowitz, Leonard. "On the Formation and Regulation of Anger and Aggression: A Cognitive-Neoassociationist Analysis," *American Psychologist*, vol. 45, no. 4, April 1990, pp. 494–503.

Bohlander, Michael, Roman Boed, and Richard J. Wilson. *Defense in International Criminal Proceedings: Cases, Materials, and Commentary*, Ardsley, NY: Transnational, 2006.

Bok, Sissela. "Early Advocates of Lasting World Peace: Utopians or Realists?" in *Ethics and International Affairs: A Reader*, 2nd ed., edited by Joel H. Rosenthal, Washington, DC: Georgetown University Press, 1999, pp. 124–147.

Brownlie, Ian. *International Law and the Use of Force by States*, Oxford: Clarendon Press, 1963.

Buchanan, Allen. "Institutionalizing the Just War," *Philosophy & Public Affairs*, vol. 34, no. 1, Winter 2006, pp. 2–38.

Buchanan, Allen. *Justice, Legitimacy, and Self-Determination*, Oxford: Oxford University Press, 2004.

Buss, Arnold, and A. Durkee. "An Inventory for Assessing Different Kinds of Hostility," *Journal of Consulting Psychology*, vol. 21, 1957, pp. 343–349.

Buss, Arnold, and Mark Perry. "The Aggression Questionnaire," *Journal of Personality and Social Psychology*, vol. 63, no. 3, 1992, pp. 452–459.

Caney, Simon. *Justice beyond Borders*, Oxford: Oxford University Press, 2005.

Case concerning Military and Paramilitary Activities in and against Nicaragua (Nicaragua v. United States), International Court of Justice, 1986.

Case concerning Oil Platforms (Islamic Republic of Iran v. United States of America), International Court of Justice, 2003.

Charter of the International Military Tribunal at Nuremberg, Annex to the London Agreement (August 8, 1945), 82 U.N.T.S. 279.

Charter of the United Nations (June 26, 1945), T.S. 993, 59 Stat. 1031, 1976 Y.B.U.N. 1043.

Chatterjee, Deen K., and Don E. Scheid, editors. *Ethics and Foreign Intervention*, New York: Cambridge University Press, 2003.

Christopher, Paul. *The Ethics of War and Peace: An Introduction to Legal and Moral Issues*, 3rd ed., Upper Saddle River, NJ: Prentice Hall, 2004.

Clark, Roger. "The Crime of Aggression and the International Criminal Court," in Jose Doria, Hans-Peter Gasser, and M. Cherif Bassiouni, editors, *The Legal Regime of the International Criminal Court*, Boston: Brill, forthcoming.

Combs, Nancy. *Guilty Pleas in International Criminal Law*, Stanford, CA: Stanford University Press, 2007.

Compact Edition of the Oxford English Dictionary, vol. I: A-O, Oxford: Oxford University Press, 1971.

Crick, Nicki R., and Jennifer K. Grotpeter. "Relational Aggression, Gender, and Social-Psychological Adjustment, *Child Development*, vol. 66, 1995, pp. 710–722.

Danner, Allison Marston, and Jenny S. Martinez. "Guilty Associations: Joint Criminal Enterprise, Command Responsibility, and the Development of International Criminal Law," *California Law Review*, vol. 93, January 2005, pp. 75–169.

Davidson, Eugene. *The Trial of the Germans*, New York: Macmillan, 1966 [reprinted by University of Missouri Press, 1977].

Dinstein, Yoram. *War, Aggression, and Self-Defense*, 3rd ed., Cambridge: Cambridge University Press, 2001.

Discussion paper proposed by the Coordinator; Part I, Definition of the crime of aggression and conditions for the exercise of jurisdiction; Part II, Elements of the crime of aggression (as defined in the Rome Statute of the International Criminal Court), UN Doc. PCNICC/WGCA/RT.1 (2002).

Douglas, Lawrence. *The Memory of Judgment*, New Haven, CT: Yale University Press, 2001.

Drumbl, Mark A. *Atrocity, Punishment, and International Law*, New York: Cambridge University Press, 2007.

Drumbl, Mark A. "Collective Violence and Individual Punishment," *Northwestern University Law Review*, vol. 99, no. 2, Winter 2005, pp. 101–179.

Drumbl, Mark A. "Pluralizing International Criminal Justice," *Michigan Law Review*, vol. 103, no. 6, May 2005, pp. 1305–1311.

Drumbl, Mark A. "Victimhood in Our Neighborhood: Terrorist Crime, Taliban Guilt, and the Asymmetries of the International Legal Order," *North Carolina Law Review*, vol. 81, 2002, pp. 1–113.

Durkheim, Emile. *Division of Labor in Society*, New York: Free Press, 1964.

Durkheim, Emile. *Emile Durkheim on Morality and Society*, edited by Robert Bellah, Chicago: University of Chicago Press, 1973.

Dworkin, Ronald. *Law's Empire*, Cambridge, MA: Harvard University Press, 1986.

Eckert, Amy E., and Mnooher Mofidi. "Doctrine or Doctrinaire – The First Strike Doctrine and Preemptive Self-Defense under International Law," *Tulane Journal of International and Comparative Law*, vol. 12, Spring 2004, pp. 117–151.

Fleck, Dieter, editor. *The Handbook of Humanitarian Law in Armed Conflict*, Oxford: Oxford University Press, 1995.

Franck, Thomas. *Recourse to Force*, Cambridge: Cambridge University Press, 2002.

French, Peter, editor. *Individual and Collective Responsibility*, New York: Schenkman, 1972.

Fuller, Lon. *Legal Fictions*, Stanford, CA: Stanford University Press, 1967.

Fuller, Lon. *The Morality of Law*, New Haven, CT: Yale University Press, 1964, 1969.

Gaja, Georgio. "The Respective Roles of the ICC and the Security Council in Determining the Existence of Aggression," in *The International Criminal Court and the Crime of Aggression*, edited by Mauro Politi and Giuseppe Nesi, Burlington, VT: Ashgate, 2004.

Gardam, Judith. *Necessity, Proportionality and the Use of Force by States*, New York: Cambridge University Press, 2004.

Gentili, Alberico. *De Jure Belli* (On the Law of War) (1598), translated by John C. Rolfe, Oxford: Clarendon Press, 1933.

Glueck, Sheldon. *The Nuremberg Trial and Aggressive War*, New York: Alfred A. Knopf, 1946.

Gomaa, Mohammed M. "The Definition of the Crime of Aggression and the ICC Jurisdiction of that Crime," in *The International Criminal Court and the Crime of Aggression*, edited by Mauro Politi and Giuseppe Nesi, Burlington, VT: Ashgate, 2004.

Govier, Trudy. *Taking Wrongs Seriously: Acknowledgement, Reconciliation, and the Politics of Sustainable Peace*, Amherst, NY: Humanity Books, 2006.

Gray, Christine. *International Law and the Use of Force*, 2nd ed., Oxford: Oxford University Press, 2004.

Grotius, Hugo. *De Jure Belli ac Pacis* (On the Law of War and Peace) (1625), translated by Francis W. Kelsey, Oxford: Clarendon Press, 1925.

Haggenmacher, Peter. "Grotius and Gentili," in *Hugo Grotius and International Relations*, edited by Hedley Bull, Benedict Kingsbury, and Adam Roberts, Oxford: Oxford University Press, 1990.

Hamdan v. Rumsfeld, 126 S. Ct. 2749 (2006), plurality opinion of Justice Stevens.

Harris, Whitney. *Tyranny on Trial*, Dallas, TX: Southern Methodist University Press, 1954, 1999.

Hart, H. L. A. *The Concept of Law*, Oxford: Oxford University Press, 1961, 1994.

Henckaerts, Jean-Marie, and Louise Doswald-Beck. *Customary International Law, Vol. I: Rules*, Cambridge: Cambridge University Press, 2005.

Hersch, Seymour. *Chain of Command*, New York: HarperCollins, 2004.

Hobbes, Thomas. *Leviathan* (1651), edited by Richard Tuck, New York: Cambridge University Press, 1996.

Holmes, Robert L. *On War and Morality*, Princeton: Princeton University Press, 1989.

Holzgrefe, J. L., and Robert Keohane, editors. *Humanitarian Intervention: Ethical, Legal, and Political Dilemmas*, New York: Cambridge University Press, 2003.

Holzgrefe, J. L., "The Humanitarian Intervention Debate," in J. L. Holzgrefe and Robert O. Keohane, editors, *Humanitarian Intervention*, New York: Cambridge University Press, 2003, pp. 15–52.

"ICTR: The MRND Trial Goes Adrift," *International Justice Tribune*, no. 31, 12 September 2005, p. 3.

International Conference on Military Trials. London, 1945, quoted in Cherif Bassiouni, *International Criminal Law*, 2nd ed., vol. 3, Ardsley, NY: Transaction, 1999.

Iriye, Akira. *Global Community*, Berkeley: University of California Press, 2004.

Jackson, Robert H. "Closing Address for the United States of America," in *Nazi Conspiracy and Aggression*, Supplement A, edited by Charles A. Horskey et al., Washington, DC: United States Government Printing Office, 1947.

Jaspers, Karl. *The Question of German Guilt*, New York: Capricorn Books, 1947.

Jokic, Aleksandar, editor. *Humanitarian Intervention: Moral and Philosophical Issues*, Orchard Park, New York: Broadview Press, 2003.

Kelly, Erin. "The Burdens of Collective Liability," in *Ethics and Foreign Intervention*, edited by Deen K. Chatterjee and Don E. Scheid, New York: Cambridge University Press, 2003.

Kemp, Kenneth W. "Punishment as Just Cause for War," *Public Affairs Quarterly*, vol. 10, no. 4, October 1996, pp. 335–353.

Kennedy-Pipe, Carolyn. "Torture, Rights, Rules, and Wars: From Northern Ireland to Iraq," unpublished paper.

King, Martin Luther. "Letter from the Birmingham City Jail" (1963), reprinted in *Applied Ethics: A Multicultural Approach*, edited by Larry May, Shari Collins-Chobanian, and Kai Wong, 4th ed., Upper Saddle River, NJ: Pearson Prentice Hall, 2006.

Klabbers, Jan. "How to Defeat a Treaty's Object and Purpose Pending Entry into Force: Toward Manifest Intent," *Vanderbilt Journal of Transnational Law*, vol. 34, no. 2, March 2001, pp. 283–331.

Klabbers, Jan. "Just Revenge? The Deterrence Argument in International Criminal Law," *Finnish Yearbook of International Law*, vol. XII, 2001, pp. 249–267.

Knight, Jack. *Institutions and Social Conflict*, New York: Cambridge University Press, 1992.

Kohler, Lotte, and Hans Saner, editors. *Hannah Arendt – Karl Jaspers. Correspondence 1926–1969*, New York: Harcourt Brace, 1993.

Koskenniemi, Martti. "Between Impunity and Show Trials," *Max Planck Yearbook of United Nations Law*, vol. 6, 2002, pp. 1–35.

Kristof, Nicholas D. "Save the Darfur Puppy," *New York Times*, Thursday, May 10, 2007, p. A33.

Krulewitch v. United States, 336 U.S. 440, 69 S.Ct. 716, 93 L.Ed. 790 (1949).

Kutz, Christopher. *Complicity: Ethics and Law for a Collective Age,* New York: Cambridge University Press, 2000.

Lackey, Douglas P. *The Ethics of War and Peace,* Upper Saddle River, NJ: Prentice Hall, 1989.

LaFave, Wayne R., and Austin W. Scott, Jr., *Criminal Law,* 2nd ed., St. Paul, MN: West, 1986.

Lauterpacht, Hersch. *The Function of Law in the International Community,* Oxford: Clarendon Press, 1933.

Lauterpacht, Hersch. "The Grotian Tradition in International Law," *British Year Book of International Law,* vol. 23, 1946, pp. 1–53.

Law Reports of Trials of War Criminals. London: United Nations War Crimes Commission, 1949

Lippman, Matthew. "The History, Development, and Decline of Crimes against Peace," *George Washington University International Law Review,* vol. 36, 2004, pp. 957–1056.

Luban, David. "Beyond Moral Minimalism," *Ethics & International Affairs,* vol. 20, no. 3, 2006, pp. 354–355.

MacPherson, Lionel. "Innocence and Responsibility in War," *Canadian Journal of Philosophy,* vol. 34, 2004, pp. 485–506.

May, Larry. "Collective Responsibility, Honor, and War Crimes," *Journal of Social Philosophy,* vol. 36, no. 3, Fall 2005, pp. 289–304.

May, Larry. *Crimes against Humanity: A Normative Account,* New York: Cambridge University Press, 2005.

May, Larry. "Grotius and Contingent Pacifism," *Studies in the History of Ethics* (an online journal), February 2006, pp. 1–24.

May, Larry. "Humanity, International Crime, and the Rights of Defendants: Reply to the Critics," *Ethics & International Affairs,* vol. 20, no. 3, 2006, pp. 373–382.

May, Larry. *Sharing Responsibility,* Chicago: University of Chicago Press, 1992.

May, Larry. *The Morality of Groups,* Notre Dame, IN: University of Notre Dame Press, 1987.

May, Larry. *The Socially Responsive Self,* Chicago: University of Chicago Press, 1996.

May, Larry. *War Crimes and Just War,* New York: Cambridge University Press, 2007.

May, Larry, and Hugh LaFollette. "Suffer the Little Children," in *World Hunger and Morality,* edited by William Aiken and Hugh LaFollette, Englewood Cliffs, NJ: Prentice Hall, 1996.

May, Larry, Eric Rovie, and Steve Viner, editors. *The Morality of War: Classical and Contemporary Readings.* Upper Saddle River, NJ: Prentice Hall, 2006.

May, Larry, and Nancy Viner. "Actual Innocence and Manifest Injustice," *St. Louis University Law Journal,* vol. 49, no. 2, 2004, pp. 481–497.

McGuiness, Margaret. "Case concerning Armed Activities on the Territory of the Congo: The ICJ Finds Uganda Acted Unlawfully and Orders Reparations," *Newsletter of the American Society of International Law,* January/February 2006, pp. 6–7 and 14–15.

McMahan, Jeff. "Just Cause for War," *Ethics & International Affairs,* vol. 19, no. 3, 2005, pp. 1–21.

McMahan, Jeff. "The Ethics of Killing in War," *Ethics,* vol. 114, no. 4, Summer 2004, pp. 693–733.

McMahan, Jeff, and Robert McKim. "The Just War and the Gulf War," *Canadian Journal of Philosophy*, vol. 23, 1993, pp. 501–541.

Meron, Theodor. "Defining Aggression for the International Criminal Court," *Suffolk Transnational Law Review*, vol. 25, Winter 2001, pp. 1–15.

Meron, Theodor. "Editorial Comment: Revival of Customary Humanitarian Law," *American Journal of International Law*, vol. 99, no. 4, October 2005, pp. 817–834.

Miller, David. *On Nationality*, Oxford: Clarendon Press, 1995.

Miller, Seumas. "Civilian Immunity, Forcing the Choice, and Collective Responsibility," in I. Primoratz, editor, *Civilian Immunity in War*, Oxford: Oxford University Press, forthcoming.

Model Penal Code (1985).

More, Thomas. *Utopia* (1516), translated and edited by George M. Logan and Robert M. Adams, Cambridge: Cambridge University Press, 1989.

Nasinovsky, Evgeny. "The Impact of 50 Years of Soviet Theory and Practice on International Law," reported in *American Journal of International Law*, vol. 62, 1968, pp. 748–753.

National Security Council, The National Security Strategy of the United States, Washington, DC: U.S. Government Printing Office, 2002.

Neff, Stephen C. *War and the Law of Nations: A General History*, New York: Cambridge University Press, 2005.

O'Brien, William V. *The Conduct of Just and Limited War*, New York: Praeger, 1981.

Orakhelashvili, Alexander. *Peremptory Norms in International Law*, Oxford: Oxford University Press, 2006.

Osiel, Mark. "The Banality of Good: Aligning the Incentives against Mass Atrocity," *Columbia Law Review*, vol. 105, October 2005, pp. 1773–1804.

Osiel, Mark. *Mass Atrocity, Collective Memory, and the Law*, New Brunswick, NJ: Transaction, 1997.

Paust, Jordan J., M. Cherif Bassiouni, Michael Scharf, Jimmy Gurule, Leila Sadat, Bruce Zagaris, and Sharon A. Williams, editors. *International Criminal Law: Cases and Materials*, 2nd ed., Durham, NC: Carolina Academic Press, 2000.

Politi, Mauro. "The Debate within the Preparatory Commission for the International Criminal Court," in *The International Criminal Court and the Crime of Aggression*, edited by Mauro Politi and Giuseppe Nesi, Burlington, VT: Ashgate, 2004.

Prosecutor v. Kvocka. Judgment of the Trial Chamber of the International Criminal Tribunal for the Former Yugoslavia, Case No. IT–98–30/1T, T.C. I, 2 November 2001.

Pufendorf, Samuel. *De Jure Naturae et Gentium* (On the Law of Nature and Nations) (1688), translated by C. H. Oldfather and W. A. Oldfather, Oxford: Clarendon Press, 1934.

Ragazzi, Maurizio. *The Concept of International Obligations Erga Omnes*, Oxford: Clarendon Press, 1997.

Rawls, John. *The Law of Peoples*, Cambridge, MA: Harvard University Press, 1999.

Reichberg, Gregory M. "Preventive War in Classical Just War Theory," *Journal of the History of International Law*, vol. 9, 2007, pp. 5–34.

Reisman, W. Michael, with the collaboration of Myres McDougal. "Humanitarian Intervention to Protect the Ibos," in *Humanitarian Intervention and the United*

Nations, edited by Richard Lillich, Charlottesville: University Press of Virginia, 1973.

Reydams, Luc. *Universal Jurisdiction,* New York: Oxford University Press, 2003.

Rodin, David. *War and Self-Defense,* New York: Oxford University Press, 2002.

Rubin, Alfred P. *The Law of Piracy,* 2nd ed., Irvington-on-Hudson, NY: Transnational, 1995.

Schabas, William. "*Mens Rea* and the International Criminal Tribunal for the Former Yugoslavia," *New England Law Review,* vol. 37, Summer 2003, pp. 1015–1036.

Schabas, William. "Origins of the Criminalization of Aggression: How Crimes against Peace Became the 'Supreme International Crime,'" in *The International Criminal Court and the Crime of Aggression,* edited by Mauro Politi and Giusseppe Nesi, Aldershot, England: Ashgate, 2004.

Schachter, Oscar. "The Legality of Pro-Democratic Invasion," *American Journal of International Law,* vol. 78, 1984, pp. 645–650.

Shane, Scott. "Terrorist Experts Cast Doubt on Qaeda Ties to London Arrests," *New York Times,* Sunday, August 13, 2006, p. A8.

Shue, Henry. "Bombing to Rescue: NATO'S 1999 Bombing of Serbia," in *Ethics and Foreign Intervention,* edited by Deen K. Chatterjee and Don E. Sheid, New York: Cambridge University Press, 2003.

Siniora, Fuad. "Give the Arab Peace Initiative a Chance," *New York Times,* Friday, May 11, 2007, p. A23.

Smith, Bradley. *Reaching Judgment at Nuremberg,* New York: Basic Books, 1977.

Statute of the International Criminal Court. Adopted by the U.N. Diplomatic Conference, July 17, 1998.

Sterba, James, P. *Justice for Here and Now,* Cambridge: Cambridge University Press, 1998.

Sterba, James P., editor. *Terrorism and International Justice,* New York: Oxford University Press, 2003.

Sterba, James P. "Terrorism and International Justice," in *Terrorism and International Justice,* edited by James P. Sterba, New York: Oxford University Press, 2003.

Stone, Julius. *Aggression and World Order,* Berkeley: University of California Press, 1958.

Suarez, Francisco. "On War," in *Selections from Three Works* (Dispation XIII, *De Triplici Virtute Theologica: Charitate*) (c. 1610), translated by Gwladys L. Williams, Ammi Brown, and John Waldron, Oxford: Clarendon Press, 1944.

Surtz, Edward, S. J., editor and translator. *Selected Works of St. Thomas More,* New Haven, CT: Yale University Press, 1964.

Teichman, Jenny. *Pacifism and the Just War,* Oxford: Basil Blackwell, 1986.

Tertullian, "The Soldier's Chaplet" (c. 210), Chs. 11 and 12, in *Disciplinary, Moral and Ascetical Works,* translated by Rudolph Arbersmann, Sister Emily Joseph Daly, and Edwin Quain, New York: Fathers of the Church, 1959, pp. 255–260.

Trahan, Jennifer. "Defining 'Aggression': Why the Preparatory Commission for the International Criminal Court Has Faced Such a Conundrum," *Loyola University of Los Angeles International and Comparative Law Review,* vol. 24, August 2002, pp. 439–466.

Treaty between the United States and Other Powers Providing for the Renunciation of War as an Instrument of National Policy, August 27, 1928, art. 1, 46 Stat. 2343, 2345–46, 94 L.N.T.S. 59, 63 (1929).

Trial of the Major War Criminals before the International Military Tribunal, Secretariat of the Tribunal, Nuremberg, 1948, 42 volumes.

Trials of War Criminals before Nuremberg Military Tribunals under Control Council Law No. 10, Washington, DC: U.S. Government Printing Office, 1949, 18 volumes.

Tuck, Richard. *The Rights of War and Peace: Political Thought and the International Order from Grotius to Kant,* Oxford: Oxford University Press, 1999.

United Nations General Assembly Resolution 3314, adopted on December 14, 1974.

United Nations Security Council Resolution 1368, adopted on September 12, 2001.

United Nations Security Council Resolution 1373, adopted on September 28, 2001.

Valls, Andrew. "Can Terrorism Be Justified?" in *Ethics and International Affairs,* edited by Andrew Valls, Lanham, MD: Rowman and Littlefield, 2000; reprinted in *The Morality of War,* edited by Larry May, Eric Rovie, and Steve Viner, Upper Saddle River, NJ: Prentice Hall, 2006.

Vattel, Emer de. *Le Droit des Gens, ou Principes de la Loi Naturelle* (The Law of Nations or the Principles of Natural Law) (1758), translated by Charles G. Fenwick, Washington, DC: Carnegie Institution, 1916.

Vienna Convention on the Law of Treaties, 1969.

Vincent, R. J. "Grotius, Human Rights, and Intervention," in *Hugo Grotius and International Relations,* edited by Hedley Bull, Benedict Kingsbury, and Adam Roberts, Oxford: Oxford University Press, 1990.

Vitoria, Francisco. *De Indis et de Jure Belli Reflectiones* (Reflections on Indians and on the Laws of War) (1557), edited by Ernest Nys and trans. by John Pawley Bate, Washington: Carnegie Institution, 1917.

Walzer, Michael. *Just and Unjust Wars,* Boston: Basic Books, 1977, 2000.

Wellman, Christopher Heath. "Relational Facts in Liberal Political Theory: Is There Magic in the Pronoun 'My'?" *Ethics,* vol. 110, no. 3, April 2000, pp. 537–562.

Wheaton, Henry. *Elements of International Law,* Boston: Little Brown, 1836.

Wilmshurst, Elizabeth. "Definition of the Crime of Aggression: State Responsibility or Individual Criminal Responsibility?" in *The International Criminal Court and the Crime of Aggression,* edited by Mauro Politi and Giuseppe Nesi, Burlington, VT: Ashgate, 2004.

Zappala, Salvatore. *Human Rights in International Criminal Proceedings,* New York: Oxford University Press, 2003.

Index